Your Client's Story

ASPEN SELECT SERIES

Your Client's Story: Persuasive Legal Writing

Second Edition

Ruth Anne Robbins

Distinguished Clinical Professor of Law
Rutgers Law School

Steve Johansen

Director of Lawyering
Professor of Law
Lewis & Clark Law School

Ken Chestek

Director, Externship Program
Assistant Director, Center for the Study of Written Advocacy
Professor of Law
University of Wyoming College of Law

Published by Wolters Kluwer in New York.

Wolters Kluwer Legal & Regulatory U.S. serves customers worldwide with CCH, Aspen Publishers, and Kluwer Law International products. (www.WKLegaledu.com)

To contact Customer Service, e-mail customer.service@wolterskluwer.com, call 1-800-234-1660,
fax 1-800-901-9075, or mail correspondence to:

> Wolters Kluwer
> Attn: Order Department
> PO Box 990
> Frederick, MD 21705

Printed in the United States of America.
2 3 4 5 6 7 8 9 0

ISBN: 978-1-5438-0370-9

Library of Congress Cataloging-in-Publication Data

Names: Robbins, Ruth Anne, author. | Johansen, Steve, author. | Chestek, Ken, author.

Title: Your client's story : persuasive legal writing / Ruth Anne Robbins, Distinguished Clinical Professor of Law, Rutgers Law School; Steve Johansen, Director of Lawyering, Professor of Law, Lewis & Clark Law School; Ken Chestek, Assistant Director, Legal Writing Program, Assistant Director, Center for the Study of Written Advocacy, Associate Professor of Law, University of Wyoming College of Law.

Description: 2nd edition. | New York : Wolters Kluwer, [2019] | Series: Aspen--Select Series | Includes index.

Identifiers: LCCN 2018041459 | ISBN 9781543803709

Subjects: LCSH: Legal composition. | Law--United States--Language. | Law--United States--Methodology. | LCGFT: Textbooks.

Classification: LCC KF250 .R625 2019 | DDC 808.06/634--dc23

LC record available at https://lccn.loc.gov/2018041459

SUSTAINABLE FORESTRY INITIATIVE

Certified Chain of Custody
Promoting Sustainable Forestry

www.sfiprogram.org
SFI-01347

About Wolters Kluwer Legal & Regulatory U.S.

Wolters Kluwer Legal & Regulatory U.S. delivers expert content and solutions in the areas of law, corporate compliance, health compliance, reimbursement, and legal education. Its practical solutions help customers successfully navigate the demands of a changing environment to drive their daily activities, enhance decision quality and inspire confident outcomes

Serving customers worldwide, its legal and regulatory portfolio includes products under the Aspen Publishers, CCH Incorporated, Kluwer Law International, ftwilliam.com and MediRegs names. They are regarded as exceptional and trusted resources for general legal and practice-specific knowledge, compliance and risk management, dynamic workflow solutions, and expert commentary.

Ruth Anne Robbins dedicates this book to her husband and daughters, who shared the writing journey with her: Steve, Shelby, and Gwen.

Steve Johansen dedicates this book to Lenore Honey Johansen.
You are the hero of our story.

Ken Chestek dedicates this book to Robin Chestek, whose unfailing support and encouragement made this project possible. FFLA.

Summary of Contents

Contents

Acknowledgments

There are many people whom we need to thank, but the first are the three lawyers who wrote the appendices of this book while they were still in law school. They are Andrew Norcott Dodemaide (Rutgers Law School), William F. Hanna (Rutgers Law School), and Naima Solomon (Indiana University McKinney School of Law).

Others who contributed, materially or influentially, to this second edition include Toni Berres-Paul (Lewis & Clark), Victoria L. Chase (Rutgers), Brian J. Foley, Esq., Blair Gerold, Esq.,the Rocky Mountain Legal Writing Scholarship Group, and of course, Michael R. Smith (Wyoming).

There were many other people who provided immeasurable assistance, either by asking students to read early chapters or by supporting our work on the book. Those people include Sarah Adams (Arkansas), Bill Chin (Lewis & Clark), Jason K. Cohen (Arizona State), Alison Julien (Marquette), Derek Kiernan-Johnson (Colorado–Boulder), Allison Martin (Indiana University McKinney), Tracy McGaugh (Touro), Debby McGregor (Indiana University McKinney), Anne Villella (Lewis & Clark), Carol Wallinger (Rutgers), and Daryl Wilson (Lewis & Clark).

Like all books, this one has been many years, many consumed Moonstruck chocolates, and many stories in the making. This book is also the result of several years spent studying and discussing Applied Legal Storytelling, and we thank the Legal Writing Institute and all of the people who have been involved with the conferences that brought us together. We are especially indebted to our U.K. colleagues Robert McPeake (City University, London) and Erika Rackley (Durham), and their efforts to bring Applied Legal Storytelling to an international audience. We also are indebted to those who have provided us feedback on our background articles—so many people in legal writing have provided us support and encouragement that we cannot hope to thank them all individually.

Finally, to our students over the years, we thank you for giving us the opportunity to teach persuasive legal writing in this manner and to learn from you as well.

Your Client's Story

Topeka, Kansas, 1950. World War II had ended five years ago. The country was turning to happier times. The Baby Boom was underway. Factories were turning out cars and refrigerators and a new device called a television. Prosperity reigned.

But not everyone was pleased with the status quo of 1950.

In September 1950, Linda Brown, an eight-year-old African-American child who lived in Topeka, Kansas, was ready to begin the third grade. Her first years of education had been spent at Monroe, an all-black school located about twenty-one blocks from the Brown home. In a modest neighborhood, the Monroe school building had been constructed in 1926. It was of brick in the Italian Renaissance style, well-cared for and ..."a credit to the community" where it was located. The Brown's home was in a racially mixed neighborhood. The children of white and other nonblack families of the neighborhood attended Sumner School about seven blocks from the Brown residence. Named for abolitionist leader Charles Sumner, the first school on the Sumner site was initially for blacks only, but in 1885 it was designated for white students. The current building at Sumner was built in 1935. It was constructed of light-colored brick with a good deal of ornamentation. The testimony of the expert witness was that the Sumner classrooms were more spacious and the facilities more ample and in keeping with a good school situation. The academic programs at Monroe and Sumner were comparable.

Bus transportation was provided for Linda and other Monroe students along a designated route. Linda boarded the bus at a pick-up station about seven blocks from her home. There was no shelter for waiting passengers, and to reach the pick-up station Linda and other black students had to walk through a railroad switchyard and cross Kansas Avenue, Topeka's main commercial street, where the motor traffic was heavy. No such hazards were encountered by students walking to Sumner.

> As the 1950–51 school term was about to begin Oliver
> Brown, Linda's father, was concerned about his daughter's
> safety and comfort, the inconvenience of her daily trip to
> and from Monroe School, and the quality of the educational
> opportunity afforded her by the Topeka school district. On
> the day appointed for her enrollment he led Linda to
> Sumner, the neighborhood school, and requested that she
> be admitted. The request was denied solely because the
> child was black and the rules of the board of education
> limited attendance at Sumner School to white, or
> approximately white, children. Linda continued to attend
> Monroe, but the events of that September morning
> commenced a series of happenings from which Linda
> Brown emerged as a celebrity and a folk heroine of the civil
> rights movement.[1]

We all know how this case turned out. In one of the most important
decisions of the twentieth century, the United States Supreme Court
ruled that separate schools for black and white children were
"inherently unequal" and therefore unconstitutional.[2] But let's stop
for a moment and consider the choices facing Linda Brown and her
father Oliver in September 1950. The law of the land was, and had
been for a long time, that separate facilities for black and white
persons were permissible so long as the facilities were "equal."[3] To
challenge that law meant that Linda and her family had to take on
not only the entire city school system, but also a long-established line

---

[1]Paul Wilson, *A Time to Lose: Representing Kansas in* Brown v. Board of
Education 8–10 (U. Press of Kan. 1995) (footnotes omitted). (Copyright © 1995 by
the University Press of Kansas. Used by permission of the publisher.) The author
of this book was an assistant attorney general for the state of Kansas in the 1950s.
He wrote the briefs and represented the Topeka Board of Education in oral
argument on the case before the United States Supreme Court. By the way, the
reference in this passage to "approximately white children" is explained later in
the book: Hispanic, Asian, and American Indian children were permitted to attend
the Sumner school. Only black children were segregated at the Monroe school. *Id.*
at 15. In Chapter 15, we return to this story, and particularly the interesting fact
about the school's namesake.
[2]*Brown v. Bd. of Educ. of Topeka*, 347 U.S. 483 (1954).
[3]*Plessy v. Ferguson*, 163 U.S. 537 (1896).

of precedents that originated in the United States Supreme Court. And the facts of her case were, overall, not shocking. At least one of the witnesses from her neighborhood described the blacks-only school as "a credit to the community," and the academic programs at the two schools were described by experts as "comparable."

Nevertheless, Linda and her family believed that enforced segregation was wrong, not only because of the inconvenience of having to travel to a much more distant school, but also because of how it made them feel. And by telling a compelling story about their experiences, they helped change our society in a dramatic way.

Stories matter.

Lawyers are paid to advocate for their clients. Advocacy is a form of communication, designed to persuade someone. Legal advocacy, consequently, is a communication designed to persuade someone to take a position about the client's legal claim. And because human beings are hardwired to think and communicate in stories, one of the central premises for this book is that stories are an effective way to advocate on behalf of our clients. We tell each other stories all the time. Stories help us imagine what that other person senses or feels, something that we cannot know for certain, other than through empathy and conjecture. A story that "feels" true to the listener is a powerful tool for persuading that listener because that feeling comes from within the listener.

We call our approach to teaching "client-centered" because we believe the role of the lawyer is to show the court the client's story. But this text is more than just a theoretical discussion of how client stories work. We have organized this book around the central reality of a lawyer's life: handling a client's case, from start to finish. That process includes

- getting to know your client (his character, his goals, and the obstacles he faces in achieving his goals);
- investigating the law;

- formulating a strategy to tell your client's story within the confines of the law; and

- implementing the strategy through written and oral communication to the decision maker.

Notice that this organizational structure starts long before you actually place your fingertips on the keyboard to write something. While you might think that a book on legal writing would focus on the final product (the brief), the actual writing process begins long before you sit down to write. You need to know what to write about, which means getting to know your client's story intimately.

But before getting to that process, it's helpful to know about some basic principles of persuasion. The first few chapters introduce you to the fundamental principles of persuasive lawyering: understanding your client, understanding the process of persuasion, and understanding how legal stories are structured through legal argument. We will explore such questions as How do readers react to what you are saying? and How do you reach into the minds of readers and persuade them?

Think of the first chapters as creating the "setting" for the rest of the book. Our ultimate objective, of course, is to teach you how to produce writing that will persuade judges to rule in your clients' favor and how storytelling techniques can help you accomplish this.

Embracing curiosity

> "Curiouser and curiouser!" cried Alice (she was so much surprised, that for the moment she quite forgot how to speak good English); "now I'm opening out like the largest telescope that ever was! Good-bye, feet!" (for when she looked down at her feet, they seemed to be almost out of sight, they were getting so far off).

Lewis Carroll, from *Alice's Adventures in Wonderland*, Chapter 2

Curiosity is an essential lawyering skill. Curiosity leads to investigation and discovery. It harnesses confusion and staves off frustration. Curiosity leads to better thinking, better ways of doing things, better solutions to problems. A good lawyer is curious about the parties to a dispute. Why did they behave the way they did? What does my client hope to get out of this? Why does the opposing party think its position is right? What facts do I need to know to understand this case? Only by answering all of these questions can the lawyer craft a credible story.

A good lawyer is also curious about the law: why, exactly, is the rule the way it is? Does the rule make sense in the context to which it is now being applied? Does the rule produce a result that is intuitively correct? Is there another way of looking at a problem, using different rules, that might produce a more satisfying answer?

A good lawyer is curious yet again about the nature of a lawsuit. What court would be the best place to file this lawsuit? How can I make sure I have sued the right party? What is the most effective way to make this claim against my client go away? By continuing to ask questions like these, a good lawyer better understands her client's story and consequently can better help resolve her client's problem.

Think about Linda Brown's lawyer, Thurgood Marshall. The rule of "separate but equal" had been settled for almost 60 years by the time the case was brought into court. But Marshall was curious: What impact did the "separate but equal" doctrine have on young children? What if the rule were different? How would that affect his client's life? Would a different rule improve Linda Brown's life? How can we make Linda Brown's story resonate with the Supreme Court?

Just like Alice, you may need to stretch yourself into shapes you never imagined in order to see things more clearly. As we will learn later, stories involve characters (typically your client) striving to overcome obstacles to achieve important goals. The obstacle might be an inconvenient fact, or it may be unfavorable law. But if the goal is worthy, it is your job to help your client find a way to achieve that goal. And that may involve stretching yourself to be able to see over, or around, the obstacle; to find a new route to success; to stay curious.

The recursive process of writing

The writing process consists of four major stages:

1. Prewriting (research and planning)

2. Writing a first working draft (a "brain dump," or getting it all on paper)

3. Revising and rewriting (rethinking, reorganizing, improving)

4. Polishing (proofreading, formatting, editing for writing mechanics, word choices, concision, etc.)

As you probably know already, this is not a simple, step-by-step process. Not all of these steps need to occur in this exact sequence, although all of them have to occur at some point. The process of writing in any field is recursive, with the writer revisiting the different stages in a looping manner. A writer might have a document's organization initially set but then decide to completely reorganize the document. The same recursive process occurs in persuasive legal writing. The process begins when a client presents a problem. The lawyer may identify the likely legal means to resolve that problem and even have some ideas about how to connect the law to the facts of the client's story. However, before the lawyer can formulate a solution, she might need more information—more facts and more knowledge of the applicable law. That information will lead to a different understanding of the best legal argument for the client. The lawyer may begin writing an outline and a draft of a document. But the act of writing may also cause her to revise her understanding of the problem. Perhaps the lawyer will discard her initial legal theories and adopt new ones. Or perhaps she will maintain her same understanding but will deepen the analysis. Each of those outcomes will cause her, in turn, to search for new information.

All of this leads to a truism that you may have heard before: **writing is thinking**. Good lawyers begin to write even before they completely understand how to best solve their clients' problems. The act of writing leads the writer to have more ideas and to further refine her analysis. Indeed, some aspects of a persuasive argument become clear to the lawyer only after she has completed at least one—and often two or three—drafts. For example, it is sometimes difficult to determine the most effective theme of the client's case until later in the revising process.

The take-home point is this: because the writing process helps you to clarify your ideas, you will want to start the writing process early, creating preliminary documents that will help you begin to put together the client's story.

If writing were linear, we might identify the stages of the writing process as shown in Figure P-1.

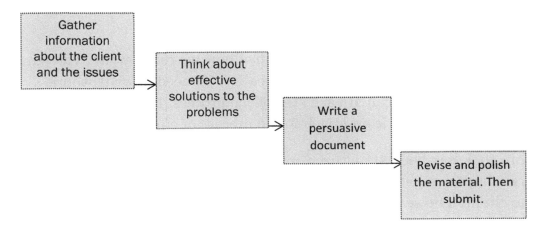

Figure P-1: Four stages of the writing process

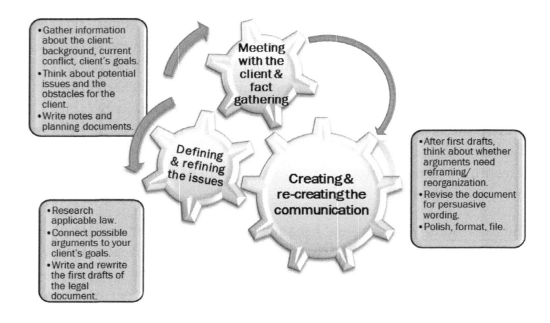

Figure P-2: Recursive writing process

This is, however, an oversimplification of how we really write. Though this is a useful *general* approach, in reality, we need to write, think, and gather information at each step of the process. Figure P-2, then, shows a more realistic approach to the process of effective writing.

This book has been structured to reflect this recursive process. The first chapter starts with the ultimate foundation of legal advocacy: the client. The second chapter then provides the foundational background about what persuades us, from classical rhetoric, to types of reader responses, to storytelling structures that deliver persuasive messages to the audience. The book next moves to the intermediate stages of researching the facts and bringing the law and facts together to form the outline and working drafts of the client's persuasive story. The third part of the book discusses revising the working drafts for persuasion. The book concludes with the last steps: completing and formatting the written persuasive document, and creating the oral argument that accompanies it.

The recursive nature of writing leads to what may be counterintuitive strategies. For example, the parts of a brief are not usually written in the same order that they will appear in the finished document. This book is written in the manner that a lawyer might approach a situation involving a brief: fact gathering, initial case planning, researching and drafting the legal arguments, and then revising the facts section of the document. Keep in mind the key idea that every stage of the writing process builds on what has come before. At each step, the lawyer gathers additional information, reflects on how that information fits with (or changes) what he has done before, and adds detail to the working drafts.

How to use this book

To demonstrate how these principles work in practice, this book uses two hypothetical cases that former law students worked on in prior legal writing courses. We chose these scenarios specifically because they are easy to imagine and represent understandable legal stories. One of the two scenarios involves a question of statutory interpretation about the phrase "dating relationship," as interpreted in an Internet situation, and the other involves a question of common-law contract interpretation and enforcement relating to unused hotel room reservations. From time to time throughout these chapters, we discuss how the lawyers representing clients in those cases might approach their various tasks. The appendices include sample briefs from these two simulation-case files, and are the result of the processes we describe in this book. The sample briefs are largely based on briefs submitted by our former law students—and for their permission to use their work, we again thank those former students. We have added annotations to those briefs to assist you in spotting the things the briefs do well.

The first hypothetical case, *Hawthorne v. Beagle*, turns on the statutory interpretation of the phrase "dating relationship" and involves a domestic violence situation. The two parties meet at a speed-dating event, correspond online via video conferencing and Facebook, and then end that correspondence unhappily. We generally refer to this example as the "Internet dating case" or the "statutory construction case" throughout the book.

The second hypothetical case, *Gloucester Hotel v. Save Our Forest Trees, Inc.,* involves two parties in a dispute over hotel rooms. The defendant, SOFT, Inc., is a small nonprofit organization that plans a conference at a hypothetical chain hotel in Indiana. It signs a contract with the hotel to reserve a block of rooms for conference attendees but does not attract enough registrants to fill the guaranteed block of rooms. The hotel sells those rooms to nonconference guests after the reservation deadline passes, but it still seeks to enforce a liquidated damages clause in the contract to the tune of about $9,000 (an amount larger than the profit SOFT actually earns from putting on the conference). We generally refer to this as the "hotel reservation case" or the "common law case" throughout the book.

Additional details about both of these cases appear in the various chapters as they become relevant. But for now, in the next chapter we see what happens when a lawyer first meets her client.

Part I

Introduction to Storytelling and Client-Centered Lawyering

Meeting the Client

In the beginning, there is the client. Lawyers exist because clients exist. Our job as lawyers is to act as a conduit between our client and the other parties necessary to resolving our client's problem. These include the opposing party, possible co-parties, and the court.

1.1 Client needs and goals in litigation

When a client first meets with us, she will rarely, if ever, say something like, "I would like to file a negligence claim for an automobile accident. There is no question of either duty or breach of that duty, though the defendant will probably argue that I was comparatively negligent. I have special damages of $87,343 and my general damages are $300,000. There may be a problem with personal jurisdiction over the defendant and the statute of limitations expires in six months."

More likely, her story will be something like, "About a year and a half ago, I was driving down Madison Street, right by the new swim center when this delivery truck came barreling down First Street, right through the intersection and broadsided me. It totaled my car and I broke my collar bone in three places. The jerk that ran into me was some guy from Lithuania, I think. I have his name and email address, but he hasn't responded to my emails. I know he was driving for Speedy Delivery, but I haven't talked with Speedy Delivery. I told the cop that came that I was texting when he hit me, but I was sure I had the green light. I wasn't able to work for three months (I'm a gardener at the golf course), and last week I got a notice from some bill collector saying something about my hospital bills being turned over to collections. I thought my insurance had paid all my bills. I'm pretty much recovered from my accident, but I just want to get all of this taken care of so I can get on with my life."

Clients don't come to us with well-defined legal issues. They come to us with problems that they need our help to solve. Clients have needs and goals, both within and outside the legal representation context. Clients who hire lawyers to represent them in transactions (such as writing a will or drafting a contract) may engage lawyers to protect their interests when things are going well. But things are rarely going well for clients who retain lawyers for litigation. Litigation usually disrupts clients' lives or businesses, sometimes in profound ways. It is the job of all lawyers to navigate the legal system to help their clients overcome these disruptions and move toward those overarching needs and goals.

Effective legal advocates always act to further their clients' goals. It is easier to remember that when the client is a living, breathing person. But not all lawyers represent individuals. For example, prosecutors represent the citizens of their jurisdiction, and corporate lawyers represent organizations. There are also times when a lawyer might not have met a client, even when that client is an individual; appellate brief writers, for example, might not have represented the client during the pretrial and trial proceedings but are working strictly from the record. In every case, however, the lawyer must understand the client's goals as well as the legal obstacles keeping the client from those goals.

To understand our client's goals and to tell her story, we must be curious. We must be open to looking at the facts and law from different perspectives. We must recognize the ambiguities in every dispute. This is the essence of good lawyering and we will explore how we do that throughout this book. But first, we need to be curious about our client's expectations on a more practical level. Before proceeding with any legal matter, we need to ask our client some very practical questions:

1. Does the client want to endure the financial and emotional expense of litigation? These costs are significant when you add up the number of hours involved with preparing a case for trial or writing an appellate brief. Even the fixed costs associated with preparing for litigation, such as investigating the facts, ordering transcripts, and copying and binding the briefs and record, can add up quickly.

2. Under what conditions is the client willing to settle the case? A settlement might help the client meet the ultimate goals about her life, even if it means giving up something that she might be entitled to legally. There's a premium on peace of mind, after all.

3. Does the client understand how long it will take to resolve the case? Trials take months, and sometimes years, to resolve and appeals take at least several months. In some jurisdictions, an appeal may not be resolved until years after the initial verdict.

4. Do you and your client agree on the legal strategies you plan to use for the case? If you and your client don't agree as to how best reach your client's goals—or as to what goals are realistic—it may be best to decline to take the client's case. Taking the time to get to know your client's expectations will save time and grief, especially if those expectations do not jibe with your own.

1.2   Ethical considerations

You are undoubtedly aware that lawyers owe ethical obligations to their clients. On the surface at least, many of these obligations are fairly obvious: lawyers cannot steal clients' money; they must respect clients' confidentiality; lawyers cannot lie for their clients. However, the duties under even these fundamental concepts can become murky.

You will study these rules in detail in your professional responsibility course. For now, we highlight some of the most important ethical obligations that are likely to guide your role as advocates for your clients.

1.2.1   Providing competent service

A lawyer's first obligation to the client is to be competent.[1] This requires that the lawyer exercise the diligence, judgment, and care of a general practitioner. While this is a necessarily ambiguous standard, all lawyers are expected to understand applicable court rules, effectively research legal issues, adequately investigate

---

[1] *See* Model R. Prof. Conduct 1.1 (ABA 2012).

factual issues, and clearly explain their client's claims through written and oral advocacy.

While our ethical rules require us to be competent, that requirement merely sets the ethical floor below which we cannot fall. We should aspire to be not just competent, but effective in meeting our client's needs. Competency requires adequate investigation of both the facts and the law. But effectiveness requires something more: curiosity.

The raw ingredients of curiosity are **unfamiliarity, conflict with something already known, ambiguity**, and **complexity**. Each of these ingredients has a ready-made counterpart in law. Whenever a client comes in with a legal question, the matter is unfamiliar. Unless the question is an open-and-shut situation, there will be ambiguity in interpreting the existing law. That ambiguity may be complicated, and it may challenge existing norms.

An effective lawyer is curious about the parties to a dispute. Why did they behave the way they did? What does my client hope to get out of this? Why does the opposing party think it is in the right? What facts do I need to know to understand this case? A good lawyer is also curious about the law: why, exactly, is the rule the way it is? Does the rule make sense in the context to which it is now being applied? Does the rule produce a result that is intuitively correct? Is there another way of looking at a problem, using different rules, that might produce a more satisfying answer? A good lawyer is curious yet again about the nature of a lawsuit. What court would be the best place to file this lawsuit? How can I make sure I have sued the right party? What is the most effective way to make this claim against my client go away? By continuing to ask questions like these, a good lawyer better understands her client's story and consequently can better help resolve her client's problem.

Linda Brown's lawyer, Thurgood Marshall, demonstrated diligence in his lawyering. The rule of "separate but equal" had been settled for almost 60 years by the time the case was brought into court. But Marshall asked questions because separate but equal conflicted with what he knew to be true—one of the ingredients of curiosity: What impact did the "separate but equal" doctrine actually have on young children? What if the rule were different? How would that affect his client's life? Would a different rule improve Linda Brown's life? How can we make Linda Brown's story resonate with the Supreme Court? Likewise, the United States Supreme Court responded by looking at the social science of segregation—the novel argument won.

1.2.2   Being a diligent advocate

You are probably already familiar with the concept of the zealous advocate. This concept was famously explained by the English barrister Lord Brougham, who said, in explaining his defense of Queen Caroline against a charge of adultery, "A lawyer, in the discharge of his duty, knows but one person in all the world, and that person is his client."

Writing in 1820, Lord Brougham captured the strength of the lawyer's duty to his client that continues to this day. A lawyer's role is not to judge his client but to advocate on her behalf even when the whole world may seem to be against her. The story a lawyer tells in the discharge of that duty is the *client's* story told from her point of view.

Zealous representation has its limitations, however. Too often, lawyers hide behind a claim of zealous representation to excuse rude, boorish, or even deceitful conduct. Zealous representation means something very different than pushing for every advantage. Zealous representation and unprofessional conduct are two different concepts. A truly zealous advocate understands that part of zeal includes professional conduct toward the court and opposing counsel. A zealous advocate also respects the legal system. Nothing about being a zealous advocate permits a lawyer to lie, destroy evidence, or otherwise violate his ethical obligations to the court, opposing counsel, and the general public. Rather, the most successful lawyers are those who are able to advocate for their clients' positions while showing respect and courtesy to those who have a different story to tell.

Perhaps the most important limitation on zealous representation is the recognition that sometimes our client's desired goal is unattainable. Sometimes the law is simply and unavoidably against our client. Other times, our client may be in the right, but the costs and risks of litigation outweigh any potential gains. In the words of the famous 19th-century lawyer Elihu Root, "about half the practice of a decent lawyer is telling would-be clients that they are damned fools and should stop."[2]

1.2.3   Respecting client autonomy

Because lawyers recognize that the client's goals are the driving force of any legal action, the profession's ethical rules also recognize that the client controls the ends to a legal matter while the lawyer controls some, though not all, of the means.[3] For example, it is the client who decides whether to enter into a contract or file a lawsuit or accept a settlement offer. On the other hand, it is the lawyer who decides whether to object to the opposing counsel's question to a witness during a trial. Thus, at least in a general sense, it is the client who decides on the goals of the lawyer-client relationship, and it is the lawyer who decides how to best achieve those goals.

However, as you might expect, this dichotomy quickly blurs because many decisions fall somewhere in between the ends and means of representation.

---

[2] Elihu Root, *quoted in* Philip C. Jessup, ELIHU ROOT 1:132–33 (1938).
[3] *See id.* at R. 1.2.

Those who take a client-centered approach to lawyering believe a lawyer's role is to advise his client as to her legal options. It is not the lawyer's role to substitute his preferences for those of his client. After all, it is the client's story, and the client will live with the consequences of how the story comes out. At the heart of the client-centered approach is a belief that a fully informed client is able to make the best decisions for herself. While the lawyer may have expertise in the law, the client necessarily has greater expertise as to what she wants. Thus, the lawyer is an advisor—he informs the client as to her options and then follows the client's direction as to which option to pursue.[4]

Sometimes client-centered lawyering is challenging. Imagine, for instance, that a client wants to accept a settlement that her lawyer believes is not in her best interest. The lawyer might believe that his client, a domestic violence victim, should obtain a restraining order and leave the batterer. But the client might ultimately decide to work out an arrangement with the batterer in which she moves back into the home. Although the lawyer might advise his client about his apprehensions, ultimately it is the client's decision to make.

In another example, suppose a client has suffered damages because of the other side's negligence. And suppose the insurance company for the defendant offers a quick settlement that the client is willing to take, but that the plaintiff's lawyer believes is a mistake for his client to accept. The lawyer is reasonably certain that the other side is almost certainly willing, or even expecting, to entertain a counteroffer from the plaintiff. Moreover, she believes the early settlement offer is grossly unfair for her client. The plaintiff's lawyer also suspects that a few months from now, with time to gain some distance from the dispute, her client would likely regret accepting

---

[4] *See* Steven J. Johansen, *This Is Not the Whole Truth: The Ethics of Telling Stories to Clients*, 38 ARIZ. ST. L.J. 961, 973–974 (2006) (citations omitted).

the offer. What can she do? Certainly, she will discuss the downsides of accepting such an offer. She may ask her client to take some time to reconsider. She might suggest the client seek the advice of a trusted friend. But ultimately, if the client insists on making a poor decision (at least in her lawyer's judgment), the lawyer must remember that it is her client's lawsuit and acquiesce to her decision.

1.2.4   Keeping client secrets: client confidentiality

Perhaps a lawyer's most challenging ethical obligation is to keep her client's secrets. The attorney–client privilege bars a lawyer from disclosing client confidences in court. Lawyers' ethical obligations are even greater, as lawyers may not disclose virtually any information about their clients that their clients want kept secret.[5] This nearly absolute duty to maintain client secrets has but few exceptions, such as when disclosure is necessary to prevent serious bodily injury or death. An illustration of the consequences of this duty is shown in the shadow box.

The Burden of Keeping Client Secrets

Sometimes, lawyers can have very compelling reasons to reveal a client's secrets. For example, in the early 1980s, Dale Coventry and Jamie Kunz were public defenders in Chicago. One of their clients, Andrew Wilson, confessed to Coventry and Kunz that he had shot and killed a man during a robbery of a McDonald's restaurant. However, Wilson refused to give his attorneys permission to disclose his admission even after he had been convicted of another murder and sentenced to life in prison.

For Coventry and Kunz, it was difficult enough to keep silent, knowing that their silence allowed a murderer to escape responsibility for his crime. However, the problem became even more difficult when another man, Alton Logan, was first arrested and then convicted of first-degree murder for the killing that Wilson had admitted to. Logan was sentenced to life in prison, narrowly escaping the death penalty.

For decades, Coventry and Kunz protected Wilson's confidential confession. They had convinced Wilson to sign an affidavit confessing to the crime. Wilson agreed to allow them to disclose his secret upon his death. In 2008, Wilson died in prison. Coventry and Kunz then revealed his confession. Twenty-six years after he was convicted of a murder he didn't commit, Alton Logan was finally released from prison.

---

[5] *See* ABA Model Rule 1.6.

Many law students (and indeed, many lawyers) are troubled by this duty to keep silent even when that silence may lead to injustice. However, there are thoughtful and compelling reasons behind lawyers' duty to maintain their clients' confidences. First, clients must trust their legal counsel. Lawyers cannot competently advise their clients if the clients withhold information. Clients need to be assured that they can discuss their legal issues frankly with their lawyers without fearing breached confidences or other adverse consequences. Remember that the vast majority of clients want to comply with the law, and those frank discussions usually lead to securing justice rather than undermining it. For particularly troubling situations, it helps to remember that the lawyer likely only learned a client's secrets because that client came to her for advice. In essence, lawyers are privileged to know clients' secrets, and to ensure that clients will continue to trust lawyers, lawyers must respect that privilege.

Attorneys must also be careful not to breach their clients' confidences inadvertently. For example, they should never talk about their clients' cases in places where conversations may be overheard. Crowded restaurants, subways, and office lobbies are improper places for discussion or calls about client matters. Likewise, it is imprudent for lawyers to talk about client matters even with trusted family or friends; once client information is disclosed, counsel loses all control over who else will hear that information.

Electronic communication has its own set of potential pitfalls. We have all had the experience of sending an e-mail to the wrong person. Most of the time, this is little more than embarrassing. However, if that e-mail contains client confidences and gets sent to the wrong person, it may be a cause for malpractice. All legal professionals, be they attorneys, paralegals, or support staff, should always check to make sure e-mails are going to their intended audience—before pressing the Send button. And Reply All should be used sparingly and with extra caution! Other forms of electronic communication, like Facebook, Twitter, and blogs, are not appropriate forums for discussions about clients.

It may also be prudent to warn clients about keeping conversations private. Some clients are compelled to discuss their legal issues with almost anyone who will listen. Such conversations may help a client work through the stress of a legal issue. However, they can also have unintended consequences. For example, a federal judge reports that at a recent pretrial conference, the defense counsel informed the plaintiff's lawyer that the plaintiff had been blogging about the details of her lawsuit, including many of the confidential discussions between the plaintiff and her lawyer. As a result of her blogging, the plaintiff had waived the attorney–client privilege with respect to those conversations!

1.3   The client as a key audience

The first principle of legal writing is that audience matters. Everything we write must be crafted with our audience in mind. One audience for virtually all of our writing is our client. When we write *for* our client, we also necessarily write *to* our client. This means our writing should be accessible to our client so that she can understand the story we are telling others. It also means that the choices we make, both in telling the factual story and in creating the legal story, must be acceptable to our client. In literary terms, our client has final approval of our story arc, even though she may rely on us to craft the details of the story.

Throughout this book, you will learn ways to keep your persuasive document client-centered. The story you write in your Statement of Facts will be your client's story. The legal analysis in your Argument section will connect to your client's story. The word choices and details you weave into your analysis will further your client's story. The headings in your document will capture the essence of your client's story. Even choices about your document's font and format may be based on furthering your client's story. Simply put, the product you will create has one primary objective—to help your client achieve her goal. In the end, as at the beginning, there is always the client.

1.4   Getting started: learning about your client

The first step of your project is learning about your client and her goals. How you do this will depend on where you enter the case. Often as a new lawyer (and even more so as a law student assigned to write a persuasive document), you will be assigned to work on a project well after your firm has accepted a client. If so, much of the preliminary work will have been done. Your supervising attorney will likely have briefed you on the details of the case and given you the case file. If you are working on an appellate brief, there will also be a record of the proceedings below; on appeal, the only facts that matter are those that are in the record. Furthermore, the only legal issues that matter are those that were preserved at the trial level. Thus, at the appeals stage of a problem, you are unlikely to do any original fact investigation. If you are dealing with an issue at trial, of course, fact investigation may be a critical part of your task.

Even though you are likely to be brought into the process well after the initial steps of representing a client, it is helpful to have some idea of how the client's problem landed on your desk. The usual first step of beginning a lawyer–client relationship is the client intake interview. This first interview is usually fairly limited. Before a lawyer accepts any client, he needs to consider several issues. Does the client have a plausible case? Can the client afford the cost of pursuing the case? Does this case create a conflict of interest with himself, his other clients, or the clients of anyone in his firm? Some of these questions cannot be answered during the initial meeting. Thus, the lawyer will gather just the information he needs from the client to decide whether he will accept the case. The intake form reproduced in Figure 1-1 shows the type of information gathered at an intake interview.

Today's date_____

Client's Full Name_____ SS#_____

Spouse's/Partner's Full Name_____ SS#_____

Street Address_____

City/State_____ Zip_____E-mail_____

Address_____

Phone (home/cell) _____ Phone (work) _____ Spouse/Partner cell/work_____

Client's Employer _____ Spouse's/Partner's Employer _____

Emergency Contact:

Name/Relationship _____ Phone _____ Email_____

Referred by: _____

Conference with Attorney regarding:

Docket Control	
Statute of Limitations Deadline	
Tort Claims Act Notice Due	
First Appearance Due	
Other Deadlines	
File Review Frequency	
Instructions	

Conflict Control	
Name/Relationship	Conflict Check Results

For Office Use Only

Fee arrangement:
Billing arrangement:

Figure 1-1: Client intake form

If, after resolving any possible conflicts of interests and other potential obstacles to taking the case, the lawyer is willing to accept the client's case (and the client wants to hire the lawyer), then they will usually meet again so that the client can provide more details and the lawyer can begin planning the representation. Of course, the lead lawyer may do considerable work before bringing you onto the project. That said, whatever stage of the project you are asked to work on, you will need to begin your work with some initial planning. This planning begins with learning about the client and her legal issue. You will need to review the information you have to learn the following:

- What do you know about your client?
- What are the client's goals beyond winning the lawsuit?
- What are obstacles to the client meeting those goals?
- What are the tentative legal issues?
- What do you already know about the applicable law?
- What are your preliminary thoughts about theme or narrative arc?

We discuss how to address these several questions throughout this book. As you progress through the writing process, you will revisit your preliminary thoughts about your client and her story. Undoubtedly, your final document will not be identical to your preliminary assessment of your client's story. But the planning document will get you started and will be useful to refer back to, especially in the early stages of research and reflection, where you are most susceptible to wandering away from your specific task.

In the next chapter, we begin to think about how the human mind works and suggest some ideas that can help you persuade your audience to your client's position.

Understanding Persuasion

Persuasion—what legal types like to call "advocacy"—is what lawyers do for a living. So, it behooves us to familiarize ourselves with its key aspects. Persuasion is a rich and complex field of inquiry that cuts across many disciplines. Thousands of articles about it are written by psychologists alone. Other scholars and professionals who study persuasion include linguists, market analysts, graphic designers, neurobiologists, and sociologists. But we all use persuasion every day, even when we're not aware of it.

This chapter explores two fundamental principles of persuasion. First, it looks briefly at classical rhetoric and the concepts of logos, pathos, and ethos. Then it looks at audience responses to persuasive arguments and the most effective way to persuade an audience to respond positively to your client's position.

2.1 Classical rhetoric

The art of persuasion traces its roots back nearly 2,500 years ago to the ancient Greeks. Aristotle is widely recognized as the father of classical rhetoric. The principles that he developed remain just as relevant today as they were at the time he was writing. Aristotle recognized that persuasion occurs in three ways: through logic (in the ancient Greek, logos), through emotion (pathos), and through the reputation of the speaker (ethos). While logos, pathos, and ethos are distinct concepts, in practice, persuasion is most effective when you use all three to appeal to your audience. Logos makes your audience think you are right; pathos makes your audience feel you are right; and ethos makes your audience trust you are right.

Ethos

Credibility component; reflected through the advocate's demonstrating good will, candor, respect intelligence, competence, curiosity.

Logos

Logical component: obtained through the argument's structure, content, and coherence.

Pathos

Emotional component: Comprised of the argument's (1) look and tone (medium mood control), and (2) the audience's activated feelings.

Figure 2-1: The Interconnectedness of ethos, logos, and pathos

Another way to remember the differences is with a cake metaphor.[1] Suppose someone bakes a birthday cake for you. The way we define the type of birthday cake it is captures the essence of logos. If we told you that it was a chocolate birthday cake, you would understand that the structure of the cake is chocolate flavored. A cake is not typically defined by its frosting but by the ingredients in the part made of flour.

And speaking of frosting, that is the pathos of the cake in our metaphor. Pathos is what helps keep the logos part from being too dry. If we offered you merely cake (logos) with nothing to break it up (nothing to drink either), you might thank us, but we are going to bet

---

[1] Thanks to Anne M. Mallgrave, Rutgers Law School of Law, for this metaphor.

that you would probably prefer it with some frosting (pathos). People may have different preferences in the amount of frosting, naturally. Some people might even prefer to eat just the frosting without any cake. Those people might also feel a little ill afterward, as if they have overdosed on sweets.

Finally, to complete the metaphor, let's talk about the person who baked the chocolate birthday cake with frosting. That's the ethos of the cake. You are much more likely to accept a piece of cake from someone you have reason to trust. If, however (and we're sorry to ruin the visual for you), the person who baked the cake washes her hands only once a month, you might not feel all that inclined to eat it.

2.1.1   Logos: the substance of the argument

Much of the reasoning that you are familiar with are just variations of syllogistic reasoning. Legal analysis follows a logical progression related to the logic used in a mathematical proof or a scientific paper. In law, math, or science, these progressions rely on the processes of induction and deduction. Induction infers general conclusions from observing specific examples. Deductions works in the opposite direction: deducing specific conclusions from general principles.

In law, the inductive process helps us pull together different legal sources to formulate the governing rule or the proffered governing rule. The deductive process involves looking at the case facts, and determining how the governing rule suggests a particular result. For example, when we apply case law through analogical reasoning, we use the syllogism, a classic form of deductive reasoning. On the other hand, we often synthesize various specific authorities (the text of statutes, regulations and case law) to establish a more general governing rule. That is the inductive process.

Showing how the prior cases used the rule might remind you of mathematical proofs—showing your work. Turning to the facts of the case file you are working on then requires you to use deduction. Deduction links the premises (the rules) to the facts, thus bringing you to a conclusion.

To illustrate the power as well as the limits of logic, let's look at how we might approach a typical legal dispute. To keep things simple, let's assume that there is no dispute of facts.[2]

- Case A establishes that the law requires this result under these facts. (Rule Explanation = major premise)

- Our case has similar facts to Case A. (Rule Application = minor premise)

- Therefore, our case should get the same result as Case A. (Conclusion)

Similarly, statutory analysis often relies on syllogistic reasoning:

- Statute B prohibits specific conduct. (major premise)

- The defendant engaged in this specific conduct. (minor premise)

- Therefore, the defendant violated Statute B. (conclusion)

Such examples are neat, tidy illustrations of simple deductive reasoning. Alas, real legal issues are rarely neat and tidy. Logic may provide a framework for thinking about a legal dispute, but it rarely resolves it completely. In the real world, legal reasoning is rarely as straightforward as a simple syllogism, although testing your conclusions with a syllogism will certainly help you find logical leaps. But keep in mind that whether a problem is governed by case law, statutes, or both, there is often plenty of room for disagreement. Parties might disagree as to what the law requires (the major premise); or they may disagree about how the law applies to the issue in dispute (the minor premise). In either case, these disagreements are likely to lead to conflicting conclusions. The conflict does not arise because the parties disagree on the proper logical framework—both accept the syllogism. Rather, they disagree on what are the correct premises from which to create the syllogism. Persuading the court toward your client's view as to the "correct"

---

[2] This assumption is a convenience of law school that lawyers rarely experience in practice. Many legal disputes are centered on factual disputes.

premises usually requires going beyond logic to a more complete argument that draws on both pathos and ethos as well.

So, what does this mean for us? It means that as we start to think about building a persuasive argument, it is often helpful to start with the logic of our argument. As we outline, our overall framework should have a structure that is consistent with the logical framework that our audience expects. Although each step of our legal analysis must be logically sound, that is only our starting point.

Demonstrating the limits of syllogisms in legal analysis

Comedian Stephen Colbert provided a humorous example of the limits of syllogistic reasoning. In 2010 the Supreme Court held in *Citizens' United v. Federal Election Commission* that corporations had the right, under the First Amendment, to spend unlimited amounts of money to support political candidates. Colbert pointed out that this decision was based on several premises, all derived from Supreme Court precedents: (1) corporations are people; (2) people have the right of free speech under the First Amendment; and (3) money is a form of speech. If you accept all of those premises as true, the Supreme Court's decision is eminently logical. But a similar set of syllogisms could lead to a conclusion that corporations also have a right under the Second Amendment to bear arms.

To see the whole clip, visit http://www.colbertnation.com/the-colbert-report-videos/249055/september-15-2009/the-word---let-freedom-ka-ching.

To see one of the co-authors of this textbook challenge the metaphoric framework of corporations as people, please see Ken Chestek's TEDx Talk, Of Metaphors and Magic Wands: Are Corporations Really People?
https://www.youtube.com/watch?v=aU4woH9gFDI

2.1.2   Pathos: appealing to our audience's emotions

Legal analysis is more than the exercise of pure logic because we have clients. In the real world, clients rarely have stories that fit into clear legal syllogisms. Rather, real legal stories often involve different understandings of the underlying facts, uncertainty about the applicable law, and competing policy considerations. Even when lawyers craft what appear to be purely logic-based stories, those stories activate emotions in the audience—both the gut-level types of emotions and the emotion of sensing cohesion and rationality to the story. In other words, there is always an inherent sense of the emotion in every lawsuit. Thus, lawyers are most persuasive when we combine logical arguments with strategies that allow our audience to understand and empathize with our client. These strategies often involve storytelling—which we introduce in the next chapter, including using a narrative structure to present logical material.

Narrative structure has three elements: a character, the character's goals, and the obstacles that stand between the character and his goals. We want our audience to empathize with the client—to understand what the character is experiencing. We establish empathy by showing how our client is like our audience, how his goals are familiar or understandable to our audience, and how the obstacles our client faces are like those our audience has faced—or perhaps will face in the future. The better we can develop empathy in our audience, the more effective our use of pathos will be.

Note that empathy is not based in logic but acts in parallel with logic. For example, no logical reason explains why a judge should rule in favor of a party merely because that party has similar goals to those of the judge. Nonetheless, judges, just like other people, are likely to include these considerations in their decision-making calculus.

Pathos is not limited to direct, substantive appeals to emotion. What Professor Michael Smith calls "medium mood control" is a secondary part of emotional persuasion.[3] (Here, the word "medium" means the mode of communication.) The tone or mood of the document is set in many different ways. Word choices convey a tone, certainly. A document that seems hostile rather than respectful can convey negative medium mood control. A document that uses polished language and is free from editing mistakes sets a positive tone. Likewise, the formatting of the document—the choice of fonts and layout—can affect readers' emotions. Things that you can't really control also contribute to the medium mood control of the document: where readers are sitting while reading the document, the lighting,

---

[3] Michael R. Smith, ADVANCED LEGAL WRITING: THEORIES AND STRATEGIES IN PERSUASIVE WRITING 11–13 (2d ed., Aspen L. & Bus. 2008).

the background noise, the time of day, and how readers are otherwise feeling.

Skepticism about emotional appeal is understandable. We have all been exposed to emotional appeals that are obviously bereft of logic. When pathos is overdone, it quickly loses its effectiveness. For example, Judge Michael Musmanno was a colorful judge on the Pennsylvania Supreme Court who became legendary for his strongly worded dissents. While Judge Musmanno was often keenly direct in his disagreements with his judicial colleagues, he sometimes seemed overwhelmed by the emotional basis of his objections. Consider his dissent in *Commonwealth v. Robin*. The issue in this case was whether banning Henry Miller's novel Tropic of Cancer violated the First Amendment. The United States Supreme Court had already ruled that it did. That didn't stop Musmanno from arguing otherwise. Here is his description of the novel:

> *Cancer* is not a book. It is a cesspool, an open sewer, a pit of putrefaction, a slimy gathering of all that is rotten in the debris of human depravity. And in the center of all this waste and stench, besmearing himself with its foulest defilement, splashes, leaps, cavorts and wallows a bifurcated specimen that responds to the name of Henry Miller. One wonders how the human species could have produced so lecherous, blasphemous, disgusting and amoral a human being as Henry Miller. One wonders why he is received in polite society.[4]

While Musmanno may have been trying to appeal to his audience's emotions—anger, outrage, fear—his overwrought attack does little beyond undermining his own credibility.

2.1.3 Ethos: the credibility of the advocate

The final element of classical rhetoric is ethos, the reputation of the speaker (or, in our case, the writer). It would be grand if, on graduating from law school, you could begin your practice with a well-established reputation for professionalism, sound reasoning, and

---

[4] *Commonwealth v. Robin*, 218 A.2d 546, 556 (Pa. 1966).

accurate and cogent writing. This, however, is not likely to happen. Rather, you are more likely to begin practice with a reputation as a new, inexperienced member of the legal community who still needs to learn a thing or two about how the world really works. And as one who still needs to establish her credibility with the courts, clients, and opposing counsel. This does not mean, however, that you will have to check your ethos at the door or will not have this tool at your disposal.

As a new lawyer, you can use ethos to persuade in several ways. First, remember that your written work says a lot about you. Your credibility is improved when your document looks professional and is free of typos, spelling errors, and similar distractions. When you are writing to a court, check the local rules for formatting and other expectations—and follow them to the letter. Design your document appropriately for your audience. (Chapter 19 looks in detail at document design.) The appearance of your writing is just as important as your own appearance. You wouldn't wear cutoffs and a dirty t-shirt to court; your document shouldn't look that sloppy or informal either.

Ethos is more than just looking good. Your document must also be substantively sound. This means that you must always remember the ABCs of legal writing: accuracy, brevity, and clarity. Your audience knows you are an advocate for a particular point of view. What you want them to also know is that you are reasonable and trustworthy. This requires that you describe the facts fairly, explain the law accurately, and recognize that there are counterarguments to even the strongest legal positions.

It may be tempting to omit troublesome facts or law from your argument. After all, it's not your job to make your opponent's argument. Resist this temptation. First, it is unlikely that opposing counsel will be so incompetent as to let your omission pass without comment. Your credibility will be damaged if your opponent points out obvious omissions or misstatements in your analysis—which she almost certainly will do. However, even if you are lucky enough to have an incompetent opponent, the judge is almost certainly not incompetent, and neither are his clerks—and they are likely to discover your efforts to paint an inaccurate picture. When that happens, you have lost your credibility—not just for the immediate case, but for a long time to come. All cases will have bad facts and bad law. Your job is not to hide them, but to explain why they do not result in a bad outcome.

2.1.4 Putting it all together: persuasion requires logos, pathos, and ethos

Though we have discussed logos, pathos, and ethos as separate concepts, in practice, effective persuasion combines all three. The importance of blending these three forms of persuasion is sometimes lost in law school. One of the first lessons we learn in law school is that justice demands impartiality and that impartiality is best met through objective, rational thinking. Though we permit lawyers to appeal to a jury's emotions to a degree, such

Whole-Brain Thinking and the Limits of Logic

In his book *Descartes' Error: Emotion, Reason and the Human Brain* (Putnam 1994), neuroscientist Antonio Damasio tells a compelling story that illustrates the point. Elliot, a patient, had a tumor removed from his frontal orbital cortex—that part of the brain that connects the rational frontal cortex to the emotional parts of the midbrain. As a result, Elliot suffered no loss of IQ. But he was no longer able to connect emotions to rational thought. His frontal cortex still functioned, but emotion no longer played a part in his decision making. One might expect that Elliot would become the perfect "judge," able to make decisions based solely on reason—a Spock-like judge, uninfluenced by emotional appeals. In fact, Elliot became unable to make even the simplest decisions. Dr. Damasio would ask him to choose a day for their next appointment, and Elliot would spend hours evaluating the reasons for choosing Tuesday over Thursday—but never be able to assess the choices and make a decision. Tragically, when Elliot was no longer able to connect his rational thought to his emotions, this previously very successful and happy man was no longer able to hold a steady job. His wife and children eventually left him. His life essentially fell apart.

The lesson to be learned from Elliot is not that we should reject reason. Rather, it is that, in the pursuit of wise decision making, we should embrace rather than fear emotions. In fact, our brains work best when we engage in "whole brain" thinking—when our rational frontal cortex works in concert with our emotional neural centers. This is what happens when we hear stories. Stories are more interesting, more memorable, and more persuasive than other narrative forms. They also engage our brain in a way that is more likely to lead to good decisions. When we make decisions based on a combination of reason and emotion, we reach better decisions than when we rely on reason or emotion alone.

appeals are tolerated, not praised. Furthermore, we expect judges, especially appellate judges, to not be persuaded by obvious emotional appeals; judges are expected to make decisions based solely on reason.[5] However, contemporary developments in cognitive science and neuropsychology suggest reason, without emotion, leads to poor decision making, particularly on important decisions about complex matters. Our brains are more likely to make wise decisions when the rational part of our brain—the frontal cortex—works in concert with the emotional part of our brain.

So, how do we effectively combine the persuasive power of logos, pathos, and ethos? We spend the rest of this book exploring how these concepts intersect in a persuasive legal document. At the outset, though, here are a few strategies to keep in mind.

2.1.4.1 *Start with the logos*

In your first semester, you may have written an objective document that predicted the outcome of a legal issue. This type of predictive legal writing is largely logos based. For persuasive documents, we'll not stop here. But to be sure, we must first have a solid grounding of the facts, the law, and the connection between the two.

2.1.4.2 *Build empathy for your client's position*

When we persuade, we are asking our audience to make a choice between competing positions. Our audience is most likely to choose our client's position when we can show how that position is consistent with the audience's own understanding of the issue and its resolution. This is best done weaving the logos of traditional legal analysis with the pathos of your client's story.

---

[5] *See, e.g.,* Antonin Scalia & Bryan A. Garner, MAKING YOUR CASE 32 (Thomson West 2008) ("Good judges pride themselves on the rationality of their rulings and the suppression of their personal proclivities, including most especially their emotions").

2.1.4.3 Establish your own credibility along with your client's

You establish your client's credibility by effectively telling her story. You establish your own credibility less directly: by telling your client's story accurately, by scrupulously following all court rules, by maintaining a professional tone, by accurately explaining the law and facts, by thoroughly editing and proofreading your document. Such attention to detail establishes your reputation as a trustworthy advocate.

2.2 Audience responses to persuasion

The goal of persuasion is to give information and guide an audience's response to it. Broadly speaking, there are three types of responses, based on creating, maintaining, or changing the audience's beliefs with respect to your position.

As part of responding to persuasive messages, the audience calls on their memories and experiences—and they do so by forming mental images and by drawing immediate—and often subconscious—connections to a series of "stock structures" of common or everyday experiences. This section of the chapter details each of the possible responses to an attempt to persuade.

2.2.1 Response shaping

Response shaping happens when the audience has no prior knowledge or experience. Children are engaging in response-shaping reactions as they learn to speak, to use utensils, and to ride a bike. An adult might have that sort of response-shaping reaction when she immerses herself in a completely foreign culture. However, because adults tend to filter new information through a lens of prior knowledge or experiences, there is less response-shaping happening naturally in adults. That's partly why the older we get, the harder it is to adapt to changing technology.

In law, unless you are dealing with a case of first impression, lawyers have little call to make a response-shaping argument.

2.2.2   Response reinforcing

Response reinforcing happens when the writer strives to reinforce what the audience already accepts or believes. Most of the messages we receive each day serve that purpose. For example, you probably know what time of day heavy traffic will slow your commute. Each time you get caught in that traffic your belief system is reinforced: "The traffic is always horrible in the afternoon; I should not have left at this time."

In law, response reinforcing is our primary mode of argumentation. The use of legal authority appeals to the judge's existing concepts of legal problem solving. The strongest legal arguments are the ones that show judges that they are following an established precedent. Asking the judicial audience to merely reinforce their existing beliefs in stare decisis is the easiest way to persuade that audience.

2.2.3   Response changing

Response changing occurs when the audience is asked to overcome, or change, its existing beliefs and form new ones. This is the most difficult form of response for an audience and therefore is the hardest form of persuasion for the writer. Simply put, if you need to change a judge's mind about how the law applies to your problem, you are probably going to lose. Nonetheless, many people think "being persuaded" means being convinced to change one's mind.

When we write a persuasive document, we should keep in mind the two primary ways we have to persuade. Response reinforcing will almost always be more successful than response changing. If we can convince our audience that our client's position is consistent with what the audience already believes, we have a much better chance of persuading our audience than if we have to change the audience's mind. One of the best ways to create a response-reinforcing argument is to create empathy for our client. If a judge can see a legal problem from our client's point of view, he is more likely to accept that point of view. Likewise, we want to show how our client's position is in line with what the judge already believes. For example, judges believe that they should follow existing precedent; we want to show that our client's position is consistent with existing precedent.

2.3 Cognitive Psychology

Throughout this book, we will bring in aspects of cognitive psychology. Persuasion is, after all, a psychological phenomenon. If an advocate has a sense of how humans typically process information, she will be much more effective at persuading the reader. We introduce a few concepts of cognitive psychology here.

2.3.1 The Negativity Bias

Many cognitive psychologists believe that people have a "negativity bias;" that is, people "spend more time looking at negative than at positive stimuli, perceive negative stimuli to be more complex than positive ones, and form more complex cognitive representations of negative than of positive stimuli."[6] They theorize that negative experiences are more powerful than positive ones across a wide range of phenomena. Think about that for a second. Are you more likely to remember, and react to, criticism or praise? And why do politicians constantly resort to negative campaign ads, when every survey shows that people hate them? Answer: because negative ads work!

The scientists believe that negative information is retained longer and affects us more because it is processed by the brain more thoroughly. This is possibly because it is evolutionarily adaptive behavior.[7] That is, bad things can kill us, while good things generally cannot. Organisms that are more attuned to detecting

---

[6] Amrisha Varish *et al.*, *Not All Emotions Are Created Equal: The Negativity Bias in Social-Emotional Develompent*, 134 PSYCHOL. BULL. 383 (2008).

[7] Roy Baumeister, *et al.*, *Bad is Stronger than Good*, 5 REV. GEN. PSYCHOL. 323 (2001).

and reacting to bad things are therefore more likely to survive. Because we are prone to processing bad information more extensively, we are more likely to remember bad things.

This phenomenon has significant implications for legal writing that we will explore in later chapters. For one thing, the negativity bias may influence the brief writer's selection of theme, something we will talk about in more detail in Chapter 9. Should the writer choose a negative theme, focusing on the negative aspects of the opponent's position? Or can a more positive theme, focusing on what is good about your client's position, be more effective?

Second, the negativity bias might lead an advocate to phrase policy arguments in terms of avoiding bad outcomes instead of promoting good outcomes, since the judge may process the negative statement more thoroughly. We address this topic briefly in Chapter 11.

Third, the negativity bias suggests that it is critically important to understand the negative facts of your case (every case has them), and deal with them effectively. Managing adverse information is discussed in more detail in Chapter 12 (although not all adverse information is actually negative).

Finally, how does the negativity bias influence the way in which we write the rule statements in a brief? Should they be worded to promote a good outcome or to avoid a negative one? We will deal with that question in Chapter 15.[8]

2.3.2   Thinking in images

People think in pictures. Our audience thinks in pictures that we create for them, through our use of details and description. Where we

---

[8] For a more in-depth look at the brain's negativity bias, *see* Kenneth D. Chestek, *Of Reptiles and Velcro: The Brain's "Negativity Bias" and Persuasion*, 15 NEV. L. REV. 605 (2015).

don't provide detailed description, the audience will simply fill in the descriptive gaps with pictures from their own experiences—actual or learned from other media.

Things that can be described:	Ways to describe things:
• Actions • Settings • Characters • Objects	• Name • Sensory information (what they look, sound, smell, taste like) • History • Function • Comparison to something else

In a study conducted in 2000, cognitive psychologists asked 50 students to recall a memory about certain random topics. The topics were provided in either single-word or short phrases. Afterward the researchers asked the participants to describe the memory and their way of accessing it. The students described how they had "relived" more than one-third of the memories that trigger words had conjured. In 98 percent of those relived memories, the students reported being able to see, hear, and feel the memory. They had activated many sensory parts of their brain. Although vision is our strongest sense, people use other senses as well when they think.

The real take-away is that readers will call on memories using their senses unless they are provided with a substitute description. This critical aspect of persuasion is vital to a good telling of the client's legal situation (Statement of Facts), as well as an explanation of how the governing rules of law have operated (Rule Explanation) or should operate (Application).

Sometimes it is important, as part of advocacy, to thoroughly describe information relevant to the lawsuit. Using a more detailed description causes readers to call on images that more closely match what the writer intends. The good lawyer understands which images are critical to the client's case and which ones can be left to readers' own imagination.

2.3.3   Stock structures in persuasion

It's a decent bet that you recalled your favorite pair of jeans as blue denim. That's because the common understanding of "a pair of jeans" is an article of clothing that are full-length pants made of blue denim.

Your favorite pair of jeans

To help understand why imagery details matter in Rule Explanation, here is a short exercise that calls upon autobiographical memories.

For 15–20 seconds, think about your favorite jeans—the best pair you ever had.

- Did you see the jeans in the memory?

- Where were you? In your home? Out and about?

- Did you place yourself in relative time—"it was sometime in my junior year of college"?

- What were you doing in your memory? Wearing them? Washing them? Pulling them out of the drawer or shelf where you stored them?

- Do you remember how they fit or used to fit or what size they were?

- Do you remember how they came into your possession? Why you stopped wearing them?

- Do you remember what color they were?

This exercise is designed to prove the point that you also access memories through sensory perception. Keep this important point in mind when deciding on which details to include when describing key points in a story. Those might be details from your client's story or from a case you are using to illustrate the application of a rule of law.

It's also a good guess that when you purchased this book for your class, you probably did not expect it to contain a science fiction novel inside.[9] Rather, you expected it to read like a textbook, providing information that supplements or anchors your professor's in-class discussions. Your expectations are based on previous experiences of

---

[9] Sorry, it doesn't.

"textbook" you have had in other academic courses and perhaps in other legal writing courses.

Likewise, on your first day of this course, you entered an assigned classroom. If asked beforehand, you probably could have guessed approximately what the room's layout would look like: a number of chairs, a surface in front of those chairs designed as a place for students' computers or notebooks, and a place in the room where the professor can write or project images. You probably also would have guessed that the room would include at least one door and a lighting system. All of those guesses would have been based on your stock structure of the concept "classroom."

We all rely on certain "standardized" pieces of information, such as settings or encounters with the world, to help us get through our day. All new experiences are understood by means of comparison to a stereotypical model. These standardized pieces of information have different names in different disciplines. Linguists refer to them as "idealized cognitive models," but in literature they are called "schemas" or "scripts." Another popular name, and the one that we choose to use in this book, is "stock structures."[10]

Part of effective persuasion is understanding how and when readers' minds activate stock structures. Understanding this allows us to activate stock structures for readers or circumvent them by substituting with our own description. Stock structures show up in almost every aspect of legal writing—from the facts we provide about the client's legal situation, to the rules of law, to the material we include in the explanations of case precedents.

---

[10] Gerald P. Lopez, *Lay Lawyering*, 32 UCLA L. Rev. 1 (1984); George Lakoff, WOMEN, FIRE, AND DANGEROUS THINGS: WHAT CATEGORIES REVEAL ABOUT THE MIND 68–76 (U. Chi. Press 1987); ROUTLEDGE ENCYCLOPEDIA OF NARRATIVE 520–521 (David Herman, Manfred Jahn & Marie-Laure Ryan eds., Routledge 2008).

2.3.3.1   *Types of stock structures*

Stock structures can come from our personal experiences or from cultural, social, or historical norms. There are two basic types of these norms, those that describe scenes and those that describe characters.[11]

> **Scenes:** These stock structures are phrases that call up mental images of places or actions. The phrase, "a playground," or "a town library" both create mental images that depend on your memories, but they will all have key structure similarities. Likewise, "brushing your teeth," "answering the phone," or "putting jam on a piece of toast," are actions that create mental images of situations we can probably all imagine. Either we have experienced it or seen it acted out in media. Keep in mind that there might be assumptions built into these things and you should try to unpack those. "Hailing a taxicab," might look different in Center City, Philadelphia, than it does at the same time in Laramie, Wyoming.[12]

> **Character (sometimes called "personal scripts"):** These have signature roles that a character may take on at any given moment. These are often useful for things like rule explanation, where they can convey a quick visual image for readers, for example, "the plaintiff's nephew" or "the employee." Generic stock structures may also convey background information about a person's special expertise, "the preschool teacher" or "the law student." Both carry a stock

---

[11] At least one other source refers to three categories: situational, instrumental, and character. We have combined the first two categories into one. *See* ENCYCLOPEDIA OF NARRATIVE 520–521 (David Herman, Manfred Jahn & Marie-Laure Ryan eds., Routledge 2008).

[12] *See* Gerald P. Lopez, *Lay Lawyering*, 32 UCLA L. Rev. 1 (1984) (describing stock structures and using the example of hailing a cab in New York City at 7:42 p.m. on a gray Friday evening).

structure about the character's credibility—that is,
ethos Keep in mind the important distinction between
stock structures, and the type of hurtful stereotypes
that an ethical lawyer tries to avoid. A stock structure
should have common underpinnings even if there are
slight variations in the precise details, e.g.,
"employee."

2.3.3.2 *Be careful: stock structures are different to different people*

A few words of caution. Stock structures do provide an extremely
useful tool for lawyers because of the shortcuts they provide. But
because stock structures call up visual images in the minds of the
audience based on their own knowledge and experience base, they
are susceptible to differences and assumptions. Take time to consider
and recognize where differences in culture or experience may have
occurred.

Remembering to look for and recognize these differences will
often make a difference. Cultural competencies are part of a
lawyer's professionalism in our communities. But differences in
stock structures can also be as simple as different experiences
based on geography, physical abilities, or age. For example,
suppose one of the key elements in a lawsuit involved someone
who was "purchasing movie tickets." The act of purchasing a
movie ticket is a stock structure, but that stock structure could
be different depending on geographical or generational
influences. For some, the stock structure of purchasing a movie
ticket might include selecting a seat (for those locales that have
reclining-seat theaters available). Someone else's stock structure
may be purchasing tickets online while another person might
first think of standing in line at the theater.

2.3.3.3   *Many legal disputes are centered in a debate about competing stock structures*

You should also recognize that just as you might be strategically employing the use of stock structures in your advocacy, so will opposing counsel. Remember to stop and unpack the assumptions in the other side's descriptions of people, things, places, and even legal theories.

Try to spot the stock structures involved in your client's case. In truth, many lawsuits are grounded in disputes about the meaning of a phrase in a statute, case precedent, or contract—in other words, conflicting stock structures. The Internet dating case provides a perfect example of that. The central dispute in those sample briefs turns not on whether there was an act of domestic violence, but on whether the family court was permitted to hear the case in the first place (i.e., whether it had subject matter jurisdiction). And the competing arguments all focus on the phrase "dating relationship." There are so many different stock structures of what it means to be "dating" that the statute is ripe for judicial interpretation. As one of the lead cases pointed out, a phrase like "dating" can mean different things to different groups of people.[13]

We talk about the relationship of stock structures to persuasion in more detail in later chapters. For now, keep in mind that when we write, our readers will mentally interpret our words to fit into their own, pre-existing images and meanings of those words. While we can override those images by providing more descriptive detail, it is important to remember that readers will be constructing mental pictures based on our descriptions, and will fill in gaps with images taken from their own files of stock images.

---

[13] For more reading, see Michael R. Smith, *Linguistic Hooks: Overcoming Cognitive Stock Structures in Statutory Interpretation*, 8 LEGAL COMM. & RHETORIC: JALWD 1 (2011).

2.3.4 Priming

An audience that has advance knowledge and is prepared for your message is more likely to accept your message. Psychologists studying the effect of a stimulus on a later response call this **"priming"** and divide the various ways of priming into two broad categories: cognitive and affective.

Cognitive priming occurs when the audience draws on previously learned material to form an analytical response to new material. For example, when a writer provides an overview paragraph, a short introduction, or even a simple heading, that information is priming the reader for what follows.

Drawing upon someone's values to transfer them to a new situation is the other type, affective priming. Affective priming is based on the audience's substantive emotions.

Readers process new information by connecting it to already-known information or to information provided recently, in context.[14] or that has recently been provided in a contextual setting. In advocacy writing, if the writer doesn't provide the recent context, the readers will automatically fill in any gaps in the new information with their prior experiences—which of course fall outside the control of the writer. Strong legal writers thus use priming techniques to steer their readers away from making guesses or assumptions based on the readers' own experiences, and to instead fill in gaps with concepts consistent with the writer's client's story. This concept becomes particularly critical to legal writers when thinking about headings, Rule Statements, and thesis sentences of any paragraph. In advocacy writing, they must all be written from the client's perspective. Priming is discussed in greater detail in those chapters that discuss organization and revising for persuasive effect, Chapters 12, 14, and 15.

---

[14] Michael J. Higdon, *Something Judicious This Way Comes: The Use of Foreshadowing as Persuasive Technique in Judicial Narrative*, 44 U. RICH. L. REV. 1213, 1218, 1220–21 (2010).

This well-known example demonstrates the visual point of cognitive priming. What is the central figure in this diagram?

If you were carefully reading the prior paragraphs, you may have thought about a "13" first rather than a letter "B." That wasn't a very large prime, however, because the paragraph's mention of the numbers was not central to the paragraph's point itself. To create a better cognitive prime might have been a textual discussion about the graphic design of numbers. In that situation, you might be more inclined to see the central figure above as the number 13 rather than as the letter B.[15]

Priming may predispose a reader to a particular perspective. That is why documents have headings, paragraphs have thesis sentences, and briefs have overviews.

2.3.5 Framing

Another cognitive psychology principle that we will discuss in more detail in Chapters 3 and 8 is the concept of "framing." It is related to the concept of "priming" in that an advocate can plant images and ideas in the head of the audience through persuasive word choices and the way the advocate chooses to describe, or "frame," both the legal and the factual disputes that the reader will need to resolve.

According to cognitive scientist George Lakoff, there are two types of frames: "surface" and "deep." Surface frames are easy to spot, and can feel manipulative. For example, a person opposed to the

---

[15] *Id.* (citing the example and explanation of Ian E. Gordon, THEORIES OF VISUAL PERCEPTION (Psychology Press 2004)) (this example uses an adaptation of the original chart).

estate tax may refer to it as a "death tax," in an obvious attempt to persuade you that it is a bad thing. "Deep" frames are harder to spot and work better, because they resonate deep within a reader's psyche. If the advocate who is attempting to persuade you that the estate tax is bad frames the issue in terms of "freedom" or "hard work," the reader is more likely to agree with the advocate, since everybody likes freedom and respects hard work.

We will return to this important concept in Chapter 8.

2.4   What type of persuasive reasoning is needed

Trying to teach persuasion as a precise cooking recipe is something like trying to teach art as a paint-by-number activity. But lawyers can draw on some rough guidelines. Persuasion is about advocacy and problem-solving towards a goal, not about bluster or intimidation. Advocacy uses certain types of legal reasoning; we will discuss those types of reasoning in more detail in Chapter 9¾.

Why do we like to say "advocacy" instead of "persuasion"? The word "advocacy" sounds better and more professional somehow. That could be because persuasion feels like it is on the same continuum as coercion. In fact, that's true. Persuasion is on the same continuum. It doesn't make "persuasion" a bad word per se, however.

Persuasion—and yes, we know this may startle or disturb you—involves indirect threats. It implies that an audience who rejects the persuader's argument may experience certain undesirable consequences. Coercion, on the other hand, involves direct and consequential threats.

Here is an easy hypothetical that illustrates the differences and similarities. Suppose a parent asks a child to clean up her bedroom and to pick up all the laundry scattered around the floor (the authors are wryly assuming that many of us were on both sides of the scenario at some points in their lives):

>   ***Persuasion statement:*** Please clean your room and put all
>   of your dirty clothes in one place. That would help me
>   because then I won't have to go searching myself or have
>   to do multiple loads as you discover more items under your
>   bed. If you do this, then I will have time to spend with you
>   doing fun things like the bike ride we have planned.
>
>   ***Coercion statement:*** If you don't clean up your room, we
>   aren't going to be going on that family bike ride.

The coercion statement is something that would happen later in time, after the attempts at persuasion have failed. But the same potential consequence exists in both statements, the loss of the bike ride.

What response do the statements create in the child? It depends on the child's knowledge base and perspective. Of course, real-world problems are rarely as tidy as bike rides. Most of the time, our client's story requires some mix of response reinforcing and response changing. As we saw earlier in this chapter, we know that the more response changing, the harder it is to persuade.

2.5   Conclusion

Developing sophisticated legal arguments brings together logos, pathos, and ethos and considers the audience's likely responses to the lawyer's attempts to persuade. As we move on to creating persuasive arguments, keep in mind that the most persuasive argument combines logic, emotion, and reputation, and that the most persuasive arguments are those that create a reinforcing response in the audience. Also remember that as the audience is reading or hearing the material, mental images are forming, either based on the lawyer's use of description or based on readers' own experiences and understandings.

There is one more critical aspect to persuasive theory: the importance of delivering the persuasive message in a story structure. Chapter 3 will introduce the fundamentals of story.

Story as a Tool for Persuasion

Just as we use persuasion every day, even when we are not aware of it, we also use storytelling in our everyday lives. Humans intuitively use stories to make decisions. It should come as no surprise, then, that storytelling is essential to good advocacy. In this chapter, we introduce basic concepts about story and storytelling. We further explore those concepts throughout the rest of this book.

3.1 What is a word like "story" doing in a serious legal writing course?

You have probably used the word "story" at least half a dozen times this week, without even being aware of it. The word "story" and its derivative, "storytelling," are ubiquitous. And intuitively, we know that stories persuade. Stories are inherently interesting. We grow up listening to stories, and we learn to tell stories to each other. We are entertained by stories. Politicians and public speakers often use stories to make points and to teach, and often to persuade. Stories are methods of delivering information. Although stories are certainly used to affect an audience at a gut level, stories are more frequently used simply as the most effective way to have the audience remember the information.

> **Try this: counting stories**
>
> If you want to test for yourself how important stories are in human interactions, count how many stories you hear in a single day. Then try to count how many stories you tell during that same period.

Because humans are hardwired to remember information when it is delivered as part of a story, much of this book—including the sections on legal argument—reads in terms of storytelling. Before we get to the specific parts of stories, however, we need to pause for a moment and define exactly what we mean by the term "story." Here is our definition: a story is a **character-based descriptive telling of that character's efforts, over time, to overcome obstacles and achieve a goal**.[1]

That the word "character" appears twice in this definition is intentional. It reflects a central tenet of cognitive science: that people relate and respond to characters' stories. We often "picture" ourselves in the situation that is portrayed by the story, and relate the experience described in the story to how we would react in the same situation.[2] If the character in the story reacts in a way that we can imagine ourselves doing, it feels "real" and we are more likely to understand and accept the character's point of view.

Think of the "story" as the whole of a client's case. The client arrives in the lawyer's office with a dispute that needs to be resolved, either because he seeks redress against some other person or entity or because somebody has claimed the client has done something wrong. That dispute involves a character (the client), an obstacle (which can be the other side of the case, or the law, or other challenges), and a goal (the client wants the dispute resolved in a way that favors him). This story is told in court over time, often in pieces. The pleadings

---

[1] This definition is derived from a definition proposed by storyteller Kendall Haven. Kendall Haven, STORY PROOF: THE SCIENCE BEHIND THE STARTLING POWER OF STORY 79 (Libraries Unltd. 2007). We recognize that there are many definitions of "story," some of which are too broad to be useful. For example, Aristotle described the "whole" of a story as a narrative with a beginning, a middle, and an end. Aristotle, THE POETICS 31 (W. Hamilton Fyfe trans., Harv. U. Press 1973). Haven's definition captures the essential elements that make stories interesting and are present in all legal disputes: characters, conflicts, and resolutions.

[2] *See* Ruth Anne Robbins, *Harry Potter, Ruby Slippers and Merlin: Telling the Client's Story Using the Characters and Paradigm of the Archetypal Hero's Journey*, 29 SEATTLE L. REV. 767, 774 (2006) ("We understand narrative because we join the story and see ourselves as part of it: we place ourselves into the story and walk with the characters."); *see also* Steven L. Winter, *The Cognitive Dimension of the Agony Between Legal Power and Narrative Meaning*, 87 MICH. L. REV. 2225, 2272–2277 (1989) ("the audience lives the story-experience, and is brought personally to engage in the process of constructing meaning out of another's experience").

(the plaintiff's complaint, the defendant's answer) are preliminary tellings of the client's story. There may be preliminary motions (supported by briefs) that tell and resolve parts of the story. There may be a trial, or an appeal, that provides a more comprehensive (and refined) telling of the story. You might think of each step of the process as a chapter of the client's overall story. Because each chapter is part of the larger story, each chapter should keep the client's larger goals in mind, even if that chapter is only a single step toward that final goal.

The possible chapters of any legal story might be depicted graphically as shown in Figure 3-1.

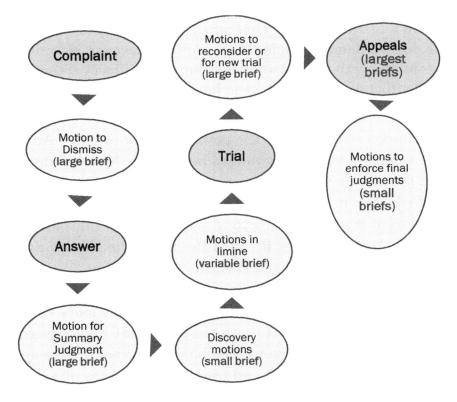

Figure 3-1: Possible chapters in a litigation story

3.2   Stories are persuasive, even to lawyers and judges

In legal education, the words "story" and "storytelling" are sometimes given a bum rap by people who believe that stories are not serious enough for legal discourse. Nothing could be further from the truth. Cognitive psychologists and neurobiologists have conducted a variety of experiments that have demonstrated that all humans process information into stories. Thus, if we want our audience to remember and, more importantly, to accept, our legal arguments, we should present those arguments in a form that will resonate with our audience. Stories resonate.

Perhaps the reluctance of some legal scholars to embrace storytelling comes from a mistaken belief that stories are incompatible with the rigorous, logical demands of legal reasoning. However, effective stories combine both pathos and logos for their efficacy. Storytelling does not conflict with rigorous logic-based reasoning, but rather enhances it.

Many legal experts recognize the power of story. Justice Anthony Kennedy suggests that many judges begin with "quick judgments" and then determine whether their judgment "makes sense, if it's logical, if it's fair, if it accords with the law, if it accords with the Constitution, if it accords with your own sense of ethics and morality."[3] Likewise, Judge Richard Posner of the United States Court of Appeals for the Seventh Circuit admits that "[i]ntuition plays a major role in judicial as in most decision making...."[4] Both jurists thereby suggest that rendering judgment is more than an exercise in pure logos. In fact, both suggests that judges begin their decision-making with a pathos-based sense of justice and intuition. And the best tool for addressing the pathos of a case is through story.

---

[3] Richard A. Posner, HOW JUDGES THINK 257 (2008).

[4] *Id.* at 107.

It's really quite simple. We should tell stories in persuasive documents because stories persuade. One recent empirical study asked judges to read two different versions of the same brief—one that confined itself to argumentation without storytelling, and one that included a strong story-based argument—and asked the judges to report which version was more persuasive. Briefs were written on both sides of the argument to simultaneously test or debunk the hypothesis that story is most useful when the case precedent leans against that party's position. In the simulation, the appellants had more than 130 years of precedent supporting their position, whereas the respondents had the better script for a made-for-television movie: trying to protect their picturesque small town feel from the non-aesthetics of a large, has-everything store.

A majority of the study's participants chose the story-based brief, regardless of whether they read the appellant or respondent briefs.[5] The limited demographics of the study also revealed a preference for the story-based brief regardless of gender.[6] Interestingly, the story-based brief was preferred by most job groups with one exception: law clerks who were recent law school graduates. Figures 3-2 and 3-3 demonstrate the findings very succinctly.

Looking at these figures, the hypothesis that "story persuades" plays out with a legally trained audience. Judges, appellate attorneys, and staff attorneys (also known as career law clerks) are all persuaded by a story-based brief more than they are by a brief that relies heavily on pure logos. Only those participants who had recently graduated from law school were unsure.

---

[5] Kenneth D. Chestek, *Judging by the Numbers: An Empirical Study of the Power of Story*, 7 J. ALWD 1 (2010).
[6] The study was not designed to include other demographics, so there are no results based on race, religion, sexual orientation, or political ideology. The study participants came from many different areas in the United States.

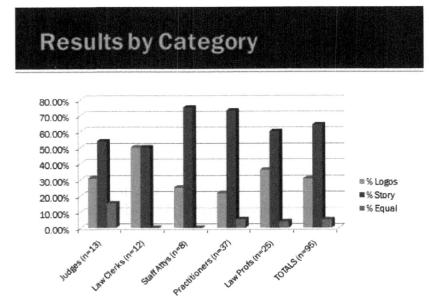

Figure 3-2: Percentage (by category) of those who preferred logos brief to story brief

Figure 3-3: Percentage (by years of experience in current job) of those who preferred logos brief to story brief

3.3   The biology of storytelling

According to several branches of the biological sciences, the only results above that have a modicum of surprise are those of the new law graduates. The other participants were all responding to the biology of storytelling. Humans—and quite likely many other animals—are programmed to accept and learn from stories, beginning at an early age. Babies, for example, focus on faces from as early as a few weeks after birth. Babies study how faces move and what emotions people are showing. They can smile in response to people's faces as early as six weeks, and they can cry if they are uncomfortable with a

---

Stories are part of response-reinforcing in our audience

The biology and psychology studies of story confirm that our audience, be they clients, judges, or opposing counsel, will automatically use storytelling strategies to build understanding. The *form* of our argument, thus, is response-reinforcing because our audience is predisposed to think in story. Moreover, when we present our client's argument in the form of a story, our audience is more likely to connect to our client and to be open to accepting our analysis.

To illustrate the power of our storytelling instinct, consider the following:

- He dropped the piece of paper into the goldfish bowl.

- Over the next six months, the company continued to make money at impressive rates.

- As the boat sped down the Columbia River, Hazel tried to forget.

These sentences have no connection to each other. In fact, they were randomly drawn from three different books.[1] Nonetheless, most of us naturally made connections between these sentences to form a story.[2] Did you make a connection between "he" and Hazel? What was Hazel trying to forget? Did she miss out on the money the company made?

If so, that's your mind logically creating a narrative to connect the three sentences. Imagine how a reader's mind will make connections when the author purposely develops the narrative! More importantly, imagine how the reader will begin to relate, to understand the perspective of the characters in the story.

[1] Jasper Fforde, THE EYRE AFFAIR, (Penguin Books 2003) at 101 ; Michael Lewis THE BIG SHORT (Norton, 2011) at 111; and RICK RIORDAN, THE SON OF NEPTUNE (Hyperion Books 2011) at 213, respectively.
[2] See Kendall Haven, STORY PROOF: THE SCIENCE BEHIND THE STARTLING POWER OF STORY at 34 (Greenwood Publishing, 2007).

new person's face. By the time the baby becomes a toddler, he can understand stories and craves them. This is the bedtime story stage. By the age of six, most children can tell a full story from memory and create their own stories. That is the stage of dressing up as characters, playing with dolls or action figures. These children are walking through stories and asking us to walk through with them.[7]

An effective story draws the audience into the story. Cognitive psychologists refer to this as narrative transportation. We travel to the author's narrative world and travel within the story as observers. Silently, we shadow a character, experiencing muted versions of what she is experiencing. When we jump while watching a movie, we experience the physical response that the character feels. Stop to consider that phenomenon. Intellectually, we know that we aren't in danger. Yet we have an empathetic response. That is because we experience stories by living them or reliving them. When J.K. Rowling, author of the *Harry Potter* series, describes a pensieve—the magic bowl in which people visit other people's memories by becoming an invisible player inside of them—she gives a form to the way we experience stories.

Recent developments in neuroscience have shown how story-telling is hard-wired into our brains. We connect stories to fundamental concepts called frames. "A frame is a mental construct that helps readers think about or organize abstract concepts. One type, "surface frames," is narrow in scope, easily identified, and easy to counteract. For example, the characterization of the "activist judge" and "frivolous lawsuit" each use surface frames that attempt to deflect attention from the actual and deeper issue. "Deep frames," however, resonate with more deeply held values, such as "freedom" or "justice" in the listener. An argument that resonates with a person's deep frame is more likely to persuade him. And presenting an argument as a story is how we connect that argument to the audience's deep frames.

---

[7] Haven, *supra* note 1, at 25.

Cognitive scientist George Lakoff describes deep frames as ideas or values that structure how you view the world.[8] Deep frames can be stated in just a few words and should evoke a predictable response from the listener. For example, Lakoff describes the word "freedom" as a deep frame. At the heart of every deep frame is what he calls an "uncontested idea"; in this case, the idea is that "freedom" is good and is something all people long for.

This textbook returns to the concept of deep frames in more detail in Chapter 9 when we explore how to choose a theme. For now, it is simply important to recognize that everybody has deeply held values, and that persuasion is most effective when you craft your client's story so that it appeals to those deep frames.

> **Surface versus deep frame example: McDonald's coffee case**
>
> In *Liebeck v. McDonald's Restaurants*, the plaintiff sued for damages suffered when she spilled coffee in her lap, which burned that part of her body. As the case went to trial, the national media picked up the story and spun it with a surface frame argument that it was an example of "frivolous litigation" that proved a need for tort reform. The jury, however, privy to the actual evidence, rejected this surface frame and awarded punitive as well as actual damages. The evidence showed that McDonald's had made a conscious choice to serve super-heated coffee, that it knew was dangerous to drink upon its purchase, because the company derived an economic benefit from the higher temperatures—the coffee would cool and be at the right temperature for those drive-thru commuters who waited until reaching work to drink it. The pictures of Ms. Liebeck's third degree burns graphically showed the risks that McDonald's knowingly took, without adequate warnings to its customers. The deep frame of health and safety won the day.

3.4 The storyteller's tool box

Storytelling has many components. We discuss several of them in this book, but we cannot hope to cover all of them. After all, this first course in written advocacy is just that: a first course.

---

[8] George Lakoff, WHOSE FREEDOM? THE BATTLE OVER AMERICA'S MOST IMPORTANT IDEA 12 (2006).

Legal stories, though nonfiction, are still stories. Although fiction and nonfiction stories have obvious differences, they both use many of the same tools. There are two categories of tools that writers can use to accomplish their purpose: structural and stylistic (sometimes called aesthetic). Both types of tools are necessary. Imagine your piece of legal writing as a house construction project. A well-built house begins with a sound structure in the form of rough carpentry: a firm foundation; strong walls; watertight roof and windows; electrical, heating, and plumbing systems. The structure remains incomplete, however, until it includes aesthetic components as well: floor and wall coverings, light fixtures, bathroom fixtures, cabinets, and appliances. A lawyer writing any sort of persuasive document (a brief, a demand letter, a proposal in a negotiation context) will use both the structural and aesthetic tools that fit the situation.

3.4.1   Structural tools for the legal writer

Recall the structural definition of story from a few pages ago: "a character-based and descriptive telling of a character's efforts, over time, to overcome obstacles and achieve a goal." Implicit to that structure are the following seven components.

3.4.1.1   Character

The "characters" are the participants in the story. Characters with whom readers empathize are "protagonists," while characters who oppose the protagonist are "antagonists." Characters who are neutral, but who may have important information to impart about the story, may be called "companion characters." Typically, your client is cast as the protagonist in the story, and the opposing parties may be the antagonists. Witnesses with no stake in the outcome of the case may be companion characters.

3.4.1.2   Conflict

"Conflict" is the fuel that drives the action forward. In most stories, the protagonist (your client) seeks to resolve the conflict and return to a satisfactory condition. There can be multiple conflicts in a story if the story is tracking more than one character's pathway or if the story explores protagonist's relationship to many characters. This is equally true in a client's legal story. The conflict might be primarily about

- the story of the parties. The plaintiff claims that the defendant injured the plaintiff in a specific way, and the plaintiff wants to be restored to some satisfactory condition. This is what we usually think of when we think about a legal story and is often the most important story line.

- the story of the law. In such story lines, the case turns on the meaning or validity of the particular law at the center of the dispute. This type of story line may have as much impact on future conduct as it does on the parties themselves, since it is often designed to effect a change in the law.

- the story of the process. This kind of story is often about things like whether a particular court has jurisdiction to decide a case or whether a controversy really exists or is "ripe" enough for a court to consider it. Such stories are sometimes told by defendants seeking to have a case dismissed without a decision "on the merits" of the underlying controversy.

The chapters in Part IV discuss these three conflict types in more detail.

3.4.1.3 Theme

In literature, the "theme" is the "moral of the story," that is, the lesson that the author wants readers to take away from the story. In legal writing, the theme is the emotional center of the case. It is the essential reason that the writer advances to convince a judge or jury that a ruling in favor of your client is fair, just, and emotionally satisfying.

"Theory of the case" is a legal concept that differs from "theme," although the terms are sometimes mistakenly used interchangeably. The theory of the case describes the legal reason why your client should win. The theme gives the court a reason to want to rule in your client's favor. The theory is logos-based; the theme is pathos-based. The differences between theory of the case and theme are explored in more detail in Chapters 9 and 16.

3.4.1.4 Setting

In standard story structure, "setting" refers to the physical and social characteristics of the time and place where the story occurs. Legal writers need to describe in appropriate detail the factual setting of the case: that is, the time, place, and background details about how the conflict arose. They also need to describe, in appropriate detail, the legal setting: the rules of law that form the legal basis for the court's ruling, as well as the facts of the precedential cases that provide context for those rules.

3.4.1.5. Perspective

While setting is the physical and social context of story, the distance and angle from which the reader sees that setting is the story's perspective. For example, sometimes we may describe the setting from a bird's eye perspective, high above the unfolding scene, where we are able to see a broader context of the physical setting. At other times, we may move our reader closer, on the ground, to see the setting in greater detail. A well-written story may move from one perspective to another, depending on the context the author wishes to convey.

3.4.1.6 Point of view

"Point of view" is related to setting and perspective in that it reveals the physical and social context of a story. Point of view is more specific in that it refers to the narrator's perspective. Sometimes the narrator's point of view is the same as the reader's. For example, some stories are told from the point of view of an "omniscient narrator," who knows everything or at least more than any single character knows. Other stories are told from the more limited point of view of an individual character in the story. In a legal document such as a brief, the lawyer will often choose to write from the client's point of view, though not necessarily with the client's voice.

3.4.1.7 Plot

Many definitions of "plot" are available, but for our purposes, E.M. Forster's definition is the most useful: plot is the causal connections between individual events that constitute the chronology of the story.[9] The overall plot of a story is made up of story "beats" (or scenes) that connect through key causal words: "then ... but ... if ... or ... so ... because ... and ..."

Note that plot and conflict are inextricably entwined. Without a conflict, there would be no need for anything else to happen in the story.

3.4.1.8 Organization

"Organization" is simply the sequence in which the events are told in the story. The narrative arc is the global organization of the story. In legal writing, the whole organization of the brief comprises the narrative arc. The parts of the arc are "order" (what the world was like before the conflict), "chaos" (the incident which upsets the pre-existing order), and "reorder" (the story's eventual resolution).

Not all stories are organized chronologically. In legal writing, stories are rarely told in exact chronological order, in fact. The facts section of the brief, for example, often establishes context by starting with the most recent events, such as the procedural history of the case, and then goes back in time to talk about earlier events. The organization of the legal argument is not chronological either but is organized around the rules of law.

---

[9] E.M. Forster, ASPECTS OF THE NOVEL 60 (1974).

Other temporal ordering devices such as foreshadowing, flashback, and flash-forward are also organizational tools, though they are stylistic ones.

3.4.2   Stylistic tools for the legal writer

A writer of fiction has a much wider array of stylistic tools available than does a writer of nonfiction. Nonfiction writers, including legal writers, are bound by the existing facts and constrained by ethos considerations. For example, literary devices like suspense or humor are rarely appropriate for lawyers to use in persuasive legal writing. Their clients have engaged the services of a lawyer for serious reasons. The lawyer also must remember the audience—mostly legal readers—have been trained to be skeptical readers and will assume that exaggerations or flamboyance are meant to cover up a lack of substance.[10]

Note that in our earlier house metaphor, the stylistic construction materials of light fixtures, bathroom fixtures, and so on were all very functional and necessary. Likewise, the stylistic decisions of storytelling are the mood-controlling aspect of the all-important pathos needed for any persuasive communication. Professor Michael Smith calls this sort of pathos "medium mood control," where the word "medium" means the mode of communication (like the word's plural form, "media").[11] Because of the more limited scope of legal writing, lawyers are generally limited to the following five stylistic tools.

3.4.2.1   Description and the selection of details

Writers have a wide variety of ways to describe characters, objects, or settings. We can refer to characters or objects in a general way such as by name or category (e.g., a driver or vehicle). When we use

---

[10] *See* Lance N. Long & William F. Christensen, *Clearly, Using Intensifiers Is Very Bad—Or Is It?*, 45 IDAHO L. REV. 171, 174–176 (2008).

[11] Michael R. Smith, ADVANCED LEGAL WRITING: THEORIES AND STRATEGIES IN PERSUASIVE WRITING 12 (2d ed., Aspen L. & Bus. 2008).

general terms to describe a person or object, we necessarily give the reader more control over the image the reader has of that person or object. Or we can incorporate more details that define the person or object more fully. Adding details gives the writer more control in creating a mental image in the mind of the audience. For example, if we describe a defendant's "1987 Ford pick-up with a shattered windshield, rusting undercarriage, and inoperable windshield wipers," we provide a more detailed picture than if we merely reference the defendant's "vehicle." The level of detail we provide will greatly influence the mood the writer creates in the minds of readers.

3.4.2.2 *Stock structures*

Writers may also choose to tap into preexisting constructs in their readers' minds, which we called "stock structures" in Chapter 2. Recall that stock structures can be things, people, scenes, or events. For example, think of a law school textbook. The mental image you immediately called up is based on your own experience, but it is very likely that if you asked a student from another law school the same

---

The difference between frames and stock structures

Stock structures, surface frames, and deep frames are related in the sense that they are all automatic, unconscious responses to stimuli and are based on how we view the world. But they are fundamentally different in that stock structures are value-neutral, while frames are value-driven.

Stock structures are neither inherently "good" nor "bad." They just are. They help us quickly understand what we see, read, and hear. They trigger mental images that help us make sense of the stimuli we perceive. Frames, in contrast, involve value judgments. They may or may not evoke mental images (what does "freedom" look like anyway?), but they do trigger emotional or normative responses, either positive or negative. For example, think of an "activist." You probably can imagine a person who passionately believes in some cause; that is an example of a "stock structure." But if you called that person an "environmentalist" or an "eco-terrorist" (depending on whether you agree with what the activist believes in), you are using surface frames to express a value judgment about that person. A lawyer representing that person might call on the deep frame of justice or freedom by including details showing that client exercising his First Amendment rights in a peaceful manner.

question, the two pictures would look roughly the same. "Textbook" is a stock structure, just as "combing one's hair" or "the annoying coworker." However, we don't all share the same stock structures for all concepts. A law student living in an apartment in Palo Alto may have a different stock structure of "home" than a Masai warrior living on the plains of Kenya.

The more general our description of an object or concept, the more likely the reader will rely on her stock structures in how she perceives that object or concept. When to rely on stock structures and when to develop more detailed descriptions are discussed in Chapter 15.

3.4.2.3 *Metaphor*

Legal writers frequently use metaphors, both consciously and unconsciously, in persuasion because almost every conversation involves some metaphor.[12] Broadly speaking, this category of devices refers to ways of conveying multiple meanings or comparing ideas. Metaphor is a nonliteral comparison of two concepts or things; analogy is a literal comparison of concepts and things. We use metaphors in language in almost every conversation. As Professor Linda Berger points out, every time we "check" our e-mail, "browse" the web, or "bookmark" a website, we have used metaphoric language.[13]

3.4.2.4 *Reference or allusion*

Related to metaphor, an allusion or a reference uses a shorthand term to stand for a broader concept. These can be internal to the document itself or external, referencing an outside document or event. Think "literary allusion" or "pop cultural reference." Allusions work at several levels in readers' minds and are powerful devices for engaging readers and invoking subliminal responses.

---

[12] On our short list of recommended readings is this article on the topic of metaphor in lawyering. Linda L. Berger, *The Lady, or the Tiger? A Field Guide to Metaphor and Narrative*, 50 WASHBURN L.J. 275 (2011).
[13] *Id.* at 279.

3.4.2.5   Tone

Writers have many stylistic devices to use, including word choices and placement, sentence length, and paragraph structure. By making careful choices in this category, the writer can create a variety of moods, tones, and emotional responses in readers. In legal writing, those choices are somewhat more limited, but setting the proper tone is still very important. The legal writer needs to set a professional tone that conveys to readers that the writer is a serious person and respectful of the opposing side to the controversy. Doing so is one important way of establishing the writer's ethos, or credibility.

Storytelling concept	Persuasive legal writing
Character	Clients (protagonists) and opposing parties (antagonists)
Conflict	(a) The factual dispute between the parties (b) The legal issue(s) in the case (c) The procedural issue(s) in the case
Setting or scene	(a) The factual setting (i.e. the facts of the case and the circumstances in which the dispute arose) (b) The legal setting (the rules of law and precedents) (c) The setting or scenes of case precedent, used to illustrate the rules.
Point of view	The narrator's perspective in the telling of the story.
Perspective	The angle and distance from which the reader views the action, setting, characters of the story at any given point.
Theme	The central purpose or reasoning in the case that exists to motivate the reader towards an outcome that favors the client

Plot, Organization	Large-scale organization of the legal writing in a narrative arc
Metaphor, reference/ allusion / stock structures	Analogy is often useful in extrapolating results from precedents, or in explaining complicated or unfamiliar facts.
Tone	Choices of wording, paragraph structure, sentence structure, document design to create a mood to the document.
Description	Details used to describe objects, characters, actions, or settings. More description will emphasize, while less will de-emphasize. Careful use of stock structures will serve as shortcuts to understanding in the readers. All of these serve to create visual imagery in the minds of the readers.

Table 3-1: Structural writing tools

In the chapters that follow, you will learn more about how a lawyer can effectively use each of the structural tools shown in Table 3-1 to persuade readers.

Developing Your Client's Story

The next several chapters in this book discusses the lawyer's role in assisting a client achieve his goal. Part II —Chapters 4–8—is structured in the same way that a lawyer in practice would approach a real case. Chapter 4 provides some background information about how different judicial audiences, whether trial judges or appellate, might view the client's story, which in turn will help the lawyer decide how to tell that story. Chapters 5 and 6 walk through the process of investigating both the facts (i.e., what happened to cause the client's problem) and the law. Understanding the facts and the applicable law allow us to begin to develop the legal theory of the case. Chapters 7 and 8 discuss ways to conceptualize the client's problem as a story, and to make some preliminary choices about how to tell that story. At this step, the theme that runs through the entire brief begins to take shape.

The process of writing a brief involves at least four steps

- Prewriting: research and planning
- Writing the first rough draft: getting it down on paper
- Rewriting and Revising: reorganizing and filling out the material, and strategizing the word choices for persuasion
- Polishing: formatting the final document so that it looks professional and readable

These Part II chapters are all about pre-writing, a process that takes significant time. There are other skills courses in law school that deal exclusively with the pre-writing phase; for example, courses that teach client interviewing and counseling, pre-trial preparation and, discovery. These next chapters will touch on some of those topics, and will provide a brief glimpse of what those other important lawyering skills include. We recommend you take those sorts of courses, and that you also practice those skills via clinics, externships and pro bono projects. Our ultimate goal in these chapters, however, is to talk about the client's story. A lawyer cannot write a good story about the client until she has a clear sense of who the client is, and what the client's goals are.

Chapter 4

Thinking About the Audience

Legal documents have multiple audiences. Chief among them are the decider (typically, a judge or magistrate), the opposing party, and the client. Other audiences may include other lawyers or personnel within your office, co-parties and their lawyers, interested third parties, including witnesses, and in some cases, the press, other lawyers or professionals who follow that area of law, or the general public.

In this chapter, we focus on the different roles that the deciders—the judges—play in writing the endings to legal stories. By understanding what the judges' roles may be, we can begin to design our client's narratives to best advantage.

Table 4-1 summarizes the differences between a trial court judge and an appellate judge. We explore these differences in further detail below.

The Trial Judge	Appellate Judges
First neutral person to review the case	Builds on work of lower court judges
Strong incentive to make "right" decision for the parties before the court	"Error correction" only part of job; also needs to consider consequences of any decision on future litigants
Facts are often fluid; usually has discretion to "find" facts based on credibility of evidence	Facts are usually fixed by the lower court; credibility issues not reviewed
"Mentor" to the parties	"Mentor" to the lower court

Table 4-1: Differences between a trial and an appellate judge

When a lawyer writes a brief to the trial court, she advises and assists the court in writing the ending to the story of his client's case. Of course, a significant part of that story will be developed at trial, where the trier of facts will resolve any dispute as to the facts of the story. Let's then think about writing a trial-level brief as part of "story creating."

When one party appeals the final decision to an appellate court, that party is asking the appellate court to write a different ending to a previously completed story. While the underlying facts are now set as "the record," the appellate court may change the ending of the story by applying the law to those facts differently than the trial court did. However, the appellate court knew nothing about the case until the completed record arrived in its office, so the lawyer's role as advocate includes bringing the appellate court up to speed on what the underlying case story is about.

4.1   Trial judge: mentor to the client

When we view a client's legal dispute as a story, it is useful to assign roles to the participants in the lawsuit. The obvious role for the client is as the hero, or protagonist, of the story, while the opposing parties and witnesses are cast as other types of characters. We introduced this concept in Chapter 3 and will return to it in more depth in Chapter 7. The lawyer acts as a narrator, not as a direct character.

In a bench trial, the trial judge decides the case.[1] In that sense, the trial judge is more than just a passive "audience" who listens to the stories told by the competing attorney–narrators of the opposing sides. Rather, the trial judge must listen to the competing stories told, decide which of the competing protagonists is entitled to the court's assistance, and then implement the relief that provides what the court concludes is the appropriate "ending" to the story.

Understanding the trial judge's role as "mentor" or "helper" to the client–protagonist of the story (if the client prevails, that is) reminds an attorney to think about what the trial judge needs to hear.

---

[1] While in many cases juries decide the facts, this book is about writing to law-trained arbitrators, trial court judges, and appellate judges. So this book confines itself to a discussion of persuasion to those types of audiences. Many civil trials are bench trials because jury trials are extremely expensive and very often cause significant delays in case resolution.

Essentially, the judge needs to understand how the law permits that judge to assist the client, but also why the assistance the client seeks is the right thing to do. As we think about the judge as audience, we should consider what we know about how judges perceive their role.

We're not writing to Judge Clipart

When we think about audiences, we often start with our own stock structures about who our audience is. When it comes to judges, we may picture Judge Clipart: an aging, white man in a black robe, surrounded by books, who has, at best, only passing familiarity with computers and other technology. However, Judge Clipart bears little resemblance to most of the actual judges that will make up your audience.

Today's judges are a far more diverse crowd than they were 10 or 20 years ago. Even today's more senior judges live in the 21st century and have been adapting to ever-changing technology just like the rest of us. Recent surveys show that over 70 percent of judges read briefs on tablets or computers. The former Chief Judge of the United States Third Circuit Court of Appeals let clerkship candidates know in advance that he tried to keep chambers as paperless as possible. The number of "paper-based" readers will undoubtedly continue to decline throughout your career. Thus, when thinking about your audience, you should consider not only who is reading your writing, but the context in which that reading occurs.

We explore the implications of technology on document design more fully in Chapter 19. But even in the early stages of thinking about our audience, we should take care to picture our audience as it is today, rather than as the staid, unchanging, anachronism we may envision from reading countless 19th century cases in law school.

4.1.1 Judges "need to know the client's story from the beginning of the case"

The trial judge is a neutral person who evaluates a case and renders a decision, or series of decisions, resolving the dispute. The judge, therefore, must focus more intensely on the parties in front of her than an appellate court might. The contexts in which a trial judge encounters the client's story vary greatly. You might think that a trial judge only needs to concern herself with the story when she sits as a finder of fact at the final disposition of the case—that is, when parties either have no right or have waived their right to a jury trial. But in fact, trial judges need to think about a client's story from the very start of the case.

Table 4-2 lists just a few possible settings in which a judge needs to understand the client's character, obstacles, and goals.

Case or Procedural Posture	The judge needs to consider:
1. Motion to dismiss civil case	Is the story told by the complaint plausible? Is the plaintiff's goal legally permissible?
2. Motion to compel discovery or for protective order	Is one character taking unfair advantage of another character in the unfolding story?
3. Motion for summary judgment	Is the evidence in the record (produced through discovery or otherwise) sufficiently credible that a jury might believe it?
4. Motion for temporary restraining order or preliminary injunction	Is the testimony at the hearing credible? Are the plaintiff's goals important enough to merit this extraordinary relief?
5. Trial or hearing on the merits (bench trial)	Which characters are telling the truth? Which ones are mistaken? How do all of the pieces of evidence fit together in a coherent story? Who should prevail?
6. Trial or hearing on the merits (jury trial)	Is one character trying to mislead the jury or take unfair advantage of other characters, or bring in inadmissible evidence?

Table 4-2: Possible procedural postures where a client's story becomes relevant

The list could go on, virtually indefinitely. The main point here, of course, is that a trial judge needs to clearly grasp who the parties are in the cases she decides, not only to rule on the merits but also to make the numerous preliminary rulings she is called on to decide from the first time a case appears in her courtroom. A lawyer therefore must seek to fully understand his client's story from the very first time he meets the client. Only then can he present the client's story persuasively, and in the correct context, to the trial judge.

4.1.2   Role of the trial court as fact finder

The client's story is inextricably bound up in the facts of what happened to cause the dispute. But the "facts" available to the trial court are different at various stages of the case, and much different from the facts available to any appellate court. Just as a professional photographer has many different lenses in his camera bag to use in different situations, the trial judge has many different lenses through which she will view the facts. The particular lens she uses depends on the context.

Consider Table 4-2. When the trial judge decides a motion to dismiss, for example, she must assume that every fact stated in the complaint is true, and she need not consider any facts that are not stated in the complaint. However, when faced with a motion for summary judgment, the judge needs to look at facts advanced by all sides of the dispute, to determine (a) whether they conflict with each other, and (b) if they do, whether these conflicts make a difference legally. In still other situations (trials, or hearings on the merits of a case, or on some aspect of a case), the trial judge needs to evaluate the credibility of the evidence presented and render a decision as to what the facts really are. Thus, at different steps in the trial process, the facts available to tell a client's story may differ considerably.

Appellate judges have far less room to maneuver in evaluating facts. For the most part, appellate judges must defer to the trial court's resolution of all questions of fact. The burden on the appellant and the standard of review are so high because the trial judge was in a far better position to assess the context of the testimony in the overall story: the trial judge saw and heard the parties in person. Thus, the trial judge is in a better position than an appellate court to make credibility decisions based on the demeanor of witnesses and other nonverbal evidence as well as the words themselves. For example, trial transcripts make no note of whether witnesses testified in calm voices or whether they mumbled, shouted, or cried.

All of this means simply that in any proceeding in the trial court, the facts are more likely to be in play than they are on appeal. Arguments about what the facts really are, and what they mean, may be very important to the trial judge. The trial advocate therefore needs to understand how the trial judge must view the facts and then be fully prepared to reason with the facts at whatever level the trial court must do so.

4.1.3   Respect for higher authority

If the trial court is the "master of the facts" of the case, the appellate court is correspondingly the "master of the law." The deference that an appellate court has for a trial court's findings of fact does not extend to any holdings of law since the appellate court is in as good a position as (if not better than) the trial court to resolve questions of law.

Of course, a litigant who makes a novel claim or challenges a well-established legal rule must still make such arguments before the trial court to preserve a right to raise the issue on appeal. When presenting a claim that runs counter to existing legal rules or precedent, the advocate needs to rely much more heavily on the client's story.[2] To effect positive change, the lawyer needs to show how the existing rule unfairly harms or limits the client or people like the client. Telling a compelling story about how that rule is harmful is the surest path to success in such cases.

4.2   Appellate judge: mentor to the trial judge?

If the role of the trial judge is to serve as a helper to the hero–litigant who appears before her, the role of the appellate court is

---

[2] Recall the story of Linda Brown, which led to the landmark decision of *Brown v. Board of Education*, discussed in the Prologue.

somewhat different. It may be helpful to think of the appellate court as a mentor to the trial court judge.

While the trial judge is primarily focused on "getting it right" so that the "correct" party wins, appellate judges must take a somewhat broader view. Certainly, a significant part of the function of the court is error correction (at least at the level of the

> **Appellate courts and facts**
>
> One appellate court described the role of factual record on appeal this way: "When practicing appellate law, there are at least three immutable rules: first, take great care to prepare a complete record; second, if it is not in the record, it did not happen; and third, when in doubt, refer back to rules one and two." *Protect Our Water v. County of Merced*, 110 Cal. App. 4th 362, 364, 1 Cal. Rptr. 3d 726 (2003).

intermediate appellate court or, in those few jurisdictions that have no intermediate appellate court, the state supreme court). Every litigant is entitled to at least one fresh set of judicial eyes to review the matter to make sure that the trial court did not make a mistake.

But another function of any appellate court is law making. The principle of stare decisis requires the intermediate appellate court to look backward and forward at the same time. It looks backward to see whether the case before it was decided correctly—its error-correction function; it simultaneously looks forward to seeing what the consequences might be in future cases of any decision it renders in this case—its law-making function. And in the United States Supreme Court[3] (as well as in state supreme courts), the law-making function is the Court's primary focus.

---

[3] The Supreme Court's website reports that its typical annual caseload (which would be primarily petitions for certiorari) is around 10,000 cases, but review is granted in only about 100 cases (or 1 percent of the petitions) per term. Website of the Supreme Court of the United States, *The Justices' Caseload*, http://www.supremecourt.gov/about/justicecaseload.aspx (accessed July 27, 2017).

This does not mean that client stories are not important in appellate courts; as Linda Brown's story illustrates, sometimes the stories are the most important part of the brief. But it does suggest that since the appellate court's function is different from the trial court's, the story that a client tells at the appellate level may differ too.

The important points for any lawyer writing an appellate brief are these: first, an attorney has somewhat less flexibility in presenting the facts and telling his client's story because the facts as found at the trial level determine the facts on appeal.

Second, even though the facts on appeal are set, they are just as important. At the appellate level, the challenge is not what the underlying facts are, but how those facts are woven into a compelling story. The story that begins in the fact section of the brief can resonate deep inside an appellate judge's mind and create an unconscious impulse to rule in our client's favor. The way the lawyer arranges and presents the available facts can go a long way toward creating this impulse, as we explore in future chapters.

Third, a lawyer must take into consideration the appellate judge's larger role in law making when he writes an appellate brief. It may be sufficient at the trial level to show a trial judge how binding precedent requires a ruling in a particular way. But on appeal, the lawyer may need to go further and point out how a ruling is consistent with sound public policy, will be easy to implement in the future, or will have some other salutary effect on the law going forward. While such arguments may be made at the trial level too, they are likely to have more impact in the appellate court.

Finally, a lawyer writing an appellate brief must keep in mind that many appellate judges were once trial judges; and even if they weren't, they believe their trial court colleagues to be competent and thoughtful. As such, they are not likely to be persuaded by ad hominem attacks on the trial court or its ruling.

In the next chapter, we turn our attention to learning about the client's story, a job that occupies a large part of a lawyer's typical day at the office.

Chapter 5

Gathering and Assessing the Facts

Facts must be gathered and assessed before they become part of a persuasive legal document.

Let's begin with a story:

> Your new client, the executive director of a small non-profit organization, is in your office. She is a passionate young woman with a degree in biology, who has decided to dedicate her life to saving rain forests in an effort to combat global warming. She formed the small non-profit agency Save Our Forest Trees, which sponsors conferences where scientists working on climate issues can exchange information and form networks. She tells you that SOFT's major source of operating revenue is registration fees for the conferences that she organizes.
>
> Recently, she organized a conference in Indianapolis, and arranged for a block of rooms at a major hotel there. However, some of the people attending the conference were unable to reserve rooms at the hotel; they were told the hotel was sold out on the nights of the conference. The executive director is now incensed because she just received a letter from an attorney for the hotel, demanding that SOFT pay the hotel nearly $10,000 for "unpurchased rooms." The executive director asks you, how in the world can the hotel charge SOFT for rooms its members had been told were unavailable for purchase?
>
> Your first and understandable instinct is likely to be, "It can't." Yet the hotel is trying to do just that. Why? Presumably the hotel has a lawyer who thinks there is a legal basis for this claim. What might that be?

Using your sense of curiosity, you realize that you need to learn more about what happened. That is, you must gather—collect—more facts.

Regardless of how knowledgeable you may be about the law in any given field, all of that knowledge is of limited use until you learn what the client's problem is. Finding out what the problem is begins with interviewing the client—but it by no means ends there. The reality is that clients bring to the lawyer only *their perception* of *some* of the facts. Thus, after hearing the client's version of the story, the lawyer must do additional factual research and some targeted research into the law. Chapter 6 will help you think about the law and strategize about what legal theories to research and assert; for now, however, we first want to focus on how to gather all of the facts that you need to effectively represent your client.

The facts that the client conveys to the lawyer during the initial client interview are usually insufficient for the lawyer to rely upon solely. They are likely deficient for a number of reasons and in a number of ways:

- The client most likely does not know what facts are relevant to the governing law. Thus, he may withhold information because he doesn't believe it is relevant.

- The client may believe that he has done something wrong or embarrassing and may prefer not to disclose those adverse facts to the lawyer. This characteristic of human nature may operate despite reassurances that everything the client says is confidential and explanations that the lawyer needs to know everything so that she can prepare the best possible presentation of his case.

> **The Spark Plug Story**
>
> It is not always the bad facts that the client doesn't reveal at first. Sometimes there are helpful facts that the client doesn't realize are helpful.
>
> Julia (not her real name) sought help from a domestic violence pro bono project to get protection from her abusive domestic partner. She told her lawyer about some mild physical abuse that caused minor injuries. The lawyer prepared a motion for a protection from abuse order, although he worried that the evidence they would be able to present might not be enough to get the order.
>
> On the day set for hearing, as they waited in the coffee shop at the courthouse for the case to be called, Julia mentioned in casual conversation that it was sometimes difficult to manage her life since she was often unable to drive. Her lawyer asked her why she was unable to drive. "Well," she said, "most of the time when my boyfriend leaves for work, he takes the spark plugs out of my car so I can't go anywhere."
>
> In the jurisdiction, that kind of criminal mischief is actionable. And in a domestic violence context, signals a deeper and more deliberate form of abusive and controlling behavior. Needless to say, the lawyer's plan for direct examination of his client changed immediately. The court granted the restraining order.

- The client may believe things that are not provable or even are not true. Clients are only human, after all. They can perceive only what they perceive. Other people may tell the client things that the client later recalls incorrectly or translates in his head using whatever filters and predispositions he may have. While the client may sincerely believe what he tells the lawyer, that version of the facts will often include information that is unsupported by the other facts.

* And unfortunately, a few clients purposely lie to the lawyer to get the lawyer to do something she would not do if she knew the truth.

At least the first three problems are not only common, they are almost universal. In practice, a lawyer who does no fact investigation beyond what the client tells her is a lawyer who is probably committing malpractice. As a result, a typical day in the life of a practicing lawyer involves the lawyer engaged in the process of fact investigation. And, that is why fact investigation is one of the most important jobs a lawyer has, regardless of the type of legal practice. A lawyer engaged in a business or transactional practice rather than litigation nevertheless needs to understand the business deal, or the family relations, or whatever kind of facts will determine how the client's rights might be affected in the future.

You can learn the critical skill of fact investigation in elective courses that include live-client clinics and externships, which allow you to engage, experientially, in actual fact investigation. Simulation courses such as interviewing and negotiations, trial strategy, pretrial discovery, and the like also teach fact investigation. Your legal writing courses cannot cover the topic in depth, and we encourage all law students to take courses that concentrate on fact investigation opportunities because the skill is so critical for your future careers. Our purpose in this section is merely to introduce you to the idea that facts are not always as they seem, and that you, even while in law school, need to think critically about what the facts appear to be, as well as what the opposing party may perceive them to be. Professor Brian Foley has described this condition as "factual indeterminacy": facts are never "fixed" and may be other than what the client would prefer.[1]

While very few *required* law school courses focus on fact investigation, the good news is that it is not hard to learn this. In

---

[1] Brian Foley, *Applied Legal Storytelling, Politics, and Factual Realism*, 14 J. LEGAL WRITING 17, 38 (2008).

fact, since you were a human being before you went to law school, you already have most of what you need: a healthy curiosity. You just need to practice using it in a legal context.

5.1   Facts require context to understand them

Imagine that a person in a uniform is walking toward you, holding a pad of paper and a pen.[2] What does she want?

Although your mind probably jumped to one conclusion, there are many possibilities, of course. To come up with the best answer, however, you need more context. Where are you as the person approaches? What are you doing? Do you know the person approaching, or is she a stranger?

Suppose you are sitting in a restaurant with a menu in your hand. Or you are in a coffeehouse, standing at a counter. The situation makes more sense now: the person approaching will be asking you what food or beverage you would like to order.

Suppose instead you are sitting on your front porch and a man in a brown uniform has just gotten out of his large brown truck, carrying a package and a clipboard. You immediately know that he is a UPS delivery man who is going to ask you to sign for a package he is delivering.

As Chapter 2 explains, you are able to fill in the details of these scenes because they are "stock structures," also sometimes called "stock stories," "idealized cognitive models," or "schema." Everybody recognizes thousands, maybe hundreds of thousands, of these stories. They help us make sense of the world around us. They represent patterns of normal human behavior that we have all seen many times before. Stock stories help facilitate human interaction. For example, imagine that we had no stock structure for "UPS delivery."

---

[2] This example was initially suggested in Steven Winter, *The Cognitive Dimension of the Agon Between Legal Power and Narrative Meaning*, 87 MICH. L. REV. 2225, 2233 (1989), although we have expanded it for our purposes here.

To make sense of this interaction, we would need a much more explicit explanation. The delivery man might have to say something like this:

> Ma'am, I am an employee of a company known as United Parcel Service. We are a company that people or other companies hire to deliver packages. A company has hired us to deliver a package to you. To prove that I have delivered this package to the correct person, the company that is shipping this package has asked me to obtain your signature on this delivery receipt. I will return this delivery receipt to the shipper once you have signed it.

And on and on. We couldn't get anything done if we always had to stop and analyze every interaction and every experience in our day. Stock structures allow us to make assumptions about a scenario and to proceed according to our understanding of what to do in analogous situations.

The lesson for legal writing, then, is this: in the absence of context, the audience will invent context, probably using stock structures that are already in their minds. Those contexts may be based on societal norms (such as what we expect when "ordering food at a restaurant"), or they may be based on readers' personal experiences. But a writer cannot know for certain what stock structure his readers will use to invent the context. For that reason, the legal writer needs to provide readers with sufficient factual detail and context to trigger the stock structure that accurately reflects the actual situation he is describing.

This also means that the lawyer must have first identified, during the interviewing process, the lawyer's own assumptions about the stock structures that she is calling on while imagining the client's situation as the client described it. To use a simplistic example, if a client says to his lawyer "I fell on the rug," it might be worth investigating where the rug was and what it looked like. Falling on a bunched-up runner in a supermarket is very different from falling on wall-to-wall carpet in the client's own house. Likewise, the picture of "falling" could trigger images of someone ending up prone on the floor or someone ending with one knee on the floor but otherwise upright. Whether a lawyer is learning the story from her client or explaining the story to the court, she wants to be sure it contains enough detail to trigger the correct stock structures.

5.2   A five-step process to thinking about fact gathering and fact assessing

Unlike the law school casebook, in the real world, facts rarely present themselves in a tidy package. Once you're a practicing lawyer, you may learn the basics of your client's story from interviewing him, but as we saw in the example above, that could easily result in an incomplete, and possibly inaccurate, account of what actually happened. You will need to dig deeper.

5.2.1   First step: what facts are legally relevant?

Just as the facts don't magically appear on your desk, the client didn't walk into your office and say, "I have a question about the enforceability of a liquidated damages clause in a contract." Her view was more like this: "This hotel that my organization had a conference at wants to charge us for rooms that they sold to other people! Can they do that?" Your job as the attorney is to elicit more of the facts from the client, to think about what the client may be overlooking, and to inquire further.

Once you have learned what you can from your client, the next place to look is into the substantive law that appears, at first glance, to govern the client's problem. Thus, in the SOFT example, you would need to learn more from the client about the dispute. Was the contract in your client's personal name or in the name of the organization? When and where was it negotiated? Was there any prior dealing between the hotel and the client? Were the terms of the contract explained to the client? Did the client read the contract before signing it? How does the client know that the hotel sold rooms that the organization might have used? What explanation did the hotel give for seeking additional payment?

Many of these questions come from what you know about the law of contracts. You are looking to find who made an offer, whether it was accepted, whether the terms were sufficiently definite, and whether the contract was supported by adequate consideration. You would also ask some questions about whether a breach occurred and, if so, whether the hotel had been damaged by the breach.

All of these questions probably popped into your head based on what you learned in your course in contracts. But you may not know the law of the particular jurisdiction or the related relevant laws of discovery or evidence. More research might be in order. And the legal research is likely to suggest that there are more facts needed to help answer the legal questions. Thus, learning the facts helps you frame the scope of the research, but the two processes are recursive. The more you research, the more facts you may discover you need to determine. The first interview with the client is unlikely to be your only interview of her.

Your initial research into the law might suggest that there was no meeting of the minds between the hotel and your client, and that therefore no contract exists. Second, you might wonder whether the contract was imposed on your client by a party in a stronger bargaining position; this would make it a "contract of adhesion" that might be voidable at least in part by the weaker party (your client). Third, your research may suggest that the clause in the contract that calls for the payment of liquidated damages in the event of a breach might not be enforceable. Fourth, you may wonder whether, if the hotel was able to sell all its rooms during the nights of your client's conference, it suffered any damages. Fifth, given your client's claim that some of her organization's members were turned away by the hotel because it was sold out on the nights of the conference, you may consider the defense of "impossibility of performance." All these legal theories will likely suggest additional questions about the facts of the case that you need to seek answers to, either from your client or from some other source.

In addition to researching the substantive law, you may need to think about the law of evidence. The only facts that will matter if this case goes to trial will be those which a judge rules are admissible. As you research the facts, you will need to think about how you would prove each fact in court. You will want to know which witness saw the event, or whether the document you are looking at can be proven to be authentic. If your client did not actually perceive the event she is describing, you may have a hearsay problem,[3] and you will have to ask your client who did see the event so that they can provide direct testimony later. Returning to the hotel reservation example, your client claims that her organization was prevented from performing because the hotel was sold out on the night of the conference. But she does not know that from her own personal knowledge; she gathered that information from other people. So you will need to ask her how she learned this, and who she can talk to in order to verify that her guests were given this information.

Asking questions that have legal significance should not end your inquiry. Instead, continue to ask questions about the relationships and interactions—these types of questions may net important information. This is where remembering to engage your curiosity can bear fruit. Ask the client questions about why the parties acted the way they did. Perhaps there is a reason why the client did not read the contract before she signed it—maybe she was distracted. Perhaps there is something happening with the hotel financially that would cause an aggressive stance with a small nonprofit company. Background details might also be useful to humanize the client and to create visual imagery in the reader's mind. Selecting which details to use in the final written product is explored in Chapter 16; but during the fact investigation phase, you need to open your mind to a wide array of possibly relevant or helpful facts. You will sort out later on which ones actually to use.

---

[3] As you will learn in your course on evidence, hearsay is an out-of-court statement by somebody other than the witness, offered to prove that what the other person said is true.

5.2.2   Second step: what is the chronology?

As we discuss in Chapter 3, we humans are hardwired to think in chronological terms; that's how we experience the world. When you hear a story out of sequence, you will struggle to rearrange it sequentially in your mind so that it makes sense to you. But given the way we gather facts and must present them at trial, it is likely that the facts of the case will come at you in random order. Your client will tell you certain things, often not chronologically. You will then fill in the gaps by talking to other witnesses, reading documents, or doing other investigation, discussed below.

At some point in your investigation, after you have gathered enough of the facts to have a sense of what is going on but before you get too far into the investigation, you will need to prepare a chronology of what happened. It is often helpful to use a visual aid of some sort—a chart, spreadsheet, timeline, storyboard, sketch—to help you see the progression of events. Table 5-1 provides an example of a chart that you might compile based solely on what the client, the non-profit organization's executive director, explained during the initial client interview.

Date	Event	Proof
Early Jan. 2017	Executive director talks to reservation agent for Hotel in Indianapolis; confirms dates for conference and room rate.	Exec Director testimony
About one week later	Proposed contract for room reservations arrives from Hotel; Exec Director looks it over briefly but does not read it carefully.	Exec Director
Jan. 24, 2017	Exec Director signs contract and mails it back to Gloucester.	Exec Director; signed copy of contract
June 2017 (approx.)	Exec Director gets calls from SOFT members reporting that the Hotel block has sold out; Exec Director suggests they book rooms in other nearby hotels.	Exec Director

Date	Event	Proof
July 19, 2017	Conference opens. Many guests cannot get into rooms on time; some guests told that hotel was sold out.	Exec Director
July 30, 2017	Exec Director receives invoice from Hotel for $8,287.88 for "attrition for unsold rooms."	Exec Director; invoice

Table 5-1: Sample spreadsheet timeline for hotel reservations case

As you do additional fact investigation, you can insert additional rows to the chart. Using a spreadsheet allows you to sort information later, an advantage because many Statements of Facts are organized other than as straight chronologies.

Sometimes, a linear chronological order may not be the best way to tell a story. This may be true when you have differing versions of the events—for example, when different witnesses contradict each other. Or, when there are different chains of events that combine to create some legally relevant event. To create a visual image of how the facts can be organized, you might create a storyboard. Write each fact on an index card and lay them out, or pin them on a board, moving them around until they are in the order you want to tell them.[4] Storyboarding can help you visualize each fact and easily move facts to create a different sequence; choose the one that is the easiest for the reader to see.

You will discover which of these organizing tools works best for you. Whether you prefer charts, timelines, or spreadsheets is less important than whether the tool you use helps you visualize the facts in a way that leads to an effective story.

Ultimately, these tools will help you write a coherent story. But their initial purpose is to help you see some of the gaps that need to be

[4] Thank you to Professors Stefan Krieger and Reza Rezvani at Hofstra School of Law for this idea. These professors teach the system to their clinic students as part of trial preparation.

filled. This step may also reveal some of the stock structures in your understanding of the facts. For example, Table 5-1 contains certain assumptions that will need some unpacking. What stock structure does the client mean when she says, "guests couldn't check in on time"? Was it fifteen minutes after the stated hotel check-in time? Two hours? And how many guests were told this? Two? Fifteen? Fifty? All of those facts might make a difference with regard to the issue of "substantial performance" and therefore might merit exploration. As you can see, this process of mapping the facts will help you see the gaps in your evidence. Filling in those gaps will change your map, and you will repeat the analysis again.

5.2.3 Third step: does it all make sense?

Once you think you have uncovered all of the legally relevant facts, as well as sufficient background details for the story to make sense, you should take a step back and look at what you have found. Think in story terms:

- Who are the characters?
- What are their goals?
- What obstacles do they face?

Then, do a thought experiment, trying to get inside the minds of each of the characters in the story. Try to determine whether the character's actions make logical sense. Are they acting as one would expect a character to act in that situation? Are there logical gaps in the action or the timing? Try to walk and perceive the situation from the perspective of each important character in the story. We discuss how to conceive the roles of the different characters in Chapter 7, but for this thought experiment, the precise role they play in the final story is less important than seeing the story from each character's point of view.

During the process, keep notes about whether the story makes sense or whether there are things that stand out to you as odd and worth further thought. Those notes will lead to more fact investigation necessary to complete the picture.

5.2.4   Step four: have you made any assumptions?

We want to stress, again, the importance of recognizing your own assumptions about the facts. Because of the way our minds operate, every story involves each listener filling in gaps with her own mental images or experiences.

Here are two simple examples to remind you:

- **Picture a parking lot**

What do you see? Is it an open, expansive lot such as one in front of malls or big-box stores? Or is it a small lot near your law school? Is it at ground level? In a multilevel structure? Is it the kind of parking lot one might find in a different country that is narrow and alley-like?[5]

- **Picture someone ripping the phone away from another person**

Again, what do you see? Who are the people? Where are they? Is the phone a cell phone? A cordless phone? A traditional landline phone? A wall-mounted phone in a person's house? Or at a large store as part of the intercom system? Was it just the receiver/speaker that was taken away or was a cord disconnected from the wall? Or, if it was the wall-mounted sort of phone, was the whole system pulled off a wall?

While these examples may seem pedestrian, they are taken from real cases where those particular facts were critical to the outcome of that case and where law students needed to conduct a thorough fact investigation to ascertain a clear picture of the events. Recognizing the assumptions we make is an important lawyering skill. Many times, the facts that your client is visualizing will surprise you because you will be visualizing something very different.

---

[5] Thanks to Jason Eyster for this example from his excellent article. James Parry Eyster, *The Lawyer as Artist: Using Significant Moments and Obtuse Objects to Enhance Advocacy*, 14 J. LEGAL WRITING 87, 96 (2008).

Fact investigation is never a linear process. Lawyers typically learn things out of chronological sequence and often need to adjust, on the fly. That is part of what makes a lawyer's job interesting: using common sense and "people skills" to identify facts that will then help solve the client's problem.

5.2.5   Step five: what story will the other side tell?

You will learn about dealing with adverse information in Chapter 12. But you should start thinking about it even while you are doing the initial fact investigation.

When you are advocating for your client, you want to tell your client's story in such a way as to put your client in the best possible light. You will be tempted to credit every fact that makes your client look good, and discount every fact that makes the client look bad. But that would be a serious mistake. Remember that the other side will be doing a thorough fact investigation too, and will be attempting to tell a story that makes the opposing side look good, and your client look bad. If you are unprepared for this, the other side might convince the judge or jury to believe their version of the facts.

You can guard against this by looking not only for the good facts, but for the potential bad facts. Your investigation should therefore sweep broadly. Ask yourself, "What is the other side going to claim? How will they try to justify what they did? Will their explanation make sense to the fact-finder?"

5.3   Tools for investigating and collecting facts

The previous section suggested ways to think about what lawyers need to look for during fact investigation. In this section, we briefly suggest methods to go about looking for those facts.

5.3.1   Two types of facts: adjudicative and legislative

First, we need to define what we mean by "facts." While the word
"facts" may seem clear and not requiring definition, most cases really
deal with two different types of facts. The most common types of
facts are what some scholars call "adjudicative facts.[6] These are the
facts of the case before the court: essentially, the story of what
happened between the parties that caused the dispute. Adjudicative
facts must be proven through admissible evidence, unless stipulated
or assumed as part of a motion. (For example, in a motion to dismiss,
the court must assume that all of the well-pleaded facts of a
complaint are true.)

Less common, but still sometimes important, are "legislative facts."
These are "outside world" facts that are not specific to the dispute
before the court but that may shed some light on an issue that the
court needs to decide. An example of a legislative fact is a census
statistic, such as the fact that June 27, 2017, was a Tuesday or that
June 2017 had some of the hottest days on record in Portland,
Oregon. Lawyers may use legislative facts to argue for a specific
interpretation of a statute, by offering those facts as context for the
problem in society that the legislature attempted to address through
legislation. Or legislative facts may describe a scientific principle
that a lawyer may use to help the court understand what likely
happened in the case. Legislative facts may also help describe the
"setting" in which a dispute takes place—the demographics, zoning,
weather conditions, or the like, which could help explain why events
unfolded as they did. We explain more about specifically writing
about these types of facts in the context of making policy arguments
in Chapter 11.

---

[6] Ellie Margolis, *Beyond Brandeis: Exploring the Uses of Non-Legal Materials in
Appellate Briefs*, 34 U.S.F. L. Rev. 197 (2000). This is another one of the articles
that we recommend reading, in full.

For the purposes of familiarizing yourself with the two different types of facts, keep in mind that adjudicative facts inform the court about the specific dispute it must resolve, while legislative facts are used primarily as background or supplemental explanation, often in the context of making a policy argument in a brief.

Second, the two types of facts require different types of proof. We must submit adjudicative facts to the court through the tools provided by the applicable rules of civil procedure. Adjudicative facts are adduced through interrogatory answers; responses to requests for production of documents; admissions in the pleadings or through a request for admission, deposition, or trial testimony; exhibits identified during depositions or at trial; documents attached to affidavits; and in a myriad other ways. Collectively, all of these materials form the "record" of a case.

Legislative facts, on the other hand, do not require proof in the same way that adjudicative facts do, but they do require authentication. The authentication could be accomplished via the credibility of the source in which they are published. Statistics housed on websites that have a .gov extension carry the imprimatur of that government entity's ethos, and a court will likely take judicial notice of the fact. In other words, lawyers who use legislative facts research and cite to reliable authorities.[7] Even when lawyers do not introduce legislative facts, judges regularly research legislative facts as a tool to help them decide cases.[8]

---

[7] With the advent of "fake news" sites in the modern world, the legal writer needs to take a great deal of care to vet the source to be sure it is reliable.

[8] *See* Coleen Barger, *On the Internet, Nobody Knows You're a Judge: Federal Appellate Courts' Use of Internet Sites*, 4 J. APP. PRAC. & PROCESS 417 (2002) (providing often-cited standards for checking source accuracy and credibility); Ellie Margolis, *Surfin' Safari—Why Competent Lawyers Should Research on the Web*, 10 YALE J.L. & TECH. 82 (2007); *see also* Lee F. Peoples, *The Citation of Wikipedia in Judicial Opinions*, 12 YALE J.L. & TECH. 1 (2009) (providing guideline suggestions).

5.3.2   Facts, inferences, and characterizations

One more distinction needs to be drawn between facts, inferences, and characterizations.

5.3.2.1. Facts

A fact is a knowable event or condition. To a lawyer, "knowable" means "provable in court with competent evidence." You will learn more about this concept in your course in Evidence, but for present purposes "competent evidence" means direct testimony by witnesses who observed the event, authentic documents, recorded video, or other reliable information proving that something happened. A police officer who testifies that he clocked a defendant's vehicle traveling at 77 MPH using a properly calibrated radar gun would be stating a "fact" under this definition.

5.3.2.2. Inferences

An inference is a deduction based on reasonable assumptions drawn from provable facts. Suppose a police officer estimated the speed of a vehicle immediately prior to a crash as 77 miles per hour by measuring the skid marks, determining the weight of the vehicle, the condition of the road, the condition of the vehicle's tires, and other factors, and doing mathematical calculations based on his training. The length of the skid marks, weight of the vehicle, and other information would be facts; the conclusion that the vehicle was going 77 MPH prior to the crash would be an inference drawn from those facts.

Inferences are important, and often essential, in resolving cases. Suppose a criminal defendant is charged with premeditated murder; his state of mind (that is, whether he planned the murder or not) is an element of the crime that must be proven. But there is almost never any direct evidence of that state of mind; it must be inferred from other facts.

We will discuss inferential reasoning in more detail in Chapter 13.

5.3.2.3. Characterizations

A characterization is really nothing more than somebody's opinion. For example, a statement in a brief that the defendant's car was traveling "fast" is a characterization. Fast compared to what? A car going 77 miles per hour on a residential street may be thought to be going "fast;" but traveling that speed on the Indianapolis Motor Speedway during a race would be very, very slow.

It is rare that you will want, or need, to include characterizations in a legal memorandum. It is better to report the facts in a neutral-sounding way and let the audience form its own opinion. It is much more powerful to say, "The defendant drove through the residential neighborhood at 77 miles per hour," than to say, "the defendant drove very fast through the residential neighborhood," because the factual statement creates a much more vivid image in the audience's mind.

It goes without saying that facts are different than misinformation, i.e., incorrectly stated facts whether made inadvertently, by omission, or deliberately. When misinformation is deliberately disseminated broadly, it is called disinformation.

The remainder of this chapter deals with determining what the facts are. We will discuss how, and where, to draw inferences in Chapters 9 and 13.

5.3.3   Formal tools for discovering facts beyond what the client knows

Most of the time, when lawyers think about how to discover the facts of the case, they focus on the formal tools of discovery provided by the rules of procedure for whatever court the case may be pending in. And certainly, these tools are very powerful and helpful; they may be the only way to determine facts that your opponent knows or believes. You have been introduced to—or will be introduced to—some of these tools in your courses on civil and criminal procedure. We do not have the ability to talk about them in detail here other than to mention them by name: interrogatories, depositions, affidavits, subpoenas for testimony or documents, and motions to compel (a last-resort technique).

5.3.4   Informal tools for discovering facts

Beyond the formal methods for discovery, there are many informal tools for discovering facts, which lawyers use every day as part of deciding whether to use more formal means to bring the facts into the official record.

5.3.4.1   Client interview

The first and most obvious source of information is your client. During the initial interview with your client, you need to accomplish several things:

- Develop a trusting relationship with the client.

- Gather information about what happened, from your client's perspective. Start to identify sources for additional information (documents, other witnesses, etc.).

- Attempt to identify your client's goal.

> **Some introductory ethos considerations during witness investigation**
>
> 1. Your contact with these potential witnesses is not protected by attorney–client privilege. Assume the opposing counsel will learn that you contacted these people.
>
> 2. If you ask too many leading questions (questions that obviously suggest the answer), you risk planting false ideas or compromising the witness's recollection. Recollection is a fragile thing to begin with. The goal of interviewing a potential witness is to gather facts, not to educate the witness.
>
> 3. People are nervous to speak with lawyers, and the more a lawyer is able to put the person at ease, the more the person will probably be able to access their recollections. The worst thing a lawyer can do is to be pushy or unfriendly: that can turn a neutral witness hostile.
>
> 4. You may not directly contact people who are represented by counsel. You must go through their lawyer. (ABA Rule 4.2)
>
> 5. If you contact people who are unrepresented by counsel, you must be clear that you do not represent their interests. (ABA Rule 4.3)

- Differentiate roles. What is your client supposed to do to assist in developing the case, and what will you do as her lawyer?

- Establish your fee arrangement and other practical details relating to the representation.

In our hotel example, we have already learned the basics of the problem (as she perceives it) from our client, the president of the nonprofit organization. The full interview with the client would include detailed questioning not only about what she knows directly about the transaction, but to identify other people who might know different pieces of the issue, including the identities of the nonprofit organization members who experienced problems and who might be able to confirm the client's story or to provide different perspectives on what happened. The lawyer does this not because she doesn't believe her client; she does it to be able to present a complete, and factually accurate, story to the court.

5.3.4.2 *Witness interviews*

Often you will next talk to other people who were present or who otherwise have knowledge of the events leading to the lawsuit. Some of those witnesses may be known to the client, and some may be easily ascertained via common sense research. In the hotel example, a quick phone call to several of the organization members might help you learn how long the guests had to wait to get into their rooms, or what they were told when they attempted to book rooms but were denied.

5.3.4.3 *Document review*

Another important source of facts will be documents, many of which you will be able to obtain without formal discovery. For example, in a contract case like the hotel reservation example, the client should have a copy of the written agreement. In a personal injury action, a police report may describe the accident, and even though your client may not have a copy of it, a simple call or visit to the police station should be sufficient to get a copy.

5.3.4.4 Informal discussion with opposing counsel

Most states have adopted some version of the Model Rule of Professional Conduct 3.2, which states, "A lawyer shall make reasonable efforts to expedite litigation consistent with the interests of the client." Lawyers representing the plaintiff in an action might not know until initial demands or complaints are sent who opposing counsel is or whether there is opposing counsel. Assuming both sides to an action have retained lawyers, there is a good chance that the lawyers will be able to work together, without formal discovery requests, to help expedite litigation through candid exchanges of information without resort to demanding the information through motions to the court. Experienced lawyers know that it is in their client's interest to voluntarily provide such information if the court would ultimately demand that they do so anyway. This saves clients both time and money.

In the hotel example, it would be unethical for the lawyer representing the nonprofit organization to directly call the hotel to ask it for booking records or other documents that might relate to the case. But if she knows who represents the hotel, perhaps from the demand letter her client received from the hotel's counsel, she might be able to call that hotel's lawyer and work out an informal exchange of relevant documents before litigation begins.

5.3.4.5 Electronic sources

Finally, in today's Information Age, electronic sources of information are readily accessible and can be highly useful. The events that are in dispute may have been reported in the news media, so there may be newspaper reports, television clips, or YouTube videos of the incident. The event may have been discussed in blogs. The possibilities here are potentially endless. You probably are also aware that lawyers—just like employers—regularly look at the websites, online bios, and Facebook or other social media pages of parties and witnesses. In some cases, a lawyer may even hire companies that specialize in unlocking the privacy controls of those pages.

In the hotel example, it might be possible to research publicly available calendars to determine if, for example, some other major event was taking place in Indianapolis around the same time as the nonprofit organization's conference that put a great demand on hotel rooms in the city. Or, you could check the website of the hotel to determine if it may have been under renovation at the time of the conference. Any of this sort of information might help explain the hotel's behavior.

> **An Opportunity (and a caution!)**
>
> A good lawyer will advise her client not to discuss her legal problems on social media or in some other electronic form. But some will anyway. Searching Facebook, Twitter, blog, or other electronic sources for things your opponent has posted could turn up useful information which is not confidential. (And of course, you will quickly learn to counsel your own clients NOT to post such information!)

5.3.5 Conclusion

As you gather facts, a picture of the case—and your client—begins to emerge. In Chapter 9, we will discuss how to incorporate all of the facts you have discovered into a coherent story for the Facts section of a brief. And in Chapter 15 we will discuss how to incorporate the facts and appropriate inferences into the Argument section of your brief, to show how the law applies to your facts of the case. But the next step right now is to think about what all of this means in the context of the law. What legal theories or remedies might be available to assist your client in achieving her goal? We take this topic up in Chapter 6.

Researching the Client's Legal Problem

None of the authors of this text have ever had a client come to our offices and tell us, "I've got a defamation per se case I'd like to talk to you about," or "I need to find out if this deed creates a fee simple determinable or a fee on condition subsequent," or "I need a restraining order against my ex-roommate, but I'm concerned about whether the family court will have subject matter jurisdiction." Rather, the clients arrive in our offices to tell us about a dispute, or to ask a general question about how to avoid a dispute by, for example, drafting a contract to protect the client's rights in the future. They tell us about the facts of their situations and then ask us to help them achieve some goal. It is up to us to figure out what all those seemingly random facts might mean, legally.

In the previous chapters, you learned about how to discover the facts of your client's situation and how to turn those facts into a coherent story about your client. But of course, that is just the beginning of your representation of the client. Now you need to apply your legal training to the problem and figure out how—and sometimes whether—the law can assist the client in achieving her goals. This is not a linear process.

In this book we refer to two related but different concepts: the "theory of the case" and the "theme." We think of the "theory of the case" as the legal rules and theories that allow your client to win; that is, the *logos* of the case. The theme relates to the emotional reason why your client *should* win; that is, the *pathos* of the case. This chapter is about developing the theory of your case; we return to developing themes in Chapters 7 and 8.

For even a relatively simple legal problem, the research process can be quite daunting. In your first year of law school, your research assignments are likely to be quite narrow, and often the scope of the issues may be defined for you. In practice, of course, this is less often the case. Thus, it is good to start developing good research practices now—when the scope of your task is manageable. This chapter will explore some specific strategies for planning, organizing, and executing your research process. If you develop a sound research process, it will serve you well no matter how complex a future research task might be.

Typically, you will begin by stepping back and taking a high-altitude view of the situation, surveying all of your legal knowledge to think about any legal issue that might be involved. You will then need to conduct more specific research to determine which of those issues are viable. But as you conduct research, additional issues may present themselves, and you will need to circle back to investigate those new ideas. This process is what we mean by developing the theory of your case. This chapter will help you navigate that process.

6.1   Identifying the legal issues

Imagine you are in an airplane, cruising at 35,000 feet en route to some distant city. Several hours into the flight, your traveling companion asks you to look out the window to find out where you are right now.

If you are not a frequent traveler or have little knowledge of geography, you probably won't be able to do much more than make a broad guess. But let's assume you travel this route often, and you do have a good idea of the local geography. You examine where the sun is in relation to the time of day and determine what direction you are looking. You look out the window for clues: you look for rivers, mountain ranges, highways, cities. You calculate how long you have been flying from the airport you took off from to get a general sense of how far you have flown. You compare what you see to your preexisting knowledge of geography. Based on this information, you can formulate an informed guess as to where you might currently be.

But this is still pretty much a guess. To pinpoint your location, you need more data. Perhaps your airline allows you to listen in to the air-traffic control frequency; as your pilot chats with various control centers, you can get a clearer sense of what city you are near. Or you may have a detailed map available to you, enabling you to look at the area where you think you probably are and then compare what you see on the ground to what is shown on the map. This lets you make a more accurate determination as to where you actually are.

Lawyers are frequent travelers; clients are our traveling companions. When a client asks, "Where are we?" she hopes that the lawyer can use his prior training and current research skills to come up with an accurate determination.

The process of thinking about a client's problem is very similar to how the frequent traveler tries to determine where the airplane is at any given moment. You begin by tapping into your background training: your knowledge of the broad areas of the law (torts, contracts, criminal law, etc.). Next, you start to think about more specific, narrow legal theories that might be involved; but then you realize how little you actually know about the specific area of the law. You need help! This suggests a four-step process for getting started.

6.1.1   Identify the domain

When you first start to think about your client's problem, thinking back to your first-year law school courses is a great place to start. Does my client's problem involve torts? Property? Contracts? A combination of these things? Be sure to leave your mind open to consider a very wide range of possibilities here; we'll start to narrow down the choices soon enough.

6.1.2   Identify possible issues within the domain

Now break it down further: if this appears to be a torts problem, what kind of tort might be involved? What kinds of property interests are affected? Make a list of the possibilities—but be prepared to expand your list when you get into the next step.

6.1.3   Research the substantive issues

Before you can determine which of the issues may be involved, you will need to conduct specific research into each one of them. A few you may be able to dismiss quickly, based on your prior knowledge of what the law is; but many more will require you to do at least some preliminary, and maybe some highly detailed, research. Also, be attentive to what you find; the cases and statutes that you discover may suggest additional issues you had not considered before.

Let's see how this works by returning to our hotel reservations case. The executive director of the nonprofit organization has just left your office after describing the demand letter she received from the hotel chain. To decide the next steps, your thought process might go like this.

6.1.3.1.   *Identify the domain*

Since the nonprofit organization signed a contract with the hotel, this appears to be a contract issue. But the careful lawyer will think about whether there are possible other theories as well, such as misrepresentations, or fraudulent conduct.

6.1.3.2.   *Spot the issues*

The contracts questions are the most obvious. The basic contracts questions from 1L year will always be the starting point even if they are answered quickly. The first thing one does is ascertain whether the contract was valid to begin with. And whether the terms are all clear and enforceable. Next, whether, in fact, the client breached the contract as claimed. If so, what the damages are.

6.1.3.3.   *Research*

Some of the questions asked in the above part will generate questions for research—for example, the question of whether there was a contract. Some contracts are considered contracts of adhesion. Unconscionable clauses in contracts of adhesion might not be enforced. Were the terms clear? The "attrition clause" that the hotel letter quotes claims to be a liquidated damages clause, but only some liquidated damages clauses are enforceable. What are the damages? A cause of action for breach of contract requires that a plaintiff prove that it has been damaged by the breach, but in our case, it looks like the hotel was sold out during the nonprofit organization's conference, so it was not in fact damaged.

As you gain experience as a lawyer, this process will become easier. But even an experienced lawyer will sometimes encounter a client problem that stumps him. When he does, the best way to start is to get back into the airplane, gain some altitude, and look around.

6.1.4 Research procedural or "side" issues including burdens of proof and standards of review

Your case does not occur in a vacuum. Some process took place to get it to the point where you are writing about it. Perhaps the judge is deciding a motion to dismiss a complaint under Rule 12(b)(6). Or maybe it is a Rule 56 Motion for Summary Judgment. But note which side has the burden of proof for the substantive issue presented. By "note," we mean write it down and think about it.

The burden of proof is different than a standard of review on appeal. The former governs the amount of evidence a party must produce, and who must produce it. The latter governs the appellate court reviewing the proceedings. Like the burden of proof, you will want to note the standard of appellate review (i.e., write it down and spend some time thinking about it). In an appellate context, the court will need to determine what level of deference to give to the ruling of the court below. Will it review the record *de novo*, or will it review only for an abuse of discretion? The latter will result in a reversal only when the moving party can overcome a significant hurdle.

Many of these procedural issues may not be controversial, in the
sense that the parties may agree that in the context of a summary
judgment motion the reviewing court must read the record in the
light most favorable to the plaintiff, or that the appellate court must
review the conclusions of law reached by the trial court *de novo*, but
will review the court's finding of fact only for an abuse of discretion.
However, you will need to tell the court what the procedural posture
of the case is and cite authority for what the proper standard of
review is, at either the trial or appellate court levels. You should
research the appropriate jurisdiction for binding authority (e.g., don't
cite a Federal Rule of Civil Procedure in a state court proceeding)
and analyze it to be sure that there are not any significant issues to
develop further.

6.2   Organizing your research

The best way of keeping track of your research is the method you are
comfortable with. Experienced researchers develop their own
preferred methods. However, if you are new to legal research, you
might want to consider one of the methods we suggest here.

6.2.1   Commercial research programs

Most major online research services, including WeslawNext,
Westlaw Edge, and Lexis Advance allow you to store research results
in a set of folders and subfolders that you define. You can store cases,
statutes, secondary authorities, or discrete quotations from any of
those sources in any folder you create. While these tools are built
into those services, they require you to be connected to the research
service to use them, and they are limited in what they do.

Several commercial products are available to help you organize
research results on your computer. The best known of these, CaseMap
by Lexis, helps you organize not only your research results but also
your evidence. You can code both your research and your deposition
transcripts or other evidence to specific issues that you define, so that

you can retrieve both facts and law relevant to any issue at the click of a mouse. Other programs, such as MasterFile, provide similar services—for a fee. All are database management systems, in which you enter "data" in the form of your notes regarding your research results. The program then helps you sort and retrieve your data in whatever form you need.

6.2.2   Create your own database

If you do not have access to CaseMap, MasterFile, or another case management program, it is relatively simple to create your own using a spreadsheet. The keys to effective use of such a system are

- identifying the key issues and sub-issues involved in the case (to help you sort and retrieve your results later); and

- carefully analyzing the cases, statutes, and other authorities you find and "coding" them to the issues in the case where they may be helpful.

This suggests you should create two spreadsheets. The first would be a simple listing of the issues and sub-issues that you may need to address; the second is a more complex listing of the cases, statutes, and other authorities that provide the legal rules that resolve those issues.

6.2.2.1.   Creating the issues list

Let's return to the hotel reservations case to see how this works. In section 6.1.2 above, you identified several major issues relating to the possible breach of contract case:

- Was there a contract at all?

- Were the terms of the contract clear?

- Are the terms enforceable?

- Did the nonprofit organization breach the contract?

- If the nonprofit organization breached, was that because the hotel sold all the rooms before the nonprofit organization conference attendees could buy them?

- Was the hotel damaged by the breach?

Note the logical progression of these issues, from broad to narrow, and in chronological order as the relationship between SOFT and Gloucester evolved. In this sense, the arrangement of the issues tells the legal story of the case.

In section 6.1.3, you did some research to refine your issues list. You discovered some new concepts that provide some more specific legal rules. You might revise your original issues list to include these sub-issues, looking something like this:

- Is there a contract?
  - Offer?
  - Acceptance?
  - Consideration?
- Is it a contract of adhesion?
  - Is there a disparity in bargaining power?
  - Was the contract offered on a take-it-or-leave-it basis?
  - Is the attrition clause unconscionable?
  - Is the attrition clause a true liquidated damages provision?
- Are damages reasonably calculable?
  - Is amount of damages specified proportional to actual loss?
  - Is provision punitive?
- Breach of contract?
  - Did the nonprofit organization breach?
  - Did the hotel suffer any damage?
- Was it even possible for the nonprofit organization to perform?

As you do more research into these issues, you may start to discern certain sub-issues, elements, or factors that courts employ in cases like this. You should constantly be revising and refining your list of issues and sub-issues; Figure 6-1 shows a more detailed list of issues, which was developed by additional research.

The main issues appear in boldface, with the bulleted sub-issues below.

Finally, to help you keep track of your research results and tie them to your issues, you should assign each issue and sub-issue some sort of code. To make it easy to sort your research results by issue, it is simplest to assign a number to each issue and sub-issue, something like the system shown in Figure 6-1.

Note that the issue numbers are not sequential. There are several reasons for this. First, identifying a main issue with a number divisible by 10 allows you to show the hierarchy of how the issues relate to each other: the first digit of each sub-issue is the same as the first digit of the main issue to which it is related. Second, leaving gaps between each major issue allows you to add more sub-issues as your research proceeds and you discover potential new sub-issues. And if you discover a new major issue, you can always add it to the bottom of your list as your research proceeds.

	Main issue
Issue #	**Sub-issue**
10	**Is there a contract?**
11	• offer?
12	• acceptance?
13	• consideration?
20	**Is it a contract of adhesion?**
21	• is there a disparity in bargaining power?
22	• was contract offered on take-it-or-leave-it basis?
23	• is the attrition clause unconscionable?
30	**Is attrition clause a true liquidated damages provision?**
31	• are damages reasonably calculable?
32	• is amount of damages specified proportional to actual loss?
33	• is provision punitive?

40	**Impossibility of performance?**
41	• Event beyond control of breaching party
42	• Absolute impossibility to perform results
50	**Breach of contract?**
51	• did the non-profit organization breach?
52	• did the hotel make the non-profit organization's performance impossible by selling all available rooms?
53	• did the hotel suffer any damage?

Figure 6-1: Issue list for the hotel reservation case

6.2.2.2.   Creating the database of authorities

Next you need to create a comprehensive list of possible authorities and the relationship of each to the identified issues. This is where a standard spreadsheet program such as Excel or QuattroPro can be very useful. If you design your spreadsheet carefully, simply using the Sort feature will help you group all of your authorities according to the issue or issues that they address.

We suggest creating a spreadsheet with the following columns:

				Issue #				
Authority name	Citation	Court	Date	1	2	3	4	Notes

A template with these columns is available as an Excel spreadsheet at the website for this book.

This list of headings, also known as a "header row," describes "fields" of a database. Each row beneath this header row should include a single authority: a case, a section of a statute, a court rule, and so on. In database terminology, these are "records." Not every cell needs to be filled out, of course. Statutes will not have an entry for "court," for example. The key to this spreadsheet is identifying which issue from your issue list the authority is relevant to. Each one may be relevant to more than one issue, of course, which is why there are four columns identified for "Issue #." Record the number(s) of the issue(s) that each authority helps with in those columns.

The final column, "Notes," is where you can record a very brief synopsis of the main point or points of the authorities. This will help you later on in selecting which authorities you need to study further.

As you encounter new authorities, just keep recording them in separate rows, going down the spreadsheet. It doesn't matter what order you put them in; you will use the Sort feature of your spreadsheet later on to put them in a more useful order.

A sample research spreadsheet for the SOFT case—based on Indiana law—might look something like Table 6-1, below. (Note that this is not intended to represent a complete database; yours will probably include many more cases and perhaps a few statutes or court rules, depending on the kind of issue you are researching.)

Unsorted database (in order of cases found)

Authority name	Citation	Court	Date	Issue # 1	2	3	4	Notes
2625 Building Corporation v. Deutsch	385 N.E. 2d 1189	Ind. Ct. App.	1979	33				Great case on facts! Involves hotel room reservations and failure to use rooms (but oral contract only); hotel not allowed to keep payment
Pigman v. Ameritech Publishing	641 N.E.2d 1026	Ind. Ct. App.	1998	20	22			Good case: exculpatory clause in contract unenforceable as unconscionable
Kincaid v. Lazar	405 N.E.2d 615	Ind. Ct. App.	1980	10				interp. of contract up to court; will enforce on its face if unambiguous

Beck v. Mason	580 N.E.2d 290	Ind. Ct. App.	1991	30	12		intent of parties controls whether clause is liquidated damages or other
Sanford v. Castleton Health Care Center	813 N.E.2d 411	Ind. Ct. App.	2004	12	21	20	failure to read K before signing no excuse; defines adhesion contract
Collins v. McKinney	871 N.E.2d 363	Ind. Ct. App.	2007	50	53		list of elements of cause of action for breach of contract
Rogers v. Lockard	767 N.E.2d 982	Ind. Ct. App.	2002	30	12		intent of parties controls whether clause is liquidated damages or other
Prather v. Latshaw	122 N.E. 721	Supreme	1919	41			act of other party preventing performance excuses breach
General Bargain Ctr. v. American Alarm Co.	430 N.E.2d 407	Ind. Ct. App.	1982	30			definition of liquidated damages clause (p. 993)
Grott v. Jim Barna Log Systems–Midwest, Inc.	794 N.E.2d 1098	Ind. Ct. App.	2003	10			presumption of free bargaining
Trimble v. Ameritech Publishing	700 N.E.2d 1128	Supreme	1998	20	22		Disapproves of *Pigman*; maybe this is not a good issue for us

Table 6-1: Raw database as cases are found

6.3   Selecting the issues to write about

Once you have finished the first round of your preliminary research, you can use your spreadsheet to help you organize your results. From there you can determine (a) whether additional research is needed, and (b) which issues appear to be viable. By the end of this process, you should have a coherent theory of your case.

6.3.1 Arranging your research results

The value in using a spreadsheet program to record research results is that you can use the built-in Sort feature to rearrange the data in any way you choose.

Sorting a database can occur at multiple levels. The top-level sort arranges each row of the spreadsheet according to the value in one of the columns (either alphabetically or numerically, depending on the kind of data contained in that column). But when more than one record (row) contains identical values in that field, all records with the same value are listed one after the other. You can then define second-, third-, and lower-level sorts to arrange the rows with those identical values according to the values in a different field.

This is easier to see by using an example. Take a look at Table 6-1, above. You can see that the researcher has listed eleven authorities. They are listed in the order in which the researcher found them (essentially, random order). But because the researcher carefully listed (or "coded") the issues that each authority related to, we can now sort the spreadsheet to gather together all of the cases that relate to the same issues.

Table 6-2 below shows the same authorities as Table 6-1, but this time they have been sorted using the spreadsheet program's Sort feature. The top-level sort was on column E (which bears the heading "Issue 1"); this grouped all of the records according to the main issue that the authority addresses. But since three of the authorities involved issue 30 (defined on the issues list as "Is the attrition clause a true liquidated damages provision?"), a second-level sort on column D (the date of the authority) arranges all three of those authorities so that the most recent cases jump to the top of the list of cases related to that issue.

Database sorted by issue and date

Authority name	Citation	Court	Date	Issue # 1	2	3	4	Notes
Grott v. Jim Barna Log Systems– Midwest, Inc.	794 N.E.2d 1098	Ind. Ct. App.	2003	10				presumption of free bargaining
Kincaid v. Lazar	405 N.E.2d 615	Ind. Ct. App.	1980	10				interp. of contract up to court; will enforce on its face if unambiguous
Sanford v. Castleton Health Care Center	813 N.E.2d 411	Ind. Ct. App.	2004	12	21	20		failure to read K before signing no excuse; defines adhesion contract
Pigman v. Ameritech Publishing	641 N.E.2d 1026	Ind. Ct. App.	1998	20	22			Good case: exculpatory clause in contract unenforceable as unconscionable
Trimble v. Ameritech Publishing	700 N.E.2d 1128	Supreme	1998	20	22			Disapproves of *Pigman*; maybe this is not a good issue for us
Rogers v. Lockard	767 N.E.2d 982	Ind.Ct.App.	2002	30	12			intent of parties controls whether clause is liquidated damages or other
Beck v. Mason	580 N.E.2d 290	Ind.Ct.App.	1991	30	12			intent of parties controls whether clause is liquidated damages or other
General Bargain Ctr. v. American Alarm Co.	430 N.E.2d 407	Ind. Ct. App.	1982	30				definition of liquidated damages clause (p. 993)

2625 Building Corporation v. Deutsch	385 N.E. 2d 1189	Ind. Ct. App.	1979	33		Great case on facts! Involves hotel room reservations and failure to use rooms (but oral contract only); hotel not allowed to keep payment
Prather v. Latshaw	122 N.E. 721	Supreme	1919	41		act of other party preventing performance excuses breach
Collins v. McKinney	871 N.E.2d 363	Ind. Ct. App.	2007	50	53	list of elements of cause of action for breach of contract

Table 6-2: Database sorted by issue and date

You can, of course, sort and resort the data on any of the fields you define in the header row.

6.3.2   Analyzing your results

Once you have sorted the data, you may notice some gaps in your research. Consider these examples:

- You may have no authority identified for some of the issues.

- You may have conflicting authorities for several of the issues (you can see that by looking at the "Notes" field for each authority listed as relating to a specific issue).

- You may have statutory authority but no interpretive case law for one or more issues.

- The authorities you have for any issue may be very old, or from nonbinding jurisdictions, or inadequate in some other way.

Any shortcoming you find in analyzing your results might suggest additional research that you should do to flesh out your legal analysis. You can just keep adding new authorities to the bottom of the spreadsheet, then resort the sheet periodically to see where you are.

Of course, some of the issues on your issues list may turn out to be based on well-settled principles of law and won't require a great deal of research or analysis. For example, in Figure 6-1, our list of issues for the SOFT case includes a series of issues (issues 10–13) involving questions of whether a contract was formed to begin with. The rules regarding offer, acceptance, and consideration are good examples of well-settled rules that have not changed much (or at all) for decades, and thus one or two cases setting those rules out may be all that you need.

6.3.3   Selecting the issues for deeper analysis

You started with a broad list of issues, just to make sure you didn't miss anything potentially important. But one of the most common mistakes made by new lawyers (and many older ones) is presenting too many issues to the court. This "scattergun" approach is generally ineffective for the following reasons:

- It makes the advocate look indecisive or lazy. The judge may see a brief listing 14 different issues and think, "This lawyer doesn't have any good argument to make at all, so he'll try anything." Or worse yet, "This lawyer doesn't understand his case very well."

- If you have a page or word count limit, using those pages or words to discuss issues with little merit

> **Judgments, not wishes**
>
> As you are sorting through your potential issues, be sure that you make your decisions about which issue to include based on sound judgment rather than on wishful thinking. For example, do not decide to omit an issue just because it is troublesome for your client. Ignoring the weak points won't make them go away and you can be sure your opponent will highlight your weaknesses. Rather, choose to eliminate the issues that are so insignificant that they do not affect the outcome of your case. Similarly, potential issues that turn out to be well-settled will warrant little or no discussion. Remember, judges are busy people; keep their attention focused on what really matters.

deprives you of the pages or words you could use more
effectively to discuss issues that are more significant.

* It is distracting. You don't want to force the reader to wade
  through a lot of "iffy" arguments to get to the gems.

Of course, deciding what is an "iffy" argument and what is a gem
is part of the art of being a lawyer.

Your research spreadsheet, if constructed well, can help you decide
which issues are worth discussing and which you should abandon.
After you sort your research results by issue, you can scan the
"Notes" field for each issue group and get a good picture of what the
rules are for each issue. This will help you understand whether the
issue works for your client or whether it is not worth developing
further.

Let's try this out on the research results for Pat Freebird and SOFT.
Recall that in Figure 6-1, the first major issue (number 10) deals with
whether a contract was formed in the first place. You may conclude,
based on your knowledge of what Pat admits she did, that all of the
elements for a valid contract (described in more detail in sub-issues
11–13) are present in the case and that this is not likely to be a very
fertile ground for defending her organization. You could then
rationally decide not to raise that issue at all in your brief, but to focus
on other issues that are more likely to result in a favorable outcome.

The second major issue (number 20), whether the contract was one of
adhesion, may be more promising. In looking over the cases you
found through your research, you might conclude that Gloucester
had a great deal more bargaining power than SOFT (sub-issue 21)
and that Gloucester drafted the initial contract and presented it to
SOFT on a take-it-or-leave-it basis, offering no real opportunity for
bargaining (sub-issue 22). But that last sub-issue, number 23 on your
list, may be problematic. Was the provision truly unconscionable?
You may decide you need to study the cases you found on that sub-
issue more closely to see what kinds of things have been found

"unconscionable" in prior cases. Then you can determine from that closer analysis whether you should raise that issue.

The third and fourth major issues may both look very good, from SOFT's point of view. It seems likely that the damages are easily calculable (sub-issue 31) since the contract itself specifies the formula by which the damages may be calculated. Likewise, the damages (more than $9,000) seem disproportionate to the actual loss (sub-issue 32) since the evidence suggests the hotel was sold out on the night in question and therefore suffered no damage at all. For the same reason, sub-issues 52 (impossibility of performance) and 53 (the requirement of damages as an element of a cause of action for breach of contract) look very promising, again because the hotel was sold out and couldn't have accommodated any more SOFT guests anyway.

From this analysis, you might now conclude that you have two viable major issues: whether the attrition clause is a valid liquidated damages provision (issue 30) and whether Gloucester may prove a breach of contract (issue 50). Both of those major issues have two sub-issues, which look pretty strong. Based on this analysis, you might reasonably forgo making any argument about whether this was a contract of adhesion (issue 20) since that seems weaker and more distracting to the judge.

6.4   Next steps

Having thus identified the theory of your case (in our example, two complementary theories), it is time to conduct more detailed research and analysis of the rules governing those issues. The next chapter will help you think about how to structure an argument in your client's favor for each of the issues you have chosen. In upcoming chapters, we will discuss how to write about these issues in the ways most favorable to your client.

Chapter 7

Representing Your Client, the Protagonist

At the heart of every story is the central character or protagonist. In a legal story, the protagonist is usually our client. It is her story that we tell, and we will want to tell it from her point of view. The first step of creating that story is to develop our protagonist–client. This chapter draws on literary theory to explore the different types of protagonists that we may choose from to describe our client. In addition, it examines the role of other characters, including the opposing party and others who play less significant roles in our story.

This chapter also examines how we begin to think about the obstacles the client must overcome to reach her ultimate goal. When we have identified the client's character, goals, and obstacles to that goal, we have the underlying structure of our story. This structure forms the foundation of our persuasive document. Later we will build on this foundation by adding the stylistic or aesthetic refinements that complete our story.[1]

As we begin to build our client's story, remember that we are in the thinking stages of the writing process. Remaining curious involves considering alternative approaches; questioning the assumptions we have made about our own mental images of the settings and actions as our client described the facts of the story to us; exploring the gaps in our legal theory; and evaluating the effectiveness of the theme

---

[1] Material in these paragraphs was adapted from Brian J. Foley & Ruth Anne Robbins, *Fiction 101: A Primer for Lawyers on How to Use Fiction Writing Techniques to Write Persuasive Facts Sections*, 32 RUTGERS L.J. 459 (2001), *citing* Robert McKee, STORY: SUBSTANCE, STRUCTURE, STYLE AND THE PRINCIPLES OF SCREENWRITING 15 (Regan Books 1997) (analogizing writing training to music training, saying that writers should think more like composers and recognize that they need formal training in the craft).

that will tie our story together. We are in a very fluid stage of the process and do not want to become locked into one rigid approach to the story too soon. While keeping our options open, we first turn to examining the core of the legal story—its characters. Not surprisingly, we begin with our client.

7.1   The client as a character in the legal story

Representing a client well, whether it be in litigation, a transaction, or any other context, requires you to understand the characters in the client's story, in both the context of the dispute and the client's overall life. The most important character, of course, is the client itself, even when the client is an organization such as a corporation or government.

No matter who the character, the same truism will exist: characters have **_needs_**, which are baseline survival fundamentals, and **_goals_**, which are aspirations. As a lawyer, you must consider both when representing a client because, after all, the client's needs and goals are what brought him to your office in the first place. Thus, your primary considerations are answers to these sorts of questions: What challenges does the client face before meeting her desired goal? How does the current legal action fit in—as a pathway to achieving the goal, or a roadblock that hinders the client from reaching the goal?

For example, negotiating a contract for the purchase of raw materials will help the client produce the finished product and reach the goal of selling that product. The contract is a pathway to help the client satisfy its need of the raw materials that are necessary to creating the finished product. Negotiating the contract moves the client forward toward the goal. In contrast, a defendant in a negligence action needs your help to get past the roadblock of litigation. Getting past that roadblock will allow the client to achieve her goal of getting back to her normal life that existed before being sued.

Lawsuits involve many characters: the client, the opposing party or parties, the various witnesses, and the fact finder. You may have noticed that "lawyer" was not on that list. That's because lawyers are the narrators of the story. They are not characters unless their actions have become part of the lawsuit itself (e.g., the rare case in which a lawyer who is an advocate for a client is unexpectedly required to testify). Remember, our legal story is not about us; it is about our client.

We already know that legally trained audiences tend to be skeptical. Judges and other lawyers all expect to learn of a client's story by the lawyer telling it from the client's perspective. However, they also expect lawyers to be reasonable. Efforts to paint the positive character of the client that are too extreme or overt make the story lose credibility. The story similarly loses credibility when the opposing party is portrayed as a villain. Therefore, lawyers must very carefully present the characters in the lawsuit as believably and reasonably as possible.

7.1.2   The client as hero

Usually, we portray our client as the protagonist of the legal story. But remember that the legal action is just one chapter in the client's overall story. The client is also the protagonist of a larger storyline or of multiple storylines. When we tell our client's story, it is often that larger storyline, of which the litigation is only a small part, that is the most compelling story we need to tell.

When considering how to portray the client, keep in mind that people respond—instinctively and intuitively—to certain recurring story patterns and character archetypes.[2] According to the famous mythologist Joseph Campbell, human nature categorizes protagonists as one of several different categories of heroes. Each of

---

[2] According to a traditional definition, archetypes are the "primary form that governs the psyche." James Hillman, ARCHETYPAL PSYCHOLOGY: A BRIEF ACCOUNT 1 (1985).

the different types of heroes is defined by the challenge or obstacle that they must face and overcome.[3] Table 7-1 shows these different heroic archetypes.[4]

Hero type	Task and challenge	Illustrative examples (cultural; legal)
Warrior	Fighting for what really matters	Prototypical Hollywood big action movie hero; Sports champion or person trying to move past serious physical injury
Creator	Gain identity through creations	Writer or artist struggling to succeed such as Harry Potter author J.K. Rowling; small business owner
Caregiver	Help others without martyring self	Religious icons or leaders such as Gandhi; Parent taking care of family against odds; Prosecutors taking care of society
Everyperson	Being able to live as everyone else can: with rights to life, liberty, and the pursuit of happiness	Rosa Parks; Plaintiff in civil rights or discrimination lawsuit
Orphan	Find way back into society after having been cut off from it	Harry Potter; Domestic violence victim seeking restraining order
Outlaw	Change what is not working in society	Robin Hood; Whistleblower in corporate corruption case
Sage/Scholar	Search for better life through study or knowledge	Jane Goodall; Student trying to do well in school

---

[3] Joseph Campbell, THE HERO WITH A THOUSAND FACES (Princeton U. Press 1990).
[4] A version of this chart originally appeared in a longer article on the same topic. Ruth Anne Robbins, *Harry Potter, Ruby Slippers and Merlin: Telling the Client's Story Using the Characters and Paradigm of the Archetypal Hero's Journey*, 29 SEATTLE L. REV. 767 (2006).

Hero type	Task and challenge	Illustrative examples (cultural; legal)
Explorer / Wanderer / Seeker	Search for better life through exploration of the world	Early colonists and pioneers and explorers Meriwether Lewis & William Clark; Advocacy groups trying to break new ground or call attention to societal issues
Magician	Understand and transform the universe at a profound level	Merlin, Gandalf, Dumbledore transformed their worlds; Steve Jobs transformed ours
Ruler	Create and maintain a thriving community	Queen Elizabeth I of England; Prosecutors are ruler heroes, trying to maintain an ordered and safe society for the citizens
Lover	Gain bliss through relationships	Cinderella variations; Loss of consortium plaintiff; Wrongful death plaintiff
Jester / Fool	Change society by exposing the absurd for what it is	Jon Stewart and Stephen Colbert; Author of a satirical publication involved in a defamation suit, such as Larry Flynt.
Innocent	Remain in safety	Dorothy from *The Wizard of Oz*; Someone who is incapacitated or is a child. **Note: this is a heroic archetype that works well only for clients who are children or who are rendered in a child-like state by illness, age, or accident

Table 7-1: Heroic archetypes

A person can be on more than one hero trajectory at a time. In fact, most of us fit within multiple archetypes at any given time. A client might be an Everyperson hero in the workplace, a Caregiver hero at home, and a Creator hero with his volunteerism. The question for you becomes which one of those heroic archetypes best portrays your client and meets her goals. Think about which hero type will be most effective in telling a particular client's story. Note that reasonable minds may differ on this point. This is not a question of finding the lone, objectively correct archetype. Rather, it is a process to make a conscious choice about how you want to portray your client in that particular situation.

7.1.3 Using your client's back story: competing considerations

Different archetypes, different stories

In choosing a heroic archetype for your client, you will likely have several options. Finding the best fit for your client will depend on the factual context, the legal issue, and the theme of your story. For example, consider the potential archetypes for the Linda Brown story from the Prologue. Was Linda Brown an Innocent child who needed protecting? An Everyperson, fighting for justice for all? An Outlaw challenging existing societal norms? Any of these archetypes could be the core of a compelling story. How might Brown's archetype change the way we would tell Brown's story?

You will probably know things about your client that are not necessarily "legally relevant" and yet are facts that you might want the audience to know. These facts could include anything from age, gender, family, education, work experience, volunteer work, military service—anything in her background that could shine a positive light on your client and help your audience understand her role in the legal story you tell.

Even when the relevance of the client's back story is not immediately apparent, it is important to investigate facts of this nature because they might become legally relevant. Or, equally important, as you learned in Chapter 5, these facts will give a more complete picture of your client as the protagonist of your story. Chapter 9 talks more about ways to weave small bits of that back story into your persuasive document. At this point in the litigation process, it is enough to collect the facts and to begin a list of things that you know about your client as well as a list of follow-up questions that you need to ask.

On the flip side, some aspects of your client's fuller story should not be used at all. At trial, certain facts cannot come into evidence for a variety of reasons. On appeal, litigants are always limited by the record developed in the trial court. Thus, you must choose an archetype that is consistent with the admissible evidence.

Hypothetical: your client, the speeder

Your client wishes to challenge a speeding ticket. According to the summons, he was traveling at 70 mph in a 55 mph zone. The penalties for going 69 mph are much lower than going 70 mph. It is your task, therefore, to try to plead the ticket down to the lower offense. Which heroic archetype is more likely to work for the case?

1. Your client won a medal in the last Olympics (Warrior hero).

2. Your client spends at least one day a month volunteering for a local charity (Caregiver hero).

3. Your client is a 3L who was on his way to a judicial clerkship interview and didn't want to be late (Scholar hero).

4. Your client wrote a thesis paper about the dangers of speeding and the error range of speed detector machines (Scholar hero).

Hero type # 1 might be appropriate if the discussion were about a person giving a motivational speech. But here it smacks of looking like an argument that some people are above the law.

Hero type #2 calls on sympathies, but the facts are disconnected from the legal action, so that the information looks like just an empty attempt to call upon emotions without reason. This heroic archetype might become the appropriate choice in a different legal action, however.

Hero type #3 and #4 both fit the legal action and add some understanding to the defense. Either one could be chosen for the circumstances. Most lawyers would probably pick #3.

7.1.4   Your client's character will have weaknesses

Just as virtually every legal dispute has unfavorable facts (or unfavorable law), every hero has her weakness. In myth, the hero's flaws are a central obstacle that the hero must overcome to succeed on the hero's journey. Those flaws symbolize the universal imperfection of being human. Likewise, in the real world, clients will have flaws. They may react to the opposing party in a way that makes you wince; they may arrive late to every appointment, including court appearances; or they may communicate poorly and therefore won't do well on the witness stand. The client's flaws may or may not be critical to the success of the lawsuit. They might influence decisions about the strategy of the case—anything from decisions about whether the client will testify to decisions about legal arguments. Chapter 12 talks about handling adverse materials, while Chapter 15 helps you decide which of these flaws you might need to address in your written advocacy.

7.1.5   The client's narrow and broad goals

Your client's most immediate goal is to win her lawsuit. However, that narrow goal is unlikely to build empathy with your audience—every litigant wants to win her lawsuit. That goal doesn't give your audience any reason to support your client over her opponent. The more persuasive tack is to see the favorable resolution of the lawsuit as a step toward a more universal goal. By taking a broader view of your client's goals, you provide a more compelling story that puts the immediate dispute in a context that will resonate with readers.

Your client's goal is also central to determining what kind of hero she is. Imagine the owner of a local restaurant who was sued for breach of contract when she canceled produce deliveries from the plaintiff, a local farmer, and entered into a new contract with another farmer. The restaurateur may have canceled the deliveries because she was having issues with quality or the timing of deliveries. She has a goal of bringing a valuable service to the community—by providing healthy food choices, creating jobs in the local community, and encouraging quality relaxation time for her patrons. This would fit with the Creator heroic archetype or even the Caregiver archetype. On the other hand, if we choose to portray her as an Everyperson hero, we would emphasize that she is working long hours to put food on her own table. Her small restaurant is her livelihood—and the trouble she is having with the food supplier is creating a problem in her ability to keep the restaurant in business. That, in turn, is preventing her from reaching the goal of stable support for herself and her family.

The above example demonstrates that these concepts work for defendants in a lawsuit just as they work for plaintiffs. It is often easier to see the goal of plaintiffs than of defendants. On the surface, the goal of most defendants is to make the lawsuit go away. But defendants have a broader story than just the legal dispute. The restaurant owner doesn't just want to get the farmer to go away. She wants to continue serving the community. If you can tell her story to show these larger goals, you help the judge understand your client's situation. And understanding is the first step toward building the empathy that will persuade the court to support your client's broader goals.

7.2   Other character roles in the legal action

Of course, your client is not the only character of the legal story. Certainly, the opposing party is an important character, and there may be other minor characters as well. While these characters will usually be less developed than the protagonist–client will be, they nevertheless play an important part in the client's story.

7.2.1   The opposing party: gatekeepers or shape-shifters

Although your client is the hero-protagonist, that doesn't necessarily make the opposing party the villain-antagonist. In a lawsuit, the audience is rarely looking to help good prevail over evil. Rather, the judge or jury is looking to resolve a dispute between two parties who are presumed to both be acting in good faith. If you portray the opposing party as evil, you are more likely to undermine your own credibility or cast doubt on your judgment than you are to hurt the opposing party.[5]

Imagine again the small restaurant owner who has been sued for breaching a contract with a local farmer. Portraying either side as a villain would look a bit absurd. The farmer and the small business owner are both sympathetic characters.

Of course, there are exceptions to this principle, but they are rare, especially in a civil dispute.

---

[5] *Id.* at 786–789 (exploring alternatives for the opposing party).

A criminal dispute may offer more opportunities for a good versus evil story, but even then, very few defendants are all bad. In fact, casting the opposing party as the antagonist can backfire because one person's villain is another person's hero. Think of the character the Wicked Witch of the West. Do you know her as the villain of *The Wizard of Oz* or as the heroine of *Wicked*?

Instead of portraying the opposing party as a villain, you could portray him as a "gatekeeper," sometimes also called a "threshold guardian." Gatekeepers are exactly what the word suggests: people who create roadblocks that could keep the hero from achieving her goals unless the hero rises to the challenge of getting past the obstacle of the gatekeeper. Gatekeepers might be unpleasant for their own reasons, but their own chief goals are about something other than simply thwarting the hero. In the classic comedy *Monty Python and the Holy Grail*, both the Knights Who Say Ni and the Black Knight are gatekeepers. A perhaps more relevant though less amusing example of a gatekeeper might be the Board of Bar Examiners. The people standing between you and the right to practice law are not evil (despite how you might feel about them in a couple of years), but do present an obstacle you must overcome to complete your journey to law practice. Similarly, the opposing party is usually not an evil villain, but merely a defender of its own turf.

When the lawyer sets up the opposing party in this gatekeeper role, she invites the judge to guide the client past this gatekeeper challenge so that the client can achieve her goal.[6] This perspective also recognizes that the opposing party may have legitimate reasons for opposing the client, even though those reasons must ultimately give way to the client's pursuit of her goal. The judge then has an easier time with the client's proposed resolution because the decision is something other than a ruling that the opposing party is completely at fault. The judge is also given some leeway in

---

[6] *Id.* at 782–786 (exploring the judge as mentor and providing examples).

fashioning a result that is acceptable to both sides of the dispute.

As an alternative to the gatekeeper, you may choose to portray the opposing party as a "shape-shifter," a character who morphs from one type of personality to another. In the restaurateur and farmer example, the farmer might portray the restaurant owner as a shape-shifter who has transformed from being a reliable and stabilizing business alliance to being a threat to the stability of the farmer's business. That's a very different—

and very reasonable—spin on the story's characters.[7]

> ### Hidden heroes
>
> You probably weren't in law school very long before you realized that someday you might have to represent someone you don't like—someone who doesn't seem very heroic. You may also be wondering about other settings where your client does not fit the traditional protagonist role of your story. For example, on occasion, you may be faced with a "pure question of law" where the real issue turns on the interpretation of a statute and the underlying facts of your client's case seem less important. While there are situations where your client will not be the protagonist, they are in fact, relatively rare. Thus, do not be too quick to abandon your client as hero or protagonist.
>
> Let's take the obvious problematic case—a criminal defendant accused of a horrific crime. An axe murderer is not a hero. And if we were defending such an unsavory, indeed, thoroughly indefensible, person, we may feel hard pressed to make him a hero. However, even one accused of an axe murder is entitled to a defense. He can still demand the prosecution prove its case. He is still entitled to the protections that all citizens are entitled to. Thus, we could tell his story as a citizen—the everyman hero entitled to the presumption of innocence and constitutional protections that are fundamental to our system. Our focus would not be on his conduct, but on his role as an accused citizen.

7.2.2 Secondary characters: Judges, witnesses, and lawyers

Parties are not the only characters our client's story. Witnesses, lawyers, and judges also have parts to play. The role of the witnesses is relatively straightforward. Witnesses who testify positively for your client are "companions," whose goals include helping the client–hero. Other companion characters could be expert witnesses since they

---

[7] For more reading about shape-shifters, see *id.* at 789.

travel with and help the hero with their own gifts. Even "neutral" fact witnesses called by the attorney are a type of companion character since they help the hero overcome some obstacle.

Other witnesses may be gatekeepers. An opposing counsel's expert witness who offers an opinion adverse to your client is a gatekeeper. So are hostile witnesses or neutral witnesses whose testimony impedes the hero in her journey to achieve her goal.

Lawyers and judges are more problematic. You, as legal advocate, should never play a role within the client's legal story. Instead, you are the story's narrator. Portraying yourself as the hero of the client is probably doing the client a disservice by putting the client in the precarious position of a victim, a party who needs to be saved. Most audiences are less understanding of a victim than they are of a hero. Because you want your audience to connect with the client's story and not your own, you should keep the client at the center of the story.

The proper role for judges may be even more problematic than for lawyers. At trial, the judge controls how the legal story will end. In that sense, she, like the lawyer, is a narrator who will write the final chapter of the story, but remains outside the story of the parties. On the other hand, the judge may be a central character in the story of the litigation's procedure.

Likewise, the role of appellate judges may vary depending on the story. Generally, appellate judges are much more concerned about the story of the law—and its impact on future cases, than on the story of the parties. The judges may write the final chapter of the client's story, but they will usually remain outside of that story in doing so.

7.3   Finding your client's archetype

Your client may represent several archetypes. She may be a Creator, an Everyperson, or a Scholar. To find the match that best tells your client's story, you will want to have a thorough understanding of the law and the facts. However, you may want to use the form shown in Figure 7-1 on pages 128-129 to get started thinking critically about your client's character.

7.3.1   Selecting a heroic archetype

Pick at least two or three heroic archetypes that you think might be appropriate for your client. Keep an open mind; more options may fit than you first imagined. Remain curious and consider a variety of potential archetypes that might fit your client. To evaluate the potential of different archetype, consider the following questions:

> **Where in the brief are the client's overall goals discussed?**
>
> The short answer: "if we include it, we keep it far away from the first paragraph of the Statement of Facts." Remember that we must be careful of how we tell the backstory because our readers are trained to be skeptical of overt attempts to persuade with blatant calls to sympathy.
>
> The backstory can certainly show up in your notes or checklists, however. And the client's overall life challenges might be woven into the client's legal story, but it will most likely need to be done in a careful and subtle way. The next chapter will talk about writing "shadow documents" and later in the book, as you are working on the revising of language to fit the case theory, we will revisit some techniques of how to use word choice and organization to convey this type of backstory information.

- What is a possible heroic archetype for my client?

- What is my client's goal that matches the archetype?

- What are the obstacles the client faces in reaching that goal? (Do those obstacles match the archetype?)

- What are the dark sides of this archetype?

- How does this archetype fit with the legal theory of the case I have chosen? (See discussion of this topic in Chapter 6.)

- What facts do I have that support the use of this archetype?
  - Use specific facts that can be cited in the record or evidentiary exhibits.
  - Leave out any opinion or judgment on the part of the narrator (i.e., your opinion).

7.3.2   Missing information and reasonable inferences

Developing archetype possibilities may reveal that some facts needed to complete the story are missing. If the lawsuit is still in the pretrial phase, more conversation with the client or potential witnesses might be needed. Likewise, you might conduct additional discovery. At the appellate stage, the record is set, of course. But you might still look for non-adjudicative facts (statistical or other legislative facts, as discussed in Chapter 5). At the same time, this exercise in archetypes could help identify additional needed legal research.

Studying the facts through this sort of lens also might help you better visualize the incidents. Doing so could lead to reasonable inferences from the facts. That is different than interpreting the facts. Here's an example. Suppose someone describing a scene says something like "everyone in the hotel stopped what they were doing to watch the argument between the woman and the registration clerk." An inference you could draw is that the argument was loud enough to catch people's attention.

As you start to put together your list of facts, be sure to ask yourself these questions:

- What information do I still need to develop my client's heroic archetype? (Remember that on appeal, you cannot add to the record.)

- What, if any, reasonable inferences about my client's character can I make from the evidence or record?

7.3.3   Repeating the steps

The first and most obvious heroic archetype that your client's story "fits" is not always the one that is the best for the lawsuit. Every domestic violence case involves a Lover hero whose relationship with Prince(ss) Charming has turned out to be a harmful one. But the client might also be a Creator hero. Suppose her start-up business is suffering because she has had to take time off due to the abuse. Or perhaps the client has cut off friendships and other family connections because of the abuse. Then the client is also potentially an Orphan hero.

Another way to visualize this is by using a chart similar to Figure 7-1, below. That gives you the option to see several choices at once.

Arche-type	Client's goal	Obstacle to that goal	Facts that could be used to demonstrate the particular archetype (cite to the record or evidence for every asserted fact)	Facts that are inconsistent with my client's heroic archetype (cite to the evidence or record for every asserted fact)	More information to investigate to round out this archetype consideration (if at appellate level, only non-adjudicative facts)	Inferences I can make about character based on the record (inferences are different than your own opinions)

Figure 7-1: Choosing your client's archetype

7.4   The client's obstacle: the conflict type of lawsuit

Finally, all stories need an obstacle or a conflict for the protagonist to struggle with and overcome before reaching the goal. This conflict engages readers by making the story interesting. (It also creates the need for a lawsuit in the first place!) If a character achieves a goal without

> **Conflict Types and Themes**
>
> As noted in Chapter 3, conflict is one of the structural tools that a writer can use to tell an effective story. In the story arc, or plot, conflict causes the pre-existing order to fall into chaos, which is what drives the plot forward. "Conflict" differs from the "theme" of the brief, which we discuss in detail in Chapter 14. The "theme" of a brief is the emotional center of the case: the "moral of the story." It captures the essential reason why the court should *want* to rule in your client's favor.

struggle, the story is dull and your readers won't care. Thus, when you tell the client's story, do so by framing it around the obstacles your client is working to overcome. The immediate obstacle your client faces, of course, is the conflict with the opposing party. However, just as the client's goals go beyond the specifics of this case, so might her obstacles. Once again, you want to construct the story in a way that suggests that its significance is greater than only winning the immediate lawsuit.

7.4.1   The types of conflicts

Literary theory scholars identify the following conflict types:

- Person versus Self
- Person versus Nature
- Person versus Society (or the flip, "Society versus Person")
- Person versus Machine (a/k/a "Person versus Institution/Leader")
- Person versus God
- God versus Everybody
- Person versus Person

For example, you experience a "Person versus Machine" conflict every time you need to talk to a customer service representative but reach only a recorded voice telling you to "press one." (Here, you confront not just the machine that plays the recorded message, but the more daunting machine of the Big Corporation.) People trying to pick up their lives after a tornado destroys their property face a "Person versus Nature" conflict. Hamlet struggling with whether to be or not to be is a "Person versus Self" conflict.

These conflict types are often readily apparent in the legal story as well. For example, a prosecutor is working on a "Society versus Person" conflict type, where the prosecutor represents the citizens of that jurisdiction trying to keep an ordered and safe society. In the prosecutor's story, the defendant is the person who has done something adverse to the order or safety of the community. In the defendant's story, however, this may be a conflict of "Person versus Society," if the theory of the case is "SODDI" (Some Other Dude Did It). Or, if the defense's theory of the case is that the police or prosecutor committed some sort of violation of constitutionally protected rights, then the defendant will portray the case as "Person versus Machine" (i.e., that the government has acted as a machine). Or, the defendant may be pleading insanity, which would be a "Person versus Self" conflict type.

We have deliberately moved "Person versus Person" into the last position on our list of conflicts because it should probably be last on your list of optimal choices. Selecting "Person versus Person" as the conflict type ensures that Person wins. Which Person? Yes, that's the problem. It's unclear. It also creates a situation where the opposing party is almost necessarily set up as a villain. One person's hero is another person's villain, and vice versa.[8]

The conflict of the lawsuit flows throughout the whole of the brief. The requested relief of the brief, in fact, is a request to the court to resolve the conflict in the client's favor. Thus, the conflict type is first seen in the Introduction or Question Presented section of the brief. It may also be spotlighted in the Statement of Facts, depending on whether the type of legal question is a factual question, a mixture of fact and law, or purely a question of law.

But no matter which type of legal issue, the Statement of Facts cannot end the legal story for readers. Remember that a story ends when readers discover—or, in the legal story, when readers decide— whether the protagonist overcame the obstacles to attain the goal. In legal writing, the end of the story occurs after readers have considered the underlying facts and the obstacle-clearing elements of the legal arguments. Thus, the Statement of Facts usually

---

[8] Also discussed in Foley & Robbins, *supra* note 1, at 472.

represents just the exposition of the story, including the origins of the conflict. It sets the stage for the rest of the story by identifying the characters, explaining the protagonist-client's goal, and showing the obstacles facing this protagonist-client. By the time readers have finished with the Statement of Facts, they may have formed an opinion about how this story *should* unfold, but they will look to the Argument section to see how it *does* unfold.

7.4.2   Identifying the central conflict your client faces

Just as you did with the potential archetypes for your client, you will want to go through the conflict types that could be involved with your client's case. Table 7-2 may be helpful as you think about which potential conflicts best reflect your client's story. It is again important to remain curious and keep an open mind; as you do the legal research and begin writing the legal argument, all of this can easily change. As you do so consider:

- The central conflict of my client's story is _____ versus_____.

- The following facts establish this conflict: (cite to the evidence or record for every asserted fact):

   _____

Conflict Type	Characteristics
Person v. Self	Hero fights an internal struggle such as mental or physical illness, self-doubt, psychological threats
Person v. Nature	Hero challenged by larger natural forces such as fierce weather, remote locale separated from society
Person v. Society	Hero challenges accepted norms of community

Person v. Machine	Hero fights against forces of technology, impersonal bureaucracy
Person v. God	Hero faces spiritual conflict; moral or existential conflict
God v. Everybody	Wide-spread societal threats such as plagues, conflict arising from hubris
Person v. Person	Hero fights against personal foe, often one who is evenly matched

Table 7.2 Conflict types

Once you have decided how you will portray your protagonist-client and the story's central conflict, you are ready to develop the rest of her story. The next chapter explores how to develop the plot of the client's story.

Starting to Write: Shadow Stories and Theme Development

In the opening pages of this book we described the four main phases of any writing project. The first phase, "prewriting," consists of research and planning. Up to this point in the book, we have been talking about the researching stage: both the facts and the law that may help resolve the story. This chapter turns to the planning part of the prewriting phase, before you transition into the phases that focus more on drafting and revising (although with any recursive process, you may still circle back to research and planning while you are drafting).

8.1 Planning for writing: sketching a "shadow" draft of the Facts section

Crafting an effective and final version of the Statement of Facts requires careful, deliberate planning that spans the whole of the document-writing adventure. The Statement of Facts is the section of a document that lawyers quite often sketch first and then rewrite last. The process of doing so allows legal writers to focus on the issues, hurdles, and possible avenues for a successful resolution.

These are the key steps in writing the facts section of a brief:

- Creating a separate "shadow story": essentially, what the lawyer wishes she could bluntly **tell** the court about her client, the opposing party, and the events. This is the prewriting, or planning, phase of the process.

- Taking the shadow story and turning it into a working draft of the facts section that blends the client's needs with the ethos of legal storytelling.

- Revising the draft so that the story is presented with cause and effect flow between the story beats, from the client's point of view, and from shifting distances and perspectives as may be necessary to **show** readers—without telling readers—the important facts that will in turn convey the theory of the case. This draft is revised to subtly and carefully convey—while refraining from bluntly *telling*—the story and theme selected by the lawyer as the most effective for the client's case.

- Polishing the section for precise word choices and to include citations to the record. Removing anything that appears to be an attorney characterization rather than a verified fact or a witness statement supported by a citation to the record.

8.1.1   What is the shadow story, and why do we need it?

The idea of the shadow story is to draft the version of your client's story that your client *wishes* you could tell. Your client may be angry, frustrated, even delusional about the opposing parties and his conflict with them. At the very least, he is likely to see the dispute from only one point of view—his! Most of the time, we would never actually write the Statement of Facts from such an obviously biased perspective because it would undermine our own credibility. However, for the shadow story, that is just what we will do: tell the story with all our client's anger, biases, and emotion. It is time to "let it all out."

Remember that this is not a writing exercise but a creative one, designed to help you plan with the actual writing. A shadow story helps to plan and shape the client's story. While it may feel a little like the second phase, writing the first draft, this is still planning (on paper) what to later write about in the working draft, using what you know from the record and trying out the heroic archetype and conflict type you have chosen for the case. To be crystal clear: this isn't a draft of the document itself. It's a method for developing the theory of the case and the story that you will include in the "real" document.[1]

Because this is a planning tool, shadow stories can be short and there is no particular format for them other than one that works for you to help you move into the next phase. If you

Why is it called a "shadow" story?

The shadow story is named after the shadow cast by an object on a sunny day. It is not the object itself, but it is shaped by the object. You can learn something about the object by looking at its shadow, but the shadow is flatter than the actual object, and is often misshapen. Just as you learn more by looking directly at the object and seeing all of its colors, dimensions, and other details, you will include in your brief the necessary details to allow the reader to see the actual object.

would rather draw the shadow story than write words, then do so. It doesn't matter, because it is a document designed to help you, and you alone. Think of it as one of the supporting documents you create

that shadow your final product in other legal projects: a facts-section version of the research log from Chapter 6, a case synthesis chart, or a course outline. Case charts are useful to help us think about the legal analysis. And that is the same reason we create the shadow story or any shadow documents in legal

What's in a separate name? Peace of mind!

Just as you keep case charts as separate documents that never touch, but only shadow, your actual legal argument sections of a submitted document, the shadow story likewise will only inform, but never appear in, the Statement of Facts. To ensure you never make a potentially disastrous mistake, save the shadow story as a separate document—perhaps even shade the whole document with a gray background—to remind yourself that this is merely a shadow of the real thing!

writing. The shadow story is a type of checklist that allows thinking. The Statement of Facts needs to be persuasive and written in a client-centered way. So, just as a lawyer creates synthesis charts to help her organize her thoughts about the rules of law, writing the

---

[1] Credit for the idea and initial teaching of the "shadow story" belongs to Victoria L. Chase, Clinical Associate Professor of Law, Rutgers Law School. Podcast, *Using Corroborating Narratives in Cross-Examination—An Effective Alternative to Traditional Cross Examination Strategies and Telling the Client's Story Effectively* (2d Applied Legal Storytelling Conference, Lewis & Clark Law School, Portland, OR, July, 2009) (available at http://lawlib.lclark.edu/podcast/?p=2067).

shadow story allows the lawyer to form ideas that will lead to the eventual finished product.

Here is how a shadow story helps transition a writer into the drafting stage. Consider the hotel room reservation example: the non-profit organization SOFT could not meet the minimum hotel room reservation guarantee at its conference, and the hotel sued for breach of contract under a liquidated damages clause, despite having no actual losses. Remember, after the reservation deadline had passed, the hotel sold rooms guaranteed to the non-profit to other non-conference guests at a higher price than the conference-contract rate. The non-profit's lawyer may wish that she could simply tell the court, "It is real hubris for that big hotel to sue my client, the little nonprofit organization, for that ridiculous amount of liquidated damages when the hotel actually *made* money from the breach of contract!!! My client essentially did the hotel *a favor!* This is just greed." Of course, she can't include those three sentences, as written, in the Statement of Facts. But she can write them down in the shadow story. Later, the shadow story will be a framework—a checklist—for choosing the facts. The shadow story will also remind the writer that she needs to create juxtaposition, that is a specific ordering of the facts, to show that feeling of incredulity in the reader about the hotel's hubris. The choice of details from the record can show the reader what the lawyer cannot tell. For example, to show that the hotel profited from reselling the room, she would perhaps include in her Statement of Facts a chart with the dollar figure profit that the hotel would have made if the organization members had rented all of the rooms they were supposed to, versus the dollar figure profit the hotel actually made on those nights.[2] These facts *show* the hubris of the hotel without *telling* readers anything about greed.

---

[2] Yes, a chart. Infographics persuade—when they are centrally relevant and designed to be immediately understood. We will talk more in Chapter 19 about visual organizers as a method of communicating persuasive reasoning.

Sketching the shadow story is not only useful, it's fun. It is the place to let the passion come out, to show your client's sense of outrage. There's no risk of losing ethos, because no one sees the shadow story but you.

8.1.2   Identifying your theme via the shadow story

Besides being fun to write, the shadow story helps you plan your document in an important way: it can help you select the theme for your brief. Once you have written your shadow story, it should be easy for you to identify the theme or themes that your story tells.

Remember in Chapter 3 you learned the difference between a "theme" and a "theory of the case." The theory of the case is the legal theory (or theories) that provide the justification of why the court can legally rule in your client's favor; this is the logos of your case. The theme, on the other hand, refers to the value-based, emotional reason why the court should *want* to rule in your client's favor (the pathos of your argument). You want to give the court a reason to think that a ruling in your client's favor is fair and just, not merely legally permissible.[3]

Chapter 3 also introduced the concept of "deep frames," which cognitive scientist George Lakoff describes as ideas or values that structure how you view the world.[4] At the heart of every deep frame is what he calls an "uncontested idea": for example, the idea that freedom is good and is something all people long for.

Examples of other concepts that might be considered deep frames:

---

[3] Professor Richard Neumann describes the theory as a "justifying argument" that shows the court how it is *possible* to rule in your client's favor, and the theme as a "motivating argument" that makes the court *want* to rule in your client's favor. Richard K. Neumann, Jr., Legal Reasoning and Legal Writing: Structure, Strategy and Style 309–310 (6th ed., 2009).

[4] George Lakoff, Whose Freedom? The Battle Over America's Most Important Idea 12 (2006).

- Light (openness; transparency)
- Strength
- Health
- Fairness/justice
- Happiness

- Love
- Truth
- Opportunity
- Independence (autonomy, self-reliance)
- Community

- Charity (helping others; unselfishness)
- Obedience (respect for authority)
- Faith/spirituality
- Discipline (hard work; focus)
- Generosity

Note that all of the above concepts are stated in a positive way. Each, however, has a negative counterpart; a "dark" side, if you will, or opposing concept. Thus, "strength" could be expressed as "weakness"; "justice" could be expressed as "injustice"; and "independence" could be expressed as "controlled" (lack of autonomy, regimented, dependence).

Chapter 2 included a discussion about the brain's negativity bias. If it is true that negative stimuli are more powerful than good ones, shouldn't a writer choose the dark-side frame? Won't a theme of "the other side is bad" require more processing by the intended audience, and therefore be more memorable than a "my client is good" theme? The correct answer, as it is with all legal questions, is "it depends." The variables include the disposition of the intended reader(s)—the more specifics you know about the audience the better, the client's preferences, the relative strengths of the positive versus

> **More on 6-word stories**
>
> The idea is borrowed from the famous but inaccurate tale about Ernest Hemingway, being challenged to write a story in only six words. According to the story (which isn't true), he won the challenge with the story, "For sale, baby shoes, never worn." The story has been debunked, but that won't stop people from repeating it anyway. Facts don't persuade, but stories do. For the research proving all of this, see Garson O'Toole, *Hemingway Didn't Say That: The Truth Behind Familiar Quotations* 183 (2017).
>
> Although Hemingway did not write that 6-word story, the technique is powerful and useful. There are whole websites and books devoted to 6-word stories. It's a technique that provides a simple, yet powerful, way to test many things in your own writing, from theme, to theory of the case, to rule explanation from a published case.

negative themes based on the available evidence, and even to some extent your own comfort with using negative versus positive themes.

If the advocate can show the court how a ruling in favor of your client advances a deep frame, the court will be more motivated to rule in favor of your client. Deep frames work at an unconscious level and therefore may trump facts. Lakoff believes that deep frames are how each of us defines common sense; they shape the way we view the world. A person who encounters a fact that is inconsistent with a deep frame is likely to reject the fact as untrue, irrelevant, or unimportant because the fact seems to defy common sense.[5] Suppose, for example, readers start with the deep frame that free enterprise is good and that businesses must therefore be free to create the jobs that provide workers with the means to support their families. Readers may then reject facts that show that environmental regulation is necessary to promote public health; such regulation costs money, which impairs businesses' ability to create jobs, which then conflicts with readers' deep frame.

The concept of a deep frame is closely related to that of **theme**. Your theme should harmonize with one likely to be held by most people, or at least by your intended readers. Your shadow story should provide a sense of the theme—does it give the readers a reason to care about what happens to the client? What deep frame is triggered?

A good way to whittle down to the theme of the case from the shadow story is to distill it into a simple phrase that is six words or fewer. For example, the defendant in the hotel reservations case might sum up the theme as "hotel getting paid twice isn't fair." The hotel might sum up the theme as "people should honor their guaranteed obligations." If you find that your shadow story does not help you identify a deep frame on the list, you may need to rethink the way you are approaching the client's story so that it does trigger one.

In the next chapter, we turn to writing the actual first draft of the Facts Section.

---

[5] *Id.* at 13.

Creating the Working Draft

In every writing project, there comes a point when it is time to push the researcher aside and start writing. Once you have met the client, investigated the facts, and completed the initial research, you are ready to begin writing the Facts and Argument sections.[1] Starting to write is often the most difficult part of the writing process: moving the ideas that are loosely defined in the writer's head to a workable written draft.

Luckily, the first writing stage involves merely the production of the workable draft. Getting to a finished draft will come later. The next seven chapters are designed to get the ideas that are in your head onto paper. Once you have completed that draft, the next step will be revising that draft into a persuasive story. Part IV of this book will discuss revising.

A. Where We Are Now

There are six steps to producing a good draft of a brief:

1. Get to know the client and his goals.

2. Gather and assess the facts of the client's story.

3. Find and assess the law that applies to the client's story (i.e., develop your legal theory of the case).

4. Identify the persuasive theme or themes.

5. Determine the facts and arguments that will best represent the client's interests; and

6. Write and organize the first draft.

In Part II of this book, you worked through the first four steps— though it is likely that you will be returning to each of them, since

---

[1] There are, of course, other parts to a brief besides the Facts and the Argument. Those other parts are discussed in Chapter 18. However, the Facts and the Argument are the heart of a brief and that is what you will spend the most time creating.

writing is recursive, not linear. Now it is time for the heavy lifting of putting pen to paper. Or, more likely, fingers to keyboards.

Part III begins by sketching out the story you want the brief to tell. Chapter 9 gets this process started by taking the shadow story you wrote in Chapter 8, and turns it into a first draft of the facts section of the brief. Chapter 9¾ is a transition as we move the narrative arc from the Facts to laying the foundation of a persuasive Argument section. This chapter explores the five forms of legal reasoning as well as common rhetorical fallacies.

Chapters 10 through 13 take a deeper look at four aspects of argument: interpreting statutes, exploring policy, dealing with adverse material, and inferential reasoning. Finally, Chapter 14 helps you put it all together in creating the working draft of the Argument section.

Writing is part of the thinking process. Getting a working draft of an Argument is hard work and there is more than one way to do it. Some people may prefer to outline the Argument before they get down to writing the actual substance. Outlining can certainly be a useful way to get started. However, even if you prefer to create an outline before you write, you should remember that writing is part of the thinking process. As you write your arguments, you may discover arguments that you had overlooked; you may discover holes in your research or reasoning; you may even discover whole new issues that change the very nature of your client's case. Consequently, after you have actually written out your arguments, you will want to revisit your planned organization. You will also need to create headings and other structural markers that will make the organization of Argument clear to your reader. At that point, Chapter 14 will be very helpful.

On the other hand, not all writers can create an outline before they write. For many of us, we need to get our ideas down on paper, and then see how they best fit together. Our first drafts may look more like a stream of consciousness babble than a coherent document. That's fine too. Our goal is to create a well-organized, perfectly written *final* draft. If we need to write a messy, disorganized first draft before we get there, no worries. Organizing our thoughts is often easier once we have those thoughts on paper.

Whether you outline before or after you write your working draft, the time has come to start writing. As you work through the next chapters, you will come across many potential strategies for creating arguments. Some of them will fit perfectly with your brief problem while others may seem less relevant. Through the writing process, you will likely discover that some arguments fall away and new arguments take their place. That is as it should be. Remember, we are not yet writing the final, perfect Argument. Though we are putting pen to paper, we are still in the thinking stage of the brief writing process.

B.   What happens next

We start writing.[2]

---

[2] Even if it's crap. Just get it on the page. Or, as Professor Alexa Chew insightfully says, "you need to write words. It is OK if they are garbage words. You can fix them later." Alexa Chew (@aznchew) TWITTER (December 20, 2017, 2:55 PM), https://twitter.com/aznchew/status/943570522406903809.

Chapter 9

Creating the Working Draft of the Facts Section

The shadow story of Chapter 8 is a key tool for understanding the client's point of view. It is an important means to an end—but only that. After capturing the client's passion in the shadow story, it's time to find ways to temper the story's presentation to maintain credibility. In revising, the lawyer looks for ways to *show* the client's passion without actually *telling* the court that the client is passionate.

This chapter transitions you through the last planning stage of the Facts section to its writing phase. Any writing process is recursive, and you will need to circle back to planning—and perhaps researching!—during the revising stages of the process. Later chapters of this textbook will return to the Facts section to walk through the recursive process of revising and polishing.

Ultimately, the Statement of Facts is a story suggesting its final ending but waiting for another author to write it.

9.1 The Facts section introduces the theme

Chapter 8 helped you develop the theme of your case through the device of a shadow story. The theme of your case is related to, but different from, the *theory* of the legal document you are writing. A theme runs parallel to the theory of the case. The *theory* of the brief provides the logical basis for your argument. In contrast, the theme of a brief should evoke an emotional response from the reader. The *theme* should explain the motivations of the characters and give readers a reason to respect and "root for" those characters. Thus, in addition to the legal theories based on the rules of law, you should strive to include a strong, pathos-based theme. The theme is the emotional core that persuades a court that ruling in your client's favor is the right thing to do. But the theme should work together with the legal theory. And the Facts section of your document is where the theme shines through most clearly.

For instance, in our hotel reservation example, one of the legal theories for SOFT, the nonprofit organization, would be that the liquidated damages clause of the contract was unconscionable. The substantive law of contract for the jurisdiction where the dispute arose would then provide the factors, standards, and rules that the court would employ to determine whether the clause was, in fact, unconscionable. This is the stuff of the legal theory of the case.

But the lawyer also needs to develop a strong theme in parallel, so that the court can determine whether the clause of the contract is unconscionable. To develop that parallel theme to the theory of the case, the lawyer representing SOFT needs to argue that it is the weaker party in the transaction: it is a small, nonprofit organization trying to raise money to promote a worthy cause, while the hotel is part of a large nationwide chain of hotels trying to maximize its profit. We like to cheer for the little person. It's part of the deep frames of both independence and discipline or hard work. To tap into those frames, the lawyer representing SOFT would draft the Statement of Facts by focusing some detail on the form contract with fill-in-the-blanks that did not appear to leave room for negotiation, and on the conversation between the president of the nonprofit organization and the hotel employee who had no authority to change any of the form language. The lawyer would also point out that the clause of the contract could result in a windfall for the hotel if it were able to resell any, or all, of the rooms the organization did not reserve by the reservation deadline. The hotel, in effect, would be getting paid twice: first by the organization and again by the actual occupant of the room. That results in an unfairness (a third deep frame), in the form of a larger profit for the hotel and less money available for the nonprofit organization to pursue its mission.

Of course, if the legal theory is "unconscionability," it is pretty easy to see how theme will necessarily play a large role in the persuasive process. Unconscionability is an equitable concept, and the entire body of equity law is based on principles of fairness and justice, which are inherently narrative based. But even if the legal theory is more solidly law based, narrative reasoning of this sort still applies in the same way. Assume that the law of the jurisdiction holds that liquidated damages clauses are enforceable only if they are a "reasonable estimate of actual damages" and are appropriate only in situations where actual damages are impossible or very difficult to prove. That test looks like a standard, elements-based legal rule, but there is ambiguity in two phrases, "reasonable estimate" and "difficult to prove." The lawyer arguing for the nonprofit organization will need to engage in some narrative reasoning about the relative expectations of the hotel and the organization at the time the contract was entered into. In that second scenario, the theme also becomes one of "fairness" by highlighting facts that show that actual damages were easy to calculate—indeed that the hotel didn't have *any* actual damages.

In short, with either legal theory, the theme permeates the case and works together with the theory of the case.

9.2   Plan the plot's arc

The plot is the overall large-scale structure of the story. Planning the plot's arc will move you into position to write. Principles of literary criticism work well by analogy in persuasive legal writing. Literary critics have studied plots for years. The five stages of plot development are generally described as

- Introduction/exposition,
- Complicating incident/rising action,
- story climax,
- falling action, and
- resolution (or denouement).

This arc of a brief is visually represented in Figure 9-1.

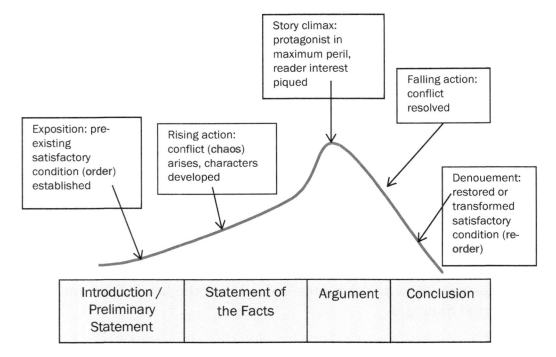

Figure 9-1: Arc of a plot

As shown in Figure 9-1, this trajectory loosely describes a well-organized legal brief. We discuss each of these components in more detail below.

Another way of thinking about the plot is to imagine the protagonist on his journey toward some worthy goal; he thinks of the starting condition as **order**. When he is knocked off his hoped-for course by some outside person or force, **chaos** results. He then seeks the assistance of the court to put him back on his chosen course (**re-order**).

The labels on the story organization elements are different than the choices you may make when organizing the telling of your client's story. Legal writers know that some kind of re-order will appear up front, setting up the legal context for the story—"this is an appeal from a domestic violence restraining order hearing." A story may be told with the chaos up front, followed by the order and then re-order.

Or it may be told blending chaos and order together. So, too, a legal story may be organized in many ways.

This path is represented graphically in Figure 9-2.

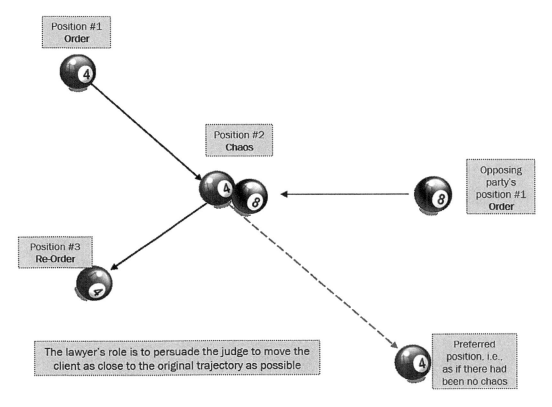

Figure 9-2: Schematic of the parties' interactions with each other

Note that since we are discussing brief writing in this chapter, we think of the readers as the judges who must decide the case. This creates an interesting opportunity for the writer because the ending of the story—the **resolution** of the plot—is ultimately in the hands of his readers. This situation gives readers even more incentive to be attentive to the details, of course, but it also means that the writer needs to think clearly about what details readers need to craft a satisfying ending to the legal story. For example, in our hotel room reservation case, the non-profit organization's lawyer wants the readers to understand from the outset that the client is a small, nonprofit organization that had little or no opportunity to negotiate

the precise language of the hotel's standard room reservation
agreement. She needs to establish this plot point in the Statement of
Facts and continue this aspect of the storyline throughout the brief.

9.2.1   Introduction/exposition

Most works of fiction—which have more leeway and a different audience
than readers of a legal brief—begin with the protagonist in a state of
repose or peace. Here, readers learn enough context about the who,
what, where, and why for the story to make sense. Physical objects,
scenes or conditions may be described so that readers can visualize
where the story takes place. Characters are introduced. Usually the story
begins with everything in stasis. Calm prevails; the protagonist is happy.

The fact section of a plot-based legal brief should likewise begin with
an introduction, in which the factual setting is revealed. Helpful
background details that explain the protagonist's and the setting
character can be included here as well. However, recall the lessons of
Chapter 7. The legal writer needs to be careful about how much detail
to include in this section because much of the detail needed for the
reader to fully understand the characters' motivation may be legally
irrelevant. Including too much background detail might be seen by
judges either as wasting their time or (even worse) as an attempt to
manipulate readers or to improperly play on their emotions.

9.2.2   Complicating incident/rising action

Once the stage is properly set, the action begins. Something happens. A
conflict arises. The status quo is upset; something is no longer right.

The conflict, of course, drives the story and grabs readers' attention,
and this is revealed through the complicating incident in any story.
The incident may be a series of incidents, one building on another
(rising action). Or it may be a single event that requires no further
development.

This is all the stuff of a compelling fact section. A good Statement of
Facts reveals not only the character of the protagonist (your client),
the antagonist (a possible role for the opposing party), and any other

characters who are not parties to the suit but who play some role in the story. The fact section also defines the factual conflict that brings the parties to the court, seeking redress.

But just like in fiction, the story need not be told in strict chronological order. A common device in fiction writing is to begin with the complicating incident (to grab the reader's attention) and then jump backward in time to show the events that have put the protagonist in peril. The "flashback" then reveals the condition of stasis that existed before the conflict arose; the setting in which the story takes place and the character of the protagonist are also developed.

Once the setting and character are introduced, the events leading up to the controversy can be filled in. Readers know what the conflict is since it was introduced in the first few paragraphs; now the details about how the conflict arose can be filled in. This "rising action" can provide further insights into the protagonist's character, painting her in a positive light as somebody deserving of the court's assistance.

At this point the rising action has begun and the factual conflict (the "chaos") at the heart of the story has been revealed. But this is about as far as the fact section can take us. The plot is far from fully developed yet. Readers are not ready for the story climax; you cannot resolve any conflicts in the fact section. You need more.

Both the introduction and the rising action must be continued in the Argument section. The fact section describes only the factual setting and identifies the factual conflict. The *legal* setting (the fixed legal rules that must be applied by the court) must be described in the Argument section, and the *legal* conflict must be explained there as well. We will pick up this discussion in Chapter 9¾, next.

9.2.3 Story climax

In literature, the climax occurs when the protagonist is at the height of peril. Things are out of kilter, making the reader uncomfortable and aching for things to get better, to return to a condition of stasis.

Readers' attention is at its peak. How will the conflict be resolved? How does the story come out?

In a legal brief, this moment occurs at the point when the reader (1) knows the characters; (2) understands the factual dispute (what happened to drive the parties to the court for assistance); and (3) understands the legal dispute, including the legal principles needed to resolve the dispute. The reader wonders: How are these issues going be resolved? How is this going to turn out? And the reader of the brief is even more interested because the reader is the person who ultimately gets to decide, or at least vote on, how the story "turns out."

Note that the story climax *must* occur within the Argument section of the brief, because only then is the legal setting and the "rising action" of the legal issue fully developed, arriving at the climax of the story.

9.2.4   Resolution/falling action

In fiction, the story climax often happens very near the end of the story because it is more entertaining that way. Once the story climax is reached, readers are usually brought back to stasis very quickly, as if riding a roller coaster. Things fall into place rapidly, and the story reaches a satisfactory conclusion.

In legal writing, this is not always true. In some situations, it might be: if the legal rule is hard to decipher or is a question of first impression, the writer may need to spend a great deal of time with the rising action to arrive at a sufficient description of the legal issue, explained clearly enough that the court can then take appropriate action. In such situations, once the difficult rule is synthesized, the application of that rule to the facts may be fairly straightforward, resulting in a very short section of falling action/resolution.

The more common situation, however, is the opposite: the governing rules of law are fairly straightforward, but the way in which they should be applied to the specific facts of the case at hand may be more difficult. In that situation, the falling action/resolution part of the plot is likely to be much more complex and lengthy, and should include appropriate counter-analysis to show the reader that you have thought about all of the possible resolutions and that your proposed resolution is the most logical and appropriate.

We will work more on the application of the law to the client's facts in Chapter 15.

9.2.5 Denouement

Readers like happy endings (known in literary terms as "the denouement"). Likewise, judges like satisfying results; it is their job to reach them. And it is the writer's job to propose a happy ending. We will learn how to do this in Chapter 16.

9.3 Putting hands on the keyboard (or the technological equivalent)

It's time to put the story planning into words. There are two key things to keep in mind, or maybe on a Post-it® near your computer screen. First, this story is written on behalf of the client; it therefore should be written with the client's point of view and desired outcome firmly in mind and perhaps even placed up front in the opening paragraph as a framing concept. Second, the story must be *shown* from the existing facts as opposed to *told* by means of the writer's speculation or judgment. Per the lessons of Chapter 3, lawyers must omit any of their own characterizations about a character's thoughts, motives, or feelings—facts are things that are supported by citations to the record or to other verified sources of information.

Sometimes what the client wishes his lawyer to include in the legal storytelling might be different from what readers need or expect from the lawyer. Thus, there may a balancing act between the two main audiences of the lawyer's work product. For example, the client may want a "pit bull lawyer." But, to maintain ethos, lawyers must be professional toward both the court and opposing counsel. The lawyer's task becomes capturing the essence of her client's story without appearing to tell such a biased version as to lose credibility—this inures to the benefit of both the lawyer and the client.

John Lennon on ethos in storytelling

Back when the Beatles were in their heyday, John Lennon was known for his brash, outspoken personality. While his outlandish statements were often tongue in cheek, he occasionally created serious controversy. Perhaps the most dramatic example was when he said the Beatles were "bigger than Jesus Christ." That statement led thousands of young fans to protest, some even publicly burning their Beatles records. Later, Lennon created more controversy as an outspoken critic of the Vietnam War.

While Lennon continued to be outspoken, as he aged he took a somewhat less extreme approach in his public statements and consequently became a more effective social critic. A more mature Lennon acknowledged the limits of outrage as a tool of persuasion in his song *Revolution:*

> *You say you want a revolution*
> *Well you know, we all want to change the world...*
> *But if you go carrying pictures of Chairman Mao*
> *You ain't gonna make it with anyone anyhow.*

Lennon's caution—that the hypothetical of aligning one's political calls for change with one of the twentieth century's harshest critics of Western culture would likely be poorly received within the same Western culture that Mao criticized—has a parallel when it comes to persuasion in the law. When we represent a client, we often develop an understanding for his position. Lawyers are, after all, supposed to be zealous advocates. Thus, we tend to see the legal dispute from our client's perspective. This is a good thing. However, lawyers must also guard against being so zealous that our reader mistrusts us. So, as we show our client's story, both in the Statement of Facts and in the Argument, we must remember the Lennon Principle—avoid "carrying pictures of Chairman Mao." Instead, we need to tell the client's legal story in a way that fosters understanding in our reader without telling a story of extremist viewpoints.

9.3.1 Be ready to throw away the pity paragraph immediately

The first paragraph of the working draft of

the Statement of Facts will likely introduce the client's situation. But the first paragraph *written* might not look like that. It might look something like an appeal to pity. The first paragraph of anything is probably the hardest one to write. So, write it, just to get it started. And, if it looks like the shadow story, or if it looks like "once upon a time my client is a hero," then know that it is OK to throw it away.

The pity paragraph can happen in the first draft because of the case planning work that has occurred so far. Once the lawyer has selected the type of story, the heroic archetype, the conflict type, and the theme, all of these things must be woven into the Statement of Facts but must be done so in a way that makes the facts relevant and that shows rather than tells the reader what impressions to take away. Putting hands to the keyboard could net an opening sentence "The theme of this case is . . .," which isn't a fact, but a characterization. Or it might net the overt heroic archetype introduction, which has nothing to do with the legal cause of action but is tempting because it paints the client in a positive light—something we all want for our clients.

That strategy, however, will very likely backfire with judges who are trained to be skeptical of overt attempts to, as Justice Scalia has put it, "appeal to emotions uninvited."[1] Forgo those opening paragraphs that set up a tear-jerker scene starring your client as a yoga-instructing mentor to small children in a hospital ward. Doing that will harden the heart of your skeptical reader. Instead, weave that scene relevantly into the Statement of the Facts at some point where it fits, narratively. Take comfort in knowing that the human mind is very good at making connections between things. It will remember and create a composite picture from the selected details you provide. That's why you don't need to tell, but only to show.

And, to give further comfort, Chapter 17 will discuss the Introduction section of persuasive documents (or Preliminary

---

[1] Antonin Scalia & Bryan Garner, MAKING YOUR CASE: THE ART OF PERSUADING JUDGES 32 (2008).

Statement, as your jurisdiction may call them), in which both the theory of the case and the theme appear very prominently.

9.3.2   Taking stock of the story's "beats"

Stories are measured in beats. Each beat represents a moment of change that may be described with an action, a character's shift in attitude, or the passage of time. In a story, a beat is analogous to a fact or statement you write down when you are researching for a term paper.

In television and screenplay writing, beats are very important because they are used to storyboard. In some places, each story beat is still hand-written on individual notecards and then pinned to foam boards or tack boards where they can be moved around as the story arc is plotted. At least one law clinic has learned the technique from television writers in preparation for trial.[2]

Creating something like notecards with story beats at the early stages of writing will help you focus on the record with more depth than you otherwise might. And it will also provide an easy way to play with the organization of the facts. It is easier to experiment with putting facts next to each other when each beat is an independent piece of paper. To create the beats, jot down each key point from the record, along with a way to track where it came from: which witness or document. Note whether it is a precise quote or paraphrase that needs precision checking later. That will save some time during the polishing stages.

At the same time, fixating on the precise wording of each story beat at those early writing stages may not be useful when the goal is simply to get writing. Come back to the story beats later, during revising stages, to look at the word choices and at the connections

---

[2] Stefan Krieger, Hofstra Univ. Sch. of Law & Reza Rezvani, Dir., Ctr. for Applied Legal Reasoning, Hofstra Univ. Sch. of Law, *One 8' x 4' Foam Board, 2,000 Index Cards, and Total Immersion: Storyboarding As An Approach to Legal Storymaking*, Applied Legal Storytelling Conference, Denver, CO, July 8, 2011 (Plenary Session).

between each beat. Focusing at that level will help smooth out the cause and effect relationship between the facts, and will give the overall story more narrative coherence.

9.3.3   Organize the beats into a cause-and-effect flow

A story shows a character's efforts over time, to reach toward a goal. To do that, the writer connects the beats in a way that shows cause and effect. The best stories will have a seamless flow in which each fact has its place and the overall structure is one of coherence and plausibility.

Each beat of the story should have a connection to the next beat. Cause and effect connection words include

• However	• Therefore
• But	• Consequently
• Nevertheless	• Then
• Yet	• Thus

When you physically sort the notecards out, have different color notecards with connections words on them. The story should flow from one beat to the next using only these words. Whether these connection words actually appear in the Statement of the Facts depends, of course, but they should be there at least implicitly.

Notice that the common word "and" is missing from this list. While it's impossible to get away from that word altogether, connecting beats with "and" will make the facts feel less like a story and more like a bullet-point list.

The Statement of Facts draft, viewed as a flow graphic, should be something like this:

Figure 9-3

The material from Chapter 2 about persuasion via imagery is now relevant. Recall our advice earlier in the chapter that you should *show* readers what is going on in the facts, rather than *tell* them. You do this by showing readers the facts in the case in enough detail that they see in their own minds what is going on and, from the words and mental images, arrive at the meanings and conclusions you hope to convey. Showing is very different from telling, which simply orders readers to think or feel a certain way about the story, based on the judgments or opinions of the writer.

9.3.4 Describe actions, settings, objects, and (sometimes) characters

To show a story, use description in key places. These four things are susceptible to description:

- Actions
- Settings
- Objects
- Characters

Increased detail emphasizes a point, whereas decreased detail deemphasizes a point. Using more description in a particular part of the story will provide greater emphasis, as readers more carefully construct their mental images. As a corollary, decreasing the descriptive detail about actions, settings, objects, or characters will permit readers to either conjure any image that comes to mind or to form only fuzzy pictures before moving on to the next words in the section.

Showing the precise image requires you to select details that will form the description. There are five types of details to choose from when describing objects, actions, settings, or characters.

- **The name**. A name can also include a category. For example, "national park" is a named category of settings.

- **The function**. This is particularly useful when representing an organization or an object.

- **The history or development**. An organization's history may be important to the legal theory. In patent cases, an object's history is extremely important.

- **Sensory information**. These are the details that specifically create visual images or that call on other senses. The look, sound, taste, smell, or texture of something are all sensory details.

- **Analogy to other objects, actions, settings, or characters**. An analogy detail describes something through comparison to other things— sometimes explicitly and sometimes metaphorically.

> The non-profit's headquarters are in Ms. Freebird's home, although she charges it no rent. Operating costs are kept to a **bare minimum** by communicating and advertising primarily over the Internet and through email.

In that excerpt, the term "bare minimum" is an explicit analogy, while the other details create a vivid mental image of a small business run out of somebody's home. This plays into the writer's theme that SOFT is a small organization being unfairly taken advantage of by a multibillion dollar international hotel chain.

The fun—and the hard work—of the facts section is choosing which facts matter to both the legal theory of the case and your chosen theme, and to then select and place the details that best describe those facts.

9.3.5 Choose the level of detail by changing the perspective of the reader's viewing of the story

Readers experience stories by traveling from their seat into the narrative world. Psychologists call this phenomenon **narrative transportation**.

Think of phrases related to story that convey narrative transportation, "I was drawn to the story" or I am "lost in the story," or "I am getting into that story" (or the corollary, "I couldn't get into it."). You want your reader to be drawn into the story, *i.e.,* be narratively transported, because it is there that persuasion with narrative can occur. The readers connect with characters, appreciate their motivations, and possibly adopt their positions.

Once the writer draws the reader inside that narrative world, the writer then positions the reader at different heights and angles from the action. A good writer knows that it is important to vary the distance from which the reader sees the scene. The reader cannot absorb and remember every detail, nor would a word count allow legal writers to include every detail even if it readers could absorb it all. Rather, the

> **When homework isn't painful**
>
> Observe the way a storyteller changes the viewing perspective of the audience by watching a movie. At the end, think about whether you remained drawn into the story or whether you are bounced out at some point. If so, why? In writing, readers may be bounced out if the writer inserts her opinions or judgments—these become distractions. The distractions often happen in the form of judgment or opinion words substituted for imagery words. Using "aggressively pushed" for description might bounce a reader out of the narrative because the adverb comes from outside the story, whereas the word "shoved" would convey an image without the external distraction.

lawyer must exercise judgment and deploy the use of details when she wants to emphasize a particular action, setting, or object.

Think about how you want the reader to see the various beats or scenes of the story. Someone looking down from 500 feet in the air has the opportunity to see an overview, a "lay of the land" but not minute details. Seeing something from across a room might provide a sense of the totality of the circumstances but not the specifics of interactions between two people. Sometimes the reader needs the 500-foot view to obtain context and to better understand how a variety of facts fit together. Other times the reader needs the close-in shot to be able to accurately judge how a rule of law might apply to the specific facts before the court.

9.3.6   Omit characterizations that consist of unsupported opinions rather than facts

The Statement of Facts exists to provide the reader with exactly that—the facts. A "fact" is a knowable event or condition that can be demonstrated with what we lawyers call competent evidence. Something that either happened in the story between or among the parties that is contained in testimonial or documentary evidence, or something that exists in our everyday world that can be verified by credible sources. By way of example, historical weather records kept by a meteorological center are facts, even if no one testifies about them in a court hearing because they can be verified. Because the Statement of Facts is limited to facts, cites to the record are required by court rules in almost every jurisdiction in summary judgment, post-trial, and appellate briefs.

Lawyers can—and should—use descriptive word choices to tell a persuasive story. These descriptions may fairly be called characterizations. Descriptions that characterize **actions**, **objects**, and **settings** are fine and even preferred. These word choices are subject to verification—they should correspond to something in the evidentiary record.

> ### The absence of facts can be a fact
>
> The absence of evidence may also be a fact. For example, a lawyer might write in your Statement of Facts "at no point during the parties' argument did the plaintiff call the police."
>
> Including an absence of fact in the Statement of Facts is perfectly acceptable, so long as you refrain from making an unwarranted inferential leap. Adding that "therefore the plaintiff wasn't really afraid of the defendant" would be one such impermissible inferential leap. That statement is a characterization, i.e., the lawyer's opinion and argument. It must be omitted from the Statement of Facts section. The same statement, nevertheless, could be used in the legal argument, and if you did so you could suggest that the court draw that inference. In the argument sections, the inference becomes permissible.

But in other instances, characterizations are inappropriate for the Statement of Facts. First, a lawyer's opinion about the merits

of the case or of the characters involved in it are simply that:
opinions. Lawyers are prohibited from testifying on behalf of
their clients. It is the lawyer's role to be the storyteller rather
than a character inside the story. In practical terms, that
translates to a caution for legal writers to leave their own
opinions and judgments out of the Statement of the Facts. This
type of characterization has no place in the Statement of Facts
section of any advocacy document.

Second, a lawyer should refrain from characterizations about the
motives, opinions, thoughts, or feelings of a **character** that do not
otherwise appear in testimony. The opinions and judgments of
characters inside the story are certainly includable—if those
opinions and judgments appear in the record.

Opinion words typically make an appearance as adjectives or
adverbs that attempt to tell rather than to show the reader what
sorts of conclusions to make about the incident:

> The plaintiff obviously wasn't scared of the defendant.

That statement is someone's opinion. It might also be a
conclusion of law if one of the legal elements involves fright on
the part of the plaintiff. If the writer cannot provide a cite to
testimony for that statement, then the writer has included her
own opinion. A better way to show the same thing would be a
sentence such as this:

> Although the plaintiff claimed at trial that she was afraid for her safety
> during her argument with the defendant, she admitted that she didn't call
> the police afterwards nor tell anyone about the incident until two days later
> when she was out socializing with friends at a happy hour.

These facts would be supported by record cites. They would lead
the reader to draw an inference about fear because that is how
the human mind organizes information. The writer could return
to this information later in the deduction section of the legal
argument, and draw the inference openly.

In the above example, you very likely noted the increase in word count. The increase isn't always a bad thing when the particular scene relates to a critical part of the analysis. If the plaintiff's lack of fear is a key part of a legal story, then adding in extra description merits those extra words because they guide the sort of mental images readers will call on, as they process the facts.

9.4   Putting down the working draft of the Facts section

Once you have completed the first working draft, you'll want to set it aside for a while to get some distance from it. Keep an open mind; a significant amount of revision happens after you write the working drafts of the legal argument. When a lawyer is certain that the shadow story and first draft represent the *only* story of the dispute, that's when she's likely to get in trouble. Remember, there's another story out there. After all, the other party is not likely to go to the time and expense of opposing the client if the client's case is crystal clear. Now is the time to put the facts down and study the legal arguments. After writing them, you might decide that the archetype you thought was your second or third choice for your client has become the best and first choice. The theme might become more sharply in focus or it may change altogether. Chapter 15 returns to the Statement of Facts and discusses the last steps: shaping and polishing.

Stop!

(You will come back to this . . .)

... we'll wait for you.

Expressing the Argument

You might assume that your next step should be drafting the Argument section. But we aren't quite there yet. First, we must pause, to assess and plan how you will be expressing the Argument. That involves knowing which types of legal reasoning you will be using, and which types of logic may be flawed. This chapter informs this important phase by providing information about the different types of legal reasoning that you may be using. You are already familiar with some of these types of reasoning from your previous coursework. For example, you have some familiarity with analogical reasoning when using case law authority, and with text-based reasoning when working with statutes. This chapter also introduces inferential, policy-based, and narrative reasoning. Later chapters will discuss these reasoning types in more depth.

In addition to looking at various types of legal reasoning, this chapter also looks at various forms of faulty logic that frequently appear in legal documents. As careful legal thinkers, we should avoid these fallacies in our thinking and be on the lookout for them in the work of our opponents.

9¾.1 Types of Legal Reasoning

In your other law school courses, you have been exposed to different sources of law and different types of reasoning used with those sources of law. These types of reasoning are not exclusive, but may be employed simultaneously or in sequence, depending on the situation.

Types of reasoning	Constitutions	Statutes and Regulations	Cases	Facts
Text-based	███	███		
Analogical	▒▒	▒▒	███	
Policy-based	███	▒▒		
Inferential				███
Narrative	▒▒	▒▒	▒▒	

Key	
Primary mode of reasoning	
Secondary mode of reasoning	

- **Text-Based Reasoning:** This type is also referred to as legislative or statutory-based reasoning, although it also includes regulations, promulgated by agencies. It starts with positive law and then moves into interpretive law. This reasoning begins with looking for other textual materials to define terms, and in the absence of those turns to plain meaning, judicial interpretations, canons of construction, and legislative history to help determine the legislature's or agency's intent as to the meaning of ambiguous terms. We will learn more about statutory interpretation tools in Chapter 10.

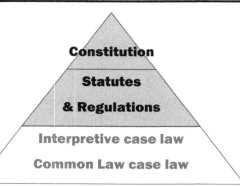

- **Analogical Reasoning:** When the text of a document is ambiguous or non-existent, the next step is turning to analogical reasoning. Analogical reasoning is used when judicial decisions or related statutes are similar enough in construct or facts to allow comparisons between that authority and current problem. It operates as a form of cause-and-effect deductive syllogism. The syllogism in its easiest form says that because compared things are similar (or dissimilar) in critical ways, the outcomes must therefore flow as a consequential result. Most commonly, analogical reasoning is employed to show how a rule of law should be applied in a client's case, based on similarities or distinctions of prior applications.

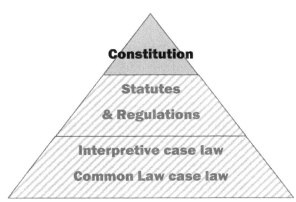

"Depth of analysis" used in conjunction with analogical reasoning typically refers to the level of sophistication of the analogies, i.e., that the lawyer has argued the rule of law's application functionally rather than superficially. The CREAC acronym of arranging legal analysis from the inductive process of the rule synthesis to the deductive process used in application works well when the legal argument uses case-based analogical reasoning. The arrangement of arguments for other types of legal reasoning will be somewhat different than the CREAC acronym.

- **Policy-Based Reasoning**: As we will see in Chapter 11, policy-based reasoning is forward-thinking in orientation. It focuses on predictions of what effect an outcome will produce, and whether the outcome will be positive or negative, usually in terms of future benefits to society. Policy arguments are interdisciplinary in nature

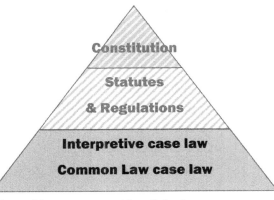

and may draw on research conducted in areas outside of the law.

- **Inferential Reasoning**: Inferential reasoning is the process of inferring facts or legal conclusions from proven facts. We sometimes call this process "reasoning with facts." For example, in a criminal case one element of the crime might be that the defendant acted "with malice." Only the defendant really knows what his state of mind was when he committed the alleged criminal act, but because of the Fifth Amendment privilege against self-incrimination, the prosecution cannot ask him what his state of mind was. (And it is not likely that the defendant would give a truthful answer anyway.) So, the prosecution must prove observable facts through competent evidence, and then allow the jury to infer that those facts prove that the defendant acted with malice. For example, evidence of what the defendant said as he was committing the act, or evidence that he stalked the victim, or that the act was especially violent, all might be provable facts that could lead a jury to infer the legally relevant fact that the defendant acted with malice. Chapter 13 discusses inferential reasoning in more detail.

- **Narrative Reasoning:** Narrative reasoning flows through the entirety of a persuasion document. It provides persuasive power through storytelling. A good story requires a consistent point of view, shows the causal connections from one point to the next, and connects characters to their effort to overcome obstacles. Narrative reasoning works best when combined with the other forms of reasoning. In a sense, the other forms of reasoning show the judge that she is *permitted* to rule in your client's favor (i.e., that there is a legal basis for the relief your client seeks); narrative reasoning gives the court a reason to *want* to rule in your client's favor (i.e., because doing so seems "right"). Always remember: a judge who believes that a particularly ruling is right, and not merely allowed, is more likely to rule in your client's favor.

9¾.2   Avoid logical fallacies

Faulty reasoning undermines the logos of the argument and your credibility as an advocate. Before we move on to specific forms of legal reasoning in the next several chapters, we are pausing for a moment to address the types of arguments to avoid making because they reflect flawed logical thinking. (Note: while you may be tempted to examine only your opponent's arguments to see if she relies on any of these fallacies, you should also carefully examine your own brief to see if you have made these same mistakes.)

When we say "logical fallacy," we often mean a "failed syllogism." As you have learned from your other courses in legal reasoning, most logical reasoning takes the form of a syllogism. The classical example of a syllogism is this:

Is Socrates mortal?

1. Major premise = All humans are mortal
2. Minor premise = Socrates is human
3. Conclusion = Socrates is mortal

In a sense, the major premise of a syllogism is a rule, while the minor premise is a fact. The conclusion flows from the application of the rule to the fact:

Issue:	Is the defendant guilty of speeding?
Rule:	The speed limit where defendant was arrested is 45 MPH.
Application:	The radar gun clocked defendant at 63 MPH.
Conclusion:	Defendant was speeding

In most logical fallacies, some part of the syllogism fails. Here is a list of 16 common fallacies, grouped by why they are fallacies.

9¾.2.1   Shallow thinking fallacies

One way in which a syllogism can fail is when the advoc⁀ with a faulty major premise; that is, the claimed "rule at all, or is poorly articulated. Here are five examples of fallacies that proceed from faulty major premises:

The False Dichotomy		
Major Premise	Minor Premise	Conclusion
People can either like Star Wars or Star Trek, but cannot like both	You like Star Trek	You do not like Star Wars
False	True	Logical but incorrect

• The False Dichotomy

This happens when someone argues that there are only two choices to a complex problem when in fact there are multiple possible choices. For example, "If you don't like chocolate, you must like vanilla." Or, "you are either a Star Trek or a Star Wars person." Some legal maxims are actually examples of this fallacy, including one of the trial lawyer's favorites: "falsus in uno, falsus in omnibus (if a witness lies about one thing, he is lying about everything)."

The Bandwagon Fallacy		
Major Premise	Minor Premise	Conclusion
All other jurisdictions have this rule	Our jurisdiction has no rule	Our jurisdiction should follow the other jurisdictions
Unproven	True	Logical but unsupported

This is a fallacy because the major premise, "the answer must be either A or B," is False.

• The Bandwagon Fallacy

"Everybody agrees with this" [implication: so it must be right]. You have probably heard this one many times or perhaps were even tempted to use it with an authority figure when you were younger. For example, the Internet is full of the faceless, nameless, "everyone says so" comments, sometimes supposedly supported by unscientific or undocumented polls. Lawyers might see this argument appear in the guise of an uncited "weight of authority" type of argument: "Most other jurisdictions do it this way!" Or, "This is a well-settled rule of law, dating back to antiquity" [no or very few citations].[1]

This one is a fallacy mostly because the major premise ("everybody agrees") is not supported by sufficient authority. The premise might be true, but the skeptical reader will likely see this sort of argument as a cover-up for a weak or non-existent rule.

The Middle Ground Fallacy		
Major Premise	Minor Premise	Conclusion
The best resolution of any valuation issue is the average of the two expert opinions	Plaintiff's expert values the property at $500,000, but Defendant's expert values it at $150,000	The property is worth $325,000
False	True	Logical but unsupported

• The Middle Ground Fallacy

Also known as the King Solomon Solution,[2] this fallacy assumes that when two parties begin from distant or opposite positions, the position squarely in the middle of those two positions is the optimal solution. The problem, of course, is that the solution disregards the possibility that one position is objectively reasonable (or legally sound) and the other is grossly unreasonable (or legally unsound). While our legal system encourages and values compromise, when

---

[1] Citations matter. Thank your legal writing professor for teaching that.

[2] In a famous Bible story, King Solomon is said to have resolved a custody dispute between two women by offering to cut the baby in half. When one of the two women then offered to relinquish her claim to the baby in order to spare its life, Solomon awarded the baby to her.

faced with this particular fallacy compromise leads to unreasonable or legally unsound results.

This kind of argument is a fallacy because the major premise assumes that both positions are equally valid. They might not be.

The Fallacy of False Equivalents		
Major Premise	**Minor Premise**	**Conclusion**
If Plaintiff's actions contributed in any way to his injury, he is barred from recovery	Plaintiff was talking on his cell phone when he walked into the intersection, and did not notice that a car was about to run a red light	Plaintiff cannot recover
Unfair	True	Logical but unfair

• The Fallacy of False Equivalents

This fallacy is similar to the Middle Ground Fallacy, except that there is no attempt to "cut the baby in half." It assumes that if one side of a dispute does something wrong, the other side must be doing it too, so that the two bad things just cancel each other out. Another version of this fallacy is that because two sides are both proven to have done bad things, both are justified even though one side's misdeeds are far worse than the other side's. One legal version of this fallacy is the former law of contributory negligence, in which the slightest bit of negligence by the plaintiff cancelled the much more egregious negligence by the defendant, resulting in no recovery for the plaintiff. Modern legislatures in most states ultimately recognized the fallacy in this old common law rule and have legislatively repealed the fallacy by enacting fairer comparative negligence statutes.

- ## The False Balance Fallacy

The False Balance Fallacy		
Major Premise	**Minor Premise**	**Conclusion**
The Earth might be flat or round	I believe the Earth is flat	The Earth is flat
False	True (he "believes")	Logical but False

This fallacy is related to the Fallacy of False Equivalents. While it is worthwhile to allow dissenting voices to be heard, not all sides of an issue deserve equal weight. Sometimes one side of a debate has little or no weight at all, and therefore deserves little or no role in the debate. Journalists are often accused of allowing air time to fallacious debates even though one side is without merit. In practice, this fallacy commonly appears in debates that involve proven science. The scientific method involves repeat experiments by different groups of scientists to verify stated conclusions. Once that has happened and conclusions have been accepted by a majority of scientists in the field, it is a logical fallacy to say that a dissenting view is equally balanced to the proved science. Allowing a debate about whether the moon revolves around the earth or vice versa would fall into this category of fallacies. As with the Fallacy of False Equivalency, lawyers can fall prey to this type of fallacy because we are taught to problem-solve through negotiation and compromise.

9¾.2.2   Insufficient evidence fallacies

Even if the major premise is valid, an argument becomes a fallacy if the rule is applied to False or inadequate evidence (that is, a faulty minor premise). Here are three examples of fallacies that proceed from faulty minor premises.

• The Hasty Generalization

The Hasty Generalization		
Major Premise	Minor Premise	Conclusion
Students need transportation to get to school	Students bounce on pogo sticks	Pogo sticks are a means of student transportation
True	True but misleading	Logical but unreliable

This is the temptation to draw big, general conclusions from insufficient or unrelated evidence. For example, "global warming is fake because we just had a record low temperature on June 21." In that example, a single data point (the low temperature on one day in one location) is insufficient to draw a big conclusion.

Another example: "Pogo sticks are the newest way of commuting to campus because I just saw a student on a pogo stick bouncing down my sidewalk." Here, the major premise is true: "Students need transportation to get to campus." But the minor premise is likely false, or at least unrelated to the major premise: "Students bounce on pogo sticks." The conclusion that students are commuting to campus on pogo sticks is therefore unreliable.

This type of fallacy is related to the Anecdotal Evidence Fallacy discussed next.

• The Anecdotal Evidence Fallacy (a/k/a Arguing from Hearsay)

The Anecdotal Evidence Fallacy		
Major Premise	Minor Premise	Conclusion
Students need transportation to get to school	A witness saw students bouncing on pogo sticks	Pogo sticks are a new means of student transportation
TRUE	Unreliable (hearsay)	Logical but unreliable

Like the Hasty Generalization, this is a fallacy because the minor premise is not proven by any reliable evidence. In the Hasty Generalization example above, the speaker did see a student on a pogo stick. But suppose the speaker said this: "Somebody told me they saw a whole group of students bouncing on pogo sticks near campus. This must be the newest form of transportation for students!" This reasoning is not only a Hasty Generalization, but also possibly based on a false report about what some other person may have seen.

- ## The Texas Sharpshooter Fallacy

The Texas Sharpshooter Fallacy		
Major Premise	Minor Premise	Conclusion
People who can shoot a bulls-eye on a target are expert marksmen	There is a bullet hole in the center of this target	I am an expert marksman
True	True but dishonest (the target was drawn after the shot)	Logical but dishonest

First the advocate shoots at a blank target. Then she draws concentric circles around the bullet hole she just made. Then she offers this as proof of what a great target shooter she is. This, of course, is a fallacy because the minor premise ("I shot a bullseye!") is entirely fabricated.

The legal equivalent of this fallacy is shallow research. A sharpshooter lawyer relies on WestLawNext or LexisAdvance to do a Google-type search, seizes on the first case that pops to the top of the results list, and then makes the whole argument about that result. ("Hey! I KeyCited/Shepardized it and no stop signs showed up, so I'm okay. Right?") Sorry, the diligent lawyer must do more than that with the research and analysis. A diligent lawyer spends the time to think more creatively and dig more deeply. Here is a great chance to indulge your curiosity!

This fallacy is related to the confirmation bias problem, where a researcher finds whatever he expects to find, and then stops looking.

- ### *Ipse dixit* (a/k/a "the Bald Assertion")

This is not merely a failed syllogism; it is not really a syllogism at all. Instead, this fallacy merely asserts a conclusion without stating the major premise, the minor premise, or either of them.

The Bald Assertion		
Major Premise	Minor Premise	Conclusion
[crickets]	[more crickets]	The defendant was negligent
Missing	Missing	Unproven

For example, the author may make the claim that "The defendant was negligent." Without more, this statement is just a bald assertion, and a logical fallacy. What was the defendant's duty (major premise)? In what way did the defendant fail to conform to the proper standard of care (minor premise)? Without those premises, the claim that the defendant was negligent is no more than a bald assertion.

Adding one of the premises does not solve the problem; both the major and minor premises must be stated. Thus, "The speed limit was 30 MPH; therefore, the defendant was speeding" is still a bald assertion, because the minor premise ("The defendant was going 45 MPH") is missing.

Avoiding this fallacy might seem obvious, but in practice it shows up with some regularity. You can find examples easily in political news.

9¾.2.3 *Non Sequitur* fallacies

A third way an argument can become a fallacy is when the major premise is applied to the minor premise incorrectly. That is, the conclusion does not logically flow from the premises; it is a *non sequitur*. Here are two examples of this type of fallacy.

- ## Correlation Equals Causation

Correlation Equals Causation		
Major Premise	**Minor Premise**	**Conclusion**
Baby Josephine received vaccinations	Baby Josephine is autistic	Vaccinations cause autism
TRUE	TRUE	Illogical

This is a fairly common fallacy in statistical analysis. It falsely assumes that because facts A and B both occur together, A must have caused B. The fact that Baby Josephine was given vaccinations, and now is autistic, does not prove that the vaccinations caused the autism. (Nor does it prove that Nicolas Cage causes people to drown in swimming pools.)[3] Causation is proved with repeat scientific studies that include controls that account for other potential factors.

_____

[3] The chart below is used with permission from the website http://www.tylervigen.com/spurious-correlations. If you want a good laugh, check out the other odd correlations that site documents.

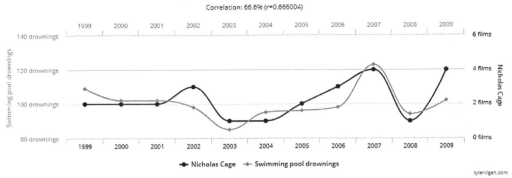

- ## The Post Hoc Fallacy

The Post Hoc Fallacy		
Major Premise	**Minor Premise**	**Conclusion**
A total eclipse of the sun occurred	I beat on drums during the eclipse, and the sun returned after the eclipse	The beating of drums will cause the sun to reappear after an eclipse
True	True	Illogical

This is similar to the "correlation is not causation" fallacy. The full Latin name of this fallacy is "post hoc, ergo proctor hoc" (because one event followed a previous event, the previous event caused the latter event). By such reasoning one can prove that the beating of drums causes the sun to reappear after an eclipse.

9¾.2.4 Avoidance fallacies

Sometimes, an argument becomes a fallacy simply because it fails to address the substance of the point in contention. Here are four examples of this type of fallacy.

• The *Ad Hominem* Attack

The *Ad Hominem* Attack		
Major Premise	Minor Premise	Conclusion
Persons who are injured in automobile accidents through no fault of their own are entitled to recovery	Plaintiff smoked marijuana in college	Plaintiff should not recover
True	True	Illogical (minor premise unrelated to major premise

This is an attack on the ethos of one's opponent (either the opposing party or that party's counsel). Rather than meet the substance of the arguments made, the *ad hominem* attack claims that the person making the argument is a bad person or not worthy of trust for some reason. The person making ad hominem attacks ends up making him-/herself look petty and small, thereby losing some of their own valuable ethos.

• The Straw Man Fallacy

The Straw Man Fallacy		
Major Premise	Minor Premise	Conclusion
Many heroin users began using marijuana before becoming addicted to heroin	Many heroin users began drinking milk before becoming addicted to heroin	Drinking milk causes heroin addiction.
True	True but misleading	Illogical

Someone using a straw man fallacy sets up a weak or absurd scenario attributed to the opposing side and then argues against it. This fallacy might take one of several forms. For example, your opponent has made an argument that you think is weak or ridiculous. You consider responding by creating a hypothetical that takes his argument to an extreme, in order to prove how weak or ridiculous the argument really is. Or, because you understand that you will gain credibility with your reader if you do counteranalysis (see chapter 12), you create a weak or ridiculous argument that you claim your opponent will likely make, in order to easily knock it down.

In chapter 11, we discuss "slippery slope" arguments as a form of a policy argument. However, if taken to extreme, a slippery slope argument can turn into straw man fallacy. For example, one might claim that since many heroin addicts began using marijuana before using heroin, marijuana use should be made illegal. Somebody opposing making marijuana use illegal might argue that most people began drinking milk before using heroin, so that milk should be outlawed too.

If you do this, however, you will ultimately lose credibility with the audience, because in the end your hypothetical or your imagined counterargument depends on being weak or ridiculous.

• Begging the Question (a/k/a the Circular Argument)

Begging the Question		
Major Premise	**Minor Premise**	**Conclusion**
Clear-cut logging is bad for the environment	Clear-cut logging destroys all the trees on the property.	Clear-cut logging is bad for the environment
Assumes the answer	True	Illogical (Unproven)

"Begging the question" actually does not refer to an answer that invites a follow-up question. It means that the answer does not actually answer the question asked; it just assumes the answer. For example, "Clear-cut logging damages the environment, because the terrain left behind has no trees on it." That just restates the problem.

- ## The Red Herring

The Red Herring		
Major Premise	Minor Premise	Conclusion
The city may prohibit loudspeaker trucks from driving through residential neighborhoods blaring political messages at times when most residents are asleep	The city is attempting to enforce its ordinance against a Green Party candidate	The city's enforcement of its nuisance ordinance is discriminatory
True	True	Illogical (doesn't address the issue)

A red herring attempts to distract or redirect the audience from the argument raised by another party, to hide a lack of a sound counterargument. Schematically it looks like this:

- **Speaker A:** Moonstruck makes the best milk chocolate sea salt caramels in the land.

- **Speaker B:** Twenty percent of people surveyed last year believe that chocolate milk come from brown cows.

- **Speaker A:** Seriously? 20%?

9¾.2.5   A final caution

Just to finish scrambling your brains, we leave you with the Fallacy Fallacy:

- ## The Fallacy Fallacy

Just because somebody has relied on fallacious thinking does not mean that they have reached an incorrect conclusion. For example, the Texas Sharpshooter is not always wrong; that case which popped to the top of her results list might in fact be the most important case or statute to analyze. But because you now understand the Texas

Sharpshooter fallacy, you know that you have to dig deeper and test out alternatives before you can be truly satisfied that she did hit that bull's eye on the first try.

Think about these fallacies for a moment. In the next chapters we move on to some more specific (and valid) argumentation techniques.

9¾.3   Tying it all together

Why do people fall for the fallacies listed above (or any other fallacy)?

In many cases, the conclusion that flows from the logical fallacy is more appealing to the reader than the answer that would flow from logical reasoning. The flawed conclusion may be more emotionally satisfying, or it may conform to what the reader thinks is true or wants to be true. Psychologists might call the latter phenomenon "confirmation bias": a researcher finds what he expects to find, without objectively considering all of the possible alternative explanations. The *correlation equals causation* fallacy is a good example of confirmation bias: one is looking for a reason to explain why some children become autistic, and vaccinations seem like they could be the cause.

We might suggest an alternative explanation: the writer has invoked the wrong form of reasoning. The *ad hominem attack* fallacy, for example, might work at the level of narrative reasoning. But the rule of law is clear in that example, and in no need of narrative reasoning to resolve the test: prior, unrelated bad behavior does not help prove whether plaintiff was injured through no fault of his own. Even the example of vaccination causing autism (our example of the *correlation equals causation* fallacy) might be appealing due to improper invocation of narrative reasoning: we feel sorry for Baby Josephine, so we seize on the emotionally satisfying explanation that an external source, namely the vaccination, must have caused her condition.

We conclude where we began: beware of logical fallacies! Consider your own legal arguments to ask, objectively, whether your line of thinking exemplifies any of these fallacies. If it does, ask yourself whether you can resolve the fallacy by

- stating a more reliable rule (major premise)

- relying on more dependable facts (minor premise)

- making sure that the conclusion you state really is compelled by objectively applying the rule to the facts, or whether alternative results are equally valid.

Also, make sure to check your opponent's writing to see if he relies on any logical fallacies. If you spot any, you should point them out to the court (while avoiding the *ad hominem attack* fallacy in your response!).

Working with the Law, Part 1: Interpreting Statutes

Many legal issues begin with statutory analysis and interpretation. The foundation of statutory interpretation is quite simple: a court must interpret a statute so that the statute accomplishes what the legislature intended. It is not the court's role to determine whether a statute is effective or premised on good policy. It is the court's job to follow the legislature's intent, unless the statute is unconstitutional.

Finding the legislative intent, however, is not as easy as it might seem. Usually, the best evidence of legislative intent is the precise words that a legislature used in the statute. Courts begin with the premise that the legislature meant what it said, and if the meaning of a statute is clear on its face, the court will apply that plain meaning. However, meaning is a slippery thing, and lawyers often disagree about the plain meaning of a statute. Consequently, we often need to look beyond the plain meaning of a statute to determine the legislative intent.

We have several interpretive tools to aid us in this task. These tools can be either intrinsic or extrinsic. By "intrinsic tools," we mean those that we use to interpret the words of the statute itself. On the other hand, "extrinsic tools" look beyond the express words of the statute for clues as to the statute's meaning, for example, by examining legislative history.

Because the words of the statute are usually the best indicator of legislative intent, we begin with intrinsic tools that examine the text and context of our statute. The text-based tools, often called "canons of construction," are simply principles for interpreting language that assist us in determining the meaning of the specific words of a statute. In addition, we have canons that are context based. We use these tools to draw meaning from the language that surrounds the disputed term or phrase. This may include the surrounding sections of the statute or related statutes that use the same terms. Finally, there are canons of general construction, principles that do not aid in interpreting specific statutory language but provide broader concepts of interpretation. For example, we prefer constitutional interpretations to unconstitutional interpretations. (Courts will assume that the legislature does not intend to pass unconstitutional laws, so it makes sense that, when given a choice, courts will opt for an interpretation that does not violate the Constitution over one that does.)

When the intrinsic tools do not resolve statutory ambiguity, a court will look beyond the text of a statute to the extrinsic tool of legislative history. Legislative history is simply the various records of the process of enacting a statute. This includes testimony before legislative committees, committee reports, various versions of a bill, and other documents that were

> ### Legislative History v. Legislative Intent
>
> Students sometimes use the terms "legislative history" and "legislative intent" interchangeably. This is a bit like confusing a hammer for a blueprint. Legislative history—that is, the record of a statute's enactment, is one tool of statutory interpretation. Legislative intent, on the other hand, is the guiding principle of all statutory interpretation. We use all of our interpretive tools, including the plain meaning, contextual canons, legislative history, and the rest, to determine the legislative intent of a statute. The legislative intent is what the legislature meant a statute to do. The legislative history is one tool that helps us figure out that meaning.

created while the legislature was deliberating on pending legislation. In addition, a court will sometimes look beyond the legislative history to the broader historical context in which legislation was enacted.

Finally, some courts will look to find the legislative purpose behind a statute. For example, a remedial statute, such as most environmental legislation, may be broadly interpreted to give effect to the goal the legislature had when it enacted the statute. Thus, the meaning of "navigable waters of the United States" is given a broad meaning under the Clean Water Act because courts interpret the legislative goal of the Act to protect as much of the waters of the United States as possible.

This chapter provides an overview of the most common statutory interpretive tools. Some of these tools may be familiar to you already.

10.1   How to read a statute

Reading a statute requires precision. Remember that most statutory disputes are about the meaning of a single word or phrase. Thus, as we first read a statute, we must remember that every word counts. It is impossible, of course, to predict which words are likely to be disputed, but we can start with a framework that can help identify the likely scope, meaning, and potential ambiguities of most statutes. There are two initial steps to getting an understanding of a statute. First, read the statute in its entire context, not just the section you found. Second, begin reading the relevant sections of the statute critically.

Before we begin, it is important to understand the difference between statutes and codes. A "statute" is what the legislature votes on and is ultimately signed into law by the executive branch. Statutes generally are broken down into discrete "sections," which serve different functions (as we will describe in a moment). A "code" is a book that publishes most, but sometimes not all,[1] of the sections of the statute. Codes are organized by subject matter, so a single code section may be made up of sections of several different statutes, passed at different time over the course of many years. Because code sections are composed of many statute sections, the individual code sections numbers usually do not reflect the numbering sequence of the original statute passed by the legislature. Often, different parts

---

[1] For example, sections that have a temporary effect, such as budgetary provisions, will not appear in the permanent code.

of the statute are placed in different "titles" or "chapters" of the code because the single statute affects different areas of the law. For example, the Patient Protection and Affordable Care Act adopted by Congress in 2010 was codified in many different titles of the United States Code because some sections of the Act affected business and labor while other sections affected taxes.

When you research, either electronically or in books, the best and easiest way to research is in the code (either federal or state). That's because the code books (especially the electronic versions in commercial databases) are updated frequently as the legislature adopts amendments to previous statutes. But remember that when you find a section of a statute in a code, what you are looking at needs to be read in the context of related sections of the code. Sometimes those sections are part of a single statute adopted by a legislature, while other times they are a combination of statutes adopted over many years. The "legislative intent" must therefore be determined by looking at the entire context of the statute, not just the single section that your research found.

10.1.1   The statutory context

When researching statutes, you will generally find specific provisions, or sections, that satisfy your search criteria. Often, your search will lead to a section that appears to be highly relevant to the issue you are researching. But that section was probably not enacted by itself. It is most likely part of a larger statute, or several statutes, that contains multiple, related sections. For example, the statutory provision that prohibits the "taking" of endangered species[2] is part of the broader statute generally known as the Endangered Species Act.[3]

---

[2] 16 U.S.C. §1538 (2010).

[3] *Id.* §§1531–1544. Note that this single act of the legislature (the statute) is codified in numerous sections of the United States Code.

Thus, even when it looks like the section you found answers your research question, you must examine the entire statutory context to fully understand how the section you found relates to your legal question.

A typical statute adopted by a legislature often includes most or all of the following sections:

- Title
- Purpose or Preamble
- Definitions
- Scope (situations to which the statute does or does not apply)
- Operative (general rule; what's prohibited or required, or permitted)
- Exceptions (if not included in operative sections, definitions, or scope)
- Enforcement (penalties or remedial provisions)
- Cross-references
- Severability or savings clause
- Effective date

10.1.2   Reading the statute critically

Once you have a sense of the overall statutory context, it is time to look more critically at the sections that are relevant to your issue. Ask the following questions for any statute you need to interpret:

- To whom does the statute apply? (The court? The state? "Any person"? Employers? Tenants?) Once you have figured out to whom the statute applies, you will need to figure out whether that includes the people involved in your dispute.

- Does the statute provide any express definitions of key terms? Many of the words used in the operative provisions may have special meanings assigned by the definitions section; these definitions may change your analysis of whether the statute applies at all, to whom it applies, or any of the questions listed above.

- What does the statute require, permit, or prohibit? All statutes affect people's conduct. Is your statute demanding some action by someone? Granting rights to someone? Restricting someone's behavior? Be sure you can identify the specific conduct that statute regulates.

- Are there any exceptions to the general rule?

- What consequences attach to noncompliance? Does the statute provide some remedy for an offended party? Require some punishment or sanction? Does it allow someone to bring a claim in court? If so, what court?

- When does the statute apply? Always make sure you are reading the relevant version of the statute. Usually, the current version of a statute is the version that applies to your problem. However, if a code section was recently amended, an earlier version of the statute may apply. You will learn how to find out when a code section was amended in your research class.

This is how it works in the Internet dating example. That case raises an issue about whether Ms. Hawthorne was a victim of domestic violence as defined by a New Jersey statute, N.J.S.A. 2C:25-19(d).[4] An experienced critical reader would first parse the statute to make it easier to see its component parts. Here's the relevant statutory section:

> d. "Victim of domestic violence" means a person protected under this act and shall include any person who is 18 years of age or older or who is an emancipated minor and who has

---

[4] New Jersey citation form is being used here. Note that as a lawyer briefing to a New Jersey court, you would use local court citation rules, as shown here, rather than general ALWD or Bluebook format.

been subjected to domestic violence by a spouse, former spouse, or any other person who is a present or former household member. "Victim of domestic violence" also includes any person, regardless of age, who has been subjected to domestic violence by a person with whom the victim has a child in common, or with whom the victim anticipates having a child in common, if one of the parties is pregnant. "Victim of domestic violence" also includes any person who has been subjected to domestic violence by a person with whom the victim has had a dating relationship.[5]

Here's how we might break this down:

"Victim of domestic violence" means:

1. A person who is 18 or older OR an emancipated minor,

   and

   who has been subjected to domestic violence by a:

   spouse; former spouse;

   or

   A present or former household member.

   or

2. Any person who has been subjected to domestic violence by a person with whom:

   The victim has a child in common;

   or

   the victim anticipates having a child in common IF one of the parties is pregnant.

   or

---

[5] **Note**: This section of the New Jersey statute has been significantly amended since the student briefs were written for this simulation. Please **do not rely on the quoted statute in this book** to be an accurate statement of current New Jersey law. It isn't.

3. A person who has been subjected to domestic violence
    by a person with whom the victim has a dating
    relationship.

Once we have parsed the statute into its component parts, it becomes
much easier to answer the questions we need to ask to understand
the scope of legal issue.

10.1.2.1.   To whom does the statute apply?

The statute identifies three potential ways to be a "victim of domestic
violence." A person must suffer domestic violence by: a spouse,
former spouse, or household member (if the victim is at least 18); the
parent of their child or potential parent if one party is pregnant; or
someone in a dating relationship with the abused.

10.1.2.2.   Does the statute provide any express definitions of key terms?

The statute defines "victim of domestic violence." However, we should
also look within this definition to see if it uses any other terms that are
defined by the statute. For example, "domestic violence," "household
member," and "dating relationship" are all potentially ambiguous terms
that may defined either within the statute itself or by case law.

10.1.2.3.   What does the statute require, permit, or prohibit?

Because this statute is a definition, it does not create any obligation
or right by itself. Once we understand the meaning of the definition,
we would need to look elsewhere in the statutory scheme to
determine how this definition fits within those parts of the statute
that do create obligations or rights.

10.1.2.4.   What are the exceptions to the general rule?

The definition does not create any explicit exceptions. If a person
does not fit with the meaning of "victim of domestic violence," she is

going to be excluded from the scope of the statute. Note that this conclusion is itself an application of the canon of construction *expression unius est exclusion alterius*, which means that the inclusion of items in a list implies that other things are excluded, which we will discuss in the next section.

10.1.2.5.   *What is the consequence of not complying?*

Again, because this is a definition provision, it does not have any penalty or sanction for not complying with it. What rights are given to people who fall within the definition are specified in the operative sections of the overall statute, so you would need to look there.

10.1.2.6.   *When does the statute apply?*

We will need to do a bit more research to find out when this definition was enacted and, more important, when was its effective date. If it was enacted after the incident giving rise to our dispute, it will most likely not apply to our case.

Once you have answered these questions, it is time to start looking for the terms that are likely to be at issue in your dispute. Of course, you already know that in the Internet dating example, the issue is the meaning of "dating relationship." However, the author of the brief could not have determined this without first carefully parsing the statute and analyzing all the potential issues. This is the heart of statutory interpretation. There are many interpretive tools at our disposal. The following sections provide an overview of the most common interpretive tools, beginning with the text of the statute and its plain meaning.

10.2   Text-based interpretive tools

Statutory interpretation begins with the words of the statute itself. This section reviews some of the most common text-based tools of statutory interpretation. This is not an exhaustive review. The first step is to consider the plain meaning of the text. Of course, opposing lawyers often disagree on the plain meaning of even the most common words in a statute. Thus, we need to look deeper into the text of the statute by relying on the canons of construction.

Note that this is not an exhaustive list of intrinsic interpretive tools. For a more thorough review, you may wish to consult a treatise on statutory interpretation.[6]

10.2.1   Plain meaning

Since the ultimate purpose of statutory interpretation is to determine the intent of the legislature, the starting point for all statutory interpretation is the "plain meaning" rule. That is, when the statute is clearly worded and susceptible to only one reasonable interpretation, that is the "plain meaning" and the court needs go no further in interpreting the statute. Stated another way, the plain meaning of a term is its ordinary and everyday usage. If a term's meaning is clear on its face, then there is no need to look beyond the plain meaning of its terms. That seems simple, but in practice is less so. For example, let's look at a simple dog bite statute:

> The owner of any dog is liable for the damages suffered by
> any person who is bitten by the dog. . . .

Cal. Civil Code §3342 (1997).

This statute would clearly include a situation involving a labradoodle. The plain meaning of "dog" would not be in question. On the other hand, the statutory term "bitten" might be arguably ambiguous. For example, if the labradoodle didn't attack but only ripped a person's jacket while playing in a dog park, was the person "bitten" per the statute? Does the statute require the dog actually to bite the person, or does biting the jacket also establish liability? What if the dog playfully put his jaws around somebody's arm, but did not break the skin?

---

[6] For a thorough examination of how one state's courts use textual canons, see INTERPRETING OREGON LAW (Jack Landau et al. eds., Or. St. B. 2009).

To determine the meaning of "bitten," we might first look to the dictionary meaning. Often courts will use dictionaries as sources of finding the plain meaning of a term. However, if a dictionary gives us insufficient guidance, we may then look to other textual evidence of the legislature's intent.

10.2.2   Canons of construction

In addition to the plain meaning rule, there are many interpretive principles, or "canons of construction," that help us give meaning to the text of a statute. While "canon" may sound like an immutable and powerful tool, these canons really are just basic principles of how we interpret text. In other words, they are specific expressions of what most would consider common sense.

These canons can be very instructive. However, as Karl Llewellyn pointed out decades ago, for every canon, there is an "equal and opposite canon" that could suggest an alternate meaning.[7] The most persuasive canon is usually that which seems most consistent with other interpretive tools. One rule of thumb is that if your interpretation of a statute suggests a meaning that is contrary to common sense, you will most certainly lose, no matter how elegantly you apply the canons of construction.

In many states, the canons of construction are common law doctrines; a few states have enacted them into statutory law.[8] Here are some of the most common canons of construction:

10.2.2.1.   *The plain meaning rule*

Yes, the plain meaning rule is a canon of construction. It is where all statutory interpretation should start.

---

[7] Karl N. Llewellyn, THE COMMON LAW TRADITION: DECIDING APPEALS 521–535 (1960).

[8] *See, e.g.*, 1 Pa.C.S.A. §§ 1921 *et seq.*

10.2.2.2.   Canons regarding specific words

* "May" is permissive, that is, it gives discretion to someone.

* "Shall" and "must" are mandatory, that is, they create a legal duty or obligation to someone.[9]

* "Or" is a disjunctive connector, establishing alternatives.

* "And" is a conjunctive connector, establishing multiple requirements (e.g., the elements of a cause of action are always connected with an "and").

10.2.2.3.   Canon regarding grammar

* *Doctrine of the last antecedent:* a referring phrase applies only to the last antecedent unless the referring phrase is separated by a comma or context suggests otherwise:

    o I saw Juan and Mary with a puppy. (Only Mary was with a puppy.)

    o I saw Juan and Mary, **with a puppy**. (Both Juan and Mary were with a puppy.)

10.2.2.4.   Canons regarding lists of things

* *Noscitur a sociis:* Interpret ambiguous words in a list by the company they keep:

> A city zoning ordinance of Michigan City, Indiana, established a height restriction of 30 feet in residential areas. A homeowner applied for, and was granted, a building permit to build a second-floor addition to his home and a 55-foot-tall tower, topped by a room enclosed in glass to provide scenic views of Lake Michigan. The homeowner claimed that his observation tower was a "tower" that could extend 25 feet above the normal 35-foot height restriction. The homeowner argued, and the city agreed, that the zoning ordinance's exception for "towers" permitted this structure to be built.

---

[9] Note, however, that a number of cases have interpreted the word "shall" to mean "may."

That controlling zoning ordinance's exception allowed "penthouses or roof structures for the housing of elevators, stairways, tanks, ventilating fans, or similar equipment required to operate or maintain the structure, and fire or parapet walls, skylights, towers, steeples, flagpoles, chimneys, smokestacks, radio and television aerials, wireless masts, electric and telephone service poles, water tanks, silos, storage hoppers, elevators or similar structures" to exceed the height restriction by no more than 25 feet. The Indiana Court of Appeals, applying the canon of *noscitur a sociis*, held that the word "tower" must be interpreted to be similar to the other words in the list: structures that are not habitable. Since the observation room atop the "tower" was habitable, the court decided that the room did not fit within the zoning ordinance's exception.

> *Ross v. Harris*, 860 N.E.2d 602 (Ind. Ct. App. 2006).

- ***Ejusdem generis:*** When a list of terms is followed by a general catchall phrase, that phrase should be interpreted to be consistent with the specific terms of the list:

    The Motor Vehicle Theft Act defined "motor vehicle" to include "an automobile, automobile truck, automobile wagon, motorcycle or any other vehicle not designed for running on rails." 18 U.S.C. § 408 (1926). In *McBoyle v. U.S.*, 283 U.S. 25 (1931), the issue was whether an airplane was a "motor vehicle." Because all of the specific terms in the list were vehicles that moved on land, the Court held that "any other vehicle" applied only to vehicles that ran on land, not those that fly. *McBoyle*, 283 U.S. at 27.

- ***Expressio unius est exclusio alterius:*** The inclusion of one thing implies the exclusion of other things not included. When a statutory list includes several things and does not include a catchall phrase, the court will not include within its scope those things that are not expressly listed:

    A statute that exempted from real estate taxes property owned by a municipal government for "streets, sewer lines, water lines, and other municipal purposes" did not exempt a power plant and electric lines operated by a municipal

government since those things were not included on the list
of exempt purposes.

Town of Pine Bluffs v. St. Bd. of Equalization, 333 P.2d 700
(Wyo. 1958).

10.2.2.5.   Other textual canons

- ***The court may not omit what has been included nor add what has been
  excluded.*** This is sometimes referred to as "every word must mean
  something," or expressed in an admonition that "a court may not
  disregard the letter of the law in pursuit of its spirit." If an
  interpretation of a statute requires adding language to the statute or
  ignoring words that are included in a statute, that interpretation is
  disfavored. This canon is premised on the principle that the legislature
  crafts statutes with care, and it is not the court's role to amend the
  express language of the legislature, or to substitute its judgment for the
  judgment of the legislative branch

- ***Construe terms consistently throughout a statute.*** When the legislature
  uses the same term in different provisions of a statute, the court will
  give that term the same meaning in every provision.

10.2.3   Contextual canons

In addition to textual canons, a court also considers the context of
the statutory term at issue. It is sometimes difficult to distinguish
between "text" and "context." Text is the specific term at issue, and
context is the text surrounding the specific term at issue. However,
for most purposes, this distinction is not important. Rather, the key
is to begin your statutory analysis with intrinsic interpretive tools,
that is, the words of the statute—including both the specific terms
and the context in which they are found. That said, there are two
kinds of context interpretive tools: the surrounding statutory context
and the historical context.

10.2.3.1 *The statutory context: definitions and* in pari materia

The statutory context includes looking at other sections of the same statutory scheme. The statutory scheme may include a list of specially defined terms as well as a statement of legislative purpose. These sections, and others as well, may shed light on the meaning of a particular term in a different section of the statute.

One section that you must always consult is the definitions section. Definitions can resolve potential ambiguity by giving a precise meaning to a statutory term. On the other hand, definitions sometimes *create* ambiguity when the plain meaning appears obvious from the text. Remember, definition sections are not a tiebreaker to resolve ambiguities arising from textual analysis. Definitions trump any other interpretive tool as they reflect the legislature's specific intent as to the meaning of the defined term.

In addition to definitions, other statutes that govern the same subject or have a similar purpose are said to be *in pari materia*. In other words, the meaning we give a term in one statute should generally be given the same meaning in a related statute. The idea behind this principle is that the legislature is aware of all of its previous enactments and if it uses the same word in a statute with a similar purpose as an existing statute, the legislature probably intended that word to have the same meaning in both statutes.

> ### How to craft an *in para materia* argument
>
> 1. **Widen the lens through which you are looking at the particular statute to come up with a broader category**
>
> One way to do this is to look at the overall indexing of the statute. Criminal statutes, for example, are often grouped together by type of crimes. If you obtained the statute electronically, you can still easily expand the search to see the broader categories (and sometimes they are just listed at the top of the page). Or, click the "Table of Contents" button at the top of the screen to see where this section appears in relation to other parts of the codified statute.
>
> 2. **Once you have that broad lens, think of other statutes that fit into the same category**
>
> This may be a repetitive step if the statute's indexing system helps you. But otherwise you will have to think creatively in Step 1 in order to get here. For example, if you need help answering a question about the Endangered Species Act, you might broaden your scope of research to include other statutes that protect animals. The Migratory Bird Act or the Bald Eagle Act might give you some clues. If they don't then you might widen the scope even further to statutes that are also designed to protect natural resources. Is there something in the Clean Water Act that could help your argument?
>
> 3. **Research those other items in the category and see if they provide some interpretive answers**
>
> These answers may come from different sources. For example, a related statute may provide a specific definition for a particular term. Or, a court may have interpreted the term in the context of the related statute. The more consistent interpretations you find, the stronger the *in pari materia* argument is likely to be.
>
> 4. **Communicate to the reader that there are analogous interpretations to the statute you are dealing with**
>
> You are going to need to walk your reader through the steps that you just took to get to the analogy.
>
> 5. **Recognize when it isn't working**
>
> It is important to note that not all statutes are appropriate for an *in pari materia* argument. For example, "residence" may have a different meaning in tax law than it does for immigration law.

10.2.3.2.   *Consider the historical context*

Sometimes a court looks to the broader context in which a statute was enacted. For example, the PATRIOT Act was adopted shortly after the September 11, 2001, attacks on the World Trade Center and the Pentagon. At that time, there was widespread concern in the United States that law enforcement lacked the powers it needed to protect citizens from future terrorist attacks. Those concerns undoubtedly played a role in the drafting of the Act, and the historical context could be useful in interpreting the statute to be consistent with Congress's intent in passing it.

10.2.4 Substantive canons

In addition to text and context, there are some canons explaining general principles of interpretation. These substantive canons are not about how to interpret particular terms, but rather reflect broader, often policy-based, principles.

10.2.4.1 Punitive statutes are to be narrowly construed; remedial statutes are to be broadly construed

When a statute's primary effect is to punish—for example, a criminal statute—that statute will be narrowly construed. On the other hand, a statute that is primarily designed to remedy a problem (for example, an environmental protection statute) should be broadly construed to meet the legislative purpose.

10.2.4.2. Constitutional interpretations are favored over unconstitutional interpretations

When a court is faced with two possible interpretations of a statute, and one would make the statute unconstitutional, the court will favor the other interpretation. For example, when the Affordable Care Act was before the United States Supreme Court, one of the issues was whether the "penalty" imposed on individuals who did not purchase health insurance was a tax authorized under Congress's taxing power. If so, the statute would be constitutional; if not, the statute would not be constitutional. Chief Justice Roberts, in writing for the majority, held that because the penalty could reasonably be read as a tax, it was constitutionally valid.[10]

---

[10] *Natl. Fedn. of Indep. Bus. v. Sebelius*, 132 S. Ct. 2566 (2012).

10.2.4.3.   The legislature does not intend absurd results

Similar to the constitutional preference canon, courts likewise disfavor interpretations that lead to absurd results. Thus, if the meaning of a statute appears clear on its face, but that meaning leads to a result that is clearly absurd, the court will reject that meaning in favor of one that is not absurd.

The absurd results canon is popular with many novice legal writers because it is tempting to argue that any result that is bad for one's client is "absurd." However, a bad result is not necessarily an absurd one. Likewise, a result that seems like bad policy is not necessarily an absurd result. Rather, an "absurd" result must be one that the legislature could not have intended. An example would be an interpretation of a statute that creates an internal inconsistency (such as requiring voters present I.D. at a polling place when a different statute requires all voting be done by mail).

10.2.4.4.   Statutes codifying the common law are to be broadly construed; statutes in derogation of the common law are to be narrowly construed

Many statutes simply mirror the existing common law. In essence the legislature enacts statutes to ensure the common law continues. In such cases, the statute is to be broadly construed to reflect the policies underlying the common law. On the other hand, when the legislature passes a law that changes (i.e., is "in derogation of") the common law, it is to be narrowly construed.

10.2.4.5.   The rule of lenity

Similar to the rule that punitive statutes are to be narrowly construed, statutes that impose either criminal or civil sanctions (such as fines) are also to be read narrowly. Ambiguous terms in such statutes should be construed so as to impose the penalties in the fewest circumstances possible. This is premised on the need to ensure the law provides clear notice as to the scope of the law.

10.3   Purpose-based interpretation

Sometimes the express text of a statute remains ambiguous even after thorough application of the canons of construction and careful review of legislative history. On occasion, an apparently reasonable interpretation of a statutory term or phrase will lead to a result that seems contrary to a fundamental goal of the statute. In these situations, a court will expand its interpretation of the term or phrase to examine the underlying purpose of the statute. If faced with a choice between one interpretation that furthers the legislative purpose and one that does not, the court may adopt the one that furthers the purpose, even if a literal reading of the statute suggests a different result.

Keep in mind two important points about purpose-based arguments. First, you need some authority to establish what the legislative purpose of a statute is. For some statutes, the legislature will include a statement of purpose or similar provision at the beginning of the statute. Such statements tend to be aspirational and may set goals that are not realistic. Thus, even when the legislature has provided an explicit expression of purpose, a court may be unwilling to further that goal when the express language of the statute suggests a different result.

The respondent's brief in the Internet dating case provides a good example of how to use legislative purpose to give meaning to a statutory term:

> The pertinent section of the statute does not provide a definition of what constitutes a "dating relationship." Interpreting courts have rejected the notion of an absolute or plain meaning to the phrase. Instead, courts will interpret it in light of the

> policy set out by the New Jersey Supreme Court to
> look at the Act through a broad lens. *Cesare v.*
> *Cesare*, 154 N.J. 394 (1998). The New Jersey
> Supreme Court has stressed the importance of a
> liberal interpretation "to achieve its salutary
> purposes" so as to "'assure the victims of domestic
> violence the maximum protection from abuse the
> law can provide.'" *Id.* at 399.
>
> Because the legislature has called for a liberal
> construction, courts have developed and use an
> expansive and liberally construed factor test to
> determine when parties are in a dating
> relationship....

In this example, the author has a particularly strong legislative purpose argument because the New Jersey Supreme Court has already relied on the statute's express "salutary purposes" to interpret the statute broadly. Because the *Cesare* court held that the statute should be interpreted broadly to meet the legislative purpose, this same principle should be applied here.

Another place that we may find evidence of legislative purpose is in the legislative history. Statements in the legislative history can be persuasive, but the usual cautions discussed above apply. Remember, unlike express statements of purpose, the legislative history is never expressly approved by the legislature as a whole.

The second point about legislative purpose is that we should not confuse it with legislative intent. Legislatures often pass a broadly worded, aspirational Purpose section of a statute, as Congress did in the Endangered Species Act. However, that broad aspirational language will only get the lawyer so far when interpreting a specific section of a statute. Remember, all statutory interpretation is aimed at finding the legislative *intent* of the specific statutory language at issue. Understanding the stated purpose of the legislation can be a useful tool in finding that legislative intent. However, what a legislature states as its broad goal is not the same thing as the mechanism it establishes to achieve that goal. If, for example, a specific term seems to be more limiting than the broadly stated purpose, a court will often give that term its more natural, limited meaning rather than stretch its meaning to fit the wider scope suggested by the stated legislative purpose. Remember that the stated purpose of any legislation is simply an aid to the court in resolving ambiguities in the operative sections. If the court finds no ambiguity in the operative sections, it will never look at the Purpose section.

10.4 Legislative history

Sometimes, application of the canons of construction and other tools of interpreting a statute based solely on the words of the statute do not yield a clear answer. In that situation, courts sometimes look to extrinsic

How legislative purpose saved the snail darter...

One of the best examples of how legislative purpose can reveal legislative intent of a particular statutory term is found in *Tennessee Valley Authority v. Hill,* 437 U.S. 153 (1978). In that case, plaintiffs sought to prevent the operation of the newly built Tellico Dam on the Little Tennessee River because the dam threatened the habitat of the endangered snail darter. The snail darter was a 3" fish, found only in this area of the Little Tennessee River. The TVA argued that Congress could not have intended the Endangered Species Act to prevent the operation of a fully-built, federally funded dam just to save an obscure fish—especially considering that there were over 130 different species of darter in the United States. However, the Court noted that the expressly stated purpose of the Endangered Species Act was the far reaching protection of endangered species:

> As it was finally passed, the Endangered Species Act of 1973 represented the most comprehensive legislation for the preservation of endangered species ever enacted by any nation. Its stated purposes were "to provide a means whereby the ecosystems upon which endangered species and threatened species depend may be conserved," and "to provide a program for the conservation of such . . . species . . . ."

Tennessee Valley Authority v. Hill, 437 U.S. at 180

This expansive purpose of the act reflected the congressional intent that the act be broadly construed to protect endangered species habitat. Even though Congress had continued to fund the construction of the dam after the snail darter had been listed as an endangered species, the Court held that the stated purpose of the Endangered Species Act would prevail despite any potential economic losses resulting from not building the dam.

evidence to determine what the legislature intended. One tool for this is to examine the "legislative history" of the statute, including testimony before committees that considered the bill, committee reports, amendments added or rejected during deliberations, and other documentation developed as the bill worked its way through the legislature.

Legislative history can be a slippery thing. For significant legislation, the history can be voluminous. It is often possible to find conflicting evidence of the legislature's intent within the history. A plaintiff may be able to find testimony before a committee that supports her position while the defendant can point to a floor debate that suggests just the opposite meaning. It is sometimes easy to pick and choose the selective legislative history that favors your position and discount that which does not. As Judge Harold Leventhal is credited with saying, "the trick is to look over the heads of the crowd and pick out your friends."[11] On the other hand, sometimes the legislative history is frustratingly silent. It is surprising how often a legislature simply didn't consider a situation that, in hindsight, seems to go to the heart of a statute. In those cases, legislative history cannot help us.

You should also remember that nobody votes on most forms of legislative history. That one witness testified as to the meaning of a particular phrase does not mean that the legislature collectively agreed with that witness. Justice Antonin Scalia, who frequently criticized the usefulness of legislative history, noted that "resort to legislative history to determine legislative meaning is at best a shaky endeavor."[12]

Justice Scalia's cautionary admonition notwithstanding, there are a few guiding principles that can help us assess the persuasiveness of

---

[11] Antonin Scalia, *Common Law Courts in a Civil-Law System: The Role of United States Federal Courts in* INTERPRETING THE CONSTITUTION AND LAWS, IN A MATTER OF INTERPRETATION: FEDERAL COURTS AND THE LAW 36 (Amy Gutmann ed., 1997).
[12] *Nat. Resources Def. Fund v. EPA*, 948 F.2d 345, 350 (7th Cir. 1991).

particular legislative history. As a starting point, remember that the purpose of legislative history is to show what the legislators were thinking when they enacted a particular law. From that starting point, we can draw a number of other principles.

10.4.1   The more the merrier

Legislative history is most illuminating when it reveals a consistent interpretation of a statute throughout the legislative process. If hearing witnesses, committee reports, sponsor statements, and floor debates all consistently suggest a particular meaning, there's a good chance that the legislature as a whole agreed with that interpretation. On the other hand, a single remark in a committee hearing would have been heard only by committee members who were present for that testimony, and there's no guarantee that they even agreed with the statement. Thus, the more consistent the evidence you can find in the legislative history, the more likely that evidence will be seen as reliable.

10.4.2   Who's talking makes a difference

Throughout the legislative process, many people may comment on proposed legislation, including the bill's sponsors, other legislators, lobbyists (who may be representing an organization pushing for the legislation), agency administrators who may ultimately be charged with enforcing the law, and other interested people. A court will not view all of these people equally. Generally, those with the most expertise or interest in the bill will be accorded the most weight. Thus, bill sponsors tend to be given more deference than other legislators. Legislators are given more deference than non-legislators. Administrative experts are given more deference than other interested citizens.

As with most legislative history principles, this general hierarchy is quite fluid and depends on the specific circumstances of the legislation. For example, non-legislators generally have less sway than legislators do. However, a spokesperson for an organization that is promoting the legislation may be given considerable deference as one who likely had considerable influence with the enacting legislature. One way to consider how much weight to give a particular speaker's statements is to think about the ethos of the speaker. The more knowledgeable, respected, and powerful the speaker, the greater the deference will be given to her assertions.

10.4.3   Not all legislative history is created equal

Some forms of legislative history are more valuable than other forms. In most instances, committee reports are the most helpful. These reports reflect the consensus of the committees that recommended a bill to the larger legislative body. They are the careful considerations of the legislators who have spent the most time working through the details of the bill and have, at the very least, been approved by the majority of the committee. Furthermore, at least in theory, every member of the legislature at least had the opportunity to read the bill before voting on the proposed law.

Another powerful source of legislative history can be changes, amendments, and deletions to a bill that occur in the legislative process. These include things like floor amendments, though they are not always made on the floor. If "black" is in the original version of a bill and the legislature changes it to "white" in the final version, we have a strong indicator that this change was intentional and that the legislature did not mean "black" when it said "white."

As a general rule, the more likely that a piece of legislative history reflects the understanding of a broad base of legislators, the stronger it indicates the legislative intent.

10.4.4   Hindsight is not insight

Sometimes a legislator or an executive who signs the bill may comment on the meaning of a law after it is passed. Such comments, even by a bill's sponsor, are generally given little weight. It is true that such statements may reveal what that particular legislator thought about the meaning of the law. However, statements made after enactment necessarily could not have influenced the rest of the legislature at the time it voted on the bill. Because the purpose of legislative history is to reveal the collective thinking of the legislature at the time of enactment, post hoc explanations are generally not helpful.

10.4.5   No one voted on this stuff

Remember that legislative history is only an indicator of the meaning of a statute. It is not the statute itself. The legislature never expressly approves statements made in legislative history. Even a clear, persuasive explanation of a statutory provision is nothing more than the author's opinion. Thus, even a really helpful statement in the legislative history cannot trump the plain meaning of a statute.

> ### . . . but amended legislation abandoned the snail darter once and for all
>
> This is what happened after the snail darter case, *TVA v. Hill*. Two years after the decision in *TVA v. Hill*, Congress passed another statute expressly authorizing the completion of the dam, notwithstanding the snail darter. The dam was completed and brought on-line. The snail darter soon disappeared from the Little Tennessee River. Fortunately for the snail darter, small populations of it have been found in other rivers.

Legislative history can reveal legislative intent; it cannot create it out of whole cloth.

10.5   Case law

For many statutory issues, we have more than just the statute itself to guide us. If a court has interpreted a statute, that interpretation becomes binding precedent that should control similar cases in the future through the principle of stare decisis. Thus, if we have binding case law that interprets a specific term that is relevant to our dispute, our interpretive task may be quite simple—the statute means what the court says it means. Of course, opposing parties may disagree as to how the court interpretation applies to a particular set of facts. In that case, our statutory issue becomes similar to a common law analysis in which comparing and contrasting precedent cases becomes important.

The Internet dating case provides a good example of how case law has refined the meaning of a statute. The statute itself does not define "dating relationship." However, through several cases, we know that the term should be broadly construed. We also know that courts have developed several factors to consider when determining whether a particular situation constituted a dating relationship. In cases like this, these court decisions effectively amend the statute and make it easier to determine its meaning.

Judicial interpretations can be useful even when they have not addressed our exact statutory question. For example, if a court addressed a related issue, perhaps interpreting a related term, or even our term in a different context, we can draw on its reasoning. If the court cited specific legislative history, that history should be persuasive in our case as well. Likewise, if the court cited the purpose section with approval, or relied on a particular canon of construction, those same interpretive tools should resonate again in our case.

Finally, it is important to remember that, at least in theory, if a court misconstrues the legislative intent of a statute, the legislature can amend the statute to correct the court.

Obviously, when the legislature effectively overrules a court decision, the original court decision is no longer good law. However, the legislature's failure to react to a court opinion can also be informative. If the legislature chooses not to correct a court decision, one may reasonably argue that the court must have interpreted the statute correctly. In essence, legislative silence implies agreement with the court's interpretation. This is particularly likely when the legislature amends other parts of a statute after a court has interpreted it, but leaves the section that the court interpreted unchanged.

10.6   Administrative interpretations

You may have had only limited experience with administrative law in your first year of law school. This is simply because of the time constraints of the 1L curriculum. Administrative law is a large and important source of law. Administrative agencies, at both the state and federal levels, have tremendous power. These powers include interpreting statutes. Indeed, many of the details of a statutory scheme are left to specific agencies to determine. For example, the subtleties of protecting the air we breathe is far too complicated for the U.S. Congress to sort out. Thus, when it enacted the Clean Air Act, it gave the Environmental Protection Agency the power to promulgate rules that establish most of the specific details of the Act. The EPA has expertise in environmental protection and thus is best equipped to develop rules that carry out the statutory purpose.

Lawyers, judges, and scholars debate just how much discretion a court should give an agency's interpretation of a statute. Courts recognize that agencies have greater expertise in their specific areas and will defer to that expertise. On the other hand, courts are experts in interpreting statutes. Just how willing a court is to defer to agencies will depend on the particular circumstances of each case. The somewhat complex principles regarding agency deference are beyond the scope of this book. You will study it in detail in administrative law classes. However, if you're working on a problem involving an administrative regulation, there's a good chance that the degree of deference a court gives to that regulation will be a central issue of your problem.

10.7   How to craft a statutory interpretation argument

You are the West Dakota state prosecutor in a criminal mischief case: a woman defendant has been charged with criminal mischief. After finding out that her spouse was having an affair, she used a sledge hammer and sulfuric acid to destroy their jointly owned vintage 1957 Chevy Impala, formerly in mint condition. The spouse has pressed charges. The criminal mischief statute in this jurisdiction defines the crime as "the intentional destruction of the property of another." The defendant has filed a motion to dismiss the charges, arguing that the language of the statute precludes her prosecution because she was an owner of the car and therefore the property was not "of another." There is no case law interpreting the criminal mischief statute that addresses the issue. Can you make an argument that is supported by persuasive legal authority?

The first argument that you may make (and should always try to make, when plausible) is the plain meaning argument. For example, the argument may begin,

> The language of the statute contains no exclusion to it. Nor is the common understanding of the phrase one of exclusion. Rather, the phrase 'property of another' is merely descriptive of one aspect of the property's ownership. As is within the average person's understanding, it is entirely possible for property simultaneously to be owned by multiple people.

This is a pretty good start. But adding a textual interpretive argument can really drive home the point. In this case, we might consider the following steps.

10.7.1   Look at the statute through a broader lens to come up with a category

One way to do this is to look at the overall indexing of the statute. Criminal statutes, for example, are often grouped together by type of crimes. If you obtained the statute electronically, you can still easily expand the search to see the broader categories or look at the table of contents to see the bigger picture. What kind of statute is similar to a criminal mischief statute? Does the indexing of the statute help? It turns out that criminal mischief is grouped under the chapter "crimes against property." That could be useful.

10.7.2   Look for other statutes that fit into the same category

This may be a repetitive step if the statute's indexing system helps you. But otherwise, you will have to think creatively in step one to get here. For example, the chapter that includes criminal mischief also includes other crimes against property: theft, burglary, larceny, and arson.

10.7.3   Research-related statutes

These answers may come from different sources. For example, a related statute may provide a specific definition for a particular term. Or a court may have interpreted the term in the context of the related statute. The more consistent interpretations you find, the stronger an *in pari materia* argument is likely to be. For this example, imagine that our research came up with a case interpreting the arson statute. The arson statute defines arson as "the intentional destruction, by fire or firebombs, of the property of another." Hot dog![13] That statute is similar just on its face.

> **Research Tip**
>
> A good place to find other statutes or cases that have interpreted a word or phrase in a different context is the *Words and Phrases* volume of the relevant West Digest.

And now imagine we found one of the cases that interpreted the arson statute:

> *State v. Ranger* (W.D. Ct. App. 2013): Appellate court affirmed trial court's denial of defendant's motion to dismiss arson charges. The defendant allegedly set fire to a building owned by himself and business partners. Defense counsel argued that the arson statute did not apply because the building was not "property of another." Disagreeing with that narrow interpretation, the appellate

---

[13] Pun was so intended.

> court ruled, "the term 'property of another' in the arson statute does not automatically exclude situations in which the actor is a partial owner of property. Rather, if any other person holds an interest, then the property is both 'owned by another' as well as owned by the actor."

Good news! Since the court held that joint ownership can be interpreted to be within the scope of "owned by another," the prosecution looks like it can now proceed.

10.7.4   Communicate to readers that there are analogous interpretations to the statute you are dealing with

Now you're going to need to walk your reader through the steps that you just took to get to the analogy:

> Although this jurisdiction has not yet interpreted the criminal mischief statute's language "property of another," our appellate court has broadly interpreted the same phrase in connection to another crime against property statute, the arson statute. *State v. Ranger*, 345 P.4th 543 (West Dakota 2013). The appellate court in *Ranger* concluded that the phrase is inclusive rather than exclusive, "if any other person holds an interest, then the property is both owned by another as well as owned by the actor."

> There is no functional difference between the destruction of property by fire and the destruction of property, generally. If the wife in our situation had set fire to the car rather than used sulfuric acid, the court would be bound to allow the prosecution, per the interpretation of the same term in the arson statute. The method of destruction of the property makes no legal difference; thus, the phrase "property of another" should be interpreted to allow prosecution of a person who is accused of criminal mischief for the destruction of jointly owned property.

10.8   Conclusion

Effective reading and interpretation of statutes requires careful attention to detail. You may be surprised at how easy it is to misinterpret a provision or at how often you fail to spot potential ambiguity in your first reading. To improve your efficiency and accuracy, practice the following steps:

- Find the operative section of the statute that applies to your issue.

- Look at the entire statutory context to see where your section fits.

- Ask these questions for every statute:

  ○ To whom does the statute apply?

  ○ Does the statute provide any express definitions of key terms?

  ○ What does the statute require, permit, or prohibit?

  ○ What are the exceptions to the general rule?

  ○ What is the consequence of not complying?

  ○ When does the statute apply?

Answering these questions will get you started. From there, you will want to decide what interpretive tools will be most helpful. Start with the plain meaning of the statute. Remember that generally, the closer you stay to the text of the statute, the stronger your analysis will be. Finally, don't forget that even the most logically reasoned statutory interpretation will not succeed if it leads to a nonsensical conclusion.

Another special problem you may encounter in writing the Argument section of your brief is whether, and how, to include policy arguments. That is the topic of the next chapter.

Working with the Law, Part 2: Creating Policy Arguments

Policy arguments examine the possible future social consequences of a particular ruling. Because policy arguments look down the road at what the net effect of a decision might be, policy arguments are used to inject consideration of "real-world effects" into the arguments. It might be the policy argument that gives your argument that commonsense spice that it needs.

Policy arguments are good choices, for example, when the particular argument seeks to elicit a response-creating or response-changing effect in the audience. We know that we have the best chance of persuading an audience when we present an argument that reinforces that audience's existing position. When writing for a judge, this usually means our strongest argument will be based on existing, binding authority. However, sometimes this option is unavailable. Sometimes we want to argue for a change in the law, or we are dealing with an issue of first impression, where we have no existing law. In other cases, we may have binding authority to support us, but it may not be as clear-cut as we would like. In these circumstances, we may strengthen our connection to existing authority by showing how our position is consistent with the policy behind the existing law.

In the right circumstances, policy arguments can be powerful tools. When used inappropriately, however, they can undermine a lawyer's credibility.

This chapter explores the what, when, and how of making policy arguments.

11.1 Future world: the uniqueness of policy arguments

Policy arguments look to the future. That makes them different from other types of legal argument, all of which look backward in time at what was. Policy arguments take a forward-looking approach to an argument, predicting what will be. Judges, especially appellate judges, are interested in policy arguments because they want their decisions to make sense in the future and be a guide to others as precedent for future cases.

But it is the very nature of trying to predict the future that causes the trepidation with which lawyers and judges approach policy arguments. We have a hard-enough time understanding our current world, much less anticipating what the future will bring. Thus, trying to convincingly argue the future consequences of competing interpretations of existing law is challenging indeed.

A common pitfall of policy arguments is that they tend to overstate the consequences of a particular decision. Think about stories set in the future. They often fall into two extreme categories: utopian (a world that approaches perfection compared to ours) or dystopian (a world that looks much worse than ours does or that is post-apocalyptic).

The reality is that the future is likely to look a lot like the present. Overstating the benefits or pitfalls of a particular ruling can undermine your credibility. Be wary of overstating consequences in policy arguments.

Though an unpredictable future can make policy arguments tricky, we need not fear them. Indeed, we make decisions every day based on what the future might hold. We choose our clothing based on what we expect the weather to be; we decide which politician to vote for based on what we think the candidate would do if elected to office. Because making decisions in the "now" based on what we think the future consequence of those decisions might be is so common, lawyers should not fear making a policy argument in the appropriate circumstance. The take-home lesson is more about wording and presentation than it is about the substance of the argument itself. The goal is to stay away from using words of hyperbole. A lawyer who tries to paint a picture of the apocalypse is a lawyer who is risking a lot of her ethos.

11.2   When to make policy arguments

Despite the cautions, policy arguments are an important part of presenting the substance or logos of an argument. Policy arguments help the reader understand how the lawyer's proposed outcome for the client fits into a bigger societal picture. Likewise, policy arguments appeal to pathos because they help round out the fairness factor of an argument. They can be a good way to reinforce the theme you have chosen for your case by tapping into the reader's deep frames (recall the discussion of themes and frames from Chapters 3 and 9).

There are no hard and fast rules about when to use policy arguments. But a good indicator is when the future impact of a decision is of particular importance. Of course, virtually all published appellate decisions will establish new precedent and thus have some impact on the future. However, some situations are better suited to policy considerations than others.

11.2.1   When one party is arguing for a change in existing law

There are times when a lawyer must ask a court to change or clarify an existing interpretation of the law. This could be because the existing law is no longer appropriate. Alternatively, a lawyer may ask the court to apply law in a context where there is no existing law (i.e., a case of first impression). And of course, lawyers frequently ask courts to clarify existing law as to how it should apply in a new situation.

In these situations, the lawyer arguing for a change in the law will want to explain how, going forward, a new rule better reflects those societal goals the issue raises. This type of policy argument is usually offered as a supplement to more direct arguments as to the meaning of existing law rather than as a substitute. Even when we are arguing for a change in the law, we have a better chance of succeeding if we can show how the change is consistent with existing legal principles. It is very difficult to convince a court to abandon common law rules based solely on a policy argument.

The classic example of lawyers arguing for a change in the law based on changing societal goals and expectations is *Brown v. Board of Education*, discussed in the Prologue.[1] In that case, Thurgood Marshall and the other lawyers representing the plaintiffs argued that express and unequivocal Supreme Court precedent (that "separate but equal" facilities are constitutionally permissible) should be overturned. Part of what makes *Brown* a landmark case is that the Court agreed. Such direct overruling of existing law is very rare.

It is not only the lawyer arguing for a change in the law that should consider policy arguments. The lawyer arguing for the status quo— for the maintenance of existing law—will argue that current law is working and maintaining the existing law will make for a better, more predictable future. The time to develop strong policy arguments is when one of the parties is arguing for a change in the law that will have a future impact.

11.2.2 When an argument is based on persuasive authority

When a jurisdiction is silent on a legal issue, but other jurisdiction have already addressed the issue, lawyers will often turn to persuasive authority to bolster their position. However, persuasive authority alone is not particularly effective. It is not enough to show

---

[1] *Brown v. Bd. of Educ. of Topeka,* 347 U.S. 483 (1954).

that another jurisdiction has adopted a particular rule. One must also show that the rule is effective and will work well in one's own jurisdiction. When relying on persuasive authority, a lawyer will want to show how the other jurisdiction's decision was consistent with policies valued by the courts in his own jurisdiction.

For example, if arguing to define a "household pet" for the purposes of zoning law, a lawyer might look to the definition of "household pet" in another jurisdiction's zoning laws. Whether that definition would be helpful in the context of this dispute will depend on whether the other jurisdiction's zoning law parallels the policy behind this jurisdiction's zoning law.

11.2.3   When the time is right

Finally, for any policy argument—for any prediction about the future—the time must be right for the court to adopt that policy. *Brown v. the Board of Education* overturned 70 years of Supreme Court precedent because the societal changes over those 70 years (including the changes in the makeup of the Court) made the plaintiffs' policy arguments resonate with that Court in 1954. On the other hand, in 1986, gay rights advocates unsuccessfully raised policy arguments for the privacy rights of gay couples to engage is consensual sexual relations within their own home and lost.[2] However, just 16 years later, those same policy arguments persuaded the Court to reverse that decision.[3] The policy arguments didn't change, but society had. In the intervening years, times had changed and by 2004, the time was right for them.

---

[2] *Bowers v. Hardwick,* 478 U.S. 186 (1986).
[3] *Lawrence v. Texas,* 539 U.S. 558 (2003).

The ancient Greeks had a word for this—*kairos*—the opportune moment. Greek philosophers differed in their approaches, but agreed that the power to persuade is dependent upon the timing of the argument. When times are right—the kairic moment—our audience is more receptive to policy arguments. This kairic moment may depend upon changing societal expectations, significant recent events, the stability (or instability) of community, and any number of other contextual factors that influence decision-makers. As you develop your policy arguments, reflect on the time and place in which you will be making them. An argument that will not resonate today may become powerful down the road. And an argument raised at the wrong time, no matter how powerful, is unlikely to resonate with an audience that is not ready to hear it.

> **Policy arguments are for trial courts too!**
>
> In Chapter 4, we discussed the differences between trial and appellate cases. We mentioned was that appellate courts tend to be more focused on the future consequences of their decisions (the precedential effects), while trial judges tend to be more focused on getting the "right" result for the litigants before her. But policy arguments can still be important at the trial level: the trial judge can and will encounter all of these four situations from time to time.

11.3   The nature and types of policy arguments

In any situation, more than one type of policy argument may work. It isn't a question of the "correct" versus "incorrect" policy argument. It's a matter of choosing the most persuasive policy argument for the particular client's situation or, more accurately, for those people who are or who will be situated like the client.

We discuss the more logos-like policy arguments first because most judges claim to be influenced primarily, or only, by logos. Thus, at least in a very general sense, these policies may be the most likely to persuade. However, although the more pathos-based social value policy arguments are presented last, lawyers rely on them as frequently as logic-based policy arguments.[4]

11.3.1   Judicial administration

This broad category of policy arguments focuses on the real-world pragmatics of a legal interpretation. The goal at the heart of this type of argument is typically "judicial economy" or a "fair and efficient judicial system." Notice how that last phrase builds in two concepts: fairness and efficiency. At times, these concepts work in harmony, but at other times, they are in apparent opposition to each other. In reality, such arguments actually appeal to both logos and pathos. Because they feel grounded in law, however, these policy arguments are among the most successful types of policy arguments.

There are several types of policy arguments that fit under this umbrella.

11.3.1.1   *The new rule should be firm (or flexible)*

The very phrasing of the heading above demonstrates the yin/yang balance between two opposing policy arguments. There are good reasons for firm, predictable rules and there are good reasons for flexible rules. They are presented together because they are so closely related. Notice how the underlying policies for firm rules parallel those of flexible rules:

Firm rules:

- A firm rule articulates a clear and predictable standard.

- Firm rules result in more consistent, predictable application, or equal justice for all. That makes them *fair*.

---

[4] For more in-depth reading about making policy arguments, see the excellent work of Ellie Margolis, *Closing the Floodgates, Making Persuasive Policy Arguments in Appellate Briefs*, 62 MONT. L. REV. 59 (2001); Ellie Margolis, *Teaching Students to Make Effective Policy Arguments in Appellate Briefs*, 9 PERSPECTIVES 73 (2001).

- Firm rules are also easier for laypersons to understand, which means that people can gauge their actions and know the consequences. That also makes the rules *fair*.

- The predictability of a firm rule makes it easy for a court to administer. Easy rules are *efficient* rules.

Flexible rules:

- A flexible rule allows courts to change and adapt the rule with new circumstances.

- Flexible rules make the system more responsive to the individual stories of a client. That makes the rule more *fair* in light of the circumstances.

- Flexible rules recognize that legislatures cannot anticipate every possible application of a statute. That makes the flexible rule more *fair*.

- People will have more confidence in a judge to interpret a flexible rule appropriately and will work within the system. That makes the rule more *fair*.

- Flexible rules do not require new legislative action for every unforeseen situation. That makes the rule more *efficient*.

11.3.1.2   The existing or proposed rule is too complex

Related to the firm versus flexible argument is this type of policy consideration. The argument, essentially, is that if lawyers and courts will have a difficult time understanding the rule, then the court will have trouble with both the efficient and fair delivery of justice.

11.3.1.3   Floodgates argument

This type of argument is based on the presumption that efficiency is very important in

Floodgates versus fairness

The defendant/appellant brief in the Internet dating example (Appendix A) uses a floodgates argument. The defendant argues that interpreting the term "dating relationship" to include situations where the parties have not interacted romantically in-person could lead to numerous restraining order applications being filed by people who have never met, except on the Internet. In that example, the writer assumes that a court will value maintaining the efficiency of an already-crowded domestic violence court system over the loss of access to the courts by people who chat over the Internet.

a particular situation, whereas the risk to fairness is not as great. In a floodgates argument, one party to the action argues that a statutory interpretation or new rule proposed by the other party creates a class of litigants entitled to relief that is so broad that the very number of cases will overwhelm the court system. That, in turn, will lead to a decrease for resources to "true" litigants.

11.3.1.4 *Slippery slope argument*

A slippery slope argument shares some traits with a floodgates argument: both predict an inevitable crowding of the court system. While a floodgates argument, however, typically talks about classes of people who will flood the courts with similar causes of action, a slippery slope argument predicts that the law itself will stretch to the point of no return. Courts won't be able to stop application to more and more cases, and that will lead to absurd results down the line. The net result will be something very different from what the court probably intends.

This makes a slippery slope argument one that focuses on fundamental fairness more than efficiency.

11.3.2 Economic arguments

Just as with judicial efficiency arguments, economic arguments are also balancing the tensions between a fair and efficient legal system. An economic policy argument prioritizes financial concerns as a method of determining fairness for society at large. Of course, by prioritizing the good of the whole, an economics approach might compromise the fairness to a particular litigant or class of litigants.

Examples of economic policy arguments beyond judicial efficiencies include:

- This proposed rule represents a fair allocation of limited resources.
- The proposed rule is fair because it spreads the economic loss over a larger percent of the population.

- This rule is fair because it assigns the loss to the party who is best able to bear it without undue burden.

- This rule encourages the economic values of this country (e.g., "save the little Mom and Pop stores from big megastores").

> **Money might be the answer**
>
> A wise person the authors know advises, "When you don't know the answer to why something is or should be, the answer is probably money." * Think of an economics argument for the project you are working on right now. What is the economic impact of your position? Of your opponent's? Does imagining the financial impact of a decision cause you to see the issues in different ways?
>
> *Steven C. Robbins, Esq.

11.3.3 Institutional competence arguments

An institutional competence policy argument evaluates which of the three branches of government is best equipped to deal with a particular issue. For example, when a court steps in to determine a legislative purpose, it acts as a judicial legislator. Thus, if one's opponent was arguing for an expansive reading of a statute, one might respond that a court is not competent to expand the scope of the statute expressed by the legislature and should therefore apply a narrower meaning in line with the express terms of the statute.

11.3.4 Social values arguments

The last category of policy argument is based on society's values (sometimes also called normative or tradition-based arguments). Professor Michael R. Smith defines social values for this purpose as "[t]he enduring belief that a specific mode of conduct or state of existence is preferable to another."[5] A policy argument along these lines argues that the proposed rule promotes or undermines shared societal values.

The very words "values" and "beliefs" quickly signal that these policy arguments are based on pathos more than the other types of policy

---

[5] Michael R. Smith, Advanced Legal Writing: Theories and Strategies in Persuasive Writing 91 (3d ed., Wolters Kluwer L. & Bus. 2013).

arguments. While that may or may not be true, the distinction is often irrelevant because, as we will soon see, social value policy arguments can be supported with logos-based authority just as much as the other types of policy arguments.

11.4   How to make a policy argument

Policy arguments have three parts: a prediction, a judgment about the prediction, and support for the prediction and judgment.

11.4.1   Prediction

Because a policy argument looks toward the future, it must include a prediction about the way the world will look if the proposed rule of law is adopted. Of course, an attorney may also predict what the world will look like if his opposing party's proposed rule of law is adopted.

11.4.2   Judgment about the prediction

A lawyer must also include a judgment about the prediction. It is a policy argument, after all. Policy arguments are not meant to be neutral but are meant to persuade. Readers should be able to tell whether the lawyer, as the client's advocate, is predicting sunshine or gloom as part of the policy argument. Note how this differs from how you were taught to approach or present policy considerations in your predictive writing course or other academic writing settings. In predictive writing, it is perfectly reasonable to consider both the pros and the cons of a prediction and to study the countervailing policy considerations. In a brief, however, one side of a policy consideration must be argued as preferable. So, for example, an attorney might argue for the fairness of a flexible rule, even though there are potential arguments supporting a firm rule.

11.4.3   Support for the prediction and judgment

Finally, as with any legal argument, the lawyer should cite authority to support the predictions and judgments about the predictions.

11.4.3.1   Legal support

We can support many policy arguments by cites to legal authority. Those legal authorities range from legislative history to analogous rules and reasoning borrowed from other jurisdictions or other similar rules in the same jurisdiction. Other sources of legal support include statistical data collected by branches of the legal system, such as court filing statistics or uniform crime reports of the jurisdiction. Many of the statistical data are available online. As a general rule, most courts will accept, as verified, data that is published on a government website (i.e., with a .gov extension).

11.4.3.2   Nonlegal support

Many policy arguments rely on nonlegal data to support the predictions or the judgments about the predictions. For example, the United States Supreme Court cited social science research about the effects of segregation on African American schoolchildren in *Brown v. Board of Education of Topeka.*[6]

Although nonlegal support most usually appears in appellate briefs and decisions, its use is not limited to just the highest courts.

Some regularly cited nonlegal materials include:

- Statistical data collected in another discipline (e.g., census data, demographic data, or economic data)

- Generally accepted medical data ("generally accepted" means by others of stature in the field)

- Social science research results that are generally accepted as using sound methodologies and reasoning

- Other materials that a court might take judicial notice of, such as historical facts, weather data, and other similar sets of information

These types of materials are sometimes referred to as "legislative facts."

---

[6] 347 U.S. 483, 494 note 11 (1954).

> ### Terminology: judicial notice and legislative facts
>
> The evidentiary term for a court accepting non-legal material is "judicial notice." It is used in a sentence like this: "The court took judicial notice of the filing statistics compiled by the Administrative Office of the Courts." Non-legal research supporting a policy argument is also referred to as "legislative facts" (see Chapter 4) or "Brandeis Briefing." The term Brandeis Briefing refers to a brief written by former Justice Louis Brandeis while he was in practice, *Muller v. Oregon*, 208 U.S. 412 (1908). In that brief, Justice Brandeis included statistics about the health effects on women who were subjected to long work hours.
>
> In contrast, facts that are part of the parties' stories are sometimes called "adjudicative facts," presumably because those facts are under consideration by the court, i.e., subject to adjudication.

Relying on nonlegal sources is perfectly acceptable in appellate practice. These sources might be nonlegal, but they are the product of research. When a court rule disallows facts "outside the record," it is limiting its analysis to facts about the parties' stories (sometimes referred to as "adjudicative facts"). Bringing in new parts of the story is disallowed because the opposing side lacks notice and an opportunity to cross-examine that evidence. But "going outside the record" of the parties' stories by bringing up unproven adjudicative facts is very different from citing factual data (legislative facts) supported by verifiable and independent sources. The authors of the Model Rules of Evidence specifically rejected a rule that would have limited judges from considering or researching outside pertinent data. Although a number of legal scholars have criticized the permissiveness, the reality is that judges are doing independent statistical research even when the lawyers have not included that data in their briefs. It behooves a lawyer to do that sort of research.[7]

---

[7]This is a repeat from Chapter 5, but because it is relevant here as well as in Chapter 5, we included it to make it easier for you to access. See Coleen Barger, *On the Internet, Nobody Knows You're a Judge: Federal Appellate Courts' Use of Internet Sites*, 4 J. APP. PRAC. & PROCESS 417 (2002) (providing often-cited standards for checking source accuracy and credibility); Ellie Margolis, *Surfin'*

The task therefore becomes finding sources that are verifiable within a discipline. If the lawyer finds this difficult to ascertain, a best bet is to consult a reference librarian, who will have more training and access to the materials or to people who will be able to assist.

The respondent's brief in the Internet dating example provides a good illustration of how to make a policy argument.

1. First, it makes a prediction about the future:

    Courts must continue to broadly define "dating relationships" and recognize that technology will play an increasingly significant role in dating practices. To do otherwise will soon render the Act largely irrelevant to the modern world.

2. The author then argues that a broad definition will be a good thing because it will be consistent with the purpose of the Act:

    This case is a perfect example of why the court must continue to construe "dating relationship" broadly. The presence of technology in this relationship is merely a sign of modern times. In every other way the bond looks like a traditional dating relationship. The Legislature, in leaving "dating relationship" undefined, purposely deferred to future courts to refine the contours of the term to reflect future understanding of dating.

3. The author then supports that policy argument with authority, citing a prior case that is consistent with the policy:

    As the appellate court in *J.S.* has signaled, modern relationships should be understood and colored by "generational influences." Skype was just a vehicle to let the parties be in the same room with each other in real time.

    Even if these parties fall under the category of "online dating," that is still within the new boundaries of this era and this Court has plenty of discretion to include online

> dating as falling within the jurisdiction of the Act. That is why the sixth "catchall" factor in the *Andrews* case exists.

4. Finally, the author buttresses her argument with nonlegal authority that provides support for her factual assertions about the evolving concept of dating:

> Online dating is a growing trend that shapes the structure of dating relationships. The *New York Times* has reported,
>
> Since the current recession began, the popularity of online dating has surged—memberships are up and new matchmaking portals have emerged to take advantage of the demand—industry growth of up to 30 percent is expected in the next year or two, according to the tracking site DatingService.com.
>
> [Scott James, *In Calculations of Online Dating, Love Can Be Cruel, N.Y. Times*, Feb. 12, 2010, at A25A.]
>
> The online dating industry generated nearly $2 billion in revenue in 2016.[8] The practice has become so common that to provide protection for online daters, the New Jersey Legislature passed the Internet Dating Safety Act in May 2007.[9] Just as the Legislature did, the Judiciary should act to provide protection for online daters.

This deliberate development of the argument combines several policy-based concepts. It expressly argues that broad interpretations are necessary to meet the purpose of the Act. It supports that assertion with existing authority. It also implicitly argues that a flexible rule is fairer than a fixed, narrow rule. Also implicit is the institutional competence policy argument: the judiciary needs to defer to the legislature's intent to have a flexible, evolving meaning

---

[8] Mary Lynn Cesar, *Of Love and Money: The Rise of the Online Dating Industry*, NASDAQ.com, http://www.nasdaq.com/article/of-love-and-money-the-rise-of-the-online-dating-industry-cm579616 (last visited July 23, 2018).

[9] The Internet Dating Safety Act requires that online dating sites tell customers whether they do background checks on their members.

of "dating relationship." Notice that it incorporated all these policy arguments without ever mentioning the word "policy"!

11.4.4   Couch the argument in terms of *avoiding* bad outcomes

Finally, recall from Chapter 2 the fact that the human brain is more attentive to negative information than to positive information. It processes such information more thoroughly and retains it longer.

Professor Michael R. Smith has proposed that, because of a combination of several cognitive phenomena including the loss aversion effect, the endowment effect, and the negativity bias, a policy argument may be more effective if phrased in terms of avoiding bad outcomes rather than promoting good ones.[10] He argues, for example, that the classic slippery slope argument can be phrased more memorably (and persuasively) as avoiding a negative outcome: "This result would prevent a flood of litigation" rather than "that other result would protect the resources and efficiency of the court." He provides numerous examples of how this is fairly easy to do, because most positive statements are able to be stated in the inverse.[11]

In the next chapter we conclude our discussion of special problems in writing the Argument section by thinking about how to deal with adverse material through counterargument.

---

[10] Michael R. Smith, *The Sociological and Cognitive Dimensions of Policy-Based Persuasion*, 22 J. LAW & POLICY 25, 76-79 (2013).

[11] Prof. Smith's advice has been proven correct in a recent empirical study by one of the co-authors of this text. *See Fear and Loathing in Persuasive Writing: An Empirical Study of the Effects of the Negativity Bias*, 17 LEGAL COMM. AND RHETORIC: JALWD 1 (2017).

Working with the Law, Part 3: Managing Adverse Material

May you have a lawsuit in which you know you are in the right.
—Old gypsy curse

Every legal dispute has at least two sides: your client's and your opponent's. And no matter how convincing your client's story is, your opponent's story, left unaddressed, may be just as compelling. In addition, your client's story will always include some adverse facts or law. If there were no adverse facts or law, then there'd be no lawsuit, just a settlement.

One of our tasks is to recognize our opponent's counterstory and provide our readers with a sound basis for rejecting it. Legal persuasion, as Kathy Stanchi notes, is not only about presenting favorable information, but about confronting and defusing adverse information as well.[1]

> **Phrasing**
>
> We have chosen the "**adverse material**" to denote information that could hurt our client's chances of successful resolution to the dispute. We believe that phrase is more descriptive than "negative material" because not all negative material is adverse or vice versa.

The process of confronting adverse information includes four steps:

1. Recognizing what material is adverse and harmful (be it factual or legal);

2. Choosing when to counter adverse material

---

[1] Kathryn Stanchi, *Playing with Fire: The Science of Confronting Adverse Material in Legal Advocacy*, 60 RUTGERS L. REV. 381 (2008). Kathy Stanchi's scholarship in this area is significant for legal writing, and we recommend reading it when you can.

3. Choosing a structure for countering that material; and

4. Conveying a rebuttal in the most effective manner possible

This chapter begins by exploring the types of adverse material a lawyer might face in the client's case, the psychology of why it is best to address and defuse adverse material, and when it might be better to leave adverse material unaddressed unless and until the opposing party raises it. The chapter then explains how we can best address the arguments that should not be ignored.

12.1   What kind of adverse material is there?

The categories of information that might be adverse to a client's successful resolution of a legal dispute fall into a few broad categories, all of them easy enough to recognize.

12.1.1 Adverse aspects about the lawsuit procedures

The easiest way for a defendant to get a case to go away is to find a procedural flaw in the plaintiff's case. If the case is not properly in front of a tribunal, then there is no day in court for the defendant to worry about. For example, if the statute of limitations has passed, the plaintiff no longer has a claim—no matter how strong it may be on the merits. Likewise, on appeal, most claims must have been preserved in the court below. If a party did not preserve its claim of error by objecting at the trial, the appellate court will not consider the party's assertion of error on appeal.

12.1.2 Relevant facts that conflict with the client's story

Opposing parties will likely disagree about the underlying stories. First, they could disagree about what happened. This kind of dispute will be decided by the trier of fact, so in most cases, this kind of disagreement will not be at issue on appeal (although it may be highly relevant in trial-level briefs). On an appeal, of course, the facts are limited by what is in the record and what the trier of fact found at the trial. Even on appeal, though, there is likely to be a counterstory. The counterstory is likely to focus on two kinds of facts. First, there are always facts that just don't seem to fit your client's narrative. For example, imagine a simple car accident where your client crossed the intersection with a green light, but was on his cell phone while driving. Being on the phone may not be the cause of the accident, but it is certainly an adverse fact that you will need to address.

Second, even if the underlying facts are not disputed, the parties will likely view the significance of particular facts differently. How the opposing lawyer tells the story—for example, from what point of view she tells the story, from what perspective does she "see" the story unfold, how does she connects the plot beats—will most certainly reveal a different, and adverse, patina on the story, even where the parties agree on the substance of the underlying facts.

12.1.3 Adverse interpretations of the applicable law and standard of review

The parties may disagree about what law applies to the legal problem. The plaintiff may argue that a precedent is "on all fours" while the defendant argues that the case is easily distinguishable. Because authority is always subject to differing interpretations, we are almost always faced with potential adverse readings of the applicable law. Even if the parties agree that a particular statute or case applies to the dispute, they very often will disagree as to *how* that law applies. Certainly, in cases of statutory interpretation, the parties will likely disagree over the legislature's intended meaning of the key terms in the statute.

12.2 Structuring the counterargument: sidedness and refutation

Once recognized, there are different ways to handle adverse material. One way, of course, is to pretend that the adverse material doesn't exist.

Another is to acknowledge that it exists, but to leave it unaddressed. Advocates of this "mentioning" approach, called the "sponsorship theory," believe that juries will attach special importance to an adverse fact if disclosed by the lawyer to whose client the material is adverse.[2] In other words, by addressing an argument, we give it credence, or sponsor it, even if we later refute it. Thus, under the sponsorship theory, the better approach is to ignore the adverse material altogether. The danger of this approach is readily apparent—we must rely on readers to refute the unchallenged argument on their own.

A third way—and the way that cognitive studies suggest is the most effective—acknowledges the existence of the adverse material and refutes it. In other words, we should "manage" the adverse material. Lawyers who support this theory argue that it is better to address the adverse material and control it as best we can. Knowing when and how to manage the adverse material is another advocacy strategy that depends on the material and the circumstances of the case.

Which ways are more persuasive? The best way to start that conversation might be visually. Figure 12-1 shows a chart that summarizes psychologists' conclusions.

When you are reasonably sure the other side will make arguments about facts/law:

Figure 12-1: Continuum of choices about handling adverse arguments

---

[2] Stanchi, *supra* note 1, at 382.

There are more complicated terms in the psychological literature, but they boil down to these three: ignore, mention, manage.[3]

- Ignoring the adverse material offers only positive information that supports the client's position.

- Both mention and manage approaches acknowledge the adverse material. Each approach would acknowledge the existence of harmful material or arguments. Notice that mentioning without managing the adverse material is worse than simply ignoring it.

> **Example of managing adverse material**
>
> - "Some people say this economic policy will increase unemployment, but that isn't so because . . ." (direct managing of adverse assertion by providing counter evidence)
>
> - "It's true that my client was convicted of robberies in the past, but past convictions are not evidence of guilt in the current case" (indirect managing—does not challenge adverse facts but counters by raising legal issue of relevance)
>
> Examples are from Stanchi, *Playing With Fire*, 60 RUTGERS L. REV. at 394–95 (2008).
>
> **Ethos bonus:** Notice how neither example openly criticizes the opposing party or the phrasing of their arguments.

- A managing response is one that goes beyond acknowledging the harmful material or opposing arguments; it responds to that material by refuting it.

- There are two ways to manage: challenge the adverse material directly or challenge the adverse material indirectly through a more oblique attack. The difference is merely one of wording. In legal argumentation, the indirect approach can be a strategically sounder choice if the tone of the indirect refutation demonstrates better ethos or respect by the advocate than a direct refutation. Ethos is always important.

---

[3] The terms used by the psychologists are "sidedness" (one-sided or two-sided) and "refutational" or "nonrefutational" responses. *Id.*

Cognitive psychology studies have demonstrated that the most effective strategy involves managing adverse material rather than ignoring it. Managing the material is more effective because it causes sustained attitude change that is less vulnerable to opposing arguments. In other words, when readers are exposed to managed adverse material, they are more likely to be persuaded by the message and less likely to change their minds when confronted with an opposing viewpoint.[4]

On the other hand, just mentioning the adverse material is the least persuasive method—significantly less effective than ignoring the opposing viewpoints entirely! If the writer is not going to manage the adverse material or arguments, then it's better to ignore them completely.

These hypotheses have been tested in at least one legal setting using one set of briefs and law clerks' reactions to that set of briefs. The law clerks reported skepticism about the use of one-sided arguments contained in the brief because those arguments failed to take into account the value of opposing views.[5]

To manage a message about adverse material, a lawyer needs to directly or indirectly refute the opposing party's stance. The lawyer may question or respond to the "plausibility of opposing claims, criticizing the reasoning underlying opposing arguments, [or] offering evidence ... to undermine opposing claims."[6] These managing messages attempt to "remove" the adverse information either by denying the truth of the opposing claims or by arguing that the adverse information is irrelevant.

---

[4] *Id.* at 393–397.

[5] *See* James F. Stratman, *Investigating Persuasive Processes in Legal Discourse in Real Time: Cognitive Biases and Rhetorical Strategy in Appeal Court Briefs*, 17 DISCOURSE PROCESSES 1, 7–13 (1994), cited in Stanchi, *supra* note 1, at 409–414. Professor Stanchi offers some critiques of the study's assumptions and conclusions.

[6] Stanchi, *supra* note 1, at 388–389, 399–402; quotation on 394 (quoting Daniel J. O'Keefe, *How to Handle Opposing Arguments in Persuasive Messages: A Meta-Analytic Review of the Effects of One-Sided and Two-Sided Messages*, 22 COMMUN. Y.B. 209, 211 (1999)).

In Section 12.3, we discuss some of the actual mechanics of how to make a managing argument.

Even in a "post-facts" world, facts nevertheless can debunk myths or falsehoods

On January 3, 2018, SLATE published a cover story outlining and reviewing the scientific studies, old and new, that have analyzed the effects of presenting facts to counter false beliefs. Daniel Engber, *LOL, Something Matters,* SLATE (January 3, 2018, covery story) https://slate.com/health-and-science/2018/01/weve-been-told-were-living-in-a-post-truth-age-dont-believe-it.html There's good news in the most recent studies. Facts have the same power we always thought they did, to help debunk false information or myths.

The new science supporting the importance of factual persuasion ironically has its own factual persuading to do. People who know a little bit about the science of managing adverse material typically rely on a small sample-size study conducted by Brendan Nyhan and Jason Reifler. *When Corrections Fail: The Persistence of Political Misperceptions,* 32 POLITICAL BEHAVIOR, 303 (2010). The study used 130 undergraduate students at a Catholic university. Two years prior to its actualy publication, the study was written up in mass-consumption media as part of the 2008 election fever. The stories tended to make dire predictions that fact-checking news stories would end up rallying people to become more firmly entrenched in their beliefs in the falsehoods. This phenomenon was termed the "backfire" or "boomerang" effect. Oxford Dictionaries selected "post-facts" as the 2016 "word of the year," based in part on these studies.

Graduate students at different universities became interested in the Nyhan-Riefler paper, and attempted to replicate them, to no avail. The new studies were 103 times larger than the studies done by Nyhan and Riefler. One set of graduate students used over 10,000 test-subjects and another graduate student group used almost 4,000. The data tended to show the opposite: none of the conditions resulted in any evidence that people adhered to their views when presented with facts that showed the opposite was true. Rather, the studies showed that the test-subjects were more likely to adapt their views to better fit the facts.

Rather than challenge the new science, essentially debunking theirs, the original scientists, Nyhan and Riefler collaborated with one of the other sets of researchers to conduct new studies. The foursome posted a 60-page article in the summer of 2017, Brendan Nyhan, Ethan Porter, Jason Reifler, and Thomas Wood, *Taking Corrections Literally but not Seriously? The Effect of Information on Factual Beliefs and Candidate Favorability* (June 29, 2017), available on SSRN at https://papers.ssrn.com/sol3/papers.cfm?abstract_id=2995128 (posted July 1, 2017). That article concludes that people are willing to update factual beliefs when presented with "counter-attitudinal informaton." However, they further concluded that updated factual beliefs might have only minimal effects on attitudes towards a political candidate. The very creators of the backfire/boomerang effect have questioned—some might say debunked—their own previous work.

12.3 Considerations when it is unclear whether the opposing party will use the adverse material

Figure 12-1 and the explanation in the previous section are premised on the theory that the opponent has made, or very likely will make, the arguments that a lawyer is planning to counter. But when a lawyer is representing the moving party, whether at trial or on appeal, she must make a judgment call whether to address the adverse material before she has a chance to see the actual arguments the responding party raises. In that case, we have to predict whether the opposing party is likely to raise particular adverse material. Though it is not always easy to know what arguments the opposing party will argue, there is a good rule of thumb: the less you want the other side to raise something, the more likely it is going to do so.

12.3.1 Inoculation against adverse material

As you just learned, a lawyer shouldn't leave the adverse material unaddressed. On the other hand, a lawyer might not want to bring up an adverse fact or make the opponents' arguments for them when the lawyer is uncertain that her opponent will use those adverse facts or raise those arguments.

In those situations, the lawyer must decide whether to "inoculate" the reader[7] by introducing the information and then managing the information by refuting it. All of that happens before the opposing party is able to make the argument. Inoculating works because it shows the audience that the adverse material is explainable. Implicitly, this shows that the adverse material is not as damaging as the audience might believe if first (or only) presented by an opposing party.

---

[7] This is sometimes called "stealing your opponent's thunder." *Id.* at 415 (citing Kipling D. Williams et al., *The Effects of Stealing Thunder in Criminal and Civil Trials*, 17 L. & HUM. BEHAV. 597, 608 (1993)).

Imagine your study partner says, "You will soon hear some pretty awful things about me, and let me tell you why you are going to hear them and what actually happened." If the explanation she tells you is reasonable, you will probably think that she is giving you a logical explanation that counters whatever the "awful things" are. This will make you less likely to react negatively to the awful things when you later hear them from another source. Your study partner has inoculated you against the bad news. That's exactly how inoculation works in a legal counterargument. In part A-1 of the Summary Judgment brief in Appendix C, the hotel demonstrates inoculation to a projected argument about adhesive clauses in contracts by arguing in its moving party brief that the failure of the non-profit organization's Executive Director to read a contract before signing it provides no defense to contract terms.

Inoculation against the adverse material works the way of some vaccines, introducing the body to a weakened or attenuated form of a disease. Your body produces antibodies and creates a memory for its immune system. That way, if the actual live and strong disease tries to infect you, your body's immune system remembers and produces a strong protective response.

In the same way, social scientists recommend inoculating an audience to the adverse material as the best way to manage it. Thus, if a lawyer concludes that the opposing party is likely to bring up the adverse fact or legal argument, then it is better to bring it up first, in a weakened form, and to refute it. That prepares the audience to see the logic of your answer when the opposing side brings up the adverse argument—thereby blunting the effectiveness of the opposing argument.

If, however, the lawyer concludes that the opponent is unlikely to bring up the material, then, the science tells us, the lawyer should not bring it up. If it comes up, the lawyer can always manage it after the fact. That is called a "post hoc refutation." You can translate that into plain English as "managing the cat after it's let out of the bag." Figure 12-2 summarizes these strategies.

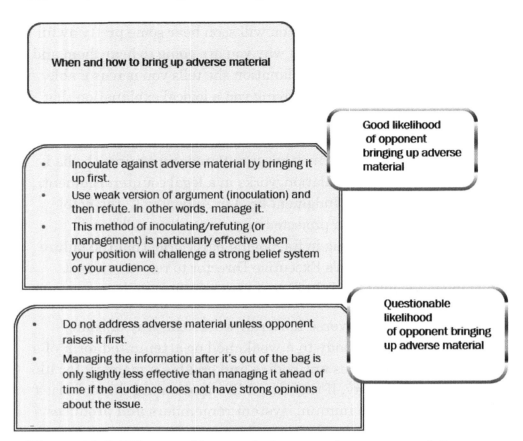

Figure 12-2: When and how to bring up adverse material

12.3.2 Deciding when to manage adverse material

So, how do you know when to assume that the opposing party will use the adverse material and that you need to manage the material by making a counterargument? That answer has a lot to do with experience in the particular area of law and in the particular practice setting. Remember, the overarching principle is that the *less* you want to talk about the adverse material, the *more* you probably need to do so.

Making the correct call comes in knowing, or making an educated guess about, what material your opponent will use. It is not always 100 percent clear that an opposing party will raise, or even knows, the adverse material that you have considered. While you can safely assume the same legal research competence (especially factoring in the duty as a lawyer to disclose controlling adverse authority), there are plenty of arguments that a lawyer may dream up that the opponent has not, or that the opponent has thought of but ultimately rejected for one strategic reason or another. That said, there are some principles to help you decide when to address adverse material.

12.3.2.1 *Address adverse material that you are ethically obligated to raise*

Of course, you always want to meet your ethical obligations. When it comes to counterarguments, one ethical duty is very clear: you must disclose binding, on-point adverse authority if your opponent fails to do so.[8] If there is a case or statute that is against your position, you have an ethical obligation to inform the court of that authority, even if it means you lose your case.

This may sound counterintuitive. After all, ours is an adversarial system; it should be up to opposing counsel to raise the authority that most helps his case. This is certainly true. And you can expect that most of the time, he will do so. But if your opponent doesn't find that key authority or somehow overlooks its importance, you cannot. In this circumstance, your duty as officer of the court outweighs your duty to advocate for your client.

Fortunately, while your obligation to disclose adverse authority is quite clear, its scope is also limited. You must disclose only binding authority. You are not required to disclose persuasive authority or authority that is not directly on point. However, as discussed below, you may *choose* to discuss adverse authority even if you are not ethically required to.

---

[8] "A lawyer shall not knowingly … fail to disclose to the tribunal legal authority in the controlling jurisdiction known to the lawyer to be directly adverse to the position of the client and not disclosed by opposing counsel.…" ABA Model R. Prof. Conduct 3.3(a)(2). Almost every jurisdiction has adopted some version of the Model Rules.

12.3.2.2 *Address adverse facts that you know the opposing party will use*

In almost every case, there are facts that you will wish did not exist. Sometimes your client acts badly. Often, the opposing party acts reasonably, at least from its point of view. And, unlike adverse authority, you have no ethical obligation to disclose adverse facts. If the opposing party overlooks facts that support his case, you are under no obligation to mention those facts. This may make it harder to decide when to inoculate against adverse facts.

You can be sure that when there's a fact that looks bad for your side, the other side is likely to raise it. You can inoculate by raising the fact yourself and putting it into the context of your client's story. Show how the adverse facts look from your client's point of view. Remember that all heroes have flaws—no one is perfect, and no case is either. But imperfection differs from reasonability. What might look unreasonable from an objective viewpoint will be better understood when seen from your client's perspective.

> **Example of a direct refutation of an adverse fact**
>
> The author of the brief in Appendix A wrote:
>
> "It true that the plaintiff posted potentially insulting things about the defendant on her Facebook page. But that just tends to show that the parties indeed were more than just casual friends and that she was reacting to the end of a romantic relationship."

If you do not know your opponent's theory of the case or are uncertain whether your opponent will incorporate specific, adverse facts, you need to exercise caution. You do not want to alert your audience to adverse facts that your opponent has overlooked or chosen to ignore. With these kinds of facts, you need to decide whether allowing your opponent to control the evidence outweighs the risk of introducing bad facts that might not have been introduced at all. How you decide this issue, of course, will depend on the specific circumstances of your case. However, a good rule of thumb is to remember that your opposing counsel is just as clever as you are.

Avoid the easy, but wishful, thinking that if you ignore problematic facts, they will just go away.

12.3.2.3   *Address and manage the opponent's strongest argument as soon as you bring it up*

Sometimes, you will look at a legal dispute and not see any significant arguments for the other side. This may give you a sense of great confidence. That confidence is misplaced. Your opponent undoubtedly has facts and legal authority that supports his position. Your task is first to recognize what those facts and authority are. If you cannot do so, you should be worried about whether you fully understand the legal issue. Put yourself in the shoes of the opposing party—what facts and authority would justify continuing the time and expense of this litigation?

Of course, often you will see your opponent's arguments all too well. Usually, there are "bad" facts or authority that you wish did not exist. But wishful thinking rarely wins in court. Instead, you must recognize these counterarguments and manage the information by incorporating effective strategies to deal with them.

Figure 12-3 will help you brainstorm responses to strong arguments.

Their argument	Your possible response
The plain meaning of the statute supports their client's preferred outcome	There is no plain meaning because the term is subject to interpretation *Or* The plain meaning is different and is favorable to our client's position because . . . (e.g., administrative regulations define the term differently or the jurisdiction's statutory scheme defines the term elsewhere in other related contexts)
Canons of statutory construction weigh in favor of their client's preferred outcome	Either the canon is inapplicable to this situation because . . . *Or* A different canon of construction is more applicable because . . .

The legislative history supports an interpretation that favors their client	The legislative history is unclear *Or* The legislative history does not tell a complete story *Or* The legislative history tells a story that contemplated a very different scenario *Or* The legislative history is slight and contrary to the plain meaning of the statute.
Policy considerations support their client's preferred outcome	More important policy reasons support your client's position because . . . *Or* The policy argument offered by opponent is inapplicable or would create a different ending to the story than what opponent suggested because . . .
Courts dealing with factually analogous situations have ruled in favor of the opposing party's position	The facts of the reported cases are different in a crucial way because . . . *Or* There are other cases that are more factually/functionally analogous to the case in front of this court and that support our client's position because . . .
There is no binding law in this jurisdiction but this court should adopt the law of *xzy* jurisdiction because . . .	The court should accept the law of [abc jurisdiction] because . . . (examples of arguments: trend of decisions, weight of authority, recency, number of highest courts, careful reasoning, policy considerations)

Figure 12-3: Table of common arguments and possible counterarguments

12.3.2.4 Avoid phantom counterarguments and look for the harder ones to manage

Novice legal advocates tend to make counterarguments that are easily rebutted. This is understandable. You have ready answers for weak arguments, and it is tempting to highlight your opponent's weaknesses as a way to bolster your own position. (This is an example of the "straw man fallacy" that we learned about in Chapter 9.75.) Unfortunately, this is rarely effective and often is counterproductive. If you represented the opposing party, what's the likelihood that you would raise those arguments? If you would not raise them, then likewise assume and expect that the opposing lawyer will also reject those arguments.

Instead, think of the best arguments for the opposing party and counter those. Remember, your guiding principle here is *the more you want to avoid an argument, the more you need to address it.* The opposite is also true. The counterargument that is obviously flawed is usually not worth rebutting—at least there's no need for an anticipatory rebuttal. If our opponent brings it up, you will have the opportunity to deal with it at that time.

> **On Being Wrong**
>
> Kathryn Schulz is a journalist and self-described "wrongologist." She notes that when we encounter people who disagree with us, we tend to conclude one of three things:
>
> 1. *They are ignorant.* If we just give that person the information that we have, they will agree with us.
>
> 2. *They are idiots.* If they have the same information that we have, they must not understand that information. Apparently, they are too stupid to get it.
>
> 3. *They are evil.* If they have the same information, and understand it, then they must be acting for their own, self-centered evil purposes.
>
> As Schultz explains, while any of these conclusions could be correct, they are not the only possible explanations for someone disagreeing with us. There are some issues where reasonable minds can simply differ. Sometimes, when viewed through a different prism of experience, circumstances will lead to different conclusions. Perhaps most frightening of all, *we* might be wrong! As lawyers, we will serve our clients best if we can remember that the opposing party is likely informed, intelligent, and well-intended.
>
> From KATHRYN SCHULZ, BEING WRONG: ADVENTURES IN THE MARGIN OF ERROR (Harper-Collins 2010).

12.4 Where to manage the adverse material

Like most things in legal writing, there is no single right or wrong answer to the question of where to manage the adverse material, other than this: put it where it needs to go. What you want to remember are the principles: inoculate and manage that adverse material.

Suppose, for example, that the dispute you face is about what the legal rule, or the scope of that rule, is. You would need to address that in the Rule or Rule Explanation section of the relevant issue. It is better practice to lead with your argument before addressing the counterargument. Often, your argument will indirectly counter the other side's position, even if not does not do so explicitly. On the other hand, once you have made your argument, you may have an explicit sentence that provides a weakened form of the opposing argument before addressing the other side's possible (or probable) counterinterpretation. This is especially helpful when you determine that you need a more overt form of inoculating the reader. In either situation, you will still have preserved the emphasis position of the paragraph for your own client's point of view.

Likewise, if the rule is fairly clear but there is a dispute as to how that rule applies to the facts of the case you are arguing, the counter-analysis logically fits within the Application section of your CREAC[9] for that issue. Again, it is usually best to present your own application first, before discussing why your opponent's proposed application is not in keeping with the letter or spirit of the law, or the comparable facts, or whatever your argument is as to why your application leads to a better result.

Just remember that the adverse material needs to be *managed*. Managing requires more than merely saying words to this effect: "This is my argument. This is the other side's argument. But they're wrong." Rather, you manage the adverse material by explaining *why* the other side's argument is less satisfactory. To do so, you will need to carefully select details and present them logically.

---

[9] You probably learned some version of the syllogistic Induction/Deduction flow as an organization acronym, e.g., CREAC, or IRAC. Chapter 14 covers argument organization in more detail.

12.5   Writing counterarguments

Once you have recognized the adverse material and the way in which the opposing party will most likely use that material, you need to plan how to write a counterargument—how, actually, to manage the adverse material.

12.5.1 Know when you have already made the counterargument

If your argument in chief already fully rebuts an argument likely to be raised by your opponent, there is no need to go any further. It is usually better to cut off a counter-argument with a strong argument that is part of your overall story than it is to rebut the counter-argument independently.

12.5.2 Avoid defensive phrasing of counterarguments

You now know that raising adverse material can help your audience resist the opposing party's efforts to use that adverse material. But you can easily work against yourself with the very wording of your managing. It is tempting, but less effective advocacy, to introduce a counterargument with a phrase like "opposing counsel will argue ..." That creates a defensive posture that may work against your advocacy rather than for it.

Here's why it works against you. That kind of wording defuses your own advocacy by creating a visual image of the opponent making a strong argument. That sort of phrasing immediately puts you—rather than your opponent—on the defensive. Consider these examples:

> **Version 1.** Defendant will undoubtedly argue that this oral agreement is unenforceable because it violates the Statute of Frauds. But that argument has no merit. The agreement is not governed by the Statute of Frauds because of an exception.

> **Version 2.** This oral agreement falls within an exception to the Statute of Frauds and is therefore not governed by it.

The first version highlights that the defendant has an argument that needs rebutting. It gives readers a visual image of the defendant (or defendant's lawyer) standing up and making an eloquent argument. That kind of visual image works against your client's case. The second version does the rebutting with an affirmative statement, and the visual image is about something better for your client. The statement anticipates the argument without explicitly making the argument. Because it asserts an affirmative legal argument rather than a rebutting one, it is less defensive and hence more persuasive.

12.5.3 Put the weakest link in the middle

When writing about adverse arguments, remember to think about the organization of a paragraph and section, and use positions of emphasis and deemphasis to help your argument. Some advocates like to set up each of their opponents' arguments and then knock them over one by one like bowling pins. The incorrect theory here is that managing the adverse material in one fell swoop will give the appearance of strength because it shows how every counterargument can be rebutted. However, that system also puts the weakest part of the argument in the most powerful position of the text—the beginning.

The better approach puts the counterargument in a relatively weaker position of the text. The "prime real estate" in writing is the beginning and end of sections and paragraphs. Thus, when you have troubling points you must address, like the opponent's strongest arguments, introduce your strongest argument in the first paragraph or two, and then discuss the counterarguments after that.

This principle applies at every level of your organization—from the overall structure of the Argument, to each paragraph of each section, though not of each sentence (the ends of sentences are the emphasis points).[10] Always strive to put the most powerful text in positions of strength—in the prime real estate locations of the document—and put the lesser material in the middle, where it will carry the least clout.[11]

Figure 12-4 shows these principles in graphic form.

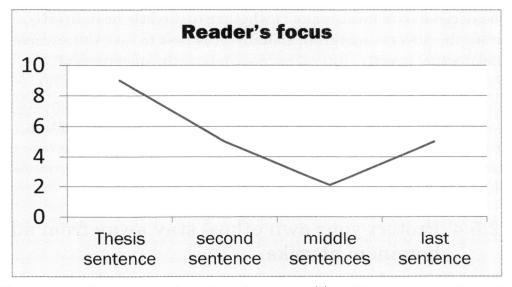

Figure 12-4: Strongest and weakest locations: (1) within a paragraph, and (2) paragraphs within a section of the brief.

The power of placement is apparent when you draft a counterargument that manages the adverse material. You must balance the need to inoculate with the countervailing consideration of making sure each paragraph is firmly written from the client's point of view. Thus, the first sentences of a

---

[10] *See* Laurel Currie Oates & Anne Enquist, THE LEGAL WRITING HANDBOOK 633–635 (4th ed., 2006).

[11] Thanks to Professor Carol L. Wallinger for the prime real estate language. See whether this Monopoly game metaphor helps: the beginnings of sections and paragraphs are the Boardwalk/Park Place of a section, whereas the middles of sections and paragraphs are the Baltic Avenues. (How many metaphors can we throw into this chapter? Apparently, quite a few.)

paragraph should place the client in a positive light. Next, you should confront the adverse material. In this way, you have put the adverse information in the middle—the weakest position. Finally, you should finish the paragraph with a direct or indirect refutation of the adverse material—putting the refutation in a position of strength.

One decision you must make is whether to directly or indirectly refute the adverse material. Usually, it is best to face the adverse information directly. But, of course, in law, the questions of professional demeanor and respect may require you to be a bit more discreet in managing an argument. So, although it appears that directly confronting the adverse material is the best option, Professor Stanchi outlines some reasons and explains some examples from advertising that show how material may be refuted with indirect arguments.[12]

12.5.4 Protect your own ethos: stay away from ad hominem attacks

Notice that the above options make no references to attacking or criticizing the opponent or opposing counsel. To do that would invite a rebound effect on your own ethos because it would show a lack of goodwill or respect.

In terms of editing, eliminate every instance of phrases such as "the other side's arguments are meritless." Those sentences tend to have little persuasive effect and are more likely to damage your own professional ethos. Even worse is descending into the world of ad hominem attacks (another logical fallacy we learned about in Chapter 9¾). If the opposing party is presenting absurd, offensive, mean-spirited, dangerous, or just downright stupid arguments, it will not be necessary for you to point that out to the judge. She will surely recognize bad arguments for what they are. You not

---

[12] Stanchi, *supra* note 1, at 394–395.

only undermine your own ethos by attacking the opposing party or its lawyer, but when the judge comes to the conclusion on her own that the other sides' arguments are absurd, offensive, and so on, she will be more thoroughly persuaded of that.

One way to think about this is to consider how you want to cast the opposing party in your client's story. It is almost always a bad idea to cast the opposing party as the villain. Judges, as impartial readers, assume both sides are acting in good faith. When you resort to ad hominem attacks, you implicitly suggest your opponents are evil villains. Readers, however, are likely to dismiss such attacks as unwarranted posturing and are likely to question the credibility of your client's story.

12.6   Read the writing of expert legal writers

Crafting a counterargument may be one of the most nuanced parts of advocacy. Reading the writing of lawyers extolled by other lawyers can only help. While there are thousands of briefs online, it is sometimes hard to pinpoint what is considered the best. Appellate attorneys write blogs, books, and discuss these issues on social media.[13] It's worthwhile to maintain a file of good writing examples—annotated—to remind yourself how you might phrase an inoculation statement.

12.7   Wrap-up: this isn't easy, we know

Your goal with any counterargument is reassuring readers that you recognize the strengths of your opponent's position, but that those positions must ultimately fail. You want to ease readers'

---

[13] For example, some of our teaching assistants will recommend Ross Guberman, POINT MADE: HOW TO WRITE LIKE THE NATION'S TOP ADVOCATES (2d. ed. 2014), a small book comprised of snippets from some of what he considers the best-written briefs taken from around the country.

potential concerns about your position. You do not want your opponent's arguments to control your legal story. Instead, you want readers to see the legal dispute from your client's point of view. The opponent's arguments are mere obstacles to be overcome; they are not the central story itself. This means that while you will address the opponent's arguments, you will keep them in a secondary role.

Counterargument requires careful strategy. There are no precise formulas, only competing considerations. This chapter is perhaps one of the most difficult in the entire book. We aren't kidding when we tell you that it is hard for any legal writer. Counterargument, as with any aspect of persuasion, is a series of factor balancing. Knowing that, however, demystifies some of the strategizing process for the legal writer.

This chapter has discussed some of the common special problems that you will encounter in expressing the legal arguments. But expressing the argument is only the first step in the induction/deduction process that you engage in. The law you develop must then be applied to the facts of your case. In the next chapter, we will discuss some special problems in handling essential facts that may not be completely proven but may be properly inferred from proven facts.

Advice from Debunking Experts

You may find useful one of the resources Daniel Engber cited in the SLATE article, JOHN COOK AND STEPHAN LEWANDOWSKY, THE DEBUNKING HANDBOOK, available for free download at https://www.skepticalscience.com/docs/Debunking_Handbook.pdf (January 23, 2012, 7 pages). The handbook focuses on the cognitive processes involved with refuting misinformation, defined as "information people have acquired that turns out to be incorrect, irrespective of why and how that information was acquired." The best approach they advise is to emphasize the core facts you wish to communicate rather than calling attention to the misinformation you are trying to dispute.

Elements, per handbook	Explanation
Emphasize core facts Place communicative emphasis on the core facts you want the audience to believe by putting them up front	Refute by emphasizing the key facts. This will create a gap in the knowledge of the audience—a hole where the falsities used to take up space. This isn't said in the text of the handbook, but the examples do mention a need for the key facts to present as a cohesive, alternative narrative.
Explicitly warn the audience Before discussing the misinformation, provide the audience with an explicit warning that they are about to read misinformation	Before mentioning the myth or falsehood, provide textual or visual cues that upcoming information is false. In legal writing-ese, this advice suggests that the writer mention the myth only after presenting the true facts. That gives the truth the position of emphasis in a subsection or paragraph.
Provide an alternative explanation Any gaps in the audience's mind left by the debunking needs to be filled. Achieve this by providing an alternative causal explanation for why the myth is wrong.	The handbook's examples show that the alternative explanation should be presented as a cohesive, alternative narrative. In other words, as you know, *stories persuade* because they are organizational scaffolds that present information as cause → effect.
Use graphics to help visually anchor the material you want to emphasize	Lawyers can and do effectively use graphic representations of facts or of legal reasoning. But, while some infographics are useful, others might be merely decorative. The writer must always balance the usefulness with the impact on persuasion. We will discuss this more in Chapter 19 of this textbook.. For more, see also Steve Johansen and Ruth Anne Robbins, *Articulating the Analysis: Systemizing the Decision to Use Visuals as Legal Reasoning*, 20 LEGAL WRITING 57 (2015), http://www.legalwritingjournal.org/2015/07/05/art-iculating-the-analysis-systemizing-the-decision-to-use-visuals-as-legal-reasoning/

Working with the Facts: Inferential Reasoning

In Chapter 9¾, we learned about the different forms of legal reasoning. Most of those forms are tools for interpreting the law. But most cases, both at the trial and appellate levels, will require you to reason by applying the law to the facts of your case. To do so, we must first critically analyze the facts. What, exactly, are the facts? What do they mean? How should they be interpreted? What story do they tell? And which facts should be included in the application of the law to the facts of the case?

Before we can use the facts in our Argument, we must first determine what the facts are. We discussed fact investigation in Chapter 5. There, we talked about how to distinguish between facts and opinions, and how to engage your curiosity in discovering what the facts of the case may be. But that chapter only addresses direct evidence; that is, facts that can be proven through eyewitness testimony, documentary or physical evidence. Sometimes the facts are more slippery, and can only be proven indirectly.

In this chapter, we begin by exploring what to do when there is a dispute as to the facts, or when crucial facts seem to be missing. Sometimes, conflicting or incomplete evidence leads to disagreement as to what the relevant facts are. This is especially true at the trial level, but fact disputes may also be relevant on some appeals. The first part of this chapter will help you reason with the conflicting or incomplete facts by trying to reconcile them with each other (a process we call "fact synthesis").

Even where the facts themselves are not in conflict, the parties will often disagree as to the conclusions that can be inferred from those facts. The second part of this chapter discusses how to use inferential reasoning to draw favorable conclusions from undisputed facts.

Finally, we note that this chapter does not deal with the situation where one party has the burden of proving a fact but fails to do so. For example, if one element of a test is not proven, the test simply fails. Instead, this chapter deals with methods for proving facts that a party needs when there is no direct evidence of that fact.

13.1 Proving facts

Reasoning with facts is similar to how a lawyer reasons with the law:

Problem	Solution: Law	Solution: Fact
Something is missing	You cannot find a directly applicable rule of law. 1. If your research is not yet complete, do more legal research. 2. If exhaustive research does not produce an answer, can you infer a rule through analogical reasoning?	You cannot find proof of an essential fact. 1. If the period for discovery is still open (trial level), conduct more fact investigation or discovery. 2. If discovery is closed (trial level) or the record is set (appellate level), or the fact cannot be proven directly, can you infer the missing fact from proven facts?
Something is unclear or incomplete	1. If the rule is unclear or ambiguous, engage in analogical reasoning to clear it up (common law rule) or statutory construction analysis (statutory rule). 2. If the rule seems incomplete or has gaps, find additional cases (common law rule) or other parts of the statute (statutory rule) that fill in the gaps, and synthesize a complete rule.	1. If the fact is unclear or it is not clear what happened, look for other facts to explain what likely occurred. For example, bias, ability of witness to perceive, etc. 2. If the fact is missing, can the needed fact be synthesized or inferred from facts that do exist?

Something is in conflict	If your research produces several different rules which might apply, and they lead to different results,	If the facts are in conflict,
	1. Is there a logical reason why one rule is binding and the other is not?	1. Can conflicting facts be reconciled with each other?
	2. If not, can you find a policy argument that supports one rule in preference to the other?	2. If not, can you explain why one version of the facts is more credible than the other?

In this section of the chapter, we will discuss the process of *fact synthesis:* the process of deducing knowable facts by combining facts from multiple sources or by reconciling conflicting facts. The next section will deal with the process of inferring necessary but unproven facts from other, proven, facts.

13.1.1 Fact synthesis

Fact synthesis is the process of establishing a knowable fact by combining a series of other facts, or by reconciling conflicting facts.[1] Consider this example:

> Brent Roberts is on trial for bank robbery. There is no witness who can testify that they saw Brent holding the gun and asking the teller for money. However, the prosecution can produce the following witnesses, all of whom know different pieces of the story:

> • Alisa can testify that a man wearing a ski mask and gloves came to her teller window, pointed a gun at her, and handed her a note telling her to put all of the money in her drawer into the canvas bag he was holding. She testifies that he was approximately 6 feet tall and of medium build, and that he walked with a limp.

---

[1] The facts that get combined in the process of fact synthesis are sometimes referred to as "circumstantial evidence." That is, they are facts that can be directly proven that describe circumstances that can lead to a relevant factual conclusion.

- Bob can testify that he was a customer at the next window, and that he saw a man wearing a ski mask hand something to the teller in another line. He said the man was wearing blue jeans and probably weighed between 200 and 220 pounds. He said he was at the bank around 1:20 in the afternoon.

- Charlie can testify that he was walking past the bank at around 1:30 when he saw a man wearing a ski mask run out of the bank, carrying a red bag. The man jumped into a "brown, older F-150 pickup" with damage to the front left fender, and sped off.

Around 5 p.m., acting on a tip, the police arrested Brent at his home. Parked in front of his home was a tan 2014 Chevy Silverado pickup truck that had been stolen that morning; it had fresh damage to the left front grille, headlight, and fender. Inside the home they found a white canvass grocery bag with the logo of a local grocery store on the side, printed in red ink. It contained about $1,800 in cash, mostly $20 bills wrapped in individual packs of 25 bills apiece. The bands around each bundle of $20 bills bore the logo of the bank that was robbed. Brent was 5'10" tall and weighed 195 pounds. He was wearing blue jeans at the time of his arrest.

Note that, while none of the eyewitness testimony exactly matches the physical evidence that the police found when they arrested Brent, the details are close enough that a fact-finder can reasonably conclude that Brent was, in fact, the man holding the gun and robbing the bank. The process by which the fact-finder reaches this conclusion is a process of *synthesis*—taking the important facts from the various eyewitness accounts, reconciling the minor variations that can be excused by the fact that each witness had only a fleeting glimpse of the events they were describing, and putting the pieces together into a coherent and plausible story.

When there is conflicting testimony or other types of evidence about a key fact, the lawyers for each side will need to argue to the court about what the court should find to be true. There are two possible ways the parties can argue:

- Some evidence is credible, and other evidence is not. The court should accept only the credible evidence and discard the rest.

- All (or at least most) of the evidence is credible and can be reconciled into a single true story.

Recall the discussion of audience responses to persuasion in Chapter 2. The first option, "choose which evidence is true," requires response shaping—the court likely has no pre-conceived idea of what really happened, and so is forming an entirely new response to the evidence. The second choice, "reconcile the evidence," relies more on response reinforcing. The court will likely start from the assumption that all witnesses are telling the truth, so that a narrative that reconciles all of the testimony reinforces that preference. Since response reinforcing is much easier than response shaping, your first task as the advocate should be to find a way to reconcile as much of the conflicting testimony as possible.

> **The Blind Man and the Elephant**
>
> In attempting to reconcile conflicting testimony, remember the famous Buddhist parable of the blind men and the elephant. In the parable, a group of blind men who had no previous experience with elephants were taken to an elephant, asked to feel the elephant, and then describe what the elephant was like. One blind man felt the tail, and said the elephant was like a rope. Another man felt the legs, and said the elephant was like a tree. Another man felt the side, and said the elephant was like a wall. Another man felt the tusk, and said the elephant was like spear. All of the men believed that their descriptions were correct and that all the other men were lying or mistaken.
>
> To some extent, then, all witnesses are blind, because they can only perceive part of the truth.

There are several principles to keep in mind as you attempt to reconcile conflicting evidence:

- Not all witnesses to the same event had the same point of view. They may have been closer to the event, or at a different angle, or only saw part of a sequence of events.

- Some witnesses may have perceptual or cognitive impairments that affect what they perceived, or what they remember. One witness may be nearsighted and wasn't wearing her glasses, for example, while perhaps another was intoxicated and unable to recall clearly what he saw.

- Some witnesses have pre-existing or later-acquired biases in favor or against one side of the other, which may color their recollection of what they perceived or the way they report what they perceived.

- Some witnesses lack sufficient context to understand what they are perceiving, and therefore may "fill in gaps" in their perceptions with stock structures that don't really fit.

These witnesses, however, could testify truthfully under oath about what they perceived, and none would be guilty of perjury.

When faced with this sort of conflicting evidence, the lawyer's first job should be to understand any limitations on the witness's ability to perceive and report what he or she saw or heard. The lawyer should then "synthesize" a version of the facts that reconciles all of the available evidence, to the extent possible. In the written brief, then, the lawyer should ensure that any statement of facts tells a story that checks mental boxes for the audience. The factual narrative should

(a) identify the relevant undisputed evidence,

(b) identify the conflicting evidence relating to the fact the attorney is trying to prove,

(c) note any evidence that suggests any impairments or limitations that might affect what each witness perceived, and finally

(d) synthesize the weight of the evidence into a statement of what probably happened.

Just like a synthesis of a rule of law, a synthesis of facts must account for as many of the facts as possible; that is, find a theory in which all evidence can be found to be true.

Of course, there will be situations in which all of the evidence cannot be reconciled. Witnesses sometimes lie, but even when they don't flat-out lie, their perception might be so out of line with other available evidence, or incontrovertible scientific facts, that it must simply be discarded. When you are in this situation, consider this strategy:

- Prefer explanations in which the conflicting testimony can be explained by a witness being simply mistaken, rather than telling an intentional lie. Again, response-reinforcing—"the witness is a good person telling the truth as he sees it"—is going to be more palatable to a fact-finder than response-shaping ("the witness is a liar").

> **Don't ignore the bad facts**
>
> In Chapter 12, we learned about how to deal with adverse information. In the context of the facts of the case, "adverse information" is what a trial lawyer might call "bad facts." Every case has them, and the lawyer who ignores them and hopes that the trier of fact just won't notice them usually ends up regretting that choice.
>
> One good way to deal with the bad facts is to include them in your synthesis, then use the other facts in your synthesis to explain why the facts aren't as bad as they seem or are actually consistent with the fact that you infer.

- Be sure to recite all facts that suggest why the witness is mistaken. Was he in a position to perceive the entire event? Was he under any perceptual impairment? Does he have a reason to favor or disfavor one side of the case?

- Be prepared to explain why some evidence is more credible (or weighty) than other evidence, using the principles described in the next section.

13.1.2 Weight of facts

As the previous discussion suggests, not all facts are created equal.

In your first semester of legal writing, you probably learned something about the "weight of authority." For example, you learned that you should rely on primary authority such as case law, statutes, regulations, and so on before you rely on the secondary authority of law reviews, legal encyclopedias, treatises, and so on. You probably also learned to cite binding authority before relying on persuasive authority.

Similar considerations go into selecting the facts you rely on in your application of law to the facts of your case:

- Physical evidence is the most reliable evidence available. As one trial lawyer tells his juries, skid marks and gouges in road and the damage to vehicles do not suffer from all of the problems associated with human memory.[2]

- Rely on direct evidence, where available—a document or object, or testimony from a witness who was present and perceived the relevant event. Note, however, that in many cases direct evidence is unavailable, and circumstantial evidence may be all you have available.

- Rely on statements against the interest of the witness in preference to self-serving statements by an interested witness. For example, if the opposing party admits to a fact that is helpful to your client's position, use that admission.

- In a similar vein, rely on testimony from disinterested witnesses in preference to testimony from one of the parties to the lawsuit who may have something to gain or lose in the case.

- Rely on facts in preference to opinions. Many opinions won't be admissible evidence (that is one of the topics that you will encounter in your course in Evidence), but if opinion testimony has been allowed, you should still recite the facts that led the witness to form that opinion.

Even where the underlying facts are not disputed, there is still likely to be considerable dispute as to the proper conclusions to be drawn from those facts. The next section explains how we use inferential reasoning to draw credible conclusions from facts. Though we may draw factual inferences in the Statement of Facts, we will also do so

---

[2] Thanks to Professor Stephen Easton, University of Wyoming College of Law, for this observation.

in the Argument section. Indeed, this is a critical skill when we are applying the law to the facts of our case.

13.2   The inferential stream (a/k/a "reasoning with facts")

An inference is a conclusion of fact reached after extrapolating from other, proven facts. Sometimes, the critical fact that an advocate needs to prove is something that cannot be proven directly. Frequently, the substantive law requires a fact-finder to determine whether somebody was "careless" or "negligent;" or whether the defendant was acting with a requisite state of mind. This kind of proof requires a jury to infer a fact from other facts that *can* be proven directly.

For example, the tort of "intentional infliction of emotional distress" is defined in the Restatement (Second) of Torts, §46:

> (1) One who by extreme and outrageous conduct intentionally or recklessly causes severe emotional distress to another is subject to liability for such emotional distress, and if bodily harm to the other results from it, for such bodily harm.

The elements of the tort thus require that, for liability to attach, the defendant's conduct must be "intentional or reckless." But how does the plaintiff prove that? It will be the rare defendant who, in his deposition, testifies that "Yes, of course I intended to cause severe emotional distress to the plaintiff!" Yet since that intent is an element of the tort, Plaintiff must find some way to convince a fact-finder that the defendant did, indeed, intend to cause the harm that resulted. In other words, the plaintiff needs to convince the fact-finder to infer the needed fact.

Drawing inferences is a logical process that begins with known facts and then proceeds through a series of generalizations that make sense to the fact-finder and that are consistent with known facts.

This process is sometimes called the "inferential stream." Let's see how this works by returning to the example of intentional infliction of emotional distress. Consider this hypothetical:

> Charles Smith is the coach of a middle school boys' basketball team. His players, in grades 6 through 8, range in age from 11 to 14 years old. One of the best players on the team is seventh-grader Bobby Jones, age 13. Bobby is very fast and leads the team in points scored on the season, but Bobby is very sensitive to criticism. Coach Smith has been critical of Bobby at practice in the past few weeks, and Bobby has noticeably grown increasingly withdrawn after hearing these criticisms. After one particularly arduous practice session, Bobby reacted to some criticism from Coach Smith by yelling "I want to quit!" Coach Smith responded by telling Bobby, "If you quit now, everybody in school will know you are a loser! You can't let me and your team down like that!"
>
> Last week, at the end of an important playoff game, the team was down by one point with only five seconds left to play. Coach Smith called a time out and, on the sidelines, designed a play to get the ball to Bobby to take the final shot. When play resumed, one of Bobby's teammates dutifully passed the ball to Bobby, but Bobby panicked, started dribbling, and failed to get a shot off before time expired. Bobby's team lost, and was thereby eliminated from the playoffs.
>
> Coach Smith looked angry, according to witnesses who were there. Many people at the game heard him scream at Bobby, "What a gutless moron you are! Why did I ever think you could make that play? You've cost all of us a chance at a championship! You'll never play another game for me! I hope your teammates take you out back and kick your butt!" Bobby burst into tears.
>
> Bobby's parents are now suing Coach Smith, on Bobby's behalf, for intentional infliction of emotional distress. One of Coach Smith's defenses is a lack of intent—he claims he did not intend to harm Bobby, but that he uses "tough love"

as part of his coaching strategy and uses it the most on the best players "as a model." Coach Smith has said that he only intended to teach Bobby a lesson so that he would play better in the future. Coach Smith has taken basketball teams to the playoffs five out of seven seasons, and under his coaching, two teams have won local middle school conference championships.

How can Bobby's parents prove the element of intent to cause severe emotional distress required by the Restatement (Second) of Torts, § 46? First, of course, only Coach Smith truly knows what his intent was; he claims that he was intending to coach Bobby and make him a better player. Because we therefore have no direct evidence that Coach Smith intended to inflict severe emotional distress, Bobby's parents will have to convince a fact-finder to infer that Coach Smith's intent was more malignant. To do so, the parents will need to begin with proven facts, and, through a series of generalizations, convince the fact-finder that Coach Smith intended to cause severe distress. The inferential stream might go something like this—and to explain the visual, the proven facts are in boldface and the generalizations flowing from those facts are shown as bullet points with arrows.

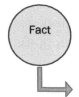 **Bobby was the leading scorer on the team.**

- Bobby was an important member of the team's chances of championship success.

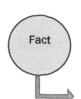 **Coach Smith told Bobby that "you can't let me down" by quitting the team, and that "You'll never play another game for me."**

- Coach Smith had a strong personal interest in the team's success.

- Coach Smith connected the team's success to his personal goals; he wanted to be known as the coach of a championship team.

• Coach Smith knew that Bobby was the leading scorer on the team, and therefore a very important person in Coach Smith's quest to become the coach of a championship team.

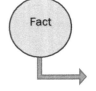 • Coach Smith sometimes holds grudges.

 Bobby's failure to take the final shot ended the season for the team.

 • Losing the game dashed Coach Smith's quest to become the coach of a championship team.

• Coach Smith's screaming at Bobby at the end of the game was because Bobby's mistake caused Coach Smith to not achieve his personal goal.

 Therefore, Coach Smith intended to cause Bobby severe emotional distress as retribution because Bobby cost Coach Smith his chance at being known as a championship coach.

This inferential stream is based on several proven facts. It then proceeds to make a series of generalizations about what those facts probably mean, leading to the final inference that Coach Smith was intentionally punishing Bobby because Bobby deprived him of a goal that was important to him. The inferential stream builds upon the writer's chosen narrative: Coach Smith is self-centered and therefore intended to punish Bobby for interfering with the Coach's personal ambition. Each step in the inferential stream seems incremental, reasonable, and supported by proven facts. The conclusion, therefore, seems perfectly logical.

But also note that the inferential stream is based on a selection of facts, chosen carefully by the plaintiff's counsel, to paint a picture of Coach Smith as a self-centered bully. Defendant's counsel would want to build an entirely different narrative based on these same facts. The inferential stream for Coach Smith might go like this:

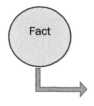

Coach Smith has taken his teams to the playoffs five of the seven seasons he has coached, and winning the conference championship twice.

    o Coach Smith has already proven that he is an excellent coach; winning yet another one is not needed to improve his reputation.

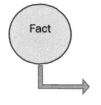

Coach Smith uses a "tough love" coaching style to get his players to perform well and focuses most on the best players "as a model."

    o Coach Smith focuses his harshest criticism on his best players because he believes they have the confidence and the talent to "take it," and therefore they have the most to gain from his harsh criticism.

    o Bobby had one more year in middle school and therefore could benefit from further instruction from Coach Smith.

Therefore, Coach Smith's intent at the end of the game was to motivate Bobby to be a better player for the team next year, which is what a coach is supposed to do.

This inferential stream, of course, establishes a completely different narrative: Coach Smith is a good coach who motivates his players to succeed.

Which inferential stream is "correct?" Although they rely on a different selection of proven facts, none of the facts are inconsistent with each other. It will ultimately be up to the trier of fact to (a) judge the credibility of the witnesses (in particular, Coach Smith's self-serving statements about his own intent), and (b) determine which inferential stream is more in line with the known facts and common sense.

13.3   Drawing negative inferences

The examples above show how an attorney might be able to infer a new fact by extrapolating from other proven facts. Additionally,   a new fact possibly can be inferred from the **absence** of other facts, under circumstances in which the facts *ought* to be known. This is known as the process of drawing a negative, or adverse, inference.

Suppose, for example, a plaintiff trips on a rug in a place of business. After suit is filed, defendant discards the rug so that the plaintiff cannot examine it to determine if it was worn or defective in some manner. Many courts would allow the jury to infer that the evidence (in this case the rug) would have been adverse to the defendant (i.e., that rug was in fact defective in such a way as to cause the plaintiff to fall).

Another example of drawing a negative inference might be when a witness in a civil case pleads the Fifth Amendment. The Fifth Amendment protects a witness in a criminal proceeding from having to offer testimony that incriminates himself. If he pleads the Fifth at his trial, the jury must be instructed that it may NOT infer that his answer would have been harmful to his defense; if a jury were permitted to draw the negative inference, the privilege against self-incrimination would be destroyed.

But what about in a civil case in which the witness's liberty is not at stake? Suppose a witness in a case has committed a crime that is relevant to understanding the dispute before the court. The victim of the crime may need to prove that the crime occurred as part of the victim's claim or defense in the civil case. In some jurisdictions, when a witness (either a party to the case or a non-party) invokes the Fifth Amendment privilege against self-incrimination, courts have discretion to allow the jury to infer that the answer the witness would have given would have been adverse to the witness.[3]

When you ask a court to draw a negative or adverse inference like these examples, you must prove the circumstances that caused the fact to be missing, then cite legal authority to show the court why it can infer the missing fact.

13.4   What's next?

Now that we have addressed some of the common special problems you will frequently encounter in writing the Argument section, the next chapter will help you put it all together and get it on paper.

---

[3] *See, e.g., LiButti v. United States*, 107 F.3d 110 (2d Cir. 110) (father's invocation of Fifth Amendment privilege in tax lien case regarding whether he or his daughter owned certain property was admissible in enforcement action against his daughter).

Organizing the Working Draft of the Argument

The previous three chapters examined what logicians call argument invention: the process of developing and refining your arguments. Arguments based in statutory interpretation, policy arguments, and adverse materials. In your first writing course, you also studied other forms of argument invention like analogical reasoning and perhaps narrative reasoning, or intent-based reasoning. The next chapters discuss the process of selecting, organizing, and arranging and organizing the types of arguments you determine will most effectively tell your client's legal story.

A *working* draft of your argument requires two things: getting your ideas down on paper and organizing those ideas into a coherent whole. It's not enough to talk about the law somewhere in the argument. Rather, good organization hallmarks good legal writing. This chapter will guide you through that critical organization process.

Back in the Prologue we included a graphic showing the writing process as one with gears that turn back on themselves. Writing is a recursive process. As you put your ideas on paper[1] and then step back to organize them, you will very likely find yourself rethinking some of your arguments, and then reorganizing your draft. The best lawyers expect that to happen—they hope it will. Writing is more than expressing crystallized thoughts. Writing is thinking itself. You put down thoughts on the page to understand what it is you are thinking. Ergo, write! It doesn't matter what your argument's first draft looks like; it matters only that it is written. For most of us, it is

---

[1] By "on paper" we also mean "on screen." Or "on canvas" or "into a recording device." The form of a first draft doesn't matter. The important thing is expressing the words so they can be rearranged.

easier to organize our thoughts once we have a first draft of those thoughts down on paper.

You have already learned that writing a legal argument is a form of technical writing. It is based on highly structured norms. Readers of legal briefs, in particular, have common expectations about how a legal argument should be structured. But while readers expect to see this logical structure, it takes you only so far when talking about advocacy on behalf of a client.

Organizing a legal argument section of a brief occurs on at least two levels, large-scale and small-scale organization. Large-scale organization refers to the overall arrangement of your chosen issues, both the major issues or prongs that must be addressed, and the sub-issues argued as part of those. Small-scale organization, in contrast, refers to the rule synthesis and analysis flow of argument any single issue or sub-issue you argue. Think of the large-scale organization as an outline, with hierarchal headings and subheadings:

1. First Major Issue to Be Argued

[Arguments relating to the first issue, with Rule synthesis and illustration [Induction], and Analysis [Deduction].]

2. Second Major Issue

[**Overview paragraph(s)** provided to Reader: Setting the context by providing any key threshold information such as governing language from a legislative/administrative source or controlling case if common law and removing from consideration or resolving any preliminary matters that may be dispensed of in the name of expediency and efficiency. Anything extraneous as may be expedient to mention. Concluding the Overview with remarks about the relationship of the sub-issues in sub-organization to each other, e.g., "two remaining elements" or "three factors."]

2.1. **First sub-issue** (organized as appropriate)

2.2. **Second sub-issue** (organized as appropriate)

In addition to choosing your large- and small-scale organizational structures, you should also distinguish in your mind between "issues" and "arguments." An "issue" (or sub-issue) is a specific legal question that a lawyer asks the court to resolve. An "argument" is a reason the lawyer advances as to why the court should resolve the issue one way or the other. This is similar to the difference between a "strategy," which refers to a person's overall objective, and a "tactic," which is a way of achieving that objective.

Another way to think about this is to recognize that "arguing" is what you are *doing*. "Issues" are what you are arguing *about*. Since arguments relate to specific issues, they are tools for thinking about small-scale organization.

For example, in our hotel room reservation example, the sample brief for the nonprofit organization identifies the first *issue* this way:

> Is the Hotel's claim for additional payment from the non-profit organization a penalty, and therefore not a valid liquidated damages clause?

When the author addresses this issue, the author makes two distinct *arguments* as to why the clause is an unenforceable penalty: (a) that actual damages for any breach would be readily ascertainable, and (b) that the amount specified as damages is grossly disproportionate to the actual damages that could be suffered.

14.1   Choosing your large-scale organization

In choosing the order in which you discuss your main points, always think independently about what structure best suits your client's needs and her story's strengths. Avoid automatically adopting the large-scale organization of an opponent's brief, for example, even when tempted to make such a point-by-point rebuttal. If you do, you are letting your opponent define the playing field. Ultimately you may end up with a structure that is similar to your opponent's (especially if there is an obvious logical flow to the issues), but that's okay so long as you make that choice after due consideration of your options.

14.1.1   "Logical flow" structure

A "logical flow" structure arranges the issues by one or more of the controlling legal issues. There may be a threshold issue, for example, that must come first. Often a court will resolve procedural issues before addressing the merits. If one of your issues is whether the court has jurisdiction (e.g., questions of ripeness, standing, personal jurisdiction over the defendant, or subject-matter jurisdiction), then logic suggests that you address that issue first. The court will certainly turn its attention to that question first, under the premise that it need not rule on the merits if it has no power to decide the case at all.

You would also use a logical flow structure when the substantive law calls for a sequential analysis. For example, in our Internet dating scenario, the substantive law calls explicitly for a sequenced analysis: first, the court must decide whether a dating relationship exists. If no such relationship exists, the case is over; but if one does exist, the court proceeds to the next step of determining whether the incident complained of fits one of the criminal categories defined by the statute as a violent act. When the substantive law directs the court to follow such a sequenced analysis, your brief should follow the same sequence.

Yet another example of a logical flow derives from how your court addresses certain types of issues. For example, some legal disputes raise both statutory and constitutional issues. Many courts will first attempt to resolve the dispute through statutory analysis. These courts will address the constitutional issue only if it cannot resolve the issue through the statutory analysis. In such a case, you should address the statutory issue first.

14.1.2   Organizing by type of reasoning

Another option for organizing your arguments is to organize them by type of reasoning. For example, you may have a mixture of rule-based, analogical, and policy-based arguments that support the relief your client is seeking. If these are truly alternative routes to the same destination, you might consider putting them in separate sub-sections of your brief and arranging them from most persuasive to least persuasive.

14.1.3   Argument chains

Many times, however, there is no obvious logical sequence to the issues. You then need to find another way to arrange the issues. In that situation, you may decide to use one of two types of argument "chains" to organize around. The first option is organizing from small to large requests. This is called a "foot-in-the-door" argument. The other option is to reverse the order and start with the largest request. This is a "door-in-the-face" approach.[2] The idea with either approach is that humans really do prefer to say yes to some sort of request. The first scenario starts a "bobble head" rhythm of saying yes to things. The second scenario starts with a pie-in-the-sky desired result and backs down so that it looks like the requester is negotiating toward something reasonable.

The difference between the two types of argument chains is very easily seen in a simple example of a child asking her parent for a pet. The child's desired result is either a dog or a cat.

Foot-in-door approach	Door-in-face approach
1. May I please have a fish?	1. May I please have a horse?
2. If you will say yes to a fish, then how about a gerbil? They are about the same amount of care in terms of daily feeding and habitat cleaning. And I can't really play with a fish.	2. If you won't agree to a horse, because of the expense and care, then how about a dog?
3. If you will say yes to a gerbil, then how about a cat? A cat isn't really all that much more work than a gerbil, and it lives longer and also is a lot more affectionate.	3. If you won't agree to a dog because of the level of care involved with walking it, then how about a cat? A cat doesn't require anyone to walk it.

---

[2]Kathryn M. Stanchi, *The Science of Persuasion: An Initial Exploration*, 2006 MICH. ST. L. REV. 411.

Another way to think of these types of structure is to think about the plot line for your brief. Your client, the protagonist, has a goal. Several routes may lead to his goal. In fiction, for example, the protagonist–hero may first choose the "safest" route that provides a successful start. After that, the hero will take a bit more of a risk on the next step, and then slowly increase the risk along the path to the final and largest hurdle. The foot-in-the-door may not lead to immediate success, but it provides a safer, more deliberate path to ultimate success.

Alternatively, our fictional hero could reverse the order. He could go for the big prize—the riskier one first, with the safer routes to be saved as a later alternative—a fallback position. If the bold but risky move fails, the hero still has the safer alternatives to pursue. This structure could be used to demonstrate to readers the seriousness of the peril the protagonist is in. This door-in-the-face approach is high risk, but it carries high rewards—success may come quickly.

The hotel room reservation case takes the foot-in-the-door approach. The attorney for the non-profit starts with the safer issue, whether the contract clause is unenforceable because it is a penalty. The brief examines the case law that defines what a "penalty" is and then applies those rules to the facts of the case. Next, the attorney makes the argument that the hotel has failed to prove any damages, one of the elements of a cause of action for breach of contract. But in fact, this issue provides a smooth transition into the riskier issue: impossibility of performance. In that section, the non-profit's attorney for points out that the hotel sold all of the rooms to other guests on the nights in question, making it impossible for the non-profit guests to purchase the required number of rooms. The message just below the surface of this issue is that the hotel is being unfair to the non-profit. It should not be allowed to be paid twice for the same rooms. While there may be some favorable facts here, the law is more difficult on this issue. Thus, the author builds to this issue by first addressing the easier issue regarding the meaning of penalty.

But note that the author could have reversed the order of these arguments and led with the impossibility argument. This would have the strategic benefit of highlighting for readers the theme of fairness. By showing readers how the hotel would be paid twice for the same rooms, they may be more receptive to the arguments set forth on the other two issues, even if the impossibility argument does not, by itself, persuade the court.

Either of these patterns could work, though in law most briefs approach the arguments with a foot-in-the-door organization.

14.1.4   "Lead with strength" is the default choice

Now suppose there is no obvious logical sequencing to the issues, and no clear argument chain appears. The traditional advice of "lead with your best argument" is good advice to follow. Of course, leading with your strongest argument will often be consistent with other approaches to argument organization. Ultimately, how you arrange your issues depends on your reading of what will be most likely to persuade the potential audience, the court. Choices like this make the practice of legal writing and advocacy more art than science.

14.2   Overviews and headings: signaling the bottom line, up front

Once you have chosen your large-scale organization, it is a good idea to let readers in on the structure you have chosen. Your job as a writer is to make readers' lives easier. This is another important way that legal writing differs from other forms of writing.

Judges or clerks reading legal briefs want information and want it quickly. Judges have very specific roles: they must learn both the applicable legal principles and the facts to which those principles will be applied, and then make a decision as to who wins. Since judges (and clerks) at all levels tend to be overworked, it is very important that you provide them with exactly the information they need to do their jobs.

Weakest issue
in middle

Anything you can do as a brief writer to assist your judicial audience in quickly locating and understanding that information will enhance your ethos—your personal credibility—with judges and their support staff.

Explicitly showing readers your chosen organization of the legal argument is a good way to assist judges in quickly locating the information they need to do their jobs. There are two ways in which good legal argument sections of briefs demonstrate organization: overviews and headings.

Educational psychologists have concluded that both headings and overviews help provide readers with the hierarchical structure of the material. Ultimately, this contributes to improved recall because readers better understand the relationships among subtopics.[3]

14.2.1   Overviews lay the groundwork for memory

Overviews, or summaries, create a knowledge base that readers can call on when later introduced to the material in more depth.[4] The information is learned the first time in the overview and placed into working (short-term) memory when the related text is read immediately afterward.

These studies have practical implications in legal documents, be they briefs, letters, offers, memos, letters, or any other document designed to persuade. A summary of the argument section or an overview paragraph between hierarchical sections of the legal argument can provide a knowledge base for the later subsection containing more detail.

The Overviews you include in a brief serve at least two functions. First, they provide readers with a brief explanation of how the law governing any particular issue is structured. Second, they provide

---

[3]Robert F. Lorch et al., *Effects of Signaling Topic Structure on Text Recall*, 85 J. EDUC. PSYCHOL. 281, 287 (1993).
[4]John A. Glover et al., *Advance Organizers: Delay Hypotheses*, 82 J. EDUC. PSYCHOL. 291 (1990).

readers with some uncontroversial, foundational legal principles that influence the rest of the law in that section.

14.2.1.1 Describing the overall legal structure and the arrangement of arguments

One way to visualize the structure of your brief is to think of a journey. You want your audience (the judge) to travel from a place of neutrality about your client's case to a place of awarding your client the relief you seek. It is your job, as the writer, to show the judge how to complete that journey in the most effective route possible—hopefully also the simplest and most direct route.

Every journey is governed by overarching considerations, and most journeys require multiple steps. Except for the lucky few who can walk to their destination, very few journeys involve one mode of transportation or one seamless route with no interruptions of turns or traffic signals. Likewise, a legal journey has overarching rules that govern it and typically involves multiple steps. There may be procedural and substantive issues to resolve, as well as alternative legal theories to consider. Certain considerations may be dispensed with immediately. The Overview signals these major organizational cues to the reader.

An Overview provides all three classical rhetorical functions. It has the *logos* function of creating knowledge about the governing statute or regulation if there is one or about the overarching rule if the case is grounded in common law. It also serves the logos function of providing the reader with an outline of the upcoming arguments. The Overview likewise serves the *pathos* function by creating an initial comfort level for the reader about the substance and that there will be a logical flow to the argument. And, because humans crave organization from chaos, providing the structure up front creates ethos for you as the writer—the reader trusts that the upcoming argument will also be well-crafted.

A global overview paragraph of an argument reveals the large-scale structure of the brief, showing the relationship between major issues and arguments you plan to discuss. A local overview paragraph reveals the structure of a specific issue, sub-issue, or theory.

Take a look at the structure of this chapter, for example. Our objective as authors is to take you, the reader, on a journey that teaches you how to organize the argument section of your brief. Immediately at the beginning of this chapter, we provide you with an overview of what the chapter is about and where we want you to go. That represents the global overview for this chapter. Now look between the 14.1 main point heading and the 14.1.1 sub-point heading of this section to see an example of a local overview.

Overviews provide specific details about argument chains. While Overviews do set forth the uncontroversial, foundational legal principles that will shape the rest of the argument, they do not provide specific details about the key principles of law or how they work. They merely alert the reader to the key legal principles that will be discussed and developed next.

The shadow box shows an example of a global overview from the non-profit organization's brief in the hotel reservation case. It describes the three main issues to be addressed and introduces the key concepts that will form the basis for the argument. Note that it does not include numbering but instead uses other language cues to signal the three main issues. The arrows point to each one. But notice one more important thing about this sample overview: it includes reference to both the client (the non-profit organization) and the opposing party. This was done explicitly, to activate the persuasion function of priming. The narrative of these parties intertwined in the Overview makes the legal material more accessible by creating mental imagery. That, in turn, makes it more memorable.

4.0 Legal Argument

The attrition clause in the contract is a penalty rather than a liquidated damages clause; it is therefore unenforceable. Payment of the invoice by the non-profit organization, S.O.F.T., would be grossly disproportionate to the damages –if any— suffered by the Hotel as a result of the shortfall in bookings by S.O.F.T. and result in a windfall to the Hotel. Moreover, the Hotel was not damaged; it was able to resell any rooms not reserved by S.O.F.T. guests, presumably at a higher price, and was therefore likely put in a better position than it would have been if S.O.F.T.'s guests had filled the 53 "unused" guest rooms at the contract rate. In addition, by selling all of the rooms not reserved by S.O.F.T., the Hotel made it impossible for S.O.F.T. to perform the contract.

> Cueing language of major issues, strategically using language of client narrative as a priming technique.

One of the most common mistakes in legal briefs is an overview that focuses exclusively on the legal rule and forgets to mention the possible impact of different choices on the client. This is an easy mistake to make; after all, this is the Argument section of the brief, where the law is explained and applied. And indeed, perhaps the most important function of the overview paragraph(s) is to help readers navigate the sometimes complex and unfamiliar rules of law. But by definition, overview paragraphs come at the beginning of a new section of the brief. Every time you change direction or topic (such as at the beginning of a new section), readers become alert: "This is new! I'm making progress here!" That means you have readers' attention— which is the best time to make a persuasive point. Thus, for example, you can show the possible impact on your client (either positive or negative) of the court's ruling one way or the other. By keeping the client front and center, judges will be reminded of why the points you are discussing in the body of each section are important.

14.2.1.2   *Setting up foundational law*

The second function of an overview is to lay out some foundational legal principles that help readers work with the concepts that follow. For example, if you are filing a brief in support of a motion for summary judgment, you will need to briefly recite the court rule that provides the summary judgment standard in that jurisdiction because the court will need to apply it to make its ruling. In a situation like that, since the standard applies to all of the sections of the brief, you would include this statement in the global overview. Similarly, in the Internet dating case example, the overview would include the specific statutory provision in the New Jersey Prevention of Domestic Violence Act that forms the basis of the entire dispute.

Another example might be where you are arguing about a well-settled elements-type of test such as common law negligence. In that situation, you might wish to state the uncontroversial elements of negligence in the appropriate global overview paragraph and then use that structure to advise readers of which elements the parties dispute and which elements are undisputed.

One example of "foundational law" is shown in the overview at the beginning of this chapter. After introducing the three main sections of this chapter, we discuss the distinction between "issues" and "arguments," a basic principle that has meaning for several of the sections to be discussed.

14.3 Headings chunk the information

Headings help readers search effectively for answers to questions about the text. They also provide the superstructure of the document, which leads to better concept recall.[5] Breaking up the information into "chunks" under headings also makes sense from a memory standpoint. Cognitive psychologists have long known that "chunking" information—grouping related information—raises memory retention rates.[6]

---

[5]Stephen C. Wilhite, *Headings as Memory Facilitators: The Importance of Prior Knowledge*, 81 J. EDUC. PSYCHOL. 115 (1989).

[6]George A. Miller, *The Magical Number Seven, Plus or Minus Two: Some Limits on Our Capacity for Processing Information*, 63 PSYCHOL. REV. 81(1956); also made

Here's an easy example that you might have heard before. Research has shown that most people can remember up to seven random numbers (plus or minus two) in their short-term memory.[7] However, it is easiest to remember seven numbers if they are chunked in groups of three and four numbers. This explains why phone numbers are broken down into "chunks" of three and four, rather than a list of seven numbers. The chunking makes them easier to remember.[8] Similarly, headings help readers identify chunks of related text, thus improving their recall of the information within each chunk.

The use of headings should be familiar to you from your course in predictive legal writing. Almost all briefs, and certainly briefs that are more than a few pages long, use headings to help readers follow the argument by chunking the information.

Be sure your point headings make a point. That is, they should make some persuasive statement instead of serving simply as a bland label denoting what the next section is about. For more information on how to write a persuasive point heading, see Chapter 15.

---

available online by Stephen Malinowski with the author's permission at http://www.musanim.com/miller1956/ (last accessed July 25, 2017).

[7] *Id.; see also* LINDA L. LOHR, CREATING GRAPHICS FOR LEARNING AND PERFORMANCE: LESSONS IN VISUAL LITERACY 206 (Merrill Prentice Hall 2003).

[8] Alas, the advent of cell phones has required most of us to now remember area codes as well. Fortunately, the same technology has made *remembering* phone numbers less important.

> ### How many headings do we need?
>
> Once we recognize that headings serve to chunk information in a way that reveals our large-scale organization, we must decide how many chunks we need to have. Generally, we should have a main heading for each cause of action or issue on appeal. When the sub-issues involve mainly analogical reasoning, then the arrangement of arguments will likely fall into something like a pattern of each subheading signaling a separate induction/deduction sequence. For example, in a legal argument about two of the four elements of negligence, each subheading would signal a separate element and for each element, the small-scale organization would include rule synthesis and illustration (the induction) and the rule application to the client's facts (the application).
>
> But headings may appear more frequently than that. When the legal argument goes beyond analogical reasoning, the headings will not neatly line up in this same way. This frequently occurs when the rule of law itself is at issue rather than the application of an existing and established rule. Headings and subheadings then serve a signpost function, even though the writer may still be in the middle of synthesizing the rule or arguing for a particular rule synthesis. Signposting provides the reader with a breathing point—a place where the reader can stop for a break. It also provides the writer with a new beginning point for emphasis purposes. Recall that persuasion lesson from Chapter 12: the reader's attention is greatest at the beginning of sections.

14.4   The visual design of headings (and why the scientific notation style?)

For headings to fulfill their principal function, they must jump out at readers, visually. They must also attract readers' attention rather than cause them to look away. Thus, you should create visually distinctive point headings. But consider that formatting choices such as ALLCAPS and underlining will distract or confuse readers. *Even italic type has its limitations.* The better choices involve the use of light and dark (i.e., boldface). You can also vary the size of headings to show hierarchy.

At the same time, headings must serve the important function of chunking the information. To do that, keep headings in proximity to the text that they modify. That means close up some of the space between headings and text. You don't need as much space between headings and the text that follows as the space you have between paragraphs. For example, in this book, the space between our headings and our text is half of the space between paragraphs. Creating proximity between headings and the modified text can end up saving you several lines in a document. That's important when you must measure length in terms of the number of pages.

This textbook's second edition has converted the headings from the first edition's outline notation to scientific numbering notation. Contracts have already begun moving in this direction. Scientific notation style provides a predictable uniformity that is missing in outline notation. Outline notations may have any variety of conventions beyond the Roman numerals and capital letters of the top-tier levels. Scientific numbering also allows reader an easier time of navigating the document because the notation carries forward the full hierarchy rather than just the lowest level of the outline. The importance of navigation facility becomes readily apparent when trying to do so with an onscreen document. Readers of your legal documents are quite likely to be reading them electronically. According to the American Bar Association statistics, nearly every law-trained reader has access to and reads some percentage of legal documents on a laptop, tablet, smartphone, or combination.[2]

Last, make sure your point headings actually make a point. That is, they should make some persuasive statement instead of serving simply as a bland label denoting what the next section is about. A point heading is a point of emphasis where you have the reader's full attention; take advantage of that moment to make a persuasive point. Look at the headings in this chapter and note the use of

---

[2] For more reading about onscreen reading and about scientific notation in legal documents, *see* Ellie Margolis, *Is the Medium the Message? Unleashing the Power of E-Communication in the Twenty-First Century*, 12 LEG. COMM. & RHETORIC: JALWD 1, 11–12 and 19–20 (2015). For more statistics about attorneys' use of technology, see the online AMERICAN BAR ASSOCIATION LEGAL TECHNOLOGY RESOURCE CENTER, https://www.americanbar.org/groups/departments_offices/legal_technology_resources.html (last visited July 25, 2017).

boldface, size, and proximity to demonstrate the hierarchy and the chunking of information.

Remember that, in an appellate brief (and maybe in a longer trial court brief, if the court rules allow) your point headings will all appear, without any supporting text, in your table of contents. If the point headings make persuasive points, then the table of contents becomes a summary of your argument: one more opportunity to persuade.

Design tips for effective headings

1. Headings should be as short as possible and still convey the point.

2. **Use boldface type so that headings stand out visually from the surrounding text.**

3. **Boldface shows contrast without altering the readability or legibility of the letters.** Underlining, on the other hand, negatively affects the readability and legibility because the underlining interferes with the tops and bottoms of letters.

4. *Italics are not quite as bad as underlining, but they aren't all that great, either.*

5. HERE IS THE WORST OPTION. WHY WOULD YOU EVER TYPE A POINT HEADING IN ALL CAPITAL LETTERS? ALL CAPS ASSAULT THE READER'S EYE, DRAMTICALLY AFFECT READABILITY AND MAKE IT ALMOST CERTAIN THAT THE READER WILL NOT READ THE POINT HEADING. WE DOUBT YOU HAVE EVEN READ THIS FAR INTO THIS TIP! IF YOU HAVE, SEE IF YOU NOTICED THE TYPOGRAPHICAL ERROR IN HERE.

6. Headings can be single spaced since you aren't going to be using more than a very few lines at most.

7. Headings should be numbered in scientific notation style, so that the reader can see the outline hierarchy with each heading, including when reading onscreen.

   7.1. Sub-topics need not be indented but can be in a smaller font size. If you must indent, be careful of how far you go, because line length changes can throw off reading rhythms.

   7.2. Remember that if you have a ".1," you must have a ".2."

8. Check your headings for symmetry with each other. If you boldface or change typeface for headings, then every heading must be boldfaced and in that same typeface. Don't suddenly switch in the middle or at a particular sub-sub level. That will throw off the reader's understanding of the heading hierarchy.

14.5   Small-scale organization

Once you have chosen the large-scale organization for your issues, it's time to fill in the content underneath each of the major point headings and subpoint headings. This is where you begin organizing the body of your Argument section.

Like any other task, it's best to have a plan before you begin. Most writers start with the big-picture concepts and then choose a structure that serves their purpose. You have seen much of this material before, in your predictive writing course. But because client-centered persuasion must always take precedence over any formulas, there might be variations on the small-scale organizational structures you have previously learned.

14.5.1   The common organizational arrangement for analogical reasoning

Most legal arguments take the form of a syllogism: you start with a major premise (a rule of law), apply it to a minor premise (the facts of the case), and deduce an answer (the result). You probably learned this induction and deduction process in your first semester, while also learning analogical reasoning. And you probably used an acronym called IRAC or some variation of that acronym.[3] When speaking about analogical reasoning, different legal writing textbooks use different acronyms, but they all represent the same one of Aristotle's rhetoric canons: arrangement.[4] Because it is too radical for us to depart from the acronyms altogether, we do

---

[3] Different textbooks use different acronyms for the analogical reasoning syllogism: CRAC, CRAAC, TREAT, TREAC, CRuPAC, etc. Pro tip: they all refer to the same inductive process. Wikipedia had 22 acronym variations listed at last count. *IRAC*, WIKIPEDIA https://en.wikipedia.org/wiki/IRAC (last visited July 26, 2017).

[4] Aristotle's five canons of rhetoric are invention (the substance of the argument), arrangement (the organization of the argument), style (the word choices, sentence structures, and creativity of the argument), memory (the knowledge and credibility the author has on a topic), and delivery (the tone and look of the communication).

references one, "CREAC," but even that we use with trepidation. In this book, the logical structure of each section of the brief is defined, of course, by the substantive law that you are discussing. This is the function of CREAC. We use the CREAC formulation for persuasive writing because it reminds us that the Explanation of the Rule is just as important as stating the Rule. The final C is a strategic choice: useful in certain writing situations but merely repetitive in others.

Novice legal writers sometimes latch onto the acronyms as the one-and-only way to organize the argument for every or for an entire brief. But the organization will depend on the type of reasoning in use. Unless the brief focuses completely on an element test with all analogical reasoning, it's unlikely that an entire brief will use that shorthand structure. Rather, the brief will very likely use multiple forms of legal reasoning, and that means the organizational structure will look different than a traditional first-semester legal writing memo.

To reiterate, a full-CREAC brief is unlikely to happen except when you are working only with an element test. If the issue involves factor tests, you might find that the CREAC structure is too limiting. (Factors tests are discussed in section 14.5.4, below.)

What is probably most important to remember about the acronym CREAC is that it sets up a method for providing readers with context before detail. The initial C—which may be the heading of the section—provides the opening context and should provide a client-centered outcome, i.e., something that translates to, "The issue resolves in favor of my client on this sub-issue . . ." The next thing that readers expect and need is to understand the law of the sub-issue; thus the next step is to include a distillation of the overarching rule of law. But law in the abstract is just that. Readers need something more concrete. Something they can see in their minds. So, logic dictates an explanation in the form of illustrative stories (e.g., cases or legislative histories) that help shed light on the rule's intent and use. Only after understanding that context can readers truly appreciate where your client's story fits.

Persuasion also is more effective when the reader is primed for the result your client seeks. Priming helps to ensure that the reader gets a preview of how the governing rile applies to the client. Think about the client's situation when developing the small-scale organization structure and language. Representing the client effectively will always be the more important principle, overriding a strict adherence to any acronym. While formulaic writing may seem easier, remember that the CREAC formula only truly works when the sub-issue involves only analogical legal reasoning.

With those cautions in mind, the rest of this section demonstrates the paradigm and then a sample of variations on the paradigm.

The traditional deduction and induction model, translated into a legal writing acronym of CREAC model, looks like this:

C   Fact-based, contextual conclusion sentence(s) that primes the reader towards a positive outcome for the client. The outcome is kept narrowed to this issue or sub-issue. The conclusion may appear in the heading, or partially in the heading and partially in the first sentence of the text if the heading would otherwise become unwieldy in length. Keep in mind that the design of the heading and text as a tight unit allows the first textual sentence to flow directly from the heading; the two can dance together as a unit.

R   Rule Statement: Multiple sentences that summarize and synthesize the particular rule that is either controlling or that you want to become controlling. Key advice: Write the Rule Statement from your client's point of view, as explained in Chapter 15.

E   Explanation (sometimes called Rule Explanation): The supporting material that explains and illustrates your Rule. Without the context of the Rule Explanation the Rule might be too abstract or ambiguous.

A proper Explanation tells stories about how courts have applied the governing Rule in other situations. It answers readers' questions about the Rule:

- What is the goal or purpose of the Rule?

- In what kinds of other stories did courts use this Rule? What were the key facts of those stories?

- Are there examples in the cases that show how the Rule can be stretched or when it should be limited?

- If a statute, are there intrinsic, textual clues that support your formulation of the rule? Does the legislative history speak to the intent? Are there statutory sections that support your formulation of the Rule?

- What equities or policies does the Rule serve?

Use in-text explanations when the Explanation is central to the client's outcome or when parentheticals do not otherwise suffice. These are discussed in greater detail later in the next Chapter.

Use parentheticals to provide information that is not crucial to the argument or when you can provide the relevant information in one sentence. These are also discussed in greater detail later in the next Chapter.

A   Application of law to facts: The argument of how and why this court should use the Rule in your client's situation.

- Use analogical reasoning to show similarities and differences between the Explanation and the client's situation. Make the analogies meaningful rather than superficial. This is discussed in the next Chapter.

- Because the Rule and Explanation provide the context before the detail of the Application, generally the Application does not start until the subsection's Rule and Explanation are fully developed.

C   Conclusion: An optional wrap-up of the legal discussion of this section. This may be necessary when there are multiple subsections leading to a common meeting point. If including this would merely add repetitive bulk, skip it and save the words.

14.5.2   Variations (avoid formulaic thinking)

Earlier in this chapter, we discuss options for large-scale arranging of issues. But even within the confines of any CREAC unit, you have choices in the arguments you raise. You also have choices on when to present counterarguments and which arguments to raise at all; these topics were discussed in Chapter 12.

A persuasive argument need not always follow a lock-step, preformed organizational structure, but may be varied to strengthen your persuasive punch. When the legal argument uses statute or intent-based reasoning, policy-based reasoning, highly narrative reasoning, or inferential reasoning, the small-scale structure may look slightly different. The goal should always be one of effective advocacy. A judge who *wants* to rule in your client's favor is more likely to do so than a judge who feels she is merely *permitted* to do so.

The most common variations on CREAC are these:

c**RE**ac

Use when Rule of Law is the focal point.

E.g. Circuit Split

Novel issue of law

This common variation happens when the controversy centers on the Rule rather than on its application. This situation can arise where the "story of the law" is predominant, as described in Chapter 3. Many appellate brief simulations used in courses and moot court competitions use these as teaching tools. In everyday practice, they may come up as part of a mix of issues, sometimes as part of interpreting a statute or a procedural rule.

Novel interpretation of a statutory phrase

When arguing for the adoption for a Rule itself, the argument will likely merit several signpost-type subheadings of Rule Explanation and a fairly short Application of the law to your client's facts. In this situation, you may subtly weave your client's story into your Rule Explanation—this keeps your client in the story.

CREAC

Use when
Analysis of client
facts (a/k/a
Application) is
very developed,
with outside fact
investigation of
non-adjudicative
facts

Another relatively common variation occurs when the rule of law is fairly straightforward, and the Application requires enough explanation to warrant signpost-type subheadings. Typically this occurs when the "story of the client" is predominant or when the Analysis includes statistical, legislative-fact research supporting a policy argument that has been woven into the Analysis.

RCEAC

Use strategically

The writer chooses to use the heading to state part of the Rule rather than an outcome. The conclusion, or client-based outcome, then appears in the first sentence of the text, i.e., changes places with what might otherwise appear in the heading. You will see this variation used with some regularity in practice. The choice is one of strategy. Part of the strategy is revealed when all of the headings appear together and are read together in the Table of Contents.

CPREAC

In this variation, the writer follows the Conclusion with a paragraph designed to Prime the reader to evoke an emotional response. Cognitive priming will happen via the organization itself and via word choice. The affective priming appeals to pathos/substance, as discussed in Chapter 2. The Priming might be a story about our client or an explanation of an overarching public policy. The goal is to motivate the judge so that she wants to find a reason to rule in your client's favor on that particular issue.

Although it is tempting to think about varying the organizational structure this way in every subsection or in every document, the impact diminishes with multiple uses. It may also become redundant with the Introduction/Preliminary Statement section of the brief. Not every brief will use it; it is the exception. Save this organizational variation for a time when you really need it.

14.5.3   An outlined argument using a common variation: Rule of Law at issue

The box below shows an example of an argument structure, when the rule itself is at issue.

Main heading	**The defendant committed criminal mischief when he destroyed the marital dining room table because "property of another" includes jointly owned property that is destroyed by only one owner.**
Global Overview	The Overview would include: • The precise wording of the relevant parts of the controlling statute (criminal mischief statute) • The conundrum. (The statute mentions destruction of property *of another*. Is jointly owned property also "property of another"?) • Overview or snapshot of the different legal reasons why the law should be resolved in the way you suggest.
Rule sub-heading (signpost). Note sub-heading doesn't state an outcome but states a sub-rule. It is using a variation.	1. **Criminal mischief is analogous to arson and theft, as part of the "offenses against property" crimes.** • Follow the normal statutory interpretation chain by looking at the cases interpreting the arson and theft statutes to determine whether those cases answer the "joint property" question for the analogous statutes.
Rule sub-heading (signpost) Note that the first textual sentence continues the idea. The	2. **The legislative history indicates that the legislators intended to include jointly owned property in the scope of the law.**

two sentences are tightly related.	They did so because the law is supposed to act as a deterrent against destruction of property.
Rule sub-heading (signpost)	3. Other states considering this precise issue have concluded that a defendant may be convicted for criminal mischief when he destroys jointly owned property. (Explain)
Rule sub-heading (signpost) Policy—this will start to include facts and therefore will blend into Application.	4. The policy of protecting married couples must be as important as protecting unmarried couples with shared property.
Application. The sub-heading plus textual first sentence are related. We could have put them together as a very long heading but why? It's better to break them up and have a shorter, more readable heading. The Application section in this type of issue-of-law might have a shorter development than with issues that rely heavily on factual nuances.	5. This court must deny the defendant's motion to dismiss the charges. Because this court should read the criminal mischief statute to include jointly owned property in the definition of "property of another," (Apply rule principles developed above to client's facts.)

14.5.4 Handling factor tests

A factors test requires considering several, often competing, factors rather than the more straightforward analysis of an elements-based legal issue.

An element test is easier to organize. In an element test, the moving party must show something like:

Simplified example of a conjunctive test	Simplified example of a disjunctive test
1st element	1st element
And	Or
2nd element	2nd element

A factor test, on the other hand, looks something like this:

Factor test to determine if parties are dating in New Jersey domestic violence law	Courts' explanations of how to use that factor test
1. Was there a minimal social interpersonal bonding of the parties over and above mere casual fraternization? 2. How long did the alleged dating activities continue prior to the acts of domestic violence alleged? 3. What were the nature and frequency of the parties' interactions? 4. What were the parties' ongoing expectations with respect to the relationship, either individually or jointly? 5. Did the parties demonstrate an affirmation of their relationship before others by statement or conduct? 6. Are there any other reasons unique to the case that support or detract from a finding that a "dating relationship" exists? *Andrews v. Rutherford* (cite).	Courts use, but should not be limited to these factors, and should consider other factors such as generational norms. *(the synthesized rule)* Each factor carries some weight, but no factor is dispositive. And there might even be other factors to consider in a particular situation.

There are two ways to approach the organization of a factors test. How you organize the argument will depend on how interdependent and interrelated those factors are to each other.

14.5.4.1   Individualized factors

The writer's first organizational choice is to address each element separately, with a CREAC structure for each factor. That choice makes sense when the factors are very distinct. In a negligence case, for example, the court may consider distinct factors to determine whether the element of "failure to adhere to a standard of care" has been proven:

* Industry standards of reasonable care

* Local standards of reasonable care

- The usual protocols of the defendant and whether they were in use at the time of the incident

- The external factors that might have affected the defendant's ability to react to a dangerous situation (e.g., time of day, day of the week, time of the year)

> **If a court sets out a factor test in a particular order, do I have to discuss them in that order?**
>
> No. You are bound only by what makes the most sense to you in advocating for your client. If you are creating a list of factors based on your own research and synthesis, then create whatever list works best for your client. If you are using a list created by a court, then you may nevertheless change the order of discussion, provided you include a sentence or two about why you are addressing the factors in an order different than what you just led your reader to expect.

In this type of a situation with individualized factors, it might make organizational sense to set out each factor individually and to separately explain and apply the law related to each factor. The small-scale organization thus may set up something that looks quite a lot like a Rule/Rule Explanation small-scale organization of element-based legal reasoning.

However, even though the factors may be unrelated, the small-scale structure may vary somewhat significantly from an elements-based analysis when it comes to the Application. In many cases, you may not analyze every potential factor individually but instead will show how the factors fit together in one Application section at the end of the several Rule/Rule Explanation sections.

Of course, in many cases, there will be some factors that simply do not apply to your situation. Those need not be addressed. Simply set out, in a local overview, which factors are applicable. They aren't elements; they aren't all required.

14.5.4.2   Interrelated factors

When the factors are intertwined with each other, as they are in the Internet dating example, you may find yourself repeating the same facts from cases as you move through each factor's individual analysis during the Rule Explanation. If that is happening, stop and think about reorganizing the explanation around the holistic stories involved in those cases.

If there are relatively few cases that you are citing for the Rule Explanation, you may also choose an alternative organization. Rather than create individualized headings for each factor with miniature CREAC argument structures, you may opt to have *no* headings, but just paragraphs of Rule Explanation. In that alternative organization, you might choose to group some of the factors together and treat them as a group to show how courts have balanced the factors in prior cases. This is how the author organized the plaintiff's argument in the Internet dating brief, Appendix B. The case law referred to six interrelated factors. The student-written brief used an organizational structure that is much more fluid or blended than six individual CREACs.

14.5.4.3   *Factor tests pop up everywhere—even in the middle of an elements test!*

Even when you have an elements test, factors frequently play an important role. For one thing, many times the presence or absence of one of the elements may itself depend on a factors analysis. For example, in our hotel reservation case, one of the elements the non-profit organization needs to prove is that it lacked bargaining power relative to the large international hotel chain. How is it to prove that it lacked bargaining power? The case law defines a set of *factors* that a court will take into consideration to determine whether the *element* of disparate bargaining power is met.

When and where to include a factors analysis depends, of course, on the substantive law that governs your case. If the substantive law requires a factors analysis, you will need to alert the reader to the fact that you are, indeed, engaging in a factors analysis, and marshal all of the factors that support your client's desired result. But do not disregard the factors that lean away from your client's preferred outcome; if you simply ignore them, you can be sure your opponent will seize upon them. Think of those factors as "adverse material" that you need to inoculate against, as you learned in Chapter 12.

14.5.5   Local overviews

The "local overview" is generally the very first thing readers encounter after the point heading introducing each section of a brief. However, you may write those overviews last since you may change your mind during the writing process about how you want to organize each section.

Because we discuss the difference between global overviews and local overviews above, we don't need to spend a lot of time here reviewing the function of the local overview. It will be helpful to remember, however, that there may be some foundational law that you need to bring in at the very beginning of any section, before you get into the detailed discussion of the legal principles involved.

One last note. As you gain more experience working on persuasive writing documents, you may (and should) start to question the existence of too many local overviews. Consider this organizational structure:

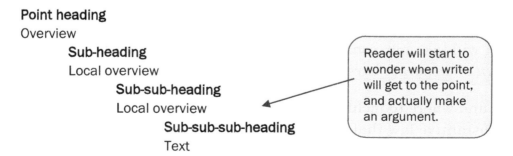

Point heading
Overview
    Sub-heading
    Local overview
        Sub-sub-heading
        Local overview
            Sub-sub-sub-heading
            Text

Reader will start to wonder when writer will get to the point, and actually make an argument.

Rather than having too many local overviews clutter up the actual argument itself, you may want to forgo some of the local overviews at the lower levels. Or you may want to reduce the amount of "mapping" information in the global overview, in lieu of doing more "mapping" in one or more of the local overviews. Readers will have a hard time remembering the sub-subcategories of information if you explain all of them on page 1 of the legal argument, even though they won't actually see those sub-subheadings until page 6 of the argument.

At this point in the writing process, you should have a complete working draft of the main parts of your brief: The Statement of Facts and the Argument section. In Part IV and the chapters to follow, we will begin to work through these drafts and turn them into polished writing that you will be proud to file with the court.

Revising, Polishing, and Finishing

Former Supreme Court Justice Louis Brandeis, himself an outstanding writer, is often quoted as having said, "There is no great writing, only great rewriting."[1]

For many writers, getting that first draft done is the hardest part of writing. But as Justice Brandeis admonishes, that is just the beginning of the process. To turn writing into "great writing" the writer must engage in the lengthy process of revising, and polishing that first working draft. Part IV of this book takes on the next two phases of writing: revising, and polishing.

Chapters 15 and 16 discuss the rewriting and revising stage. Although all sections of the brief must go through that stage, the longest time is spent on revising the Argument and Statement of Facts. Lawyers organize and shape the wording during the revising stage, by focusing on the client's point of view.

Chapters 17 and 18 focus on other formal, sections of the brief. Chapter 17 describes how to write make a good first impression in the Introduction to the brief, and a powerful final impression in the Conclusion section, which is the last thing the reader will see. Chapter 18 deals with shorter, but still vitally important, sections of the brief.

Finally, Chapter 19 will focus on the "polishing" phase of the writing process, by providing some basic principles of document design and formatting.

---

[1] There are many wonderful quotes about the pain of writing and rewriting. Here is another, from author John Irving: "More than a half, maybe as much as two-thirds of my life as a writer is rewriting. I wouldn't say I have a talent that's special. It strikes me that I have an unusual kind of stamina." One of the textbook author's favorite writing quotes is this one by Nathaniel Hawthorne, "Easy reading is damned hard writing."

Revising the Argument: Persuasive Rule Statements and Other Persuasion Techniques

At this point, you should have a working draft of your Argument section. You should be reasonably confident in the strength of your analysis, and the organization should be clear. The next step is making the working draft as persuasive as it can be. That is done by carefully revising the working draft to make sure that the client's point of view is evident throughout the Argument.

The precise wording of legal arguments matters a great deal. The language must convey the argument from your client's point of view. That point of view perspective guides the language choices across the whole of the legal argument: the headings, the rule statements, the rule explanation, and the application. This critical concept, if kept front and center in each section of the Argument, will make the legal argument that much easier to revise. And doing so will make the Argument client-centered and therefore more persuasive.

15.1 Cognitively priming your readers

As you learned in Chapter 2, "priming" your reader to receive the information you are about to convey often makes the reader more receptive to what you have to say. That is good news for advocates who need to persuade their readers.

In legal writing, strategically choosing precise words primes readers toward your client's point of view. Certain places in the legal argument lend themselves especially well to creating these types of

persuasion pressure points:

- Rule statements
- Headings
- Rule explanation "Bottom Line Up Front" thesis sentences
- Application thesis sentences

In this chapter, we look at each of these persuasion pressure points to explore how to revise an Argument to make it more persuasive. Notice that each of these pressure points is a beginning: headings begin sections; Rule Statements begin the distillation or synthesis of the governing law; "Bottom Line Up Front" sentences, in the Rule Explanation, introduce an illustration or group of illustrations; and thesis sentences connect the Rule to the client's case in the Application. This makes each of these occurrences excellent and important opportunities for priming.

15.2   Persuasively wording the rules

Like headings, Rule Statements will do a lot of the heavy lifting for your persuasion if you write them in a way that is client-centered in tone and context. The goal of your rule statement drafting should be a clear, pro-client formulation of the governing rule of law, so that a court need change only a very few words to adopt it as a holding.

When drafting rule statements, imagine the holding you want the court to write. If the holding looks very much like your own formulations of the rules, then you have written it in a client-centered way. If, however, the court has to completely rewrite or "turn around" your rule statement for your client to prevail, then you need to revisit your approach. To formulate a client-centered rule that easily translates into a holding, begin by thinking about the visual images your rules create.

15.2.1   Use client-centered imagery

Why does a persuasive rule statement strategy work? For the same reasons stated earlier in this chapter: rule statements prime readers for the examples you will illustrate during the rule explanation of the legal argument. Writing in a client-centered way also puts your readers into your client's frame of thinking. Finally, a client-centered statement will likely use some sort of imagery or metaphors that will help anchor the information in readers' minds. That imagery may be stock structures the readers call upon or images that you deliberately create with description.

Consider these two statements, both describing the same time of year:

> It was almost spring. The sun was shining, and the trees were budding. The whites and pinks of blooming trees were only a few weeks away.
>
> *versus*
>
> Winter appeared to be ending. The snow had melted and the trees were no longer bare.

Different images are formed in readers' minds for each of these descriptions. In the first, readers will likely visualize a sunny day in a season that looks something like the stock structure of "spring." (Stock structures are described in Chapter 3.) Readers are left with an impression of the season that is to come—trees in bud and about to bloom.

In contrast, readers of the second statement have a much harder time coming up with that same picture. Even though the writer's statement talks about the same period, the second statement will likely imprint an image of winter. Although the second statement talks about winter in the past tense, to get to a picture of almost-spring versus ending-winter, readers must do a great deal of original visualization work to imagine the almost-spring images contained in the first statement. Readers of that second statement will instead visualize winter, with snow and bare trees. Did you? Notice that the second sentence states the snow had *melted* and the trees were *no longer* bare! To get from there to an image of spring, there's much more effort involved. On the other hand, if the writer wants readers to visualize the end of winter instead of the beginning of spring, the second example will be more effective.

Notice, too, that in the winter and spring examples, the writers relied on assumptions of the readers' stock structures about those two seasons. That worked well in the example, but suppose you read this phrase:

> Derek spoke by phone with Nantiya, who told him where to meet her for lunch.

How do you think Derek is holding the phone? Or is he even holding it? Different people may respond differently because they have different stock structures. This may be unimportant to a Rule Statement or Rule Explanation, but if it is critical, then consider whether to overcome stock structures by using a word or two that will clarify which mental image the reader should take from her mental filing cabinet.

> While Derek was scrubbing pots and pans, he spoke by phone with Nantiya, who told him where to meet her for lunch.

Now, using inferential reasoning, the picture seems a bit clearer. Derek is very likely on a speaker phone and not holding the phone at all—unless Derek likes to take chances dropping his phone into water.

The same priming potentials exist when discussing the governing rule in an argument section. A writer can write the rule of law in a way that makes it easy for readers to imagine the writer's client prevailing. Or the writer can leave it to chance, risking a rule statement that leaves readers in a position of having to work harder to reach a conclusion that favors the writer's client. Obviously, we recommend writing the rule statement by favorably setting the context in the way that makes it easiest for the client to succeed.

What does it mean to write in a client-centered way? It means two things. The first is writing the Rule Statement in a way that favors your client or setting up a thesis sentence for the Rule Explanation that immediately creates a sense of the Bottom Line for the reader, i.e., why that image is important to the case. While you cannot rephrase the precise wording of a statute, you are not bound by the precise wording of language from a case, nor are you prohibited from including an opening contextual sentence that sets up the Rule in your client's favor. Those sentences should use or overcome stock structures accordingly. Second, have the client make a brief appearance in the Rule Statement or Rule Explanation. Have that connection between the Rule and the client begin early, not in the middle of a subsection where the readers are paying less attention.[1] We walk through examples in the next section.

15.2.2   Statutes and common law rules: the same advocacy principles apply

A lawyer's role—to analyze the governing law and to advocate for a client based on the situation—clearly extends into the communication of the governing rule of law. If the governing legal rule was so absolute as to defy advocacy, there would be no dispute. The parties would settle, since the very fact that there is a dispute must mean that the rules of law (or at least the application of the law to the facts of the case) are subject to interpretation. And thus, you must write Rule Statements with care. They are much too important to leave to a mechanistic formula of cutting and pasting from authority or, even worse, to leave to the opposing party to formulate.

This is true even when the rule you are formulating involves the interpretation of a statutory or regulatory term. While the applicable part of the statute or regulation itself must be quoted precisely, there

---

[1] Recall Figure 12-4 in Chapter 12, showing the graph of Reader Focus.

would be no dispute unless the interpretation was somehow at issue. And it is this interpretation that allows the writer to create a persuasive formulation of the rule statement.

Likewise, as you learned in the introductory semester of legal writing, if the governing rule comes from common law, the lawyer's job involves more than just quoting from the case language. A lawyer is paid to explain the analysis. In persuasive writing, that might mean generating a rule statement that is told from a different point of view than the one used by courts in that case precedent.

Below are a series of examples that demonstrate how you can revise your rule statement to reflect the client's point of view. After each example is a table explaining what certain word choices were designed to do.

15.2.2.1. *Writing about statutory law*

Even when the rule derives from a statute, lawyers still prime readers with advocacy in the way that the statute is introduced. Here is one example from a student brief on the Internet dating case. In that case, the applicable statute defined "victim of domestic violence" to include individuals who had "been subjected to domestic violence by a person with whom the victim has had a dating relationship." The issue the students were analyzing involved whether a couple whose primary contacts had been via Skype, Facebook, and other social media were in a "dating relationship." One student wrote a priming rule statement in this way:

> The New Jersey Legislature specifically called for a broad interpretation of the state's Prevention of Domestic Violence Act because of its protective purpose. Thus, courts interpreting the definition of "dating relationship" in Section 19(d) will take jurisdiction over a case such as this one, when the parties are in the type of relationship that is either family or family-like.

Here is how this client-centered formulation works:

Trigger words	Persuasive purpose
broad interpretation	The theory of the case "broad reading" is up front and center to prioritize the statutory analysis tools and to show the discretion of the trial court
protective purpose	Provides a reminder of the plaintiff's need for help
"dating relationship" in section 19(d)	Exactly quote the key phrase from the statute. We must include this in our rule statement.
take jurisdiction in a case such as this one, when the parties . . .	Wording makes it seem like taking jurisdiction is pro forma—like a permit or license. Notice, too, that the writer's **client makes a brief appearance in this rule statement.** That's perfectly acceptable in a brief in which the document exists to advocate.
when the parties . . .	The word "**when**" is more persuasive than the word "if" because "when" suggests that the action will happen. There's more certainty to it than the speculative word, "if." Your takeaway lesson is to revise **if → when**
are in the type of relationship that is either family or family-like.	"type of relationship" seems like a pretty broad tent. The "either family or family-like" phrasing is also designed to show how large a tent jurisdiction is. Parties don't have to be family. Just "family-like." Notice also how visual the statement is: the reader certainly has a mental image of what a "family" looks like, as well as a desire to protect a "family."

The judge can easily convert this formulation into a judicial decision:

> "We interpret the definition of 'victim' in Section 19(d) to allow jurisdiction over a case such as this one, when the parties are in the type of relationship that is family-like."

By carefully crafting the argument from her client's point of view, the writer has made it easier for the court to rule in her favor. First, of course, the court will look at the dispute from the client's point of view—and be more likely to adopt that same point of view. However, there is a second way that point-of-view writing helps the judge see things your client's way—the precise word choices give judges a framework for their own work. With this kind of rule statement, the judge can easily turn this into a holding with very little editing. There are very few changes in wording between the writer's rule and the court's decision.

The other party to this dispute could likewise write a persuasive rule statement. That writer, however, would develop a different theory of the case and therefore would tell a different story, even while introducing the same statutory language. Here is an example, showing the opposing story to the first example:

> Because the New Jersey Prevention of Domestic Violence Act is expansive in the scope of its relief, the appellate courts are increasingly cautious about the overstretching of the jurisdictional boundaries in Section 19(d) of the Act by expanding the scope of "dating relationship." The most recent decisions have limited the types of people who may bring an action. Trial judges must dismiss a case such as this one when the parties have only a mere casual relationship that is outside the scope of close and family, or family-like, interactions.

Trigger words	Priming purpose
Because...	Reader is primed for a policy rationale for the interpretation the writer is about to offer.
Increasingly cautious . . . over-stretching	Suggesting this court likewise be cautious and consider the particulars of a given situation (as opposed to a liberal, broad application) *Notice too, the use of visual imagery here. "Over-stretching" feels like a rubber band that has stretched too far and is weakened as a result—perhaps about to break.
Expanding the scope of "dating relationship"	Again, exactly quote the key statutory phrase.
Most recent decisions . . .	"most recent" is a powerful way to synthesize a decision or a series of decisions.
limited outside the scope mere casual relationships	Using the terms "limited" and "outside the scope" as counter-words to the opposing party's use of "broad" is much more effective than using the antonym "narrow." Particularly if the word "broad" appears in the case law and "narrow" doesn't. It's very important, when seeking to counter a particular phrase, to find words that are supported by the case law rather than simply choosing the antonym. "limited" as the antidote to "broad" is a good example of that lesson on efficacy. Notice also how these words evoke visual images. The judge is invited to see boundaries and edges; she is also invited to discount a "mere casual relationship" as not worthy of protection, because it is outside of those boundaries. She will see the relationship as merely transitory, unserious.
Trial judges must dismiss a case such as this one when . . .	Notice how the rule statement builds in the preferred outcome for this particular client.

Here is how this opposing formulation works—an easy conversion into a judicial decision:

> "The case is dismissed because the parties have only a mere casual relationship that is outside the scope of close and routine family or family-like interactions."

As with the first example, this writer's presentation of the rule statement has made it very easy for the judge to convert the writer's words into a judicial decision.

15.2.2.2. *Writing about common law*

Similarly, in a common law context, the writer can state the applicable rule of law in several ways. Below are examples, taken from the two opposing briefs in our hotel reservation example, showing how writers for the two parties made different persuasive choices in stating the same rule of law:

From the brief for the nonprofit organization:

> [A] contract provision that claims to be a liquidated damages clause will not be enforced when it merely punishes the nonperforming party. This determination is made on a case-by-case basis, without the benefit of strict guidelines, but using a number of factors. *Gershin v. Demming*, 685 N.E.2d 1125, 1127–28 (Ind. Ct. App. 1997).

Trigger words	Priming purpose
claims to be a liquidated damages clause	The word "claims" focuses the reader's attention on the possibility (which the writer advocates) that the clause really is not a liquidated damages clause, but a penalty.
will not be enforced	This language leans in the direction that the advocate wants: do not enforce this clause.
when it merely punishes the non-performing party	The client appears here, albeit somewhat indirectly, as "the non-performing party." But notice how the client (SOFT) is presented: it is at risk of being "punished." Courts should be leery of imposing unjust punishment (that's the policy behind this rule, after all), so this statement asks the court to proceed with great caution before enforcing the clause.

| case-by-case basis, without the benefit of strict guidelines | The writer knows that the reasoning of this case tilts against his client; the contractual provision, on its face, seems to obligate his client to pay the claimed damages. But the facts of the client's particular situation create a strong argument in its favor. A non-profit organization can ill afford to lose the money, while the hotel would barely notice if it were paid or not. This sentence lets the court know that facts matter, and that it has some freedom to decide the case in whatever manner seems just. |

Here is the same rule statement from the brief for the hotel:

> Whether a contractual provision stipulating damages in the event of a breach is a valid liquidated damages clause or a penalty is a question of law for the court. *Mandle v. Owens,* 164 Ind. App. 607, 610–11, 330 N.E.2d 362, 364 (1975). In determining whether the non-breaching party may recover a stipulated sum on breach of a contract, the court will consider the facts, the intention of the parties, and the reasonableness of the stipulation under the circumstances of the case. *Nylen v. Park Doral Apts.,* 535 N.E.2d 178, 184 (Ind. Ct. App. 1989).

Trigger words	**Priming purpose**
a contractual provision stipulating damages in the event of a breach	The writer wants the court to focus on the fact that this is a contract, and that it has been breached. Also, since "liquidated damages" sounds a little too much like a powerful party is taking advantage of a weaker party, the writer has described the clause as an agreement to "stipulate[e] damages," which sounds more like two equals reaching an agreement.
valid liquidated damages clause or a penalty	Here, the writer could not avoid the term "liquidated damages" since that is a term of art used by all of the court decisions. However, the writer has primed the court for a favorable ruling by placing the adjective "valid" before "liquidated damages."
In determining whether the non-breaching party may recover a stipulated sum on breach of a contract	The client shows up in this statement as "the non-breaching party." The court is reminded that it was SOFT, not the hotel, which failed to perform, and that the hotel is merely trying to "recover" from that "breach."
the court will consider	Here, the writer chooses active voice to describe the role that the court must play in deciding the case. In the SOFT brief above, the writer recited this same standard in a direct quote from a case, using the passive construction "are to be considered." This suggests that the writer of the hotel brief is recruiting the court to agree with the hotel, by directly acknowledging the court's role in the dispute.

All of these choices are subtle, but important. And just as in the statutory examples above, both rule statements are worded so that it would be easy for a court to lift the statement right out of the lawyer's brief and drop it into the court's opinion.

15.3   Persuading through headings and introductions

Priming also happens at the beginning of each subdivision of the argument.

15.3.1   Writing persuasive point headings

Headings provide contextual clues for readers, the "you are here" signals. They also stand out, visually. That means readers' eye will naturally be drawn to headings. Headings are thus perfect opportunities to persuade readers toward your client's position. Your working draft should already have headings that accurately reflect your organization. Now is when those headings are revised to better prime readers for your client's story.

Headings require careful attention. Choose the language strategically to lead readers toward the desired response: the finished and polished headings will be client-centered and will provide answers up front. The design and length also need to draw readers in rather than intimidate them. You want the audience to read your headings, not skip over them.

To start working on a persuasive heading, think about boiling the essence or purpose of that argument section down to a six-word story. Focus on exactly what that section needs to demonstrate for your client to move ahead in the argument.

To illustrate how to use the six-word story to revise a heading,

> **Try this: headings short enough for Post-its**
>
> Come up with a six-word story for each major subsection of your argument. Write it on a Post-it note and put it on your computer screen as you write that subsection.

consider opposing lawyers writing on the Internet dating case. Assume Defendant, Mr. Beagle, wants the court to focus on the limitation of the meaning of "dating relationship"— a question of law. On the other hand, Plaintiff, Ms. Hawthorne, wants to focus on the broad discretion of the trial court to determine whether a dating relationship exists—a question of procedure.

Here is what the six-word stories might look like for the headings on this point. Remember that six-word stories can be extremely informal. They exist simply as vehicles to boil down ideas to their essence.

> Defendant (Mr. Beagle): "Skype kissing isn't dating relationship-y enough."
>
> *versus*
>
> Plaintiff (Ms. Hawthorne): "Statute, judge's discretion—both are broad."

Now, compare these two headings from two student-authored briefs from the same case and about the same issue, but from opposing parties:

> Defendant (Mr. Beagle): The parties' online-only interactions never created a relationship beyond a mere friendship.
>
> *versus*
>
> Plaintiff (Ms. Hawthorne): The court has properly interpreted the expansive scope of "dating relationship" when it took jurisdiction over the case.

Notice how these headings, with each pointing toward opposite outcomes, aren't framed as mirror opposites of each other. They work toward opposite outcomes using different storylines. The first heading promises a fact analysis (i.e., the story of the parties) that will show how absurd it is for courts to allow online communication to form the basis of a "relationship" in a domestic violence scenario.

The second heading, on the other hand, is centered on the procedural story, that this case and issue was already properly decided by the trial judge, who was there to assess credibility and nonverbal behaviors. Although these two headings do not mirror each other, they both set up their argument from the perspective that best supports their client's position.

Keep in mind that, in the end, both subsections will discuss the same law. It is the frameworks that are presented differently. Both writers seek to prime readers toward a different conclusion because each writer has a different client who seeks a particular outcome. All of this comes across simply by wording the point heading to reflect the client's point of view.

> **Try this: rehearsing the skill of headings**
>
> Go back to an earlier document you wrote in your legal writing course. Imagine you now represent that client and are writing a persuasive brief. Write a persuasive heading that points toward a particular outcome that helps your client's

It is certainly possible that both authors could have constructed client-centered headings without first drafting a six-word story. However, that intermediate step—of forcing oneself to boil an argument down to its essence—can bring even the most complex analysis into crisp focus. It is a simple but effective tool for crafting persuasive headings.

The main point to keep in mind here is that headings should be told from the client's point of view. But the way in which they are presented matters too. The format and style of headings depends to some degree on writer or reader preferences or customary practices in your jurisdiction. For example, a major point heading might merit a full sentence, complete with a "because" clause that explains, succinctly, the basic reason for the outcome. Other writers might prefer shorter headings that are phrases rather than complete sentences. For subheadings and sub-subheadings, shorter phrases probably make more sense for both visual and content purposes.

(Refer to the shadow box in Chapter 13 for a discussion of some of the stylistic considerations for point headings.)

Remember that, in an appellate brief (and maybe in a longer trial court brief, if the court rules allow) your point headings will all appear, without any supporting text, in your table of contents. If the point headings make persuasive points, then the table of contents becomes a summary of your argument: one more opportunity to persuade.

15.3.2   Bottom Line Up Front (BLUF) writing

Too often, the drafting process ends before the writer moves the bottom line conclusion from—well—the bottom to upfront, where it does the work of cognitive priming. An easy acronym to use as an editing checklist reminder is "BLUF" or "bottom line up front."

Many writers start the section of an argument with a contextual client-centered sentence stating the conclusion for that section (the initial C of CREAC). Other readers put that conclusion in the point heading and begin the textual discussion with a statement of the governing rule.

Is it necessary to have an initial contextual setting (a "C") sentence in the text of the section? The answer, of course, is: it depends! Many times, the point heading is already a contextual and client-centered conclusion. If it is, there's no need to repeat the information in the text. You may lose readers' attention and interest if you do. Other times, you may start the context in the heading but include something additional in the first sentence—if that

> **Cutting and pasting cautions**
>
> If you cut and paste text straight from the Overview into the opening context of the argument subsection, you are almost guaranteed to lose credibility with your reader. Cutting and pasting is obvious and conveys a tone of disrespect—a reader assumes that the writer did not trust the reader to have read the material the first time.

happens, make sure the two are connected but not repetitive.

There's also another pragmatic reason to refrain from being repetitive between the heading and the first sentence of the subsection: it saves space. That can make a critical difference if the document is subject to a rule about maximum pages, length, lines per page, or maximum word count.

There are, however, times when it makes perfect sense to start the text of the section with the conclusion:

- When the heading is simplified for length/readability purposes, thus suggesting a need for a longer textual sentence up front. The goal here is one of readability in the heading. Headings are so important, and so easy to throw off balance with their font size and boldface, that if you see a heading that is extending too many lines, opt for a shorter one and a longer first textual sentence. The first sentence of the subsection and the heading "dance" together so it's perfectly acceptable to opt for brevity with the headings. Longer headings are often visually overwhelming.

- When the writer chooses to make the heading a statement of law rather than a client-centered statement. That's an acceptable use of headings and a common variation on the traditional CREAC paradigm (look back at Chapter 13 for those variations).

- When the person supervising your work prefers the repetition because she has doubts the headings are read with the text. Some readers do read headings separately from text, even when headings are visually close to the text. Thus, some writers prefer to repeat their conclusions in the first sentence of text to make sure that readers who skim over the headings still have the context of the argument. But even then, don't repeat the conclusions word for word. Instead, rephrase the same idea.

15.4   Rule explanation: illustrating the rule with precise details and stock structures

The same visual imagery and cognitive priming principles apply when providing readers with concrete illustrations of the rule's usage or development.

These two principles combine when a legal writer provides illustrations from case law or the like. Specifically, the purpose of providing those illustrations is to allow readers to create visual images, using either the specific details provided by the writer or stock stories or schemas. Recall from Chapter 3 that a writer uses stock stories to shape the way that the audience draws on their existing experiences, memories, or shared community understandings.

15.4.1   The storytelling of the rule explanation

Although it's critical in each argument section to provide a statement of the governing rule or section of the rule, that alone will be too abstract for readers. The analogies that the legal writer draws on for the heart of a legal argument must draw on readers' concrete concepts of the actual workings of that governing rule.

This is where story comes in again. Because humans learn best from information delivered in story form, the rule explanation part of a legal argument is best communicated as pure storytelling. Tell readers stories of what happened in other scenarios when the courts used that governing rule or subpart of the rule. That is called a case illustration, or, if it helps remind you of what you are trying to do, a "case story." Stories of the legislative intent and process can also

> **Deciding what to include in a case illustration**
>
> • What details and stock structures can you use that will put an indelible image in the reader's mind?
>
> • What unique facts of a case story did the court rely upon to decide *this part* of the governing rule?
>
> • Did the court comment on the importance of those unique facts, or signal their importance, using detail in the description?
>
> • Did the court imply importance or imply a lack of importance by using or not using detail in the description?
>
> • How do those unique facts (or lack of unique facts) ultimately measure up to those of your client's situation?

form part of the overall rule's explanation when you have a statutory issue.

To keep the client's point of view front and center, the legal writer must choose carefully which details to focus on and, most importantly, to have readers focus on.

Think back to Chapter 9's discussion of description and the four things that can be described:

- Actions
- Objects
- Settings
- People

Readers will want to know a general sense of where or when the key events took place and who or what was involved. The whole story of the case need not appear in the rule explanation, but parts of it will.

Because the legal writer typically needs to convey the illustration in a relatively few number of words, using stock structures to convey meaning takes on a special significance. The reader wants to know, *generally*, the types of characters or objects involved, the setting, and events, but the writer will want to rely on common understandings of many of those things. That permits him to guide readers toward only those specific details that really matter to understand that particular subsection's rule.

This means that the careful writer needs to strike a balance. On the one hand, the writer can't skimp on the information because that will leave readers with the need to read the authority for themselves to understand the writer's reliance on it. But, at the same time, the writer has to take care to avoid overloading readers with information that might clutter or distract them from the unique facts that are important to that particular subsection's argument.

This generally translates into providing three pieces of information to readers with each cited case: the basic story of the conflict, the holding of the case and any important reasoning, and the outcome of the case (meaning who won).

For example, in the Internet dating case, the respondent relies on the case *J.S. v. J.F.* The first draft of writing a case illustration for that case might forget to include the priming language up front. That would make it less effective. It looks like this:

In *J.S. v. J.F.*, 983 A.2d 1151, 1152 (N.J. Super. Ct. App. Div. 2009), the defendant claimed that the parties were not dating because he allegedly paid for the plaintiff to accompany him to his family's Thanksgiving dinner. But, testimony demonstrated that the parties had multiple dates, dinners, evenings together, and other regular interactions as a couple. The state appellate court found that, even if the defendant had, in fact, paid for the plaintiff's company, the evidence also described multiple other dates, dinners, and evenings together. And, the court held that arrangements to pay for the "dating" do not necessarily end the dating inquiry. The appellate court affirmed the trial court's denial of the defendant's motion to dismiss the action.	These are the basic facts without priming Here is the court's holding and reasoning This is how the case came out

While that case illustration is completely accurate, it is fairly neutral in tone—it does not provide priming context for the reader. A more persuasive way of illustrating this case, with the cognitive prime, would be something like this:

In one recent case with a relationship much more traditional than the one in front of the court today, the court ruled that the parties in that case were in a common form of a dating relationship. *J.S. v. J.F.*, 983 A.2d 1151, 1152 (N.J. Super. Ct. App. Div. 2009). In that case, although the defendant claimed that the plaintiff was merely someone whom he had paid to accompany him to his family's Thanksgiving dinner, the testimony at the final restraining order hearing demonstrated a typical relationship involving multiple dates and evenings in each other's company. Even if the defendant had, in fact, paid for the plaintiff's company, the court held that fact did not preclude further inquiry into the nature of the relationship.	Important information (outcome and holding). Note also: priming. Basic facts Reasoning, Note use of detail.

Note the priming language, "with a relationship much more traditional than the one in front of the court today." The facts then go on to discuss a dating relationship of multiple dates the parties had. The Thanksgiving dinner details were really beside the point. The author chose to emphasize these details to show that even peculiar relationships (who pays for someone to go to Thanksgiving dinner?) can be part of dating when the parties are with each other multiple times. The case reader is primed to understand that this case is distinguishable. Perhaps more important, it makes the story of this case memorable.

Of course, how a writer puts these elements together is a strategy decision and will depend on how much reliance or weight the lawyer wants the reviewing court to give the case.

15.4.2   Write about case illustrations by putting the bottom line up front

In this part of the analysis you also want to use a thesis up front. Readers' attention waxes and wanes throughout the reading process. Generally, audience attention increases when the reader encounters new things.[2] A point heading marks the beginning of something new, just as a paragraph does. The writer must take advantage of these moments of attention, or "positions of emphasis," to make persuasive points.

As with any other position of emphasis, the thesis sentence that introduces the case illustration will likewise focus readers on those details that matter. It is much more persuasive to start the rule explanation with the bottom line up front rather than with the case name and citation. In the argument section of an advocacy document, these illustrations are there as part of the advocacy. Begin them with advocacy statements.

Compare this thesis sentence to a case illustration:

> In the case of *XYZ Corporation v. Random Individual*, 341 O.Y. 792 (2015) the court discussed the question of whether corporations have free speech rights.

---

[2] Again, refer to Chapter 12, Figure 12-4, showing a chart of the reader's focus.

with this better one:

> Because the First Amendment protects speakers and not
> speech, corporations have the right to spend money in direct
> support of political candidates. *XYZ Corporation v. Random
> Individual*, 341 O.Y. 792 (2015).

Which thesis statement has more impact? The second one: the important information appears up front.

Omit the phrase "In the xyz case" to avoid lists of blurbs. A thesis instead will help you move away from writing about cases in a "list-y" manner. Notice, how, in the second example, the case name and citation appeared after the sentence rather than serving as the lead off. Placing the case name and citation in the position of emphasis in a paragraph is a waste of the prime persuasion real estate of that paragraph. Revise these descriptions so they work for your client rather than serving as a book-report. Advocate instead of summarizing.

15.4.3 Choosing the length of the rule explanation: in-text versus parentheticals

A writer has choices about how much space to use for writing about a particular case's story. Those choices range from a clause (a parenthetical) to in text sentences, paragraphs, or pages. In some situations, only a brief statement of what the case stands for, followed by a citation, is necessary (typically where the rule stated is well settled, easy to apply, and uncontroversial). In other cases, some context about the facts of the case is necessary to help readers understand how the rule works. That context might be as little as a parenthetical explanation following the case citation or as much as one or more paragraphs, or even pages, providing a great deal of background and discussion about the case (a case illustration). These choices lie along a continuum; different situations call for different choices along that continuum.

There's no need to allot a full paragraph to each case discussed in an argument section. In fact, it's often a much stronger arguing technique to discuss several cases together in a single paragraph that starts with an overarching thesis sentence.

Deciding whether to use parentheticals or in-text explanations really depends on how much information readers need to understand about that case and how important the case is to the outcome of that subsection of argument. There are no hard and fast formulas, but only competing strategy considerations. For that reason, a good brief will have a mix of case explanation lengths.

At some point, the length of the document starts to become an important consideration. There's also a limit to how much a writer wants to include from a particular case in any one subsection. Only part of the case story is important for that subsection. It's at that point that the writer has a choice between in-text or parenthetical presentation of the case information.

15.4.3.1   *Will an illustration help readers at all?*

A great deal of the time, the answer to this question is yes. Only in the simplest of situations can a writer allow stock structures to carry the day. One test is how debatable the point being offered is. As noted earlier in this textbook, there's generally not a lot of debate, for example, about whether a labradoodle is a dog for the purposes of interpreting a dog bite statute. If you were citing a case for that point, a parenthetical is all you would need. On the other hand, the writer might need to use more detailed case explanations to talk about whether a dog licking someone falls under the definition of "bite."

An example of an effective use of a parenthetical instead of a full case illustration is found in the hotel's brief in our hotel room reservation case:

> In some cases, a dispute has arisen as to whether a
> liquidated damages provision is the exclusive remedy or

> whether a nonbreaching party may seek relief in addition
> to liquidated damages. *See, e.g., Beck v. Mason*, 580
> N.E.2d 290, 293 (Ind. Ct. App. 1991) (holding that
> describing an earnest money deposit in a real estate
> sales contract as "liquidated damages" was sufficient
> proof that the parties intended to limit their remedies to
> that clause).

15.4.3.2   *How important is the case to the argument?*

If the case is central to the dispositive argument, then it is better to opt for a more detailed illustration for that case. If the case illustration is not dispositive but is merely supportive of the argument, then it is possible that a single sentence or a parenthetical clause may suffice.

15.4.3.3   *How complicated are the facts of the case?*

Even if a case is not dispositive, the context of the facts may still take a few sentences to explain to readers. In that situation, opt for better writing: choose to use in-text sentences. Remember that the choice can still be one sentence, two sentences, three sentences, or more. A writer is never committed to a full paragraph about a case unless she wishes to commit that much space.

15.4.4   Drafting parentheticals

Parentheticals appear at the end of a citation sentence. They are typically clauses or phrases, as opposed to full sentences. Parentheticals might use single words or single descriptors. They might also borrow a quotation from a case that helps explain the rule further.

There are common pitfalls to parentheticals, the most prevalent of which is using a parenthetical to restate the abstract rule rather than using a story or a piece of a story to illustrate an example of the rule's use. Because this is such a common error, it's a good idea to check parentheticals for their content.

There are three different ways to use parentheticals. Some are more common than others. The bottom line for any legal writer is to choose among these and to draft accordingly.

15.4.4.1 Narrative parentheticals

Narrative parentheticals are the most common type. These substitute for an in-text rule explanation and provide enough detail about the story of the case to give readers a sense of what happened as it pertains to the subsections' rule statement. Often, but not always, this is the parenthetical that begins with present participles: the *-ing* words. For example, the brief of the Gloucester Hotel in our hotel reservation case includes this citation:

> *See, e.g., Beck v. Mason*, 580 N.E.2d 290, 293 (Ind. Ct. App. 1991) (holding that describing an earnest money deposit in a real estate sales contract as "liquidated damages" was sufficient proof that the parties intended to limit their remedies to that clause).

15.4.4.2   List parentheticals

List parentheticals are shorter forms of narrative parentheticals. These parentheticals can provide the relevant case information in just a word or two. Something like this:

> Oregon courts cast a wide net when contemplating what constitutes a pavement hazard that gives rise to a commercial owner's duty. *Gardener v. Portland Nursery*, 321 P.3d 622 (Or. 2004) (overgrown rosebushes); *MacTarnahan v. McMenamin*, 814 P.2d 802 (Or. 1982) (beer keg); *Blumenauer v. Wyden*, 409 P.3d 112 (Or. App. 2010) (spilled recycling can); *Beard v. Ringside Restaurant, Inc.*, 248 P.3d 624 (Or. App. 2002) (bag of root vegetables).[3]

---

[3] Do not rely on these cases as authority. We made them up!

15.4.4.3   Quote parentheticals

This last type borrows exact language from a decision. Quotes used in this last—and rarest—type of parenthetical often are where a writer mistakenly restates the legal rule. Instead, quote parentheticals should show a particular turn of phrase that adds concreteness to an otherwise abstract rule. One situation where it makes sense to use a quote in a parenthetical is where a metaphor has become central to a legal principle, like this:

> *Reynolds v. U.S.*, 98 U.S. 145, 164 (1878) (recognizing Jefferson's metaphor of the "wall of separation between church and state").

When your authority provides precise language like a metaphor or term of art, it is appropriate to quote that precise language in a parenthetical. Still, be careful that you are quoting language that helps explain the asserted legal principle rather than merely restating the principle itself.

Consider this passage from the hotel's brief in our hotel reservation example. In discussing when liquidated damages provisions in contracts are appropriate, the author notes the rule that such clauses are valid when the specified damages are not grossly disproportionate to the damages that would likely result from a breach. The brief goes on:

> [I]t is important to remember that this determination is evaluated as of the time of the signing of the contract, not at the time of breach. *Rogers*, 767 N.E.2d at 991 (liquidated damages clauses are unenforceable where the payment specified "is grossly disproportionate to the loss *which may result* from breach") (emphasis supplied); *Gershin*, 685 N.E.2d at 1128 (liquidated damages clauses are enforceable where the payment specified "is not greatly disproportionate to the loss *likely to occur*") (emphasis supplied).

The writer chose to cite two cases to emphasize the point that the determination is viewed from the point of view of the parties at the time they signed the contract. Since different courts expressed that concept in different language, the writer chose two different formulations of the rule to show that it is well settled and uncontroversial.

15.5   Application to the client's facts

So now you have written your Rule Statements and Rule Explanation, so that they favor your client's position. Now it is time to apply those rules to your client's case to show why the law supports a ruling in favor of your client. Many of the same principles discussed above about drafting a persuasive rule statement also apply to drafting a persuasive application.

The first thing that a reader should see in any paragraph of Application is a thesis sentence. A Bottom Line Up Front. Just as writing a case illustration as a "case story" helps readers retain information about the case, including vivid details of the client's story helps readers see how a ruling in favor of the client will assist that client in achieving his worthy goal, whatever it may be. The connecting of the rules to the client's facts is a golden opportunity to overtly shape the client's story, or at least some important part of the story.

Application can be straightforward, such as where there is a clear statute directly on point or a nearly identical case. Or, as is more likely, it can be more complex and nuanced, such as where the applicable authority is unclear or novel. In either scenario, the writer's primary goal in application is to connect the client's case to the governing rule, as explained with the authorities used in the rule explanation.

The best lawyering will involve analogies that go beyond the surface, and will instead focus on form or function. A **functional analogy**, also known as a **structural analogy**, looks at how something works rather than just at the surface-layer similarities. For example, one can draw a functional analogy between an iPhone and a filing cabinet. They might look very different, and they aren't precisely the same things, but they do perform similar functions at least in one regard. That type of analogy requires a bit more depth of understanding to it than an analogy between an iPhone and a landline phone.

The analysis or application is not based in absolutes, either, but is susceptible to interpretation. This is where advocacy truly matters, which also helps explain why the synthesis must be situated up front. To illustrate this point, here is a visual exercise. Create a single enclosed space by connecting all four of these dots:

Which answer is correct?

All of them! The difference will lie in the contextual sentence that begins the discussion.

Most people would connect the dots in the most obvious way—by drawing a square. That is activation of the stock structure of being presented with four dots in that sequence. However, nothing in the instruction required this. In fact, there are an endless number of ways to connect the dots that would be consistent with the instruction. The stock structure can be overcome and sometimes might need overcoming. This is very different than misrepresenting or misleading a reader. It is the very nature of advocacy—asking a decision-maker to sometimes connect the dots in a different way. That's also the take-home message about connecting dots in legal analysis: sometimes you need to look beyond the obvious or superficial connections between your authorities and your case. Doing so can reveal new and meaningful insights.

In the application, it is best to craft your writing to be as response reinforcing as possible, rather than response changing. Remember back to Chapter 2 and the idea that response reinforcing is the easiest way to persuade somebody because the audience will be predisposed toward accepting the argument. The more you can show how your client's position is consistent with the judge's likely perceptions (or "frames") about what is fair and just, the easier it will be to persuade the judge that the client is right. This, of course, invites the question, how do we build a response-reinforcing argument? Following are situations you may find yourself in, including how to find response-reinforcing ways to apply the law to your facts.

15.5.1   Show how your legal position is consistent with existing precedent (arguing by analogy)

If the rule of law you are applying is a common law rule, it is obviously easiest to persuade a court when the facts of your client's case are materially identical with the facts of binding cases that were decided in a way that favors your client's

> **A time to tell**
>
> Throughout this text, we have suggested that you should "show" your client's story to the reader, through the use of good visual detail, rather than "tell" the reader what the story is (or how to feel about it). In application, however, there is a bit of an exception. If you have previously shown the court what the case is about, in applying the law to the facts you can do a bit of telling.
>
> Thus, it would be perfectly okay to write something like "our case is just like the *Jones* case because, like *Jones*, the plaintiff in our case was similarly desperate to find the right shade of auburn hair."

position. When you have such a case (which lawyers describe as a case being "on all fours" with your case), writing the application is easy: you just show how the facts of your case are materially identical and argue that the same result should apply.

However, clients are rarely that lucky. More often, a dispute exists because there is more than one way to interpret and apply existing law and reasonable minds may differ on the most appropriate interpretation of existing law. Where novice legal writers sometimes fail is that they are unable to get beyond the surface of the precedent cases to reach a deeper understanding of what the existing law really means. Often a lawyer can find a more persuasive application of the law by looking for different ways to explain how the client's case is similar to the case law than might appear at first blush. Consider this passage from the Rule Explanation in the brief of the non-profit organization in our hotel reservation example:

> In one case, a hotel was required to refund the plaintiff's deposit because of the otherwise disproportionate loss that the plaintiff would have suffered. *2625 Bldg. Corp. v. Deutsch*, 179 Ind. App. 425, 385 N.E.2d 1189 (1979). In that case, the plaintiff reserved six hotel rooms during the weekend of the Indianapolis 500 race and, upon doing so, paid $1,008.00 to the hotel, representing the full cost of the rooms. Two months prior to the reservation dates, the plaintiff cancelled the reservations and requested a refund. The hotel refused to return any of the advance payment. *Id.* at 1190.

Note that the case is introduced with a BLUF sentence.

> Although the contract in that case was oral and thus included no express liquidated damages clause, the court held that allowing the hotel "to retain damages representing payment for use of all the rooms, regardless of the fact that damages could be ascertained, would be to enforce a penalty or forfeiture." *Id.* at 1192. Moreover, "assessing Deutsch for the full amount of his room payments would cause him to suffer a loss which was wholly disproportionate to any injury sustained

by [the hotel]." *Id.* at 1193. The court therefore ruled that the
defendant hotel was required to refund the plaintiff's deposit.

Recall that the issue in our case is whether a liquidated damages
clause in a written contract should be enforced or held to be an
unenforceable penalty. At first glance, the case of *2625 Building
Corp. v. Deutsch* appears to be unhelpful because the hotel
reservation in that case was made orally and there was therefore
no written liquidated damages clause to interpret. But look at the
reasoning of the court: "retain[ing] damages representing
payment for use of all the rooms, regardless of the fact that
damages could be ascertained, would be to enforce a penalty or
forfeiture." And doing so "would cause him to suffer a loss which
was wholly disproportionate to any injury sustained" by the
hotel. This sure sounds like the same rationale used by courts in
interpreting written liquidated damages clauses. So, the author
of the non-profit brief chose to include this case, along with other
cases that did involve written contracts, and thereby managed to
connect a case with very similar facts (i.e., a hotel getting paid
for rooms not used by the party reserving them) to the facts of
her own case, hoping that the case would reinforce the response
the judge likely shares: it is unfair for the hotel to keep
somebody's money when it can resell those rooms to somebody
else. Then, in the application of the rule to the client's facts, the
author applied the lesson of *2624 Building Corp.* like this:

> It is true that just as the court in *2625 Building Corp.* found
> that damages in the event of a breach were easily
> ascertainable, damages in this case
> are easily ascertainable: the Hotel
> sent an invoice to SOFT for exactly 53
> unused guest rooms. Freebird Dep.
> Ex. 3. More important, however, just
> as the court in *2625 Building Corp.*
> held that charging the patron who
> reserved the rooms but did not use
> them for the full value of those rooms was wholly

> **Functional analogy** in use
> here. Some of the facts on
> the surface may look similar.
> However, it's the prior court's
> reasoning using those facts
> that truly matters in this
> situation. The case helps the
> non-profit organization.

disproportionate to any injury sustained by the hotel, charging SOFT with the full value of the rooms its members did not use is similarly grossly disproportionate to any loss the Hotel might suffer. This is because the Hotel admittedly resold the rooms not reserved by members of SOFT. Pl.'s Answer to Req. for Produc. of Doc. ¶6.

15.5.2   Show how your position is materially different from precedent, and therefore should have the opposite result (arguing by distinction)

The opposite of a case "on all fours," or a "bullseye" case of course, is a case that appears to reach a result contrary to what your client wants, on similar but not identical facts. In this situation, your comparison takes this form: "The case precedent says *x*, but the following dispositive facts are different. Since those facts were so important to the court's reasoning, and our case lacks those facts, the result in our case should be negative *x*." This is called "reasoning by distinction." It is another example of reasoning by function rather than by surface characteristics.

Here is an example of reasoning by distinction based on (but for the purposes of brevity, altered from) a description in the Defendant's brief in the Internet dating example. This example also reasoning by comparison to a group of cases rather than to individual ones. Recall that in that case, the Defendant, Mr. Beagle, was trying to prove that he was not in a "dating relationship" with Plaintiff, Ms. Hawthorne. One of the applicable cases could be illustrated like this:

In *Andrews,* the plaintiff and defendant were in a relationship for five months while the woman defendant had another boyfriend. 363 *N.J. Super.* 252 (Law. Div. 2003). The parties held themselves out as a couple in front of the plaintiff's family, but because of the defendant's other boyfriend, they hid their relationship from

> The importance of putting these facts up front will become obvious in the application. Reader has a sense "five months of many

> the defendant's family. *Id.* at 260. They were seen kissing, hugging, and being affectionate, and they went out at least 15 times over the course of a few months. *Id.* They would spend nights together, and they attended a number of social gatherings together. *Id.* at 261–62. The defendant argued that because she was in another relationship at the time, she could not be held to be in a dating relationship with the plaintiff. *Id.* Nevertheless, the court found that the sum of the circumstances sufficiently established that a dating relationship existed. *Id.* at 265.

Later in the brief, in applying that case, along with others, to his own facts, Defendant, Mr. Beagle writes to distinguish that case from his own situation:

> Previous cases have shown that there is usually a significant period of time, and frequent contact between the parties, before a dating relationship can be found. In *Andrews,* the parties dated for four months, went out on at least 15 dates, were seen hugging and kissing, and on occasion spent nights together. 363 *N.J. Super.* 252 .... Since Mr. Beagle and Ms. Hawthorne met briefly in person only twice (once at a speed dating event and a second time by chance at a New Years' Eve party a few weeks later) and were never physically intimate, Ms. Hawthorne is unable to establish that the parties were in a dating relationship.

> The *structure* and *function* of the relationships in the cases—as a group rather than individually—are compared and distinguished from the situation in front of the court

The most important thing to remember here is that, for reasoning by distinction to work, the distinction must be material. Distinguishing on the structure of the relationship—time, number of interactions—is material. Surface comparisons would not persuade as effectively. Thus, you would most likely never win by saying "The plaintiff in that case had red hair. Since my client has black hair, that case does not apply." Make sure that there is something in the reasoning of the court that suggests that the facts you are distinguishing made a difference, and be sure to quote that reasoning in the case illustration so that you can refer to it in the application. The petitioner in the example above did this by reporting the facts that the court in *Andrews* apparently found persuasive in determining that the parties were in a dating relationship, and then contrasting the facts of his own case with the facts reported in *Andrews*.

15.5.3   Show how the plain meaning of a statute directly supports the result your client wants

When instead of a common law rule you are dealing with a statutory rule, if possible, show the court how the statute unambiguously requires the court to rule in your client's favor.

In rare situations, that requires little more than reporting the facts of the case and showing the court how the express and unambiguous language of the statute requires the result the client seeks. This is rare because, if true, the parties would likely settle instead of bring suit. But if there is some ambiguity as to whether the statute applies or what it means, then the writer must examine and explain the rule more fully through statutory interpretation techniques, as described in Chapter 10. Once that is complete, the application is simply a matter of connecting the explanation of what the rule is to the specific facts of your case, similar to the manner of comparing precedent cases to the facts of your case.

15.5.4   If a statute appears to contradict the result your client wants, show how the statute does not apply

This is the corollary to "arguing by distinction" where the governing law is a common law rule. The only difference here is that you need to look for definitions within the statute, or previous court interpretations of the statute, that show why the statute does not cover your client's situation. The same caveat also applies here: make sure the difference between your case and what the statute covers is material.

After polishing the Argument section of your brief, it is time to rework the Statement of Facts in similar fashion.

Revising the Story to Strengthen the Theme

The working draft is now complete. The persuasion pressure points are in place. The brief looks like … a brief. It is time to start revising the working draft. Revising, in the latter stages, focuses on word choice and precision. Start with sections you wrote first so that you can account for any drift in the theme or the theory of the case that occurred during the later stages of writing the working draft.

The Prologue of this book began with the truism that **writing is thinking**. So many "A-ha!" moments happen while composing at the keyboard, that it is quite natural for legal writers to shift the original theory of the case or theme during the writing and revising stages. Now is the time to go back to the parts of the brief you wrote early on and conform them to the later-written sections. Budget a few days to do some additional work on the Statement of Facts. Doing that work will make it much easier to see what revising needs to be done in the Argument section. At the end of this process, and as the last major step, the other sections are added to the brief—the Introduction and any other parts required by the governing court rules.

16.1 A sequence for revising across the major parts of the document

Although there is no set order to revising and conforming the various sections of your brief, this chapter models one method of walking through the process. The sequence, shown in Figure 16-1, may appeal to you or you may decide to create your own. The real lesson here is to create and use a method of some sort that makes sure you ultimately have a completed document that is a coherent whole.

Figure 16-1: Late revising sequence

- Start by revisiting the **Facts section** of the brief.

- Afterward, go back and revisit the narrative explanations of the cited cases in the **Rule Explanation**. Did you choose the unique facts that illustrate why the court ruled the way it did? Because you have just read the Facts section again, new ideas may jump out about what the critical or relevant unique facts are from those cited cases that can be and should be used. Even at this late stage, remaining curious about new ideas can pay dividends. Remember that the facts of the cited cases are there to provide concrete—again, unique—examples that illustrate stories about the synthesized Rule statements; they are also there to be compared to your client's facts in the **Application** portion of your argument.

- As you are revising the **Rule Explanation**, the wording of the synthesized **Rule Statements** might also need some revising. Similarly, the wording of the **headings** might need some touching up. Look carefully at the language of both the Rule statements and the headings to assess whether it is presented affirmatively, from your client's point of view.

Last, because the whole legal argument may have shifted since the

> ### Avoid pitfalls when describing a character
>
> Be particularly mindful of including too much description about a character in one place in the Statement of Facts, especially in the opening paragraphs of the Facts Section. Including too many details about a character could easily create the legal reader's skepticism because those details can look like a blatant appeal to pity rather than to relevancy.
>
> Instead, if you want to include information about your client's science fair coaching, or going back to college while a single parent, sprinkle those details throughout the Statement of Facts and connect them as relevant to other actions or settings you describe. "Changing the tires meant that he could not get home from the campus, where he takes college classes, in time to pick up the two sons he is raising alone."

last reworking of the global and local overviews, reread those and check for consistency with the headings and the rule statements. Also read the overviews for repetition—if the Rule statement in an Argument section also appears verbatim or close to verbatim in the overview, decide the appropriate locale, and eliminate or condense the wording in the other locale.

16.2   Revising the facts

Because some time has probably elapsed since your last rereading of the Statement of Facts (or equivalent), the section may seem a bit stale, in need of a makeover. That section should now—hopefully—read as almost unfamiliar, as if someone else wrote it. This disconnection phenomenon is a useful asset to the writer in the late revising stage of the writing process. Because the writer's connection to the material has been broken, it's now possible to more accurately read the material as a first-time reader would. Critically assess: will the reader understand the client's story being told and the storytelling goal? What are the takeaway story moments?

16.2.1   Reworking "telling" to become "showing" description

In the early working drafts of the facts section of the brief, you replaced the "tell" words in the shadow story with evidence and detail that "show" the story. Use this later revising process to look at any remaining judgment or opinion words, other than those that have cites to the record or those that are quotations of the parties. Does the description include your judgment? Those will distract the reader, and lead her to fall out of the story (*see* Chapter 9.3.5). Eliminate your opinion, substituting words of pure imagery. Figure 16-2 illustrates the difference between words that tell and words that show.

"Tell" phrase that shows judgment		Revised to "show" phrases, showing description
a perfect day	⟹	a crisp late-October day with a breeze and temperatures in the mid-50s.
a huge and heavy piece of furniture	⟹	A 5-foot-high china cabinet of solid oak, fitted with brass handles, and filled with two 12-person place settings of china.
Jane is a sweet, elderly lady who has been sued by cantankerous neighbors who claim that her house addition has disturbed their right to quiet enjoyment of their own property.	⟹	She is 83 years old, and has lived in the same house that she and her husband bought, together, 50 years ago. She added a 9' x 12' screened porch to her home, with the money she saved from decades of making jams and jellies and selling them at local farm stands. On that porch her two Corgis like to sleep at night.

This also works in the legal argument section		
The opposing counsel's reliance on that case is wholly without merit	⟹	Although it may first appear that the case is similar, the facts are actually very different from this situation [fill in details about the differences].

Figure 16-2: Words that tell vs. words that show

Remember, we show by adding specific details that illustrate what our conclusions tell.

16.2.2   Organizational revising: Using headings to prime the reader

Recall that the beginnings and ends of sections and paragraphs are emphasis points. They are the places to highlight key and helpful material. Show the facts with detail and use other emphasis techniques such as active voice. The middle of sections and paragraphs, in contrast, are the de-emphasis places. In those places you should minimize your use of detail. Other de-emphasis techniques include the strategic use of passive voice, dependent clauses, and longer, more complex sentences and paragraphs.

To create more beginnings and ends within the Statement of Facts, consider including headings. Headings in the Statement of Facts are optional. They may help show a transition, if the story is told topically as well as chronologically. Headings will also add more beginning points, which in turn creates more possibilities for emphasis. And, of course, headings themselves provide pressure points in persuasion because they are visually distinct from the text. Note that in the hotel reservation case sample briefs, the two parties made opposite choices here. The nonprofit organization SOFT included headings in its Statement of Facts (Appendix D), while the Gloucester Hotel did not (Appendix C). This is probably because the organization arranged the story topically and used headings to introduce each new topic; the hotel chose to tell its story chronologically.

On the other hand, headings might detract from the section by interrupting the story's flow. And there's another caution to heed. Headings in the Statement of Facts must be factual, just as the text. Unlike the headings in the legal argument section, this section's headings should use descriptive "show" wording rather than the conclusory "tell" phrases that are more appropriate for headings in the legal argument section of the brief.

16.3   Revising across the brief

These next several revising steps are useful for both the Statement of Facts and the Argument sections of the brief.

16.3.1 Visual impact moments in the Statement of Facts

Professor James P. Eyster recommends that, while revising, legal writers think about what visual images from the client's story linger the longest in the mind.[1] These might be images that were created because the writer described certain events, settings, objects, or characters in the most detail. Or they might be images that the writer deliberately created by including unique, incongruous, or unexpected facts.

Each party in a case wants readers to have a different take-home visual image about the facts of the case—those memorable moments that crystallize the case and perhaps influence the outcome. These are called "visual impact moments." Think carefully about what your client wants the visual impact moments to be. Revise accordingly. Also think carefully about what the opposing attorney may set up as the visual impact moment for her client.

> **The Incongruous in Linda Brown's story**
>
> Reread the story of Linda Brown excerpted in the Prologue. Note that the whites-only school that was closest to Linda's house was named the Sumner School. Its namesake, Charles Sumner, was an abolitionist leader. The irony that the school was later designated for whites only is an incongruous—and therefore memorable—detail that sticks with the reader. Did you just see, in your mind, the name "The Sumner School" on a school building you recalled from your mental filing cabinet of memories and images? The writer intended that. This is an example of a writer's deliberate use of an unexpected visual object, meant to create a visual memory for the reader.

Consider this example from the brief of the Gloucester Hotel in the hotel reservation example. The following brief passage is taken from the Statement of Facts section of the hotel's brief:

> [The hotel manager] prepared the standard hotel contract for a group reservation and mailed it to SOFT's headquarters in Eureka, California. *Id.* at 11:10–14. It was returned by mail about ten days later, and the reserved block was entered into the hotel's reservation system. *Id.* at 12:3–6.

---

[1] James Parry Eyster, *The Lawyer as Artist: Using Significant Moments and Obtuse Objects to Enhance Advocacy*, 14 J. LEGAL WRITING 87 (2008) (an excellent discussion of visual impact moments and unexpected visual objects).

Nothing at first seems remarkable about that passage. But if you got the image that Eureka is located in a particularly scenic part of the country, near giant redwood trees, and that the organization was not in a major hurry to get the contract in place (since it took "about ten days" to sign and return the contract), then the writer has accomplished her visual purpose.

The details are there to help create a visual impact moment. In the Argument section, the hotel lawyer's choice to use detail in the Statement of Facts becomes apparent when she mirrors the amount of detail in a case illustration. There, the author discusses the case *Sanford v. Castleton Health Care Center*. Her case illustration for that case includes this description:

> In *Sanford v. Castleton Health Care Center*, 813 N.E.2d 411 (Ind. Ct. App. 2004), the plaintiff sought to avoid enforcement of an unambiguous provision of a contract with a health care institution for the care of her mother. The plaintiff brought her mother to the Castleton Health Care Center for treatment. During the admission process, her mother, who suffered from Alzheimer's, became agitated and aggressive; in addition, the plaintiff had to care for her own children who were with her as she completed the form. As a result, she signed the health care contract without reading it, although she admitted that nobody at the care facility prevented her from doing so.

The plaintiff in *Sanford* unsuccessfully attempted to argue that because of the chaos during the admission process, she should be excused from enforcement of an onerous provision of the contract because she hadn't had time to read the contract before she signed it. But the court enforced the contract anyway. This sets up a wonderful *a fortiori* type of argument for the Gloucester Hotel:

> Here, SOFT has even less reason to avoid the unambiguous contract language than did the plaintiff in *Sanford*. Ms. Pat Freebird, the SOFT Executive Director, testified that she received the contract in the mail in her office in Eureka, California, and that she had enough time to review its provisions to be sure they conformed to her understanding of the reservation she wanted to make. Freebird Dep. at 9:2–10:14. There was no chaos or

> confusion, or really any sort of time pressure; the contract was
> returned to the hotel ten days after it was sent. Mason Dep. at
> 12:3–6. Accordingly, the contract is enforceable on its own terms.

Readers are treated to two contrasting visual impact moments: the chaos of admitting an agitated, mentally impaired woman in need of immediate care to a nursing home, compared to the calm and tranquility of reviewing a contract in the comfort of one's own office, nestled amongst giant trees. If the first situation was not a reason to avoid a contract term, certainly the second could not succeed either.

The non-profit organization, of course, wants readers to have a completely different mental image about the moment when the contract was formed. The organization's theme is something of a David vs. Goliath story: a huge, multibillion-dollar international corporation that would never miss $9,000, against a small organization of people passionate about environmental causes, to whom $9,000 is a very large amount of money. One of the legal theories the organization advances in its defense is that the amount stated as liquidated damages is really an unenforceable penalty. One of the factors a court considers in determining whether the stated amount is a penalty is whether the amount stated is "grossly disproportionate" to the amount of anticipated damages. So, the organization describes itself in its Statement of the Facts this way:

> Ms. Pat Freebird, now thirty-two years old, formed Save Our
> Forest Trees (SOFT) shortly after being awarded a bachelor's
> degree in biology and volunteering her time with other
> nonprofits and environmental advocacy groups. While her
> title is Executive Director for SOFT, in fact she is the
> organization's only employee, working long hours to realize
> its mission of connecting scientists and environmentalists to
> share their research findings and discuss ways to bring
> awareness to the problem of deforestation and climate
> change. Freebird Dep. 2:14–3:9, Aug. 20, 2013.
>
> SOFT's headquarters are in Ms. Freebird's home, although
> she charges no rent to SOFT. Operating costs are kept to a
> bare minimum by communicating and advertising primarily

> over the Internet and through e-mail. Ms. Freebird herself
> earns only $30,000 in income, although she is a full-time
> employee. *Id.*

This creates a very different visual image than the one that Gloucester tries to paint, and sets up SOFT's theme that it is being taken advantage of by a much larger and far more powerful organization.

16.3.2   Connecting the Facts to the Argument

One purpose of the Statement of Facts is to set up the theme that makes readers *want* to rule in your client's favor. On the other hand, the Argument provides the denouement to the story; it gives the legal justification for readers to rule for your client. The two major sections must work in tandem. Now is the time to test that. Check to see whether each fact that the legal argument relies on is included in the Statement of Facts. If there are pieces missing in the Statement of Facts—introduced for the first time only in the legal argument's application material—they must be added to the Statement of Facts.

Once you have ensured that all the facts referenced in the Argument section are also included in the Facts section, the next step is to ensure that the theme comes through both sections. This can be difficult, but there are a few things you can do to ensure the two sections are meshing effectively:

- **Reread the Argument section quickly, then summarize the essence of the argument in a single sentence.** That sentence should reflect your theme. For example, the theme of the Dating Relationship brief in Appendix B might be "the Legislature intended 'dating relationship' to be broadly construed to protect all victims of domestic violence."

- **Next, reread the Facts section. Is the story's conflict connected to the theme of the Argument section?** The Facts section should set the stage for the Argument section. Thus, a critical reader should be able to anticipate the theme of the Argument just from reading the facts. For example, in the Facts section of Appendix B, the story highlights the extensive relationship between the plaintiff and the defendant. While that relationship existed primarily on-line, the story shows it developing much like a more typical, in-person relationship. That story of a budding romance gone wrong primes the reader for the arguments that follow.

- **Make sure the inferences flow from the facts.** Review Chapter 13 for the discussion of inferential streams.

- **Check for a match between key word choices in the Facts statement with key word choices in the Argument section**. The specific, detailed descriptive words in the Facts sections should be repeated in the Argument. The more general stock structure phrases should also match in both sections. Our goal should be to match the tone, or feel, of the Facts with that of the Argument. If, on the other hand, the story seems to get left behind in the Facts section, and the Arguments seems to stand independent and unconnected to the Facts, this is a sign that further revising is needed. In that case, work through the Argument, looking for ways to connect the arguments to the story in the Facts.

The priming function of the Statement of Facts works only when all of those critical facts are introduced to readers before they are used in the Argument section.

16.3.3 Choosing the way to refer to the characters

As the theme and theory of the case evolve, so might the way you refer to different characters in the legal story. Although the characters have already been named in the Statement of Facts, those names or descriptive designations could change throughout the drafting process. Which stock structures do you want to use? This is the time to make those final choices.

Using stock structures rather than party designations will also humanize the characters because they will call up mental images. Humanizing characters allows readers to connect more easily with them. Readers are more likely to identify with named persons than they are with characters who are only referenced by their party designations. Balanced against that, however, is the relatively common inability people have to remember too many proper names. For this reason, it is important to rely on stock structures for many of the supporting characters. For example, a witness might be referred to in terms of her relationship to one of the litigants: "The Gloucester Hotel's business manager" or "Plaintiff's sister."

> **Descriptors vs names in case illustrations**
>
> In the case explanation or illustration of the Rule it is almost always better to use a descriptive stock structure for a character rather than a proper name. The use of proper names becomes far too unwieldy given the other names the legal writer asks the audience to remember. Which descriptor to use becomes a strategy decision for the lawyer. At times, "Plaintiff" might be the best option. In many other situations, however, it is useful for the lawyer to summon a mental image for the audience with a word or phrase of description about that plaintiff. For example, "Plaintiff, a law student . . ." would certainly catch your attention and make that case illustration a bit more memorable, wouldn't it?

There are no formulas for determining how to refer to characters, including the opposing party or even one's own client. Lawyers must consider what each option conveys in terms of the tone or stock structure or visual image. A first name might convey a sense of familiarity, as if the person should be viewed in a casual manner. That may be appropriate in a particular type of case. It is common in family law cases, for example. Using someone's title might convey more formality—which might be the appropriate tone for a client in a business dispute.

Similarly, the choice of nomenclature for the opposing party is a careful strategy decision that depends on the theory of the case. That is why it is a late decision. The phrase "defendant" carries certain stock structures in our culture—ones that are not necessarily positive. Thus, if your client is a defendant, you might want to use different nomenclature.

One last caution about party nomenclature—you should be consistent in your approach. It might be tempting to refer to your client as "Widow Jones" and to the opposing party as "the defendant." After all, this approach humanizes your client and dehumanizes her opponent. However, this is also a rather transparent ploy that readers will quickly recognize. If you choose to refer to your client by her name, it's best to refer to the opposing party by name as well. And Widow Jones still looks pretty empathetic against, say, "Acme Loan Sharks."

16.3.4 Strategizing word choices

Certain types of words create especially vivid mental images for readers. The English language is filled with nuanced meanings that a writer can call on to create mental images. The more precise an image the writer needs to create, the more precise the word needed.

Broad	Narrow	Precise
Telephone	cell phone	iPhone
he fell	he plunged	he plummeted
busy customer agreeing to hotel contract	**distracted** customer agreeing to hotel contract	**harried** customer agreeing to a hotel contract

Of course, different word choices convey different levels of precision. Which one you choose depends on the circumstances. Sometimes, for example, the most precise word is critical. At other times, a very precise word might be too distracting. But most words fall on a continuum of broad to more precise.

Here are some general guidelines:

- Verbs often create powerful images, especially when used in the active voice. "The storm **raged** around the farm, **obliterating** the wheat crop." To deemphasize, consider using a less specific word and passive voice for verbs, but use the latter strategy judiciously. Every legal writer is taught this technique, which means that every legal reader (such as a judge) knows how to spot it, too. An example is "the wheat crop was lost" (leaving open the questions by whom? how?)

> **How to understand the persuasion of active versus passive voice**
>
> In general, active voice focuses on the character doing the action ("The judge overruled the objection."). Passive voice, in contrast, focuses on the action, with the character fading into the background ("The objection was overruled."). Passive voice works as a persuasive strategy when the action is more important than the actor. But, much of the time the legal writer wants to create a mental image of a character doing the action. The differences become important when the character doing the action is being studied to determine a burden of proof or a standard on appeal.

- Nouns, especially precise ones, also aid mental imagery. For example, what image does this sentence evoke?

Nora felt she could trust the man at her door.

Now consider this similar sentence:

Nora felt she could trust the police officer at her door.

The second sentence, which uses a much more specific noun, creates a very different mental image. Nouns create the specificity.

- Adjectives and adverbs can describe or can convey opinion or judgment. Although these sorts of descriptor words are problematic in the Statement of Facts (unless used as part of a quotation from the record), they can be acceptable in the Argument when used within the bounds of respect and professionalism.

- Pronouns are useful shortcuts but can be confusing if they do not refer to the most recently used noun. For example, consider the following sentence: "Rob told Jason that as soon as his ship came in, all his troubles would disappear." Whose ship is coming? Whose troubles will disappear?

That shape-shifter word, "not"

The word "not" will probably appear dozens of times in early drafts of your persuasive document. It's a very hard word to avoid using. But then, cold and flu viruses are numerous too, and nobody thinks they are advantageous. Take note: It's a bad strategy to balance the weight of your persuasion on the word "not." This small word is easily forgotten or misplaced, and it may actually give your opponent's argument an unintended boost. "Why?" you ask.

Picture this: **It did not rain today.**

Did you first picture rain? Many people do. This response is common because the readers' minds easily let go or omit the word "not," at least as a starting point to form the image. Other more memorable words in the sentence take over.

Compounding the issue of having a lack of imagery is the length of the word "not" itself. It's easily omitted or inserted accidentally. Many writers discover this type of error only after they have finalized their document—or when someone else discovers the error for them. Whether "not" is mistakenly omitted or inserted, readers are left to understand the sentence means exactly the opposite of what the writer intends.

The spoken "not" carries less of this risk because the speaker can use inflection to add tonal emphasis and therefore make it more memorable in the sentence. But, in writing, it is both impractical, and also unprofessional, to boldface, underline, or italicize every appearance of "not" in a document.

And then there's the tone to the word "not" as a counter to the opposing party's point of view. Writing a story that is merely the opposite of your opponent's is much less persuasive than telling a different and competing story. Whenever possible, the better strategy is to change the sentence structure altogether, so it becomes an affirmative statement of something descriptive that favors your client. Doing so almost guarantees that the story or the rules of law are told from your client's perspective.

As a demonstration of changing a sentence's entire structure, go back to the sentence, "It did not rain today." Here are some options that tell a more affirmative story from a different perspective:

- It was sunny today.
- It failed to rain today.
- The drought continued into today.

Keep in mind, though, that sometimes a writer deliberately chooses to use the word "not" (e.g., when she *wants* you to think about rain).

A writer cannot entirely eradicate the word "not" from a document of any length. It's too prevalent in our language. But it's important to keep an eye on the usage overall, and to substitute as often as possible. The most critical places to substitute something else for "not" are in the **headings** and **thesis sentences** of the legal argument. The student-authored sample briefs in the appendices offer strong examples.

It's worth spending a few extra words (and minutes) to make substitute for "not."

16.4   What happens next in the writing process?

After these sections and major persuasion pressure points are reread and revised, the legal writer typically adds in the last sections of the brief. The whole document is then formatted—visually designed for persuasion—and then polished.

Chief among those last sections is the Introduction, which provides readers with an opening contextual frame for the writer's case theory. The next chapter discusses Introduction in more detail.

Making the First and Last Impressions: The Introduction and the Conclusion Sections

In persuasive documents, we want to take advantage of every opportunity to persuade our reader. Recalling Chapter 12, the beginning and end of any piece of writing are positions of emphasis and often our strongest persuasion opportunities. However, many briefs forego these opportunities by writing perfunctory Introduction and Conclusion sections. This chapter explores how to bookend persuasive documents with powerful and persuasive Introductions and Conclusions. We begin, though, with a visit to the movies.

17.1 The Power of the Introduction

Think about the movie trailer. In two and a half minutes, a trailer has to convey to the audience enough information about a movie to convince the audience to see the new movie. From a typical trailer, we learn the movie's genre, the central characters, the location both in time and space, and the essence of the plot. More important, we get a "feel" for the movie—and know whether it's likely to be

> **Speaking of trailers . . .**
>
> Have you ever wondered why they're called movie "trailers"? Back in the early days of the movie industry, the promotions for the upcoming attractions were shown *after* the feature film; that is, they trailed the movie. However, the movie moguls soon realized that most of the audience didn't stick around to see the trailers. Soon, they began showing the trailers before the movie, when they had a captive audience.
>
> Though for different reasons, a legal writer should recognize that, like movie trailers, the Preliminary Statement is best placed before the feature length version of the client's story!

a movie we want to see. A good movie trailer is itself a mini-story, designed to sell the much bigger story of the movie.

In a brief, the Introduction section (sometimes called the **Preliminary Statement**) is similar to a movie trailer. It is an opportunity to introduce the essential elements of the argument in a condensed form. It is not, however, merely a summary of the extended analysis of the Argument section. Rather, it is a carefully crafted, free-standing version of a client's story. Like a good trailer, it may reveal some of the essential scenes of the upcoming story, but more importantly, it will introduce the central characters, the context for the story, and the theme that will carry through the rest of the brief.

There is another parallel between movie trailers and Introduction sections. Both can be critical to the success of the larger project. First impressions matter because they prime the audience. Just as a movie trailer creates expectations in the viewer about the upcoming movie, an Introduction prepares the reader for what is coming in the remainder of the brief. In other words, a good Introduction section primes reader to agree with the arguments that follow (see discussion of priming in Chapter 15). Consequently, the Introduction section should be crafted with care, specifically designed to show the audience the strength of the client's cause.

Introduction sections in briefs are a relatively new phenomenon. Many briefs filed in both state and federal courts now include them. They are based on the same cognitive science and theory of priming—both cognitive and affective—that we introduced in Chapter 2. While we discuss the formal parts of the brief, as required by various rules of courts, in the next chapter, this section of the brief deserves special attention because of the strategy choices that lawyers have.

Many court rules, especially appellate court rules, neither require Introductions, nor even mention them as a typical part of any brief. The Federal Rules of Appellate Procedure have no such reference, for example. But that does not mean that the rules prohibit them; indeed, an increasing number of federal appellate briefs now include them as a first section. The persuasive value of making a strong impression with the first substantive thing readers will see suggests that you should always include an Introduction as an opening section of your brief,[1] unless your local court rules specifically prohibit you from doing so.

17.1.1   Planning the Introduction

The first step toward creating a successful Introduction is to identify the central theme of the case. By the time you are ready to write the Introduction, that central theme should be well defined (*see* Chapter 9). Next, determine how to best convey that theme in a short statement. To do so, think about the many moving parts that make up your persuasive Argument section. You know that the structure of every story consists of a leading character, that character's goals, and the obstacles between the character and her goals. Usually, that leading character, or hero, is going to be your client.

Every story also has conflict, and that conflict drives one or more plots and subplots (*see* Chapters 3 and 9). However, as we learned in Chapter 3, every lawsuit has potentially three intertwining conflicts or plots: the conflict giving rise to the client's storyline; the conflict in the law's storyline; and the conflict within the lawsuit's storyline, i.e., a procedural conflict.

Though you may think that your client's conflict is the most important, that may not always be the case. Thus, it is useful to think about all three possible storylines when developing your

---

[1] A recent empirical study in which judges read different Introductions to the same brief led those judges to very different first impressions of the case, proving that Introductions are very powerful tools for persuasion. Kenneth Chestek, *Fear and Loathing in Persuasive Writing: An Empirical Study of the Effects of the Negativity Bias*, 17 LEGAL COMMUNICATION & RHETORIC: JALWD 1 (2017).

Introduction. One way to do this is to chart the three storylines of your case and then decide which one is the most important at the current phase of the lawsuit:

	Character	Goal	Obstacle
Client's storyline			
Law's storyline			
Lawsuit's storyline			

Complete the chart with the specific elements of each storyline. You should already be familiar with your client's story—that is the whole reason for the brief, after all—and the obstacles that are hindering the client from reaching his goal. However, to help achieve that goal, you may also need to explore and resolve conflict within the law. What was the legislature's goal in passing a statute? What was the court's goal in establishing precedent? Likewise, the client's lawsuit may be at a point of procedural conflict. How have the parties progressed to this point in the litigation? Is the complaint sufficiently pleaded? Has a statute of limitations expired? What other procedural obstacles might be relevant at this stage?

Not every case will present all three storylines, at least not at the same time; but some cases will involve two or all three storylines. The relative importance of a storyline depends on the specifics of the particular case. But for the Introduction, select the theme for the brief by focusing on the key elements of the conflicts presented.

For example, consider the respondent's Introduction from the Internet dating case. Here's how you might build the story chart in this case:

	Character	Goal	Obstacle
Client's storyline	Plaintiff (Ms. Hawthorne)	Getting on with her life safely	Threats of abuse from Defendant (Mr. Beagle)
Law's storyline	Legislature, appellate judges	Protecting victims of domestic violence	Anticipating potential domestic relationships warranting protection
Lawsuit's storyline	trial judge	Properly apply statute	Appellant's misunderstanding of judge's discretion

As this chart shows, the author of this brief has three storylines—the conflict arising out of the parties' relationship, the conflict about the scope of the law, and the conflict about the trial court's discretion in interpreting the law (a procedural question). It is possible that all three storylines will appear throughout the brief. However, for the Introduction, the author will want to focus on the storyline that is most important to the case, usually the story line the author judges most likely to lead to success for the client.

At first blush, it may seem that the relationship between the parties is the most powerful storyline. After all, the respondent, Ms. Hawthorne, is an empathetic character, and the petitioner, Mr. Beagle, is an abuser. However, we also know that the characterizing of their interactions as a "dating relationship" is the weak link in this case. Focusing on the parties' relationship could be problematic. On the other hand, the respondent, Ms. Hawthorne, has already won in the trial court. The trial judge has broad discretion to interpret this statute that should be broadly construed. In fact, it looks like the procedural storyline—emphasizing the judge's discretion—may be the best story line for Ms. Hawthorne. Here is how the author translated that storyline into the Introduction:

Introduction

Plaintiff-Respondent, Ms. Elaina Hawthorne, began this domestic violence case in January 2010, seeking a Temporary Restraining Order (TRO) against Defendant-Petitioner, Arthur Beagle. The TRO was granted, and, per standard procedures, the date for a full hearing on the merits of a Final Restraining Order (FRO) was set for two weeks later. Ms. Hawthorne sought this protection based on Defendant-Petitioner Arthur Beagle's threatening and harassing conduct toward her just after the parties' breakup. Prior to the scheduled FRO hearing date, Defendant-Petitioner filed a motion to dismiss, challenging this Court's jurisdiction to hear the matter. This Court held a hearing on the sole issue of whether the parties' relationship falls under the jurisdictional category of "dating." At the end of that proceeding, and after hearing testimony from the parties, plus two other witnesses, this Court issued a written opinion, concluding that the parties did, in fact, have the requisite dating relationship, pursuant to N.J.S.A. 2C:25-19(d), and that Ms. Hawthorne was entitled to a hearing on the merits of a Final Restraining Order.

Nevertheless, Defendant-Petitioner has filed, also at the family, trial level, this Motion for Reconsideration of this Court's written opinion finding jurisdiction. This response brief, thus, is filed on behalf of Plaintiff-Respondent, Elaina Hawthorne, in opposition to that Motion for Reconsideration. By liberally construing the Prevention of Domestic Violence Act, this Court's opinion properly gave effect to the Legislature's intent and followed the guidance of prior appellate case law. Accordingly, Ms. Hawthorne respectfully requests that this Court deny Defendant-Petitioner's Motion for Reconsideration and move forward with the scheduled hearing on the merits of her application for a FRO.

Notice that the first paragraph goes into considerable detail about the procedure leading to the FRO. This detail suggests that the court has followed all the steps necessary to issue the FRO. Mr. Beagle has had the opportunity to make his case and lost. The trial court did its job. Without going into extensive detail, the Introduction established the theme of the case: this appeal should be dismissed on procedural grounds.

Notice also what is missing in the Introduction. There is very little mention of the relationship between the parties. Ms. Hawthorne's lawyer mentions Mr. Beagle's harassing conduct, but provides no insight into the parties' dating relationship. Surely, the lawyer for Ms. Hawthorne will need to address this storyline in the Argument, but she wisely chose not to mention that at the outset. Having primed the audience for the strongest part of her Argument, the author has set the stage for the rest of the brief.

The Introduction doesn't need to explain every part of all three potential storylines. Rather, it needs only to bring out the core theme of the broader story. Here, that was the trial court's properly exercising discretion—the procedural storyline. In a different dispute, the core theme may depend on understanding the client herself or the conflict underlying the substantive legal issues. By charting out the intertwined storylines, it is easier to identify the core of the story that you want to use to build the Introduction.

17.1.2. Expressing the theme of your Argument

Once you have decided on what storylines you want in your Introduction, you need to decide on how you will tell that story to effectively reveal the theme of your Argument. Remember, the purpose of the Introduction is to make a strong first impression— to get readers thinking about the legal issues from your client's point of view.

Usually, the most important part of a story is the central character. The identity of that character depends on the conflict you are describing, however. For the story of the parties, the leading character is likely your client. On the other hand, for the story of the law, the leading character is often the legislature (for statutory issues), or the courts (for case law). The leading character of the story of the procedure may be the judge, a party, or even a lawyer, depending on the nature of the issue. But, whether your primary focus is the conflict between the parties, the conflict within the law, or the conflict within the lawsuit, your Introduction should be sure to introduce the leading character.

17.1.3.   Developing the character in an Introduction

If the chosen theme focuses on the conflict between the parties, the leading character is most likely your client. Thus, introduce your client in a way that makes the first impression you want readers to have about the client. For example, notice how one lawyer introduced the client in a case before the United States Supreme Court to set up the rest of the Introduction:[2]

> Petitioner Michael Turner was incarcerated for 12 months after a South Carolina family court held him in civil contempt of a court order to pay child support for respondent Rebecca Price's (now Rogers's) minor child. The contempt order provided that Turner could purge his contempt and gain release from jail if he paid his arrearage in full (nearly $6,000), but Turner, who is indigent, was unable to pay, and he served the full sentence.
>
> Turner was not represented by counsel at the contempt hearing, nor did the court advise him of his right to counsel. Had counsel been appointed, Turner could have made the evidentiary demonstration and legal arguments necessary to establish that he could not pay the thousands of dollars he owed, which, under South Carolina law and this Court's decisions addressing civil contempt, would have been a complete defense precluding his incarceration. Instead, Turner was left to defend himself (to no avail) and was jailed, in effect, for being too poor to pay.
>
> This 12-month sentence was neither the first time nor the last that Turner has been incarcerated for failure to pay child support without the aid of counsel. Because Price had received public assistance benefits, she assigned her right to child support to the South Carolina Department of Social Services (DSS), and the child-support enforcement proceedings against Turner became subject to automatic procedures carried out by DSS and the family court. Each time Turner's account fell into arrears, the court was required by

[2] *Turner v. Rogers*, 564 U.S. 431 (2011).

law automatically to issue a rule to show cause why Turner should not be held in contempt. Turner has been incarcerated in this manner several times, and so long as he continues to owe unpaid child support, he will continue to face automatic contempt proceedings and the threat of incarceration. Indeed, Turner is presently in jail again for failure to pay child support.

In the decision below, the Supreme Court of South Carolina rejected Turner's argument that he was constitutionally entitled to appointment of counsel at the contempt hearing. Notwithstanding this Court's decisions that have found a right to counsel in both criminal and civil proceedings that carry with them the "awesome prospect of incarceration," *In re Gault*, 387 U.S. 1, 36–37 (1967), the court held that the right to counsel applies only in criminal contempt proceedings. In reaching that conclusion, the court relied on the assumption that a civil contempt sanction is "conditional" and may be avoided through compliance with the underlying court order. But whether Turner in fact had the ability to avoid incarceration by complying with the child support order—and thus whether he could be sentenced to jail for coercive purposes in a civil proceeding at all—was the precise question before the family court. As a matter of fundamental fairness, Turner should have been afforded the assistance of counsel to show that he could not. The state court's contrary decision cannot be reconciled with this Court's teachings on the right to counsel, the special character and purpose of civil contempt, or the requirements of due process. This Court should reverse the judgment below.[3]

The short opening paragraph quickly tells us important facts about the client: he was incarcerated for a year for contempt of court; he is indigent. The next two paragraphs reinforce these facts: the petitioner is indigent and the only reason he was repeatedly incarcerated was that he was too poor to pay his child support and too poor to hire legal counsel. In three paragraphs, the writer has

---

[3] Petrs.' Br., Michael Turner, *Turner v. Rogers*, 2011 WL 49898 at *2–*4.

established the central character of this story and developed
empathy for him; readers can put themselves in his shoes—the
government has disrupted his life because of his poverty.

This example illustrates techniques for developing the character of
the story. First, the central character, the petitioner, is the first
character introduced—indeed, his introduction is where the author
begins. In most stories, the central character is the first party we
meet. By introducing the petitioner at the outset, readers are quickly
oriented and know who this story is about.

Look at the words used to describe the petitioner and his challenge.
He is "indigent." He was "incarcerated" for being "too poor to pay."
The author has not chosen words that are obvious appeals to
emotion. Instead, this appears to be an objective, matter-of-fact
description of the client. This not only creates empathy for the client,
but it also builds the author's ethos because she is not presenting an
overtly biased description of the central character. She does not
oversell her client's story.

The final paragraph then briefly connects the story of the client to the
legal and procedural conflicts within the case. Notice that there is only a
brief mention of the underlying legal analysis. Instead, the central theme
of this case is one of fundamental fairness: the government should not be
putting indigent people in jail merely because they are too poor to pay
their child support. While the writer needs to show how that theme is
consistent with the law, she need not make that connection in the
Introduction. The writer has set the stage—revealed the essence of the
case—and now readers are primed for the Argument that follows.

17.1.4.   Developing the conflict and the goal of the story

If you have chosen to focus on the story of the law instead of the parties'
storyline, you may not need to develop the character as much.

For example, if the key storyline is the conflict about the meaning of a statute, the central character (e.g., the legislature) may not be the most important aspect of the storyline. If you have a statutory interpretation issue where both sides agree on the underlying facts but disagree as to the meaning of the statute, you may want to write your Introduction to highlight the legislature's *goal* in enacting the statute. Of course, you may also choose to focus on the conflict about the law plot-line when your client is not particularly empathetic but has a strong legal position.

If you are trying to resolve a conflict within the law, it is likely that the main character will be the legislature that enacted the statute or the courts that have developed the law through cases. Statutory issues require determining the legislature's intent. In other words, you must find the goal of the legislative body that is the central character of the story. Consider this opening paragraph from a case before the United States Supreme Court:[4]

> The Torture Victim Protection Act of 1991 ("TVPA" or the "Act") provides that "[a]n individual who ... subjects an individual" to torture or extrajudicial killing under color of foreign law shall be liable "to that individual" or "to that individual's legal representative, or to any person who may be a claimant in an action for wrongful death." 28 U.S.C. §1350 note §2(a). The question in this case is whether the term "individual" in that statute means what it almost invariably means in ordinary and legal usage—a natural person or human being. That question all but answers itself. While "person" often encompasses corporations and similar entities, "individual" does not. Indeed, Congress replaced the word "person" in an earlier draft of the statute with "individual" precisely to exclude organizations from liability.[5]

---

[4] *Mohamad v. Palestinian Auth.*, 132 S. Ct. 1702 (2012).
[5] Respt.'s Br., Palestinian Auth., *Mohamad v. Palestinian Auth.*, 2012 WL 293720 at *1–*2.

This opening paragraph simply identifies the relevant statute and states the question before the court. But in doing so, the author primes readers to assume the answer to that question. The issue is posed as one of whether "individual" means what "it almost invariably means in ordinary and legal usage …." Legal readers will likely intuitively extract the author's primary argument: Congress intends statutory words to be given their plain meaning. This point is reinforced in the last two sentences of the paragraph that provide further explicit details that reinforce the goal Congress had in enacting this statute.

In his first paragraph, the author identifies Congress' goal as to the meaning of "individual" in the statute. The rest of the Introduction goes on to develop this idea:

> The TVPA brings certain international human rights violations within the civil jurisdiction of U.S. courts. Mindful that it was creating a private cause of action with extraordinary extraterritorial reach, Congress proceeded carefully, tailoring the statute to achieve a limited but important purpose. By imposing liability on the responsible "individual," the Act prevents human rights violators from seeking safe haven in the United States. But by precluding suit against organizations alleged to be responsible for the individual's conduct (often the state itself), Congress limited the risk of international discord and potential interference with the Executive's conduct of foreign policy. Giving "individual" its ordinary meaning respects the careful balance Congress struck. The judgment of the court of appeals should accordingly be affirmed.

In this final paragraph, the author keeps his focus on the goal of Congress. And it appears to be a very thoughtful Congress indeed. It was "mindful" and "proceeded carefully" to create a statute that "limited the risk" of international discord and in doing so struck a "careful balance" that demands interpreting "individual" as the author proposes. The author has established his theme by telling the story of the law. The central character of that story is Congress.

More important, the goal of that character—to find a balanced approach to regulating human rights violations—demands that the court resolve this conflict in favor of the author's client.

17.1.5. Wrap-Up

The Introduction should capture the theme of your brief. Think about the three potential storylines in your lawsuit: conflict between the parties, conflict about the law, and conflict about the procedure. Within each of those storylines are characters, conflicts, and goals. One storyline is likely to lie at the heart of your argument. That is what your Introduction should express.

An Introduction sets the stage for your entire brief. It needs to identify the central theme of your argument and prime readers for what follows. It does not need to tell the entire story, however. That will come later. In fact, an Introduction that is too long may undermine its force. Like a good movie trailer, a good Introduction will leave your audience curious, wanting to know more about your client's story. It should not leave your audience thinking that it has already seen the entire story.

> **Hearing your theme**
>
> As we write, it is sometimes difficult to tell if our theme is coming through our words. One simple test of the effectiveness of your theme is to read your Introduction aloud. Hearing our words can help us better judge how our reader is likely to "hear" our words. If reading the Introduction makes you feel how you want your reader to feel (empathetic, curious, supportive?), then you are on the right track. To test this, try reading aloud one of the Introductions in this chapter to see if you find it persuasive.

17.2 Making the final impression: writing a persuasive conclusion

It is time to bring the story to an end. In terms of the plot of the brief, we now need to write the denouement, the appropriate and satisfying ending. The legal argument demonstrated a logical and plausible way to resolve the conflicts and to return the characters to a state of calm. The resolution can be a return to the prior condition of stasis (a *restorative* resolution) or to a new, yet tranquil and satisfying, condition (a *transformative* resolution).[6]

In a typical brief, the Conclusion section does not finish the story. Rather, the Conclusion asks the court to finish the story by ruling in favor of the party who wrote the brief. A common Conclusion section might look like this:

> For the reasons stated, this court should grant the Defendant's Motion to Dismiss.

Per the Federal Rules of Appellate Procedure and many state rules as well, that single sentence constitutes a perfectly good Conclusion section. It complies with the admonition that an appellate brief includes, "a short conclusion stating the precise relief sought." But those court rules are permissive rather than mandatory. You may write more than one sentence, although you should heed the admonition to keep things very short.

Recall again from Chapter 12 that positions of emphasis occur every time the reader encounters something new: the beginning of a section, the beginning of a paragraph; but they can also occur at the end of things, when the reader expects a "big finish." The analogy here is a song. Some end with a repeat and fade out, such as many songs mixed for radio play; the reader is not quite sure the precise second the song ends... Other songs end definitively with a more satisfying resolution, through the device of recapitulation (a return to the main themes developed in the song) or a coda (some interesting variation of those themes), or a big a "ta dum!" such as with show tunes.

The one-sentence Conclusion that most attorneys write is a type of a repeat and fade, without the "repeat." After working through page

---

[6] Anthony G. Amsterdam & Jerome Bruner, MINDING THE LAW 113–114 (2000).

after page of sophisticated and articulate legal analysis and persuasion, the reader deserves a more satisfying ending. One appellate attorney blogger talks about the one-sentence Conclusion as looking like the writer is simply too tired of the brief to do more than bring it to an end.[7] The late Justice Antonin Scalia, along with his co-author Bryan Garner, called the one-sentence Conclusion "hopelessly feeble."[8] Instead, they called for writers to include a true conclusion, "one or two paragraphs encapsulating your winning syllogism in a fresh and vivid way."[9]

Take a look at the Conclusion of the brief on behalf of the Hotel, in Appendix C:

Conclusion

SOFT freely entered into a contract in which it reserved the exclusive right to book a specific number of rooms at the Gloucester Indianapolis Hotel for its guests. The Gloucester Hotel, relying on that promise, gave up other business opportunities, in exchange for a reasonable liquidated damages provision expressly proportioned to estimate the actual loss that might occur if SOFT failed to sell the number of rooms it promised to sell. The mere fact that SOFT may now regret its agreement is not a sufficient reason to avoid the contract. This Court should enforce the liquidated damages clause and enter judgment in favor of the Gloucester Hotel in the amount of $9,480.38.

Appendix D contains a similarly-styled Conclusion on behalf of the non-profit organization.

While this Conclusion does not conform to the typical practice of writing a simple, one-sentence conclusion, it is hard to argue that this paragraph violates FRAP 28(a)(9). It is short (just one simple paragraph), and it states the precise relief sought (entry of judgment

---

[7] Mike Skotnicki, *The Conclusion May Be at the End, But That Doesn't Mean It Isn't Important*, BRIEFLY WRITING BLOG (April 16, 2012), https://brieflywriting.com/2012/04/16/the-conclusion-may-be-at-the-end-but-that-doesnt-mean-it-isnt-important/

[8] Antonin Scalia and Bryan Garner, MAKING THE CASE 38 (2008).

[9] *Id.* at 100.

in the client's favor in a specific amount). Stated another way, the one-sentence Conclusion may be sufficient to satisfy FRAP 28(a)(9) and similar state rules, but it is not optimal.

Since you have the reader's attention at the very end of the brief, take advantage of it. Because it is short and at the end, the reader's attention will be focused. There's an opportunity for persuasion at a point of visual emphasis. Use the Conclusion to:

- Remind the reader of your theme (i.e. why the court should feel good about ruling in your client's favor)
- Remind the reader of the legal theory of the case (i.e., why the court is permitted to rule in your client's favor
- Remind the reader of the critical fact(s) unless doing so would be highly repetitive of prior sections
- State specifically what it is you want the court to do.

In the Conclusion to the brief written on behalf of the Hotel, quoted above, the writer reminds the court of the major themes (freedom of contract, personal responsibility, and fairness) as well as the law of contracts on which its claim is based. And the final sentence precisely states the relief sought. Ta dum!

To do this in your own writing, have the Conclusion touch very briefly on the main issues discussed in the Argument section. Ideally, the Conclusion will tie them all up in a neat package that is consistent with your chosen theme, and that neat little package will take up very little space. No one wants to read a full page of Conclusion. Distill, as quickly as possible, the nugget of takeaways of each major issue you discuss, bringing in the key facts from your client's story to show why the conclusion is emotionally satisfying. Then conclude with a statement specifying what you want the court to do. In some ways, it is like a summary for an audience now well-versed in the facts and law.

Although a well-crafted metaphor or pithy wrap-up statement in this section can make an argument more memorable, the Conclusion is not a place for hyperbole or snark. Being too aggressive can also backfire. Judges are among the most skeptical of readers, and generally react badly to being told what they "must" do. Couch the ultimate conclusion in terms of what is right or fair or just; not what is required:

> **Troublesome language in a conclusion:** Because the Appellant has failed to carry the heavy burden of persuasion in this case, this Court necessarily must affirm the judgment of the court below.

> **Better language in a conclusion:** Because the evidence cited by the plaintiff fails to meet the required clear and convincing standard, this Court should affirm the judgment of the court below.

A final caution: remember that while the conclusion need not be only one sentence, it must still be *short*. It cannot be a complete rehash of the Summary of the Argument or even as detailed as a global overview. The goal is a concise and powerful finish that captures the essence of your Argument.

We are nearing completion of the brief-writing process! The next chapter helps you with the more formal and logistical parts of the brief, including tables, issue statements, and other sections that may be required by the applicable rules of procedure (either appellate or trial level).

Finishing Up: The Other Parts of a Brief

By this point in your legal career, you know the importance of rules—seemingly the law is nothing but! However, many law students, and surprisingly even some lawyers, overlook an important set of rules—those governing the documents submitted to courts. But since you are reading this chapter, this certainly won't be you.

18.1 Overview: the contents of a brief depend on the rules of the court

The large-scale requirements of a brief are governed by a jurisdiction's court rules. These rules typically differ, depending on whether the brief is trial level or appellate.

Looking at the governing court rules is a critical step. The wise lawyer looks at those requirements early rather than just before filing the brief. Courts are sticklers for those rules, and for that reason, lawyers must also be sticklers. A lawyer we know told us this story about an appeal he worked on early in his career:

> Back in the days when virtually all court documents were only available in hard copy, I had a case before the United States Federal Circuit Court of Appeals. This was the first time our firm had appeared before this court. Naturally, we were very careful to follow the court rules for how to prepare briefs and records. As it turned out, the court rules required that the page numbers of the record appear at the bottom center of the page. The transcript of the hearing below had the pages on the top right-hand corner. Accordingly, we very carefully added a second set of page numbers to the bottom center of each page. Shortly after we attempted to file the brief, the court administrator notified us that our brief was rejected because it had page numbers in two places. We

> had to reprint and resubmit all 50 copies of the briefs
> after whiting out the page numbers in the corner.

As should be apparent from this story, when you file documents with a court, you should pay strict attention to the rules governing those documents.

Each jurisdiction has its own unique set of rules. The rules for a trial-level brief in Oregon will require different things than the rules for a trial-level brief in New Jersey. And the rules for a trial-level brief in Wyoming will require different things than the rules for an appellate brief in Wyoming.

In addition to looking at rules governing the type of brief (i.e., trial level, summary judgment, appellate, etc.), there are also often two sets of rules that apply to court documents: those rules that apply across the applicable legal system (for example, the Federal Rules of Appellate Procedure) and those that apply only to the specific court, colloquially referred to as "local rules" (e.g., the Rules of the Seventh Circuit Court of Appeals). Within these sets of rules are two types of rules: those that govern the substance of a document and those that cover the form of the document.

This chapter deals primarily with the rules for appellate briefs since those rules are typically more specific than rules for trial-level briefs. In fact, many trial courts have no rules, or only very minimal rules, for what should go into a brief. Our best advice is to look at the local rules for the court where you will be filing your brief, and follow them. And don't be surprised if you can't find rules for the substance of a trial-level brief.

18.2   Requirements of the Federal Rules of Appellate Procedure

To illustrate what you are likely to find in the court rules, this section walks through the Federal Rules of Appellate Procedure

(FRAP). Of course, the rules that apply to your particular legal issue will depend on your jurisdiction. Most states have fairly specific rules of appellate procedure, some of them modeled after the FRAP. Before you begin to write, you should find and review the applicable rules for your jurisdiction. Plan to return to the rules several times through the drafting process.

In the federal system, the content of an appellate brief is governed by FRAP 28. Rule 28 identifies 10 sections that must be included in an appellant's brief. These include rules that address procedural issues as well as the ultimate legal issues. Obviously, you will spend the most time on the Argument section. However, do not underestimate the

> **Important reminder**
>
> There is no need to write the individual sections of your brief in the same order as they appear in the documents. In writing appellate briefs, for example, you begin your research and writing by focusing on the Statement of Facts and the Argument sections. Those sections, however, are preceded by introductory or procedural sections, which should be written later in the process.

importance of the other sections. Sometimes, the most significant legal issue is rendered moot because of procedural problems. The text that follows reviews the required sections of both the appellant's brief and the respondent's brief.

18.2.1   Appellant's brief

18.2.1.1   Corporate Disclosure Statement

If a party is a corporation, it must include this disclosure statement that identifies any parent corporation or corporation that owns more than 10 percent of its stock.

18.2.1.2.   Table of Contents

Every brief includes three versions of the argument on appeal—the brief version, the briefer version, and the briefest version. The Table of Contents is the briefest version.

The Table of Contents lists all parts of the brief and their beginning page numbers. In this respect, it is like every other Table of Contents you have seen. However, in an appellate brief, the Table of Contents also presents an opportunity to begin persuading your audience. The Table of Contents includes the point headings for each of the arguments on appeal. If the point headings are well done, readers will understand the brief's theme just from reading the Table of Contents. Many judges consider this to be the most important part of the brief because it establishes the essence of the appellant's argument. While the Argument section will fill in the details of those arguments, this is the place that you can begin persuading by priming your audience by effectively capturing both the logos and pathos of the arguments on appeal.

The Table of Contents is also likely to be the first place to establish your ethos. If the point headings are concise and clearly written, readers will begin to trust you. If they are poorly written or uninformative, that, too, sends a message to readers—but not the one you want. The Table of Contents is the place where your writing makes its first impression. You'll want to make sure that impression is a positive one.

The Table of Contents not only reveals the essence of your argument, it also reveals your organization. The headings and subheadings appear there in outline form.

Although the words themselves need to precisely match the headings in the body of the brief, the formatting does not need to match. Nor should it. For example, within the brief itself, headings might differ in size and many or all of them will be boldfaced. If the entire Table of Contents appeared in boldface, however, it would be practically unreadable. The best choice is to make sure that each level of the outline is visually distinct, but that the page still uses plenty of white space. For example:

1.0 Major headings may still be in bold unless your brief contains no subpoints. (Remember, your table of contents should never appear in all bold type.)

1.1   If the question presented is divided into subparts, those subparts in the Table of Contents could appear in italics

1.1.1   If the subparts are further divided into sections, those sub-subparts could appear as regular, unbolded, unitalicized type, and sized down a little bit.

1.1.2   Don't forget the basic rule of outlining: at any level of your outline you must have at least two sections. (If you have "Section 1.0," you must have "Section 2.0.")

1.2   The subparts may identify the different elements of a cause of action that are disputed on appeal.

1.3   Creating the table in this way does two things:

1.3.1   It creates an appearance of an organized argument.

1.3.2   It shows readers the specifics of that organization.

The several major word processing programs include a feature to help you automatically create a Table of Contents, although you may find it necessary to reformat the table after it is created. For that reason, you may find it easier to create the table manually, after completing the final revisions to the brief (when the page numbers and point headings are finalized).

18.2.1.3.   Table of Authorities

The Table of Authorities sets out all the authorities that the brief cites with references to the pages of the brief where they are cited. This is a helpful resource to readers who are looking for a particular case or statute within the brief. Both the judges who read the brief and their clerks who check your research will look closely at the Table of Authorities.

Frankly, putting together a Table of Authorities can be tedious. While all major word processing programs can automate the process of generating the table, you must still decide what needs to be included in the table and enter the correct computer codes so that the table is accurate. All the authorities must be properly cited, according to the citation rules of the jurisdiction. (Yes, citation rules vary from court to court—make sure you know the citation rules for your particular court!) While the Table of Authorities may not advance your substantive arguments, it does affect your ethos. A carefully compiled table reveals your attention to detail, increasing your credibility with readers.

In most jurisdictions, the rules do not require a specific, detailed format for the Table of Authorities. For example, FRAP 28 requires the table to include only cited "cases (alphabetically arranged), statutes, and other authorities—with references to the pages in the brief where they are cited." The rules leave the formatting details to the discretion of the author. Two principles should guide your formatting decisions:

- Make it easy for readers to understand

- Be consistent

Although you have considerable discretion in formatting your Table of Authorities, a few pointers may make this task easier:

- Many authors prefer to separate the cases by level: Supreme Court cases; Court of Appeals cases; and District Court cases. Though not required by Rule 28, it may be helpful, particularly when the brief includes citation to many cases.

- It is not necessary to include subsequent history in your case citations. It is inappropriate to include pinpoint cites in your table.

- If your brief cites extensively to regulations or to legislative history, you may include separate sections for those authorities. Otherwise, they may be included in the "Other Authorities" section.

- "Other Authorities" includes secondary sources such as law review articles, dictionaries, and treatises. If your brief does not include cites to such sources, it is not necessary to add them just to have this section in your table. Include "Other Authorities" only when your brief requires them!

18.2.1.4. *Jurisdictional Statement*

The Jurisdictional Statement is a concise statement that identifies the basis for the court hearing the appeal. It requires four specific statements:

- The basis for the trial court's jurisdiction

- The basis for the appellate court's jurisdiction

- The filing dates showing that the appeal is timely

- An assertion that the appeal is of a final order or judgment, or that the court has jurisdiction on some other basis

18.2.1.5. *Statement of the Issues*

This section identifies the specific issues on appeal. In some jurisdictions, this is known as the "Questions Presented." This is a critical section, as whoever asks the questions gains significant control over the answers. You may have learned about writing Questions Presented for objective, predictive writing in your first-semester legal writing course. Questions Presented in persuasive

Well, when you put it that way . . .

For an example of how appellants and appellees can present very different versions of the issue on appeal, consider, *Hishon v. King & Spaulding, 467 U.S. 69 (1984).*, where the issue concerned whether federal sex discrimination laws applied to law firms' decisions with regard to promoting associates to partners. Here is how the plaintiffs framed the issue:

Whether large institutional law firms that are organized as partnerships are, for that reason alone, exempt from Title VII of the Civil Rights Act of 1964, and are free (a) to discriminate in the promotion of associate lawyers to partnership on the basis of sex, race or religion; and (b) to discharge those associates whom they do not admit to partnership based on reasons of sex, race or religion under an established "up-or-out" policy.

On the other hand, the law firm framed the issues from a different perspective:

1. Whether law partners organized for advocacy are entitled to constitutionally protected freedom of association.

2. Whether Congress intended through Title VII of the Civil Rights Act of 1964 to give the Equal Employment Opportunity Commission, a politically appointed advocacy

writing are similar to those used in predictive writing, with one important difference: in persuasive writing, the Question Presented is an opportunity to *persuade*. The way a question is phrased can have a lot of significance in how it is answered. Thus, you want to craft a question that leans favorably toward your client's position without tilting so far as to mislead the court or misstate the actual issue. In writing an effective Question Presented, you need to consider three factors: an appropriate form, an accurate and specific phrasing of the issue, and detailed and persuasive word choices.

• Formatting the Question Presented

Traditionally, a Question Presented is written as a single sentence that includes the specific legal question, the applicable law, and the specific facts of the case that establish the narrow issue before the court. This is a lot of information to fit into one sentence and can easily result in a very long, structurally complex sentence. To make this approach manageable, many experts recommend the "under, does, when" structure. This is a structure that works for virtually any Question Presented and ensures that, even when the sentence is long, it will be readable (and actually a sentence!). As you might expect, this structure has three parts:

Under [state the applicable law],

  does [pose the specific legal question]

    when [incorporate the key relevant facts]?

For example, in the hotel room reservations case, the hotel might pose the Question Presented like this:

> Under Indiana law, is a liquidated damages clause enforceable in a contract for the reservation of 150 hotel rooms when both parties were free to negotiate its terms and where, at the time it was signed, the hotel could expect to spend an undetermined amount of money on advertising and discounted room rates if the other party did not fulfill its obligation to use the rooms?

This question identifies the applicable law, specific issue, and the important facts that suggest the liquidated damages clause should be enforced.

Now, strictly speaking, this would not be the narrow question before the court of appeals. The court of appeals is reviewing the decision of the trial court. Thus, some attorneys would state the question in terms of what the trial court did:

> Did the trial court correctly rule that a liquidated damages clause is enforceable in a contract for the reservation of 150 hotel rooms when both parties were free to negotiate its terms and where, at the time it was signed, the hotel could expect to spend an undetermined amount of money on advertising and discounted room rates if the other party did not fulfill its obligation to use the rooms?

Though this deviates slightly from the "under, does, when" format, it retains its general structure and still results in a readable, persuasive sentence.

Some attorneys find this traditional format a bit clumsy, especially when the question on appeal involves a complicated legal or factual context. Consequently, they abandon the single-sentence format. Instead, they introduce the question with one to three declarative sentences, followed by a shorter statement of the legal issue. This "statement, statement, question" format allows for greater flexibility in crafting the Question Presented. Still, under this approach, one would incorporate the applicable law, specific legal issue, and key facts. For example:

> Indiana courts will enforce liquidated damages clauses where the potential damages resulting from a breach of contract are uncertain at the time the contract is bargained. At the time the Gloucester Hotel entered into its contract with the non-profit, the hotel was unaware of what it would cost in advertising and reduced room rates should SOFT fail to use all the rooms it contracted to use. Is the

> liquidated damages clause the parties negotiated
> enforceable?

Either format for the Question Presented is acceptable. More important than which format you use is that you make sure your Question Presented is readable and persuasive.

How's the Whether?

Some attorneys prefer to begin a Question Presented with the word "Whether." For example:

> Whether a floating structure that is indefinitely moored, receives power and other utilities from shore, and is not intended to be used in maritime transportation or commerce, constitutes a "vessel" under 1 U.S.C. 3, thus triggering federal maritime jurisdiction.[1]

Petitioner's Brief in *Lozman v. City of Riviera Beach* (May 8, 2012) available at 2012 WL 1651366.

Although this is a common practice, many writing experts advise against it. One common complaint about this format is that beginning a sentence with "whether" necessarily means that whatever you write will not be a question. Indeed, it is not even a complete sentence. To ensure the Question Presented is a sentence, some writers will begin with "The Question Presented is whether..." This, of course, still doesn't put the Question Presented in the form of a question.

Despite the protests of these experts, the use of "whether" persists. If you prefer to avoid sentence fragments and like to pose Questions Presented as questions, you should feel free to avoid this structure. If you find such objections pedantic and tiresome, you will be in good company.

• Stating the legal issue

Of course, the most important purpose of the Question Presented is to inform the court of what issue you are asking it to decide. The issue must be stated accurately and precisely. To begin, think about what you want the court to do. If you are the appellant, you want the court to reverse the lower court on a particular legal issue. This usually means you are asking the court to correct a misapplication of the law to the facts of your case—as those facts were found at trial. In the rare case where the issue is a pure question of law, you are asking the court to correct a misinterpretation of the law itself, so that it can then correctly apply that law to your facts.

If you are the respondent, you are not asking the court to correct anything. You are merely asking the court to affirm the lower court. This usually means you are in a position of strength (appellate courts affirm lower courts much more often than they reverse them). Typically, the respondent will state the issue to suggest that the court need do little more than recognize the lower court resolved the issue correctly. Like the appellant, the respondent must also state the question accurately and precisely. Of course, the respondent has less flexibility because it is the appellant who decides what issues to raise on appeal.

Whether you are the appellant or the respondent, you usually will state the legal issue in terms of the existing law. If the issue is statutory, include the key word or phrase of the statute in the question. For example:

> Under N.J.S.A. 2C:25-19(d), are two people in a "dating relationship" when ...

Or, if using the "statement, statement, question" form:

> The New Jersey Domestic Violence statute, N.J.S.A. 2C:25-19(d), defines "victim of domestic violence" to include a person who is in a "dating relationship" with someone who abuses that person ...

Sometimes the parties will disagree as to what is the legal issue on appeal. Often, however, this part of the Question Presented is undisputed. Where the persuasion opportunity usually lies is in how you frame the legal issue by putting it in context. Putting the legal issue in context usually means incorporating key facts that refine the issue. In some cases, it may mean incorporating key policy considerations, especially where the issue is a pure question of law.

- **Framing the Issue by adding informational context**

Framing the Question Presented is best done by carefully choosing the key facts that will narrow the focus of the question. Even though the facts are not in dispute on appeal, how you characterize those facts or which facts you emphasize can affect how the court perceives the issue before it. For example, consider how you might describe your client if you were appealing the conviction of an environmental sciences graduate student who was convicted of trespassing while protesting a proposed clear-cut on federal forest lands. Is she a "student"? a "scientist"? an "environmentalist"? an "environmental activist"? Each of these words may accurately describe your client, but they also carry different connotations and you would choose the term that best fit your theme and theory of the case. (You probably wouldn't call her an "eco-terrorist," but the prosecutor might.)

The goal of framing the question is to establish the theme of your Argument in a concise and readable way. The ideal response of your readers is "if this is the question, I know what the answer *should* be." To capture your theme, use concrete, specific terms that direct readers to the answer you want without being so strident that they believe you have overstated your case.

Let's look at a few examples from our sample briefs:

Example one:

> Under Indiana law, is a liquidated damages clause
> enforceable in a contract for the reservation hotel rooms?

This example asks the correct legal question, but it includes no context. Not only does it fail to state the question narrowly, it misses the opportunity to persuade by putting the question in a context favorable to the author's client. One measure of persuasion is whether we can tell, just from reading the question, which party wrote the question. Either party could have written this example.

Example two:

> The Gloucester Hotel is part of a huge multinational conglomerate with untold millions of dollars at its disposal. SOFT is a small band of scientists dedicated to solving the most pressing problem facing the all inhabitants of our planet, global warming. Is the Gloucester Hotel entitled to demand SOFT pay it thousands of dollars in so-called "damages" even though it profited mightily as a result of the contract between it and SOFT?

This Question Presented goes well past the line of effective advocacy. While you want to include persuasive facts, if you overstate your case, the court is likely to reject your framing of the question or, worse, conclude that you are so biased that you cannot be trusted to speak reasonably in the rest of the brief.

We can do better than these examples. Consider a better framing of the issue from the non-profit's point of view:

> Under Indiana law, is a liquidated damages clause in a contract an unenforceable penalty when the actual amount of damages is easily calculable according to the formula specified in the contract, the hotel was not damaged because it was able to resell all of the rooms not used by SOFT to other guests, and the damages claimed in the amount of $9,480.38 are grossly disproportionate to the actual damages of zero?

This example incorporates specific facts without resorting to vitriol. It includes facts that point toward the elements of an unenforceable liquidated damages clause without merely stating legal conclusions:

Legal element	Supporting fact
damages easily calculable	"formula specified in contract"
no actual damage	"hotel resold all rooms to others"
grossly disproportionate	$9,480.38 is way bigger than zero

By showing the relevant facts, in a rational tone, the author establishes her credibility and primes the judge to view the issue from the hotel's perspective.

As you draft and edit your Question Presented, keep in mind the following questions:

- What is the precise legal issue before the court?
- What story is most important to that issue?
- What characters are central to that story?
- What word choices will best capture my client's perspective?

18.2.1.6.   *Statement of the Case*

Under the federal rules, the Statement of the Case includes both a summary of the Facts and the procedural history of the case.

If you have told the client's story effectively, readers should have empathy for your client and her cause by the time they have finished reading the facts in the statement of the case.

In addition to telling a compelling story, there are a couple of other things to keep in mind when writing the Facts section. First, on appeal, the facts usually are no longer at issue. You must accept the facts as they were found by the trier of fact below. Thus, every assertion must be in the record established at trial and be cited to the record. Second, the Facts section, while a great place to persuade, is not a place to argue. This is the place to tell the story. The legal significance of that story will come in later sections. Developing the factual record is discussed in Chapter 5. Writing the Facts section is discussed in Chapters 8, 9, and 16.

The Statement of the Case also explains the procedural nature of the case, the course of proceedings leading to the appeal, and the disposition of the court below. This section covers the procedural bases, but it is not a place for argument. It should be a precise, accurate, and objective explanation of how the case has gotten to this point.

In some jurisdictions, the Statement of the Case includes many of the sections that stand independently under the federal rules. For example, in Oregon, the Statement of the Case includes the following subsections: the procedural posture, the jurisdictional statement, the judgment of the trial court, the Questions Presented, the Summary of the Argument, and the Statement of Facts.[1] In other jurisdictions, the Statement of the Case may include just the Statement of Facts. Or it may be called something else such as "Procedural History." As always, you need to check the local rules of the applicable jurisdiction to make sure you have all the preliminary pieces in the right place.

18.2.1.7. *Summary of the Argument*

This is the *briefer* version of the argument. It is considerably more fleshed out than the point headings or the Preliminary Statement, but far less than the full discussion that is the Argument section.

Many students struggle with finding the right level of detail for the Summary of the Argument. If it is too detailed, it seems redundant to include a summary that is essentially the same as the full Argument that immediately follows it. On the other hand, if it is too brief, it seems to be little more than unsupported legal conclusions that only leave readers demanding more. There are a few principles that may help you find the right middle ground.

First, leave behind any expectations that readers will read the brief from front to back as if it were a novel. Rather, the different sections serve different functions. When readers want to understand the specifics of your argument (such as when they are reading it for the first time), they will look to the detailed Argument

> **Advice from law clerks**
>
> Judicial clerks we know tell us that the Summary of the Argument is the first section of the brief that they read. For at least those types of readers, then, the Summary of the Argument section is your chance to make a first impression on the reader. Make sure it is a good one.

---

[1] Or. R. App. P. 5.

section. However, when they are looking to merely refresh their memories of the case (perhaps when preparing for oral argument), they may need to read only the Summary that highlights the key issues and authorities. This means that a good Summary will follow the same organization and make the same key arguments as the Argument section.

The level of detail to aim for in the Summary is similar to the detail you would put in the global roadmap section of your Argument. You definitely want to address every issue raised in your point headings. You may reference the key statutes and cases, but do not provide an extended explanation of them. As a general rule, you can omit counterarguments from the Summary. In this section, readers are looking for a clear statement of your conclusions but are not expecting all the underlying analysis that will support those conclusions.

18.2.1.8.   *The Argument*

You have now reached the heart of the brief. Here, you explain the details of each of your contentions, complete with citations to authority and the record. How you do that is, of course, the focus of most of the rest of this book.

In addition, for each issue, you must include a statement of the applicable standard of review.[2] Rule 28 allows you to do this either as part of your discussion of the issue or under a separate heading placed before the discussion of the issues. Because the standard of review is often misstated—and sometimes mistaken for the substantive legal standard—it should usually be explained under its own heading.[3]

As you have probably discussed in your civil procedure course, the standard of review defines the degree of deference the appellate court

---

[2] In this context, we are talking about standards for *appellate* review. There are different standards for motions at the trial court level.

[3] Some appellate courts have rules that require a separate section explaining what the proper standard of review is. *See, e.g.*, Pa. R. App. P. 2111(a)(3).

must give to the trial court. While different jurisdictions may use different terminology, there are generally three categories of standards of review: de novo, clearly erroneous, and abuse of discretion.

When an appellate court has "de novo" review, it reviews the issue on its own, giving no deference to the trial court's decision. The most common de novo review situation is when the appellate court is interpreting a pure question of law, such as the meaning of a statute. In that case, the court will interpret the statute as if it were the first court to review it. The appellate court would not defer at all to the trial court interpretation.

The "clearly erroneous" standard usually applies when the appellate court is reviewing findings of fact of the trial court. The appellate court will defer to the trial court on these findings unless findings are clearly inconsistent with the record. Generally, if there is any evidence to support a finding, the appellate court will defer to the trial court, even if, taking the evidence as a whole, the appellate court might have found differently.

The most deferential standard is "abuse of discretion." This standard is applied to administrative decisions of the trial court. For example, if the trial court refused to grant a request for an extension of time, that decision would be reviewed under the abuse of discretion standard. The abuse of discretion standard may also be applied to trial court decisions that involve balancing tests or a mix of facts and law. For example, in a child custody case, the court will consider several factors in determining what is in the "best interest of the child." Generally, the appellate court will not second-guess the trial court as to the proper balance of those factors and will look only for an abuse of discretion. This is a very difficult standard for an appellant to overcome. It is not enough that the appellate court might have reached a different result from that of the trial court. The appellate court recognizes that reasonable minds might differ, and it will not substitute its judgment for the trial court's unless there is essentially no basis to support the trial court decision.

In many cases, the standard of review is central to the appellate court's ultimate decision. Obviously, an appellant wants the appellate court to apply the de novo standard—giving no deference to the court below. On the other hand, the respondent would much prefer a deferential standard of abuse of discretion. Thus, to the extent possible, an appellant will frame issues on appeal as questions of law while a respondent will frame issues as questions of the trial court's exercise of judgment, limiting the appellate court's review to an abuse of discretion standard. Whether appellant or respondent, you want to make sure to identify the correct standard of review and keep it in mind as you fashion your argument.

18.2.1.9.   Conclusion

The Conclusion is a short statement stating the precise relief sought. It is not a summary of the argument, which you provided earlier. Chapter 17 discusses in more detail how to write a concise and persuasive Conclusion.

18.2.1.10.   Signature

Rule 32 requires that all documents filed with the court include the lawyer's signature. By signing the brief, you attest that, to the best of your knowledge, everything included within the brief is accurate. Thus, before you put your name to the page, be sure to review the entire brief one more time to correct any errors that might have escaped your previous reviews.

18.2.1.11.   Certificate of Compliance with Rule 32g(1)

If you use a modern typeface (and unless you are using a typewriter, you do), you will need to include a brief statement that affirms that you complied with the word or line count limits. Generally, under the federal rules an appellant's brief is limited to 13,000 words or 1,300 lines of text, although many states have different rules. As always, check the applicable rules! Note that Rule 32, as discussed below has additional rules about the format of the brief.

18.2.2   Appellee's brief

FRAP 28 requires the appellee's brief[4] to include most of the same sections as the appellant's brief. However, it permits the appellee to omit some sections unless the appellee is dissatisfied with the appellant's statement. These sections include

- the Jurisdictional Statement;
- the Statement of the Issues;
- the Statement of the Case; and
- the Statement of the Standard of Review.

Although the rule permits the appellee to accept the appellant's version of these sections, it is almost always unwise to do so. The appellant will certainly frame the issues and describe the facts in a light most favorable to his position. By conceding to this version of the story, the appellee loses a significant opportunity to tell her version of the story. It is far more likely that the appellee will want to reframe the issues and almost certainly will want to provide a different perspective of the facts.

18.3   Formatting rules

For appeals in federal court, FRAP 32 governs the form of briefs. In addition, each circuit court has its own local rules. You will need to check the local rules for your jurisdiction, as local rules are, well, local! The details vary, and each court has its own idiosyncratic expectations. Even if you are familiar with the practices of a particular court, you will need to review the current local rules as minor changes occur routinely.

---

[4] The federal rules refer to the appealing party as the "appellant" and the responding party as "appellee." To avoid confusion, we have generally used the terms "appellant" and "respondent" in this text. The proper terminology varies from jurisdiction to jurisdiction.

In many jurisdictions, there are different rules governing a midlevel appellate court and the jurisdiction's highest court. The United States Supreme Court Rule 33.1 governing briefs is different from FRAP 32. But in state courts, the rules of appellate procedure may be the same for both appellate levels. The point, as should be clear by now—check the rules for your court!

Following formatting rules is a bit like cleaning your house before a party. If you do a good job, no one is likely to notice. If, on the other hand, you neglect to dust the furniture or vacuum the floors, that will get your guests' attention—and not in a good way. Similarly, if you follow the formatting rules carefully, readers may not notice how carefully you have cleaned and polished your brief, but they will focus their attention on the substance of the brief instead of the formatting details. On the other hand, a brief that does not comply with the formatting rules will, at the very least, distract readers and undermine your credibility on more significant aspects of your brief. More problematic, it will sometimes get your brief bounced out of court, costing someone a great deal of extra time and money to reformat and refile the brief.

Rule 32 has seven subsections that cover a variety of formatting issues, including the following:

- Reproduction: how the brief is printed, paper stock.

- Cover, including the content of the cover and the color for each type of brief.

- Binding: briefs must be able to lie flat when open.

- Paper size, spacing, margin size: briefs are to be printed on 81/2″ × 11″ paper, double spaced, and with 1″ margins.

- Typeface: briefs may be either monospaced or proportional spaced. A proportionally spaced text must use a font with serifs. (For more details about choosing an effective font, see Chapter 19.)

- Typestyle: briefs must use a plain roman-style type. Italics or bold may be used for emphasis. Case names must be in italics or underlined.

- Length: this rule is complicated by the various acceptable typefaces. A brief is limited to 30 pages, although the rules include alternative word count or line count options: a brief using proportionally spaced fonts is limited to 13,000 words, while a brief using a monospaced font (which we strongly recommend against) is limited to 1,300 lines of text. In addition, the author must certify that a brief using either of these alternatives complies with this rule.

In addition to Rule 32, each federal court has its own rules regarding briefs. For example, the Seventh Circuit has rules regarding the number of copies to be filed, electronic filing, and citation to unpublished opinion. In addition, it requires the appellant to include an appendix with a copy of the lower court decision. On the other hand, the Supreme Court requires that briefs use a font from the Century family.

Whatever court you are submitting to, be sure to check for all the rules that apply to that court. In the federal system, that could include the Federal Rules of Civil Procedure, the Federal Rules of Appellate Procedure, and the local rules of the particular court to which you will submit your document.

Within the rules, there are many ways that you can make your document more reader friendly. Of course, whatever formatting decisions you make must comply with the court's local rules. Those rules can cover everything from page limits to font size to how to fasten the papers of your document. The local rules are available on the court's website. Chapter 19 discusses formatting strategies in detail.

Comparing court rules

Court rules for briefs vary widely among jurisdictions, and between trial and appellate courts. To illustrate that variety, the following table lists the required elements for a typical state trial court, a typical state appellate court, and a federal appellate court.

New Jersey trial court	Oregon Court of Appeals, Rule 5	US Circuit Court, Rule 28
Motion for Summary Judgment: Statement of material facts.	Indexes	Corporate disclosure statement
	Index of contents	Table of contents
	Index of appendices	Table of authorities
	Index of authorities	Jurisdictional statement
	Statement of the case	Statement of the issues
Other motions:	Statement of the nature of proceeding to be reviewed	Statement of the case
No content specified	Judgment sought to be reviewed	Summary of the argument
		Argument
	Date of judgment below	Standard of review
	Date appeal filed	Conclusion
	Question presented	Signature
	Summary of argument	Certificate of compliance
	Statement of Facts	
	Assignment of error	
	Preservation of error	
	Standard of review	
	Argument	
	Conclusion	
	Signature	
	Proof of Service	

Creating Ethos: Tone and Branding by Good Visual Design

The tone of a document contributes to its medium mood control, or pathos. So does its look. The look of a document includes its design, its adherence to the local court rules governing the filing of documents, and its technical flawlessness.

No document is perfect, but it should be as free of technical errors as possible. Errors are noticeable and distracting—and subtract from a writer's ethos. Most judges believe they are good legal writers and good legal thinkers. (And indeed, most of them are!) Consequently, lawyers who want to persuade judges must take the time to edit carefully, and to proofread carefully. You don't want a judge thinking, "If she can't even run this through a spell checker, how can I trust her reasoning?" Just as you do not want to have to change a judge's mind about the substance of the argument, you don't want to have to change the judge's mind about the quality of your work. A well written, well-formatted document allows your reader to focus on the merits of your argument rather than be distracted by a poorly executed document.

The first semester of legal writing courses often includes a discussion of the importance of polishing documents for grammar, citation, rules, and typographical accuracy. This textbook will not review those critical aspects to writing. Rather, this chapter is devoted to the document's design or the "beauty factor" in persuasive legal writing documents. That is, we will discuss what the document actually looks like. Courts and practitioners care about document design a great deal more than you might otherwise suspect.

To be read, documents must be readable. This chapter briefly discusses readability in documents that, like briefs, are all or nearly all, text, as opposed to documents with lots of pictures, graphs, charts, and other non-text material. The idea of this chapter is to explore a few fundamentals of good document design when you are managing a lot of text on the page.

This chapter will also include tips for a few general techniques in word processing that, once learned, will save you time and improve your document design. Most of these word processing techniques can be learned in just a few minutes.

19.1   Document design principles

Making a textual document visually effective means making the document as readable as possible. The more readable the document, the more likely readers are to remember the content. Fortunately, there are many scientific studies that support the textual design concepts we discuss next.[1] Graphic design experts incorporate the findings into four principles for all-text documents: contrast, proximity, alignment, and repetition.

19.1.1   Contrast with size and weight

As we have written in previous chapters, headings are a key part of written persuasion. They need to stand out in a legal document, and that means that headings should visually contrast. Providing visual contrast goes a long way to further that principle. You have probably already incorporated contrast into your legal writing documents by making headings look different from text. And, within levels of hierarchy—sections and subsections—you probably varied something about the way the headings were presented.

To present a hierarchy in the information, graphic designers choose deliberate contrast, either with typeface or with size, weight, or color.

---

[1] You can find a summary of and cites to scientific studies in Ruth Anne Robbins, *Painting with Print: Incorporating Concepts of Typographic and Layout Design into the Text of Legal Writing Documents*, 2 J. ALWD 108 (2004), and reproduced, by invitation, on the website of the United States Court of Appeals for the Seventh Circuit from 2004–16), http://www.ca7.uscourts.gov.

Notice what wasn't mentioned. *Italicizing*, underlining, and ALLCAPS. In ascending order, each of those emphasis choices makes it harder to read at our normal rate. Using all capitalization is the worst thing you can do if you want your headings to be legible and easy to read. Oregon and South Dakota have recognized this phenomenon and limit the use of all capitals in briefs.[2]

Slowing readers down is no way to persuade them. Think of *italics*, underlining, and ALLCAPS as walking on a flight of stairs in which each stair is the wrong height or depth. Steps that are set too high will exhaust someone much faster than properly set stairs—and many people will prefer to skip it and wait for an elevator. A flight of stairs that is too shallow is just as difficult. Stair climbers have to watch their feet the whole time to make sure they don't trip.

As an alternative to ALLCAPS, graphic designers suggest we develop contrast by varying the look of the letters. There are two ways to optimize contrast on the black and white printed page: vary heavy/dark/boldface lettering with light lettering, and vary the style of the letters, or fonts. An easy way to do this is to use boldface for headings and unbolded text (called "Roman style") for the body of the material. To show different levels of the organization hierarchy, use a different font size for different levels of your outline headings.

This textbook uses the same font for headings and text but uses boldface for the headings. The chapter titles are larger than the major point headings of each chapter, and those are larger than the next level of subheadings. The sample briefs in Appendices A through D use the same technique.

---

[2] Or. R. Sup. Ct. 5.05(4)(f) ("Briefs printed entirely or substantially in uppercase are not acceptable."); S.D. R. App. Ct. 15-26a-66(b)(1) ("The use of all-capitals text may be applied only for case captions and section names.").

**Off-black is the new black
(for certain things)**

There are many choices in the intensity of black in a black and white document. Modern word processing gives you multiple options to decrease the depth of the black—just pull up your font color palette and look at the several options for black.

There's no need to have as much contrast with certain things like bullet points. The bullet points themselves are not the focal point of the list—rather, it's the information set off by the bullet point. You are able to set the color (and shape and size) of bullet points and it only takes about 3 minutes to learn how to create and change bullet points (we timed it). The bullet points in this book are a medium shade of off-black.

You can do the same thing with underlining and with the lines of tables: there's no need to use a pure, 100% black. On the other hand, there are sometimes reasons to make certain lines thicker or more decorative. The borders and shadings settings of tables allow you to change these things.

Another way to create contrast is to vary the font itself between heading and text, while still using the dark/light contrast. The shadow boxes of this textbook use a different font than the body of the text, as part of a deliberate design to look different. Likewise, the shadowing sets off those boxes from the rest of the text. The two different fonts come from different font families—the text is set in a serif font ("with wings") and the shadow box material is set in a sans serif font ("without wings"). If you choose to vary the font as well as the size and weight, make sure the fonts come from different families so that there's enough contrast. Otherwise, the result can look something like wearing black pants with navy socks. A fashion faux pas. At the same time, the fonts from two different families should be in harmony—which can be hard to do. Things like the shapes of certain letters (a, e, g, and o) are things to look at.

19.1.2   Proximity: keep related items related with appropriate spacing

Proximity derives from the premise that when items are aligned on the page, they dance together as a cohesive unit and provide visual continuity. For example, a heading that is followed by too much space before reaching the text looks like it is unrelated to or floating away from the text. From a readability standpoint, it also causes a lowered retention rate of the information. From an organizational standpoint, the moving of things closer together demonstrates, visually, the relationship of the material.

Line spacing also affects the relative readability of a document. Look at any book, magazine, or newspaper. Do you see double spacing? It's doubtful. That's because educational psychologists and graphic design researchers have concluded that the most comfortable line spacing for reading is something approaching 20 percent larger than the size of the font. In word processing language, that translates to 14 points of space with a 12-point font (120 percent × 12 = 14.4 or 14 points of space). In practice, many print documents are slightly tighter than that. This textbook uses a line spacing that is slightly larger than a 1.2 multiple.

> **Setting exact line spacing**
>
> In word processing programs, you can—and should—manually set the spacing by the exact number of points or by a multiple of the font size. In the line spacing options, choose the "exact" setting in the line spacing options and type in 14 or whatever other number you may want. Or, choose the "multiple" setting and type in 1.2 or any other number you may want. This book uses line spacing that is approximately a 1.15 multiple.

Here are the places in a brief where you should pay attention to spacing:

- ***After headings and before the start of the text.*** Close up that space to something small. We use spacing in the range of 3 to 6 points between headings and the start of the text. Over the course of several headings, that adds up quickly to several lines of recaptured space. When you are faced with a maximum page limit (as some states still require), those saved lines can be critical.

- ***After a section ends and before the heading of the next section.*** We use 12 to 24 points of spacing to show the chunking.

- ***Between paragraphs.*** This is typically set at the same size as the font. Just twice pushing the Enter key on your keyboard creates that space. A better way to do this is to set the "after" line spacing to the same size as your font size.

- *Line spacing between lines of a paragraph.* This textbook uses a multiple spacing of 1.2 (1.2 times the font size), which is the same multiple that the United States Supreme Court requires in briefs.

- *Line spacing in the headings.* Multiple-line headings still need to maintain their weight/darkness to effectively show contrast. For that reason, it is better to keep the space tighter than the text's line spacing. It is perfectly acceptable to use single spacing in headings.

- *Post-sentence spacing.* The rules about two spaces after periods derive from the days of typewriters. Think about the mechanics of typewriters. They worked like pianos. Every letter was individually set on its own piece of metal, which then hammered the paper through a ribbon loaded with ink. The effect was that the letter "i" used the same width of paper as the letter "w" even though an "i" is a much narrower character. Punctuation was set on the same individual pieces of a metal, which meant that there was no difference in width between a "w" and a period. For that reason, a typist had to use a second space to alert the reader to the ending of the sentence. But we have computers now, and individual characters take up only as much width as the shape of their character requires. There's no need to use that second space after sentences because we can all see the end of the sentence without it. The second space after periods can visually detract with "rivers of space." Moving to one space after periods might save you a line or two in a longer document.

19.1.3   Alignment: justification and tables (and some resume tips)

A frequent question about alignment is whether to use left or full justification. Unless you have professional desktop publishing software, left justification is the easiest to choose. The full justification setting changes the spacing between letters inside or between words to maintain the straight lines on the left and right margins. In legal writing, this causes some odd-looking and distracting spacing within citation sentences. The fix for that, called "kerning," can be problematic in common word processing software. It's not impossible, but it won't add to the document's readability either, at least according to the studies we have seen.

One alignment tip we offer now, to save you years of frustration later, is a better way to create a caption in a legal document. Figure 19-1 shows what a caption typically looks like. Rather than using tab stops to create this, use a table and then remove the borders of that table after it is completed. Figure 19-2 shows that same caption, with the table borders, revealed.

Elaina Hawthorne,	:	Superior Court of New Jersey of Camden County
Plaintiff,	:	
	:	Chancery Division – Family Part
v.	:	
	:	
Arthur Beagle,	:	Docket No. FV 010-171696
Defendant.	:	
	:	**Defendant's Motion for Reconsideration.**
	:	
	:	*Sat: Hon. Wali Dodes, J.S.C.*

Figure 19–1: Caption, set up as a three-column table, with no table borders showing.

Elaina Hawthorne,	:	Superior Court of New Jersey of Camden County
Plaintiff,	:	
	:	Chancery Division – Family Part
v.	:	
	:	
Arthur Beagle,	:	Docket No. FV 010-171696
Defendant.	:	
	:	**Defendant's Motion for Reconsideration.**
	:	*Sat: Hon. Wali Dodes, J.S.C.*

Figure 19-2:   Three-column caption using center column for the center line (table borders revealed)

Another way to do it is by using a two-column table and removing all but the internal vertical border line, which you can turn into a dashed line or just leave solid. Figure 19-3 shows this technique.

Elaina Hawthorne, *Plaintiff,* *v.* Arthur Beagle, *Defendant.*	Superior Court of New Jersey of Camden County Chancery Division – Family Part Docket No. FV 010-171696 **Defendant's Motion for Reconsideration.** *Sat: Hon. Wali Dodes, J.S.C.*

Figure 19–3   Table showing internal border used to separate the information

Hopefully you can see other immediate applications. For example, you can use tables to help create the "letterhead" of your resume. You will save some vertical space that way. The table lines are left in, but only to show you where they are. Omit them in your own resume:

Jane L. Student	444 Cherry Tree Lane • Rutgersville, WY• 99999 555-555-5555 • <u>Janestudent@address.com</u>

Try this: document design and résumés

While you read this chapter, recall that one of the most important persuasive documents you are always rewriting is your own résumé. Document design principles are very relevant when you have only one page to convey information.

With a quick Internet search, you can see many wonderful examples of well-designed legal résumés. The most important advice we can give: have more white space and balance it across the whole of your page, not just on the right side.

Techniques to pay attention to are things like columns (best set up by inserting a table to give you max control), the use off-black for things like bullet points, and specialty shadow boxes (a text box). While we don't necessarily advocate using all techniques in all résumés, it's useful to see what is possible.

19.1.4   Repetition and document consistency

The last principle of document design, repetition, is the easiest one to implement. Keep all formatting consistent. If the point headings are set in a size 14 boldface, then all point headings must be set in size 14 boldface. If the headings use a different font than the text, then every single heading must use that same different font—don't go back and forth.

19.2   Application and limitations in legal documents

Chapter 18 noted that every jurisdiction has its own formatting rules. Those formatting rules govern briefs. As with any rule of law, they are susceptible to analysis and interpretation. And, like any other rule, they are subject to change.[3] Many courts' procedural rules will not allow you to use all of this chapter's design principles, particularly in appellate briefs. As nonsensical as it may seem, the longest of legal writing documents—the appellate brief—is often mandated to be the least readable. Many court rules are simply historical artifacts predating the computer. Court rules relating to formatting were first developed when lawyers no longer had to rely on professional printers to typeset their appellate briefs. Those professional printing days ended with the development of the mass-produced typewriter. Many court rules, even today, still reflect the typewriter era. If your jurisdiction is one that still speaks in characters per inch, pica, or requires a font like Courier or Courier New, you are working in a jurisdiction that has yet to fully embrace the advent of computers and word processing programs.[4]

---

[3] As of the date of this book's publication, many of the court rules committees in the country still would benefit from updating their formatting rules to reflect the science behind readability. Judges in the court systems, particularly at the appellate level, are spending more hours per week reading briefs than they would if the formatting rules were changed to allow optimized document design.

[4] Mass production of typewriters began in the 1880s. Mass production of computers began in the 1980s. The authors have faith that all of the courts in our country will eventually catch up.

When no court rule is governing your document design, you should be employing the same analysis and persuasion judgment that you do with other aspect of lawyering. The mediocre lawyer uses defaults. The effective lawyer thinks about effective presentation. Times New Roman appears in many jurisdictions' court rules because those rules reflect the standard of MS Office and WordPerfect through 2007. In fact, Times New Roman was designed for a London newspaper's narrow newsprint columns in small sizes below twelve-point. Even that newspaper doesn't use it anymore. Using a default font when it isn't required is the same thing as abdicating choice, and typically signals to those in the know that the document's writer lacks a persuasive visual strategy.

Put another way, you should include document design in the list of persuasive techniques but should also research the precise rules governing that document. If the court rules are silent on a particular point, or if the document you are writing is unbound by any court rules, then it is fine to design the document as you deem appropriate for the client's situation. For example, if no typeface rule is mentioned in trial court rules, then choose a typeface that brands your office (unless your office already has its own visual identity system, as many larger organizations already do). Or, as Professor Derek Kiernan-Johnson posits, choose one that sets the tone of the client's story.[5]

Remember that there are many other legal writing documents that could use your distinctive document design:

---

[5] For much, much more about the tone of font and its use in legal writing, see Derek Kiernan-Johnson, *Telling with Type: Typography and Narrative in Legal Briefs*, 7 J. ALWD 87 (2010).

- Trial-level briefs in some jurisdictions
- Pleadings
- Agreements

- Contracts
- Letters
- Intra-office documents

- Resumes
- E-mails
- Documents for presentations
- Public relations and publicity documents

Finally, branding is an important consideration. If your office has its own logo or icon, then it is fine to use it, miniaturized, as part of the signature block of the document. That includes e-mails and presentation handouts as well.

What should your e-mail look like?

E-mail is projected on a screen and will be easier to read in a sans serif font. Which font depends completely on the tone you are trying to set. Some fonts look more informal than others.

Design experts advocate using more horizontal rather than vertical space for e-mail signature lines. The accepted industry standard is no longer than four lines. Career specialists also suggest including no more than two job titles (to include more apparently diminishes the sender's overall ethos). To accomplish these suggestions, the snail-mail address can be condensed to one line, separated by a symbol or bullet point or colon. If you have multiple titles, choose which ones to use depending on the situation.

19.3   Writing for onscreen reading

With the advent of electronic filing, lawyers will need to adapt their documents for an audience reading materials on screens rather than paper. The American Bar Association's annual Technology Survey shows that technology is ubiquitous in law practice, with all lawyers reporting that they do some legal practice online. Judges also read online, with over 50 percent reporting that they read briefs primarily onscreen.[6] Lawyers practicing in the Third Circuit are well aware that the Judge Theodore McKee—the former Chief Judge of the Circuit—keeps his judicial chambers completely paperless—everything is done onscreen.

Reading online requires a different approach to document design because the eye and brain process projected material differently. While this textbook cannot hope to cover all of the differences, we do think it appropriate to call this to your attention, and to suggest that you factor into your document design some considerations about the medium of the communication.[7]

19.3.1   Scientific numbering for navigability

Professor Ellie Margolis advises legal writers that the shift to electronic reading necessitates a shift in the way we approach the organization of written materials. Too easily readers can become lost while navigating a long document online.[8] The traditional outline methods of Roman/Arabic numerals with letters does not assist that navigation. Other disciplines have migrated to a scientific numbering system. In law, we have

> **Hyperlinking headings to the Table of Contents**
>
> Your onscreen readers will also thank you for learning how to hyperlink your headings to the Table of Contents. The MS Word help function will assist you. There are also many YouTube tutorials available.
>
> The same is also true for your linking your internal citations to your Table of Authorities.

seen a shift to scientific numbering in transactional documents, but litigation documents are only slowly beginning to follow suit. The shift will and should happen. This textbook is set up in scientific numbering

---

[6] Ellie Margolis, *Is the Medium the Message? Unleashing the Power of E-Communication in the Twenty-First Century,* 12 LEGAL COMM. & RHETORIC: JALWD 1 (2015).

[7] *See, e.g.,* Mary Beth Beazley, *Writing for a Mind at Work: Appellate Advocacy and the Science of Digital Reading,* 54 No. 2 DUQUESNE L. REV. 415 (2016); Mary Beth Beazley, *Writing (and Reading) Appellate Briefs in the Digital Age,* 15 J. APPELLATE PRAC. & PROCESS 47 (2014); Ellie Margolis, *Is the Medium the Message? Unleashing the Power of E-Communication in the Twenty-First Century,* 12 LEGAL COMM. & RHETORIC: JALWD 1 (2015).

[8] Margolis *supra,* note 6, at 18–19.

and hopefully you have noticed that you can always tell where you are—in which chapter, major subsection, and minor subsection.

19.3.2   Incorporating visuals into your document

Access to word processing and graphic design software has allowed lawyers to incorporate visuals into what have traditionally been text-only legal documents. Furthermore, judges are increasingly opining that the way lawyers have historically approached document design should not continue. Former Seventh Circuit Judge Posner, for one, has also called for more lawyers to use visuals in their briefs.[9] Chief Judge Theodore McKee of the Third Circuit Court of Appeals has told one of the authors of this book that he sometimes uses graphic design software for note-taking purposes while he is reading lawyers' briefs.[10]

Research in neuroscience reveals what we already knew intuitively: visual or graphic representations resonate with readers. The cognitive boost that visuals provide has been noted over thousands of years of observation and discussed in copious numbers of scientific and social research texts.[11] Studies have repeatedly found that the general population is approximately 65 percent visual in learning and communicating styles. In

---

[9] Richard A. Posner, *Judicial Opinions and Appellate Advocacy in Federal Courts— One Judge's View*, 51 DUQ. L. REV. 3, 23 (2013). Judge Posner specifically criticized the intellectual property bar for thinking that "a word is worth a thousand pictures," particularly when the case turns on visual resemblance. *Id.*

[10] Phone conversation of Ruth Anne Robbins with Chief Judge Theodore McKee, Third Circuit Court of Appeals, May 2, 2014 (in follow up to email thread with Professor Ian Gallacher of Syracuse University College of Law about same).

[11] Simonides (556–448 B.C.E.) supposedly taught people to use imagery as a way to enhance memory. A century later, Aristotle wrote about the role of searching for an image in recollection. Aristotle, *On Memory and Reminiscence*, *IN* THE BASIC WORKS OF ARISTOTLE 616, ¶ 453-15 (Richard McKeon ed., 1941), *available at* http://www.sas.upenn.edu/~cavitch/pdf-library/Aristotle_OnMemory.pdf. Visuals aid in our recollection: much of our sensory cortex is devoted to image processing, whereas a much smaller portion of our brain processes words. For an easy summary of the science, see Haig Kouyoumdjian, *Learning Through Visuals*, PSYCHOL. TODAY, July 20, 2012, *available at* http://www.psychologytoday.com/blog/get-psyched/201207/learning-through-visuals.

contrast, one three-year study reported that 47 percent of attorneys have visual learning and communicating styles.[12] For good reason, we are drawn to visuals in lawyering when we see them.

19.3.2.1 *Documentary evidence presented as visuals*

There is a rich and valuable literature about trial attorneys' use of visuals as documentary evidence.[13] Litigators—and judges presiding over trials—are familiar and comfortable with the creation and use of visuals that are introduced as documentary evidence. These include photographs, charts, maps, graphs, presentations, and videos. When presented as evidence, these must all meet standards of relevance and reliability that are governed by the jurisdiction's rules of evidence. Attorneys also use documentary evidence outside the courtroom in pre-complaint demand letters, settlement offers, or contract negotiations. And, documentary evidence is sometimes included in briefs, pleadings, and judicial opinions. Federal appellate briefs, for example, may include "photographs, illustrations, and tables" to be reproduced by any method resulting in a "good copy of the original."[14] State appellate and trial level court rules may vary in wording, but we know of no court rule that expressly disallows visuals in briefs or motions. Rather, timelines and maps regularly appear as exhibits to filed documents.

19.3.2.2 *Analytical reasoning presented as visuals*

Legal writers may use visuals not just as a form of evidence, but also as a form of legal reasoning. Such visuals are called analytical

---

[12] Animators at Law, *Attorney Communication Style Study* (2011) (materials on file with Authors and available for download at http://www.a2lc.com/download-free-court-communication?&__hssc=&__hstc&hsCtaTracking=2794ef02-65d1-43d5-b88a-7ec22407c9a6|6d41d5f7-306f-4673-a4aa-4e0f92835899) (study included 387 lawyers and 1657 non-lawyers).

[13] *See, e.g.,* William S. Bailey & Robert W. Bailey, SHOW THE STORY: THE POWER OF VISUAL ADVOCACY (2011);

Jessica Silbey, *Images in/of Law*, 57 N.Y.L. SCH. L. REV. 171 (2012–2013); Shelley Watts, *Technology Creates Winning Visual Evidence*, 36 TRIAL 68 (2000); Jennifer L. Mnookin, *The Image of Truth: Photographic Evidence and The Power of Analogy*, 10 YALE J.L. & HUMAN. 1 (1998).

[14] FED. R. APP. PROC. 32(a)(1)(C)

visuals.[15] Analytical visuals do not attempt to prove the facts of what happened in a legal dispute. Rather, they argue for resolution of the client's case by creating a visual understanding of the legal analysis. An analytical visual might be used to illustrate:

- the meaning of statutes, cases, and other authority;
- the application of that authority to the facts; and
- the policy implications of resolving the legal dispute.

Analytical visuals include charts, graphs, infographics, and images. Analytical visuals should be designed to show patterns, illustrate inferences, or otherwise clarify concepts in ways the reader might not otherwise see. An analytical visual, then, walks the reader through some aspect of legal reasoning with the use of a chart, graph, photograph, or other visual element. Including visuals at key junctures in legal documents enhances the efficacy of the reasoning itself.

The functions boil down to three main categories of visuals: organizational, interpretive, and representative.

- **Organizational visuals** present information in a hierarchical way. This bulleted list is an organizational visual. Other examples are common: visually stylized outlines or charts that show levels of relationships. In the legal context, a brief's Table of Contents is an organizational visual. An organizational visual can also be something as simple as an arrow, pointing at a key phrase in statutory text.

- **Interpretive visuals** help learners better understand technical or complex concepts. These include a flow chart, a Venn diagram, a pie chart, matrices, and other infographics showing relationships. A five-day weather forecast is an interpretive visual that viewers quickly understand.

---

[15] This section adapted from Steve Johansen & Ruth Anne Robbins, *Art-iculating the Analysis: Systemizing the Decision to Use Visuals as Legal Reasoning*, 20 LEGAL WRITING 57 (2014) available at http://www.legalwritingjournal.org/2015/07/05/art-iculating-the-analysis-systemizing-the-decision-to-use-visuals-as-legal-reasoning/

- **Representative visuals** typically convey the same information that text might but uses a pictorial or photographic image to anchor the information.

Analytical visuals lie on a continuum of usefulness to the audience's understanding of the author's legal reasoning. At one end of the continuum are those that are merely **decorative**—perhaps interesting, and adding to the tone of the document, but not very useful in helping the reader's understanding. At the other end of the continuum is a **transformative** visual, which fully changes the way the reader perceives an issue. A transformative visual is generally the most useful to the legal writer in helping the audience understand the legal reasoning and argumentation. In comparison, truly transformative visuals do more than reinforce our written words; they open our readers to a new perspective, literally allowing them to look at an issue differently than they had before.

Just because a visual may seem like a good idea at the time does not mean that all visuals should be included in a final submission, however. Too many can clutter a document. Moreover, some are not as necessary or as central to the key legal concept as others. Inclusion is always a balancing act. Figure 19–4 shows a chart of considerations.

Is the visual effective at enhancing the reader's comprehension of the analysis?	Does the visual improve the document's overall design?	Does the visual meet professionalism norms?	In or out? The verdict.
• Determine where each visual falls on the continuum between decorative and transformative. • Ensure that each visual effectively conveys the *precise* legal analysis point and that it contributes to the overall theory of the case.	• Look critically at the quality of each visual. • Consider the overall number of visuals—will the reader become overwhelmed? • Assess the gestalt of the document.	• Consider the tone of the visual. • Review ethical and professionalism considerations.	• Does the visual assist in effective advocacy for the client?

Figure 19-4: Considerations for including an analytical visual

19.4   Further Readings

Turn to these resources for more information on the topic:

- Mary Beth Beazley, *Writing for a Mind at Work: Appellate Advocacy and the Science of Digital Reading*, 54 No. 2 DUQUESNE L. REV. 415 (2016).

- Mary Beth Beazley, *Writing (and Reading) Appellate Briefs in the Digital Age*, 15 J. APPELLATE PRAC. & PROCESS 47 (2014). Available at https://lawrepository.ualr.edu/appellatepracticeprocess/vol15/iss1/5/

- Matthew Butterick, TYPOGRAPHY FOR LAWYERS (Jones McClure 2010), and http://www.typographyforlawyers.com

- Steve Johansen & Ruth Anne Robbins, *Art-iculating the Analysis: Systemizing the Decision to Use Visuals as Legal Reasoning*, 20 LEGAL WRITING 57 (2014). Available at http://www.legalwritingjournal.org/2015/07/05/art-iculating-the-analysis-systemizing-the-decision-to-use-visuals-as-legal-reasoning/

- Derek H. Kiernan-Johnson, *Telling with Type: Typography and Narrative in Legal Briefs,* 7 J. ALWD 87 (2010). Available at http://www.alwd.org/lcr/archives/fall-2010/kiernan-johnson/

- Linda Lohr, CREATING GRAPHICS FOR LEARNING AND PERFORMANCE: LESSONS IN VISUAL LITERACY (2d ed., 2008).

- Ellie Margolis, *Is the Medium the Message? Unleashing the Power of E-Communication in the Twenty-First Century,* 12 LEGAL COMM. & RHETORIC: JALWD 1 (2015). Available at http://www.alwd.org/is-the-medium-the-message-unleashing-the-power-of-e-communication-in-the-twenty-first-century/

- Ruth Anne Robbins, *Conserving the Canvas: Reducing the Environmental Impact of Legal Briefs by Reimagining Court Rules and Document Design Strategies*, 7 J. ALWD 193 (2010). Available at http://www.alwd.org/lc&r.html

- Ruth Anne Robbins, *Painting with Print: Incorporating Concepts of Typographic and Layout Design into the Text of Legal Writing Documents,* 2 J. ALWD 108 (2004). Available at http://www.alwd.org/lcr/archives/fall-2004/robbins/

- Edward R. Tufte, VISUAL EXPLANATIONS: IMAGES AND QUANTITIES, EVIDENCE AND NARRATIVE (1997),

- Robin Williams, THE NON-DESIGNER'S DESIGN BOOK (4th ed., 2014).

Oral Argument

In some cases at the trial level, and in many cases at the appellate level, the written brief is the end of the process. The lawyers submit briefs, and the judge or judges use those briefs to make the decision. Approximately 74 percent of all federal appeals cases are resolved on the briefs, without the benefit of oral arguments. In a few jurisdictions, federal and state, the court rules permit oral argument only when lawyers specifically request it or the court itself orders it.

But, at both the trial and appellate levels, it is possible—and sometimes probable—that the reviewing court will want the opportunity to speak with the lawyers about the arguments contained in the briefs. Lawyers may be scheduled to attend a session of court in which the judge or judges ask the lawyers to present the arguments orally, and to engage in a discussion of the arguments and positions the lawyer has advanced for the client.

Part V of this book discusses effective oral presentation of the client's in a formal oral argument to the court.

Persuading in Person: Oral Argument

Many judges rely on oral arguments to help them sort out the issues, think through the arguments, and make preliminary conclusions about how to rule. Although not all courts routinely grant oral arguments,[1] when they do, it likely means that something about your case has caught the eye of one or more judges. The case is likely a close one, so oral argument may be the key to winning or losing the appeal.

One textbook on the art of oral persuasion suggests four themes:

1. Good oral advocacy is "usually balanced, positive, factual, calm, clear," and logical.

2. The credibility of the advocate is hugely important. "Listeners value …

demonstrations of judgment[] and a sense of fair play."

> **Briefs are the coin of the realm**
>
> It is probably true that the most important part of appellate persuasion happens in the written brief. After all, it is the brief that remains on the judge's desk, as she writes the opinion in the case, and serves as a reference for the arguments. Moreover, in many appellate courts, oral argument is not routinely granted. In those situations, the briefs may be the only tool the lawyer has for persuasion. In those situations where oral argument is granted, the lawyers are given an additional, and important opportunity to persuade—through the answering of the panel's questions.

---

[1] For example, in the United States Courts' annual report for the period ending September 30, 2016, the percentage of cases where oral arguments were heard in each circuit ranged from 5.9% (Fourth Circuit) to 46% (D.C. Circuit) (this doesn't include cases disposed of on procedural grounds). The average across the other Circuits was a little over 20%. That means most cases—even in the D.C. Circuit— were decided on the briefs alone. Administrative Office of the U.S. Courts, 2016 ANNUAL REPORT OF THE DIRECTOR: JUDICIAL BUSINESS OF THE UNITED STATES *Courts* tbl. B-10, available at http://www.uscourts.gov/sites/default/files/data_tables/jb_b10_0930.2016.pdf. Comprehensive statistics for state court appeals are not readily available, but probably vary widely.

3. "Bitter, overstated, angry, sarcastic, biting, emotion-dominated rhetoric usually backfires."

4. Effective use of stories and visual images "transform the forgettable into the memorable."[2]

This chapter begins with an overview of the differences between oral arguments at the trial and appellate levels. It then offers some strategies that can help you persuade, regardless of what level of court you are appearing before, by employing the four themes suggested above.

20.1   Setting the stage: the purpose of oral argument

Because the functions of trial courts and appellate courts differ, both the structure and purpose of oral arguments at those levels differ too.

It is hard to generalize about the purpose of oral arguments, especially at the trial court level, since the variety and procedural posture of cases that judges hear vary widely. However, recall the discussion in Chapter 4 about the difference between the role of the trial court and the appellate court. Usually the trial judge is the first neutral person to hear all sides of a dispute and render a decision. Therefore, the trial judge may be particularly attuned to the facts of the case, more so than an appellate judge, who may be more focused on the law. This is especially true when the trial judge sits as fact finder and must make decisions about credibility of witnesses and determine what really happened. Appellate courts, on the other hand, must accept the facts as found by the trial judge or the jury, so they have much less discretion in determining what happened.

You might be tempted to conclude that a trial court, which is more likely to be faced with a case in which the facts are not yet

---

[2] Robert N. Sayler and Molly Bishop Shadel, TONGUE-TIED AMERICA: REVIVING THE ART OF VERBAL PERSUASION 4 (2011).

determined, is going to be more attuned to the story the lawyer tells in her brief. And to some extent, that may be true. But do not discount the power of story in appellate briefs. As one scholar observed,

> On appeal, you are not writing for a jury but rather for a judge, who is well versed in fact-law interrelationships. The judge does not, however, know anything about your client's unique facts. If you can present these well—making them leap off the page to engage the judge's interest and spirit of justice—then you are that much closer to winning the appeal.[3]

Think about this for a moment. While every case requires a sound legal theory, the client is better served by the lawyer including an appealing theme as well. Give the judges a reason to feel good about ruling in the client's favor. Oral argument is another opportunity to showcase that theme.

Judges have jobs to do: they must decide the issues presented to them. They want to do their jobs well and reach decisions that they believe are both fair to the parties and in full compliance with the existing law. This is often a difficult thing to do, so judges are looking for help from the lawyers. They read briefs carefully, and they ask questions that help them understand the immediate issues before them. Sometimes, especially in an appellate court, they ask questions to help them understand the future consequences of any decision they might make; that is, what kind of a precedent might they set with any possible ruling?

This suggests that a lawyer should approach oral argument as a discussion among professionals about the case. In fact, "oral argument" is an imprecise term at best. Instead, think of this

---

[3] Laurie A. Lewis, *Winning the Game of Appellate Musical Shoes: When the Appeals Band Plays, Jump From the Client's to the Judge's Shoes to Write the Statement of Facts Ballad*, 46 WAKE FOREST L. REV. 983 (2011).

experience as a conversation between the judges and the lawyers. Both the lawyer and the judge have important roles in the case, and an equal interest in doing a good job. Both are trained in the law and can learn from each other by engaging in a high-level, intelligent conversation about the law and how it applies in this specific case.

During oral arguments, judges will often want to discuss the law with you, especially in a situation where the law itself is unclear. When on that turf, judges and lawyers are on relatively equal analytical footing. Both have read the applicable statutes, cases, or other rules of law and can apply the tools of legal analysis to argue for—or reach—a particular conclusion. But when it comes to the facts of the case, lawyers are at a distinct advantage in oral argument. In most cases, lawyers have lived with the case from its inception. They have met the clients, interviewed the witnesses, taken the depositions, reviewed the documents, maybe even tried the case. In short, they know (or should know) the record of the case, cold. Judges know the facts of the case only from the briefs and perhaps from the record, if they have reviewed it. While most judges will have read the briefs before the argument, it is a very rare judge who will have read the entire record of the case. And even a reading of the paper record provides only a glimpse of the living controversy that the lawyers have been intimately involved with.

Thus, it is likely that when the law meets the facts in an oral argument (that is, when the court considers how the law applies), judges will ask the lawyers for help. And this creates opportunities for any advocate, at oral argument, either at the trial or appellate level, to tell the client's story.

There are three broad categories of things that you may try to accomplish during oral argument:

1. Emphasize the key arguments and facts of your client's case

2. Rebut arguments or claims made by the opposing party

3. Answer the questions and concerns of the court

Perhaps counterintuitively, the third thing is the most important: oral argument is all about satisfying the concerns of the judges who will decide the case. But lawyers cannot just walk up to the podium and ask the court, "Do you have any questions?" Rather, lawyers need to have something to start the conversation with, which could be either of the first two points on the list. At the same time, lawyers cannot try to do too much during oral argument; they simply don't have enough time. Preparation is key.

20.2 Preparing for argument

The time needed to prepare for an argument is greatly disproportionate to the amount of time you will actually have to argue. Although you may have anywhere from 15 to 30 minutes to actually argue the case in court, you will need to spend many hours preparing for those few minutes.[4] Here is a checklist of things you should do to prepare for the argument:

☐ **Reread all briefs.**

Carefully review all of the briefs of all parties to the case, either supporting or opposing your position. Doing so will help you think about questions that the judge may need help with during oral argument.

☐ **Review the law.**

Review the key sections of any statute involved. Reread the key cases that you or other parties have cited. You might want to jot down a few lines of notes about each key case or statute, on an index card, that you can then affix to the inside of a manila folder to help you quickly find those authorities if you are asked about them in oral argument. (See the "Try this: using note cards" shadow box below for tips on how to do this.)

---

[4] Sometimes lawyers are given no time limits or are given more than 30 minutes. The average time, however, falls within the 15– to 30–minute range.

☐ **Review the record.**

As noted above, you likely know more about the record than the court does. For that reason, you are likely to get many questions from the court about what is, or is not, in the record. Again, keeping notes about the key parts of the record on 3″ × 5″ note cards may help you quickly locate those items during the argument.

☐ **Determine your best arguments.**

Once you have done all of the above, it is time to start planning how to use your limited time during oral argument. There is no way you will be able to restate, orally, all of the points you made in your brief; that would not be a good use of your time even if you could do it.

Remember that the court will always have your brief to review after the argument is over. You do not waive any issue or argument you make in your brief by failing to address it at oral argument.

☐ **Think about your theme.**

Ask yourself, why should the court want to rule in my client's favor? What is the emotional center of the case, and how can I bring it to life by telling my client's story? This should be easy; after all, you have intentionally chosen a theme while you were writing the brief. Remind yourself of that theme and think about the facts of your case that help you show that theme to the court. Then make a list of those facts for easy reference during the argument.

☐ **Choose your strategy.**

Use the three broad objectives you might have at oral argument (make your best points, rebut your opponent's points, answer questions from the court). You can't always anticipate questions, and you need to have a plan for how to start the argument, so think about the first two possibilities. Do you want to begin by making your own case as strongly as you can, or do you want to begin by attacking your opponent's case?

Don't be afraid to take on your opponent's best arguments directly. By the time you get to oral argument, you will have had ample opportunity to review all of the briefs in the case. If you are the appellant and did not anticipate an argument actually made by opposing counsel in appellee's brief, oral argument may be your best opportunity to refute the argument. But do so fairly. Don't present a caricature of what the opposing argument is, just so you can knock it down as a straw person argument. That will cost you credibility with the court. On the other hand, ignoring your opponent's actual arguments may signal that you are afraid of them or that you have no effective rebuttal.

Professors Robert Sayler and Molly Shadel suggest that audiences quickly tire of negative attacks, "particularly those that are personal or mean-spirited."[5] Thus, while it is important to address opposing arguments, it must be done respectfully.

☐ **Outline your presentation.**
Make a list of the major points you want to cover, in the order you want to cover them. You will want to decide which points to actively raise and which points to hold in reserve, ready to respond if your opponent or the court raises them. But while you should prioritize the major points, understand that you will almost never get to all of them or be able to take them up in the order you prefer.

> **Try this: Using notecards and folders**
>
> Some advocates find it helpful to take notes about the important cases, or parts of the record, and write them on note cards. Then, take a blank file folder and affix these cards to the inside of the folder. Staple or tape only the tops of the cards; that way, you can flip them up and read what may be on the back of the card, or on the card underneath. Doing this can help prevent a disaster if, in your nervousness at approaching the podium, you accidentally drop your stack of papers or note cards.
>
> Another tip, if you decide to type up your notes, staple or tape those notes to folders so that they cannot come loose, and so that they do not rustle in shaking hands. If you do decide to go strictly with papers, it is often easier to manipulate them by stapling them as a booklet rather than using one staple in a

---

[5] Sayler and Shadel, *supra* note 2, at 141.

You should plan to open strong and end strong. Just like in written advocacy, first impressions matter because they can engage the listener's attention; and the last thing you say will be the most easily remembered.[6] Thus, whether you plan to spend most of your time advancing your own presentation or attacking the other side, plan to make your strongest point clearly and succinctly both in your opening comments and in your planned closing.

☐ Prepare your notes.

Avoid the temptation to write a speech. You will never get to deliver it to the court (and you would be very ineffective even if the court allowed you to read your speech). A good oral argument involves lots of questions from the court, which will change the order of your presentation frequently. Rather than write down what you intend to say, make a list of the main points you intend to cover, filling in the broad outline you wrote in the previous step. Then be prepared to jump around in your outline as questions from the court direct you in different directions.

☐ Anticipate questions from the court.

This is both the hardest, and most important, part of preparation. As previously noted, the best use of your time during oral arguments is engaging the court in a conversation about the case. But that conversation begins when the court asks a question. This often means that there is some aspect of your analysis that troubles or confuses the court. So, the more you can do in advance to anticipate those questions, and to plan out your answers to those questions, the better.

Even though many questions may seem to be challenging your position, that is not always the purpose. Sometimes, the judge agrees with your position and is merely seeking clarification—or perhaps even trying to help you state your position more clearly. Always listen to the question and think about why the judge asked it *before*

---

[6] *Id.* at 20.

you start your answer. The best time to think about your answers is when you are preparing, long before you actually enter the courtroom.

Probably the best source of potential questions comes from reading the opposing briefs. Those briefs were written by somebody with a different perspective than you, so they can be very instructive about what the weak points of your case may be. But the court will view briefs by all parties as equal and will want to find a way to reconcile what may appear to be conflicting interpretations of the law or the facts. Thus, courts frequently will pose questions that invite the lawyer to respond directly to the claims made by the other side.

Another way to anticipate questions is to think back to the struggles you may have had in writing the brief. Was there some issue that you felt unsure about or had a hard time understanding? If you had those thoughts when writing your brief, don't be surprised if the court has those same thoughts. The court may ask you for further explanation.

Try to put yourself in the shoes of the court. If you were a judge and had to decide this case, what would bother you about it? What would you find surprising about the arguments you have made? What concerns might the court have about setting future precedents? Think about the potential future consequences of the ruling you are seeking, and expect questions about those consequences.

Once you have come up with a list of potential questions, think about how you would answer them in a way that reassures the court that ruling in your client's favor is not only fair and just, but logical. Your answers should subtly invoke the theme you have chosen for your presentation. Jot them down on note cards too, if you like; but it is better to have these answers programmed in your head so that you don't have to fumble around during the argument looking for the right note card.

20.3   Conduct of oral argument

While the purpose of oral arguments in trial and appellate courts overlap in many ways, the form of the arguments can vary widely. Trial court arguments in particular take very different forms, depending on the preferences of the trial judge. In general, trial court arguments tend to be more informal and less structured than appellate arguments. Here is a brief table to help you think about the differences you may encounter between trial level and appellate arguments:

Trial Court Arguments	Appellate Court Arguments
Usually before a single judge	Almost always before panel of three or more judges
Sometimes in judge's chambers, sitting down	Almost always in courtroom, at podium
Judge may direct order of presentations	Prescribed order for presentations
Often flexible as to time	Usually strict time limits enforced

The best advice we can give is to read the court rules for any court you will be arguing before. If the rules do not specify how oral argument is to be conducted, contact the court clerk's office or the judge's chambers (at the trial level) to find out what the judge's preferences are for oral argument. Or talk to other attorneys who have appeared before a particular judge.

Regardless of which level of court you are appearing in, here are a few tips on how to approach the argument:

☐ **Dress professionally.**

There are many different ideas about what "professionally" means, and there are undoubtedly regional differences about what is appropriate or not. "Appropriate" is different from "bland." The only universal guidance we can give here is that you want the judges to pay attention to your argument rather than your appearance. Lawyer attire signals respect for the seriousness of the occasion. Appropriate attire can go a long way in helping you establish credibility with the court, a key part of persuasion.

☐ **When arguing in a courtroom, take a minimum of stuff to the podium with you.**

You don't want to be fumbling through a lot of paper at the podium. If you must, you can take your brief to the podium, but preferably you will know it inside and out and can leave it at counsel table. If you did a folder with note cards attached inside, take that with you, along with any outline you have. You might also take a blank pad of paper and a pen with you in case you need to jot down some notes during the argument. The briefs and record should be in the courtroom, at counsel table, and perhaps tabbed for any point you anticipate or wish to make. But typically, these things stay behind, though at the ready.

☐ **Introduce yourself and state the party you are representing.**

Especially in a more formal appellate proceeding, it is unlikely that all of the judges on the panel know you. In law school moot court arguments, if you are arguing with a partner, the first person to speak should also introduce the partner. (Real appellate arguments rarely involve two attorneys speaking for the same client.)

☐ [Appellate arguments only] **Appellants: reserve time for rebuttal.**

Rebuttal exists to allow the moving party to respond to something the panel asked the responding party. Most appellate arguments have fairly strict time limitations. Since you, as counsel for the appellant, don't know what might come up during the appellee's argument, it is a good idea to always reserve a few minutes of your time to give a brief rebuttal to whatever was asked or said during the appellee's argument. You can always waive rebuttal later if nothing happened during appellee's argument that you feel the need to rebut, but you cannot ask for additional time if you did not initially reserve a few minutes for rebuttal.

❑ **Start with a pithy opening that sums up the case and then move into the overview or introduction to argument.**

The first sentence or two of your argument should shape the argument. Use a strong opening that catches the judges' attention—something that advocates but stays away from schmaltz. After that, outline the points you want to make. An informed listener is a good listener. Tell the court very briefly the main points you hope to cover (preferably no more than three). This is your chance to establish your main legal theories.

❑ **The opening can come be an ultra-abbreviated, boiled down, two-sentence version of the facts.**

Your strong opening can come from the record rather than from the law if it works for your case. But avoid falling into the trap of sounding like a moot court competition. Sometimes moot court competitors are given the coaching advice to begin by asking the court if it "would like a brief recitation of the facts of the case." The question is a moot court fiction and is very different from the actual practice of law. No advocate does that in a real oral argument.

That being said, the beginning of your argument is still a good opportunity to *tell* a piece of your client's story, to establish the case theme—unless there is some clear indication from the judges that they are uninterested. Yes, we did just say "tell" this time. But it must be brief! Judges typically are fine with a few sentences (i.e., less than a paragraph). If you open that way, use the few sentences to include those key facts that show both what the controversy is about and why a ruling in your client's favor would be fair and just.

❑ **Start from your outline (remember your objectives).**

If you have gotten this far without a question from the court, now is the time to begin making your legal arguments. Start with your first main point and keep going until you get a question from the court.

❑ **Avoid hyperbole or exaggeration.**

This doesn't work any better in oral argument than it does in written advocacy.

☐ **Answer all questions.**

Judges, particularly appellate judges, will tell you that the question and answer process is the most important part of oral argument. Judges don't ask questions just to harass attorneys; they ask questions because they want some help in doing their jobs properly. You actually want the court to ask questions. There is nothing worse during oral arguments than a silent bench, also called a "cold bench."

You should begin your answer, if you can, with a direct "yes" or "no." Then you should explain your answer fully. It is the explanation that the court really wants to hear.

Never, ever, say "I was planning to cover that later in my argument, Your Honor," and then go back to what you were saying before. The judge is interested in hearing about it now, and you should honor her request. On the other hand, do not attempt to butter up the judge by saying something like, "That's a really good question." Transparent attempts at flattery like that will cost you credibility.

If a question is based on an incorrect premise, correct it politely. As we said earlier, the judge wants to do his or her job well, and that can only happen if the judge correctly understands both the facts of the case and the legal arguments. If you don't fully understand the question asked, it is okay to ask the judge for a clarification, respectfully. For example, you could say something like, "Are you asking me whether ..." and then rephrase the question in terms that you understand. But do not do this to avoid answering a perfectly clear question that you would prefer to ignore.

If you get a question you had not anticipated, do your best to think about it on the spot and come up with an answer. If the question is about the record or the facts of the case, use your theme to help you think about how to answer the question in a way that will help your client. If the question is about the law, think back to your basic legal theory and search for an answer there. If you are unable to come up with a satisfactory answer, do not try to guess the "right" answer; that will lead to disaster more often than not. Simply tell the court that you had not thought of that question before, and that you would be happy to file a supplemental brief answering that question if the court would like you to.

☐ Stop talking when a judge begins speaking.

As soon as a judge speaks, you should immediately stop whatever you are saying and listen. Let the judge control the direction of the conversation; by so doing, you can learn a lot about what the judge is thinking or might be troubled by. Do not interrupt the judge; let the judge finish asking the question before you speak again. If the question is a multipart question (which is fairly common), you may wish to jot a quick note on a pad of paper at the podium so that you can be sure to answer all parts of the question.

☐ Go with the flow.

Often, one question and answer will lead to another, and another. Just let it roll; keep answering the questions posed by the court. Once you complete an answer, however, if there is no follow-up question, you should steer back to wherever you were in your outline when the first question was posed. Or, better still, if the questioning has led you into another area that you had planned to cover anyway, it might be a good idea to jump into that portion of your argument since you now know that the court is very interested in that topic.

☐ Accept all gifts.

Remember that not every question posed by the court is a hand grenade. It may be an attempt by one judge to recruit another judge on the panel to a position you and the inquiring judge share. These are known as "softball" questions, where the judge asks you a question that he or she knows you will answer easily and forcefully in a way that might persuade that other judge down the bench. If you spot such a softball, don't hesitate to agree with the judge asking the question and make your point. (But make sure it really is a softball first; it is sometimes hard to know why a judge has asked such a seemingly easy question.)

□ **Leave out issues or cases that were not briefed.**

But you may answer questions from bench even on topics not in your brief. Likewise, if you are the appellant, anything in your opposing counsel's brief that you had not anticipated when you filed your original brief is fair game.

□ **You are not required to fill the time allotted.**

If you get through your entire outline of points you wanted to cover, and there are no more questions, it wastes the court's time by going back and repeating something you have already said. Instead, be willing to concede the extra time. Have a strong "sit-down" line prepared, telling the court exactly what you want it to do and why, then deliver the line and sit down. For example, it's perfectly acceptable to say, "if your Honors have no further questions, [reiterate a key point and the requested relief] ... Thank you."

20.4   Tips on presentation

Many moot court competitions provide students with suggestions on how to make a good appearance at the podium. Some of this advice is useful; some, not so much. Primarily, we believe that if these "toastmaster tips" consume so much of the advocate's attention that he or she loses track of the substance of the argument, those tips can be more harmful than helpful. The substance of the argument is the most important thing. Most judges will forgive, or not even notice, minor tics or habits if what the advocate is saying is substantively compelling.

One of the most common "toastmaster tips" given to student advocates is to avoid using interjections like "um" or "uh." Aside from the point that those verbalizations are often very difficult to avoid, there is some evidence that these interruptions may actually serve several useful purposes in an oral presentation. As one attorney who has studied the subject puts it,

Students are being told (through textbooks, public speaking classes, moot court feedback) that they should eliminate the use of *uh* and *um* in their oral arguments. This is consistent with generally accepted principles of public speaking and reflects the teachings of organizations like Toastmasters. Notably, however, it's not the advice given by judges who actually hear oral argument. Instead, those judges plead with lawyers to stop making speeches and to engage in a conversation with the Court. Most of all, judges just want lawyers to answer the Court's questions. Whether we use *uh* or *um* in those answers seems to be the furthest thing from the judges' minds.

Linguistic study has demonstrated that listeners typically are unaware of the *uh's* and *um's* that pepper our speech, at rates as high as 2% of every spoken word. It's only when we shine a light on *uh* and *um* that people become aware of these so-called "verbal fillers." And it may only be when we declare fillers to be "bad" that people form negative opinions about people who use them, which turns out to be virtually everyone. In fact, verbal fillers may actually increase our comprehension of speech. Studies have shown that verbal fillers function as low-level signals to listeners that can provide a range of valuable information. For example, saying *uh* may function as a warning that the speaker is encountering difficulty in word retrieval or sentence structure. But listeners don't discount what the speaker is about to say (unless they've been trained to do so). Instead, *uh* primes listeners to pay careful attention, because something new or complex is coming their way. Accordingly, listeners who hear *uh* or *um* grasp and remember complex information more quickly than listeners who hear an empty pause. *Uh* may also function as a turn holder, signaling that the speaker has not finished her

thought and that the listener needs to remain
patient.[7]

Another "toastmaster tip" that seems to have a lot of adherents is
that the advocate should stand quite still at the podium and refrain
from excessive hand motions or gestures. But if you are a person who
commonly shows animation and engagement by "talking with your
hands," trying to stop yourself from doing so may be overly
distracting to you and cause you to feel stiff or unengaged. We doubt
very many arguments have been lost because an advocate was
animated; instead, that seems like a good way to signal to the court
that you believe in what you are saying, and the court should, too.[8]

This is not to say you should start to intentionally inject "ums" and
"uhs" into your presentation, since that can be very distracting and
detract from your message. Nor do we suggest that you should start
flailing about at the podium; too much gesturing will look phony and
contrived, and therefore less persuasive. All we mean to say here is
that you should not obsess about these minor quirks about your
presentation. They may be serving you quite well, so long as they are
natural and restrained.

Having said that, evidence supports that coupling a strong substantive
message with expressive nonverbal communication is more powerful
than the substance standing alone. Just as a brief with both a sound
legal theory and an appealing theme is more persuasive than a brief
with just good logos, an argument with solid substance and good

---

[7] E-mail from Barbara K. Gotthelf, Esq., to authors (July 28, 2012) (copy on file
with authors). Based on, Barbara K. Gotthelf, *The Lawyer's Guide to Um*, 11
LEGAL COMM. & RHETORIC: JALWD 1 (2014).

[8] Michael J. Higdon, *Oral Argument and Impression Management: Harnessing the
Power of Nonverbal Persuasion for a Judicial Audience*, 57 KAN. L. REV. 631,
645(2009) (another excellent article to read; citing studies that show speakers who
attempted to speak without such gestures were less persuasive to their audiences
because their speech "lost its intonation, stress[,] and expressiveness; ... there was
a jerkiness to the speech, and a reduction of the number of words used.").

forensics will be more persuasive. The substance of the argument may help convince the court of the legal merit of your case (a very important aspect, indeed), but the nonverbal messages can help convey your feelings toward the case (i.e., the story).[9]

Here are a few forensic tips that we agree you should try (although, again, not at the expense of losing sight of the substance of what you are saying):

□ **Speak clearly, at a normal conversational rate, and with practiced pauses.**

Audio-record yourself speaking in a conversation. What rate of speed do you use? Slowing down to a conversational rate might be hard to do, if you are the kind of person who speaks quickly when nervous or under pressure. It takes some practice. If you have that problem, imagine yourself speaking more slowly—even if it feels unnatural at the moment. If you are enunciating clearly, you are probably at a natural rate. Find the happy medium. And know that if the court has trouble understanding you, the judge will ask you to repeat your answer. That is never going to be a deal breaker about your argument.

In your notes, and as you practice, include pause marks to emphasize words or phrases you want the judges to remember. Pause marks are forward slash marks, and each slash mark represents one beat of time. Practice pausing for effect. Place one slash mark / in front of a word or phrase you want to slightly emphasize. Your notes will likely have several of those one-beat pauses /. A middle-length pause is signified by // or two beats. In oral argument, use those to command attention when you have something that should be remembered as key to the analysis. You will want to use those sparingly. The most dramatic effects are marked by a three-beat pause: ///.[10] That is what comedians use before

---

[9] *Id.* at 634.

[10] Susan D. Miller, BE HEARD THE FIRST TIME: THE WOMAN'S GUIDE TO POWERFUL SPEAKING 127–34 (2006).

punchlines. Because three-beat pauses are dramatic, they probably don't make an appearance in every oral argument.

☐ **Maintain eye contact.**

As we have mentioned before, judges want to have a conversation with the lawyers during arguments. In the United States, at least, it is more natural for people conversing to look at one another. Looking somebody in the eye when speaking to them shows sincerity; avoiding eye contact signals avoidance or insincerity.

☐ **Show confidence.**

This might be hard to do if you don't actually feel confident in the positions you are taking. But use the fact that you have researched and written a brief on the matter to believe in the legitimacy of your argument. Make it confidently, without apology. After all, if the court senses that you don't even believe in your argument, why should the court believe in it?

You can show confidence at the podium by maintaining an upright, but relaxed posture; by speaking clearly and directly in a normal tone of voice; by subtly varying the pitch and volume of your voice; and by maintaining good eye contact with the judges.[11]

☐ **Speak in conversational tones rather than reading tones.**

Speaking tones vary, depending on how the speaker is accessing the material. Reading material takes on a different rhythm and tone than a conversation. As noted above, you should internalize as much of your argument as you can so that you can converse with the judges rather than speaking at them. Besides, if your head is down, looking at your speech laying in front of you at the podium, you are not making eye contact with the court.

---

[11] Sayler and Shadel point out that "audiences respond to confidence," but note also that "there is a difficult balance here—over-the-top delivery can backfire, but telegraphing, 'I'm just going through the motions because I get paid to do this' is worse." Sayler and Shadel, *supra* note 2, at 140.

☐ **Address the court, not opposing counsel.**

This is easier to do when you are arguing in a courtroom, rather than in the judge's chambers, since opposing counsel will be seated at counsel table, outside of your line of sight. But in either setting (courtroom or judge's chambers), avoid the temptation to look at opposing counsel or speak to him. This is not a personal grudge match between you and opposing counsel. It is a professional discussion among colleagues. You need only to persuade the court; opposing counsel's job is to not be persuaded by you. Don't even try to persuade opposing counsel.

☐ **The number one tip on oral argument: be your confident self!**

Everybody has different presentation styles, mannerisms, and quirks. That's okay. That's being human, and stories are all about humanity. If you take on airs or try to pretend you are somebody other than yourself, you will come off as phony. Per the principles of ethos, phoniness is the *last* thing you want to convey as an advocate. Be yourself but be strive to convey the confident version of yourself.

Epilogue

As we write this epilogue, the baseball season is winding down. The playoffs are well underway, and many stories are coming to their conclusions.

One stereotypical baseball story is that of the slugger who comes to the plate, bottom of the ninth inning, bases loaded, two outs. His team is down by three runs. In an epic battle with the other team's best relief pitcher, he fouls off pitch after pitch until he gets the pitch he wants: a fastball, low and away. With one mighty swing, he sends the ball over the fence for a game-winning grand slam. He is a hero! (A warrior hero, to be precise.)

But of course this imagined scene very rarely happens. In real life, most games are won by "small ball": a combination of singles, walks, and other seemingly minor events that allow one team to score enough runs to win the game. Even the slugger needed his teammates to get on base so he could send them home with his heroic swing. Most baseball games are won by every-player heros.

We opened this book with the legal equivalent of the baseball slugger who saved the team with one mighty swing: the story of Linda Brown, who against all odds challenged the status quo of "separate but equal" schools and ended up changing society. But even her victory would have been impossible without the many smaller wins by countless other litigants whose names are lost to history.

Linda Brown's story, representing as it did so many other schoolchildren in similar situations, had a powerful effect on the court. Big changes in the law only happen because a powerful story convinces a court that the pre-existing law is flawed in some significant way. But that does not mean that stories are only useful in the "big" cases that change the world. Every case is "big" to the in the "big" cases that change the world. Every case is "big" to the litigants. We should use our most powerful persuasive tool, story, to help all of our clients.

The appendices that follow are typical of cases that lawyers handle every day, and that have great significance to the parties to those lawsuits. They were written by law students, and demonstrate capable representation of clients through brief writing. Read them and study how each writer made choices about how to tell the client's story. And think about how you, too, can become a client-centered legal storyteller.

We leave you now with our best wishes for many successes in your own legal writing endeavors.

Defendant Arthur Beagle's motion for reconsideration

(student brief)

Elaina Hawthorne,	)	Superior Court of New Jersey,
Plaintiff	)	Camden County
	)	
	)	Chancery Division — Family Part
v.	)	
	)	
Arthur Beagle,	)	Docket No. FV 010-171696
Defendant.	)	
	)	**Petitioner-Defendant's**
	)	**Motion for Reconsideration.**
	)	
	)	*Sat: Hon. Wali Dodes, J.S.C.*

Preliminary statement

This brief is filed in support of Petitioner, Arthur Beagle's motion for reconsideration based on this Court's lack of subject-matter jurisdiction to hear Elaina Hawthorne's application for a restraining order pursuant to the New Jersey Prevention of Domestic Violence Act ("the Act"). Previously, Mr. Beagle filed a motion to dismiss the action, arguing that the online chats that these parties shared are far below the type of "family-like" relationships that the Legislative Declarations discusses in the Act, N.J.S.A. 2C:25-18. This Court denied that initial motion and has scheduled a date for a hearing on the merits of the final restraining order.[1]

---

[1]This brief uses New Jersey local rules of citation, which is what a New Jersey court would expect to see.

As a matter of law, however, this Court should have concluded that the parties' computer conversations were outside the category of "dating relationship" per Section 19(d) of the Act, N.J.S.A. 2C:25-19(d), and the Court had no legal jurisdiction over the parties in this matter. The parties were simply online "chat" friends, whose communications eventually soured. They have seen each other in person only on three occasions, and the sum total of their time in each other's physical presence adds up to perhaps ninety minutes, even though they live within an easy driving distance of each other. Ms. Hawthorne herself declined any opportunity to go on a date with Mr. Beagle. To construe those interactions as a "dating relationship" was in error, unsupported by the existing law.

Statement of facts

Arthur Beagle is a student at the New Jersey State Police Academy. (R. at 22–23.) Mr. Beagle lives in Gloucester County, New Jersey, and has many friends in law enforcement there. (R. at 23.) Although he takes classes during the week and drives to and from Ocean County, he nevertheless enjoys a "moderate" social life. (R. at 23.)

As a way to improve his networking skills, and also to meet women, Mr. Beagle likes to spend time online in chat rooms related to novels. (R. at 23.) He also attends speed-dating events and singles events. (R. at 23.) At one of these speed-dating events in November 2009, Mr. Beagle met at least three women, one of whom was the Plaintiff, Elaina Hawthorne. Mr. Beagle went out on a number of dates with the other two women, and he also began to speak with Ms. Hawthorne over the Internet using a video chat program called "Skype." (R. at 24, 30.)

The parties spoke online two or three times a week for roughly six weeks. (R. at 29–30.) The conversations usually lasted for half an hour, but one or two of the conversations lasted for two hours. (R. at 15.) They talked about their jobs, common interests, and childhood memories, and they had inside jokes. (R. at 4, 18, 27.) The parties both know mutual acquaintances at the Gloucester County Prosecutor's Office, where Mr. Beagle spent a few weeks last summer and where Ms. Hawthorne is currently externing as a third-year law student. (R. at 5, 23, 30.) Mr. Beagle's "dream job" is to try to work for either the Sheriff's Office or the Prosecutor's Office as a detective, but he may become a member of a SWAT team. (R. at 23.) Ms. Hawthorne likewise hopes to work for the Gloucester County Prosecutor's Office after graduation. The parties thus had some stories to exchange about their experiences.

During one of their online conversations, because Ms. Hawthorne was wearing a scarf that made it difficult for Mr. Beagle to understand her, he asked her to take it off. (R. at 25.) She jokingly offered to take off more clothing, and so Mr. Beagle joked in turn that she should remove everything. (R. at 25.) Ms. Hawthorne began to remove her sweater, and so Mr. Beagle stated, "keep on going just as much as you want." (R. at 25.) Ms. Hawthorne then stopped removing clothing and put her sweater back on. (R. at 25.) Mr. Beagle joked about Ms. Hawthorne removing her clothes on a later occasion, but Ms. Hawthorne was unreceptive. (R. at 25.)

At some point a few weeks after they met, Ms. Hawthorne put a quote from *The Time Traveler's Wife* on her Facebook wall, which read, simply, "Why is love intensified by absence?" (R. at 6.) Mr. Beagle, who belongs to a Yahoo chat room devoted to that book, recognized the quote, and therefore clicked on the "like" indicator, which placed a thumbs' up symbol on her Facebook wall. (R. at 25.) When posting the quote, Ms. Hawthorne did not explicitly say that she meant absence from any particular person. Mr. Beagle did not understand the quote to have any personal meaning beyond its literary allusion. (R. at 24.)

During their online chat sessions, Ms. Hawthorne used the computer in her family's den. Plaintiff's sister, Sara, was frequently in the room during those chat sessions and sometimes sat in on them. (R. at 18.) Sara, when questioned at trial, was unable to say that the parties were in a dating relationship—only that they "seemed interested in one another." (R. at 18.)

In fact, Mr. Beagle was interested and for that reason, on at least three occasions, asked Ms. Hawthorne to go on a date: a dinner or a movie. (R. at 24.) She refused each of his three requests for a date—without ever offering to go out at another time. (R. at 24.) And so, the parties have never been out on a date together. (R. at 24.) Mr. Beagle's understanding was that Ms. Hawthorne was too busy to go out on a date with him but yet was puzzled that she happily flirted with him and engaged in "goodbye kisses" over the Internet as well as a long kiss or two. Mr. Beagle, however, thought that the kisses were "corny" and "weird," so he stopped that practice. (R. at 24.) He was also confused why she told him she had no time to go out on dates with him, yet had some other activities that she fit into her schedule, such as the occasional movie with friends and all-afternoon Sunday gym workouts. (R. at 26.) Eventually he assumed that she wasn't really interested in dating him, although he was happy to continue talking to her via Skype. (R. at 27.)

Having no other plans on New Year's Eve, Mr. Beagle attended a singles event with his friend, Al Gero. (R. at 26.) Ms. Hawthorne and her sister also attended the event. (R. at 26.) Although the parties had spoken during the week before New Year's Eve, neither mentioned the singles event to the other. Neither had they made any plans for what is traditionally a date night. (R. at 7.)

Mr. Beagle did not immediately register that Ms. Hawthorne was in the room, but instead first noticed her sister, Sara. "I saw a cute girl and I was about to introduce myself to her—and then realized she was standing next to Elaina and that this was Elaina's sister, Sara." Mr. Beagle guessed that Ms. Hawthorne might be upset by that and said to himself, "Self, this is NOT going to be your night for romance." (R. at 26.) Mr. Beagle guessed correctly: Ms. Hawthorne was upset with Mr. Beagle because she thought "it looked like maybe he was looking to meet other women," and so he attempted to calm her down by holding her hands and by saying "why do I need to look for anyone else when you are right here?" (R. at 8.) Ms. Hawthorne was not responsive to these attempts. (R. at 27.) Sara Hawthorne said that she saw Mr. Beagle nuzzle Ms. Hawthorne's neck while the parties were talking, but no one else, including Ms. Hawthorne, mentioned this in testimony. (R. at 22.) After Mr. Beagle was finished speaking with Ms. Hawthorne and Ms. Hawthorne left the singles event to have dinner with her family, Mr. Beagle and Mr. Gero met two other women and went out to dinner with them. (R. at 27.) The four spent the rest of the night together celebrating New Year's Eve. Mr. Gero testified that he did not believe the parties were in a dating relationship. (R. at 34.) He noted that even with a little bit of hand holding that he saw on New Year's Eve, he had concluded that Mr. Beagle "wasn't all that interested" in Ms. Hawthorne, especially because Mr. Beagle was so willing to go out with other women that same night. (R. at 34.)

Subsequently, Ms. Hawthorne called Mr. Beagle "weasely" on her Facebook account. (R. at 27.) Mr. Beagle had previously told Ms. Hawthorne that he connected being called any kind of animal name to memories of being routinely taunted and bullied as a child, both for his last name (a dog breed) and for his first name, Arthur (the name of a cartoon aardvark). He acknowledged the reaction as somewhat irrational, but nevertheless painful. (R. at 27.) As a result, he was upset by Ms. Hawthorne's comments. (R. at 27.)

More important, Ms. Hawthorne's comments were relayed to people at the Gloucester County Prosecutor's Office, and one person asked him how badly he had treated Ms. Hawthorne to warrant being called a weasel. (R. at 27.) Mr. Beagle also received comments on his own Facebook wall that Ms. Hawthorne had been calling him a "scumbag" at her externship. (R. at 28.) Mr. Beagle had not previously realized that Plaintiff was "Facebook friends" with members of that office and felt that Plaintiff was deliberately trying to harm his professional standing in the very office where he hopes to work one day.

Distressed, and not wanting to have any more online communications but needing the negativity to cease, Mr. Beagle decided that it would be best to talk to Plaintiff in person. (R. at 28.) He bought flowers during his lunch hour because he wanted to handle the situation "in a nice manner." (R. at 28, 32.) Unfortunately, he left the flowers in the car for several hours and the January cold snap froze many flowers in the bouquet. By the time he arrived at Ms. Hawthorne's house that night, a few of the flower heads fell off and, in retrospect, "the bouquet was looking kind of sad and ... [Mr. Beagle] probably should not have given them to her." (R. at 28.) When Mr. Beagle arrived at Ms. Hawthorne's door, he knocked loudly with his knuckles, "as per his training." (R. at 29.) Although Mr. Beagle was trying to explain how he felt about her ad hominem comments, "That can hurt a person's professional reputation. I am really good at what I do," the conversation devolved into a shouting match. (R. at 28.) Mr. Beagle ended up leaving after less than half an hour, and the parties have not spoken since that time.

Although the parties do not have the need to see or speak to each other again, Ms. Hawthorne decided to seek a restraining order in the Camden County family court, claiming that she was the victim of domestic violence between two parties in a dating relationship. The judge hearing Ms. Hawthorne's ex parte application for a Temporary Restraining Order ("TRO") granted it and set a hearing date for a Final Restraining Order.

Prior to that date Mr. Beagle filed a motion to dismiss the action, arguing that the parties had never been in a dating relationship, and that any dispute between them was outside the jurisdiction of the family court. Family courts may grant domestic violence restraining orders only when the parties' relationship is domestic or family-like enough to warrant the extraordinary relief permitted under the Act. N.J.S.A. 2C:25-18. After a hearing on the sole topic of the parties' relationship, Judge Dodes, in a written opinion, concluded that the parties did have enough of a relationship that Ms. Hawthorne could apply for a restraining order under the Act. Mr. Beagle has filed this motion for reconsideration of that ruling.

The total time that the parties have been in each other's physical presence is under ninety minutes, when one counts the speed-dating meeting, the chance encounter on New Year's Eve, and Mr. Beagle's visit to Ms. Hawthorne's home. Ms. Hawthorne herself has rejected the idea of the parties going on a date. And so, the parties have never been on a date. It seems illogical at best that Ms. Hawthorne can reject Mr. Beagle's offers of dates and then later claim that she was dating Mr. Beagle.

Legal argument

Section 19(d) of the New Jersey Prevention of Domestic Violence Act is designed for people in certain and very specific relationships under its definition of "victim of domestic violence." The statute provides that a victim of domestic violence includes any person who has been subjected to domestic violence by a person with whom the victim has had a "dating relationship." N.J.S.A. 2C:25-19(d). The statute leaves undefined "dating relationship," and so the courts have taken the responsibility of applying a commonsense definition of the term. *Smith v. Moore*, 298 N.J. Super. 121 (App. Div. 1997). Situations that stretch beyond that commonsense definition are ineligible for a hearing in a New Jersey family court. This case—two people conversing only with technology and not in person—represents one of those ineligible situations. As such, because this Court has overlooked or erred in its usage of the controlling law, Petitioner-Defendant, Arthur Beagle, requests that this Court grant his Motion for Reconsideration per *R.*4:49-2 and dismiss this case for a lack of subject-matter jurisdiction.

A.   The court's decision went beyond the boundaries of "dating relationship" as interpreted by the precedent.

Because the Act is remedial in nature, the courts look beyond a literal interpretation of its provisions. *See Tribuzio v. Roder*, 356 N.J. Super. 590 (App. Div. 2003); *Cesare v. Cesare*, 154 N.J. 394 (1998). The statute's remedial purpose is to protect potential victims against abuse. N.J.S.A. 2C:25-18; *Cesare*, 154 N.J. 394; *Smith*, 298 N.J. Super. 121. Accordingly, the courts will construe the Act to grant subject-matter jurisdiction when there is a special need to protect the plaintiff against future violence. *Carfagno v. Carfagno*, 288 N.J. Super. 424 (Ch. Div. 1995).

Although the Act is remedial in nature, and otherwise carries broad interpretations, those broad remedies exist for people who qualify as victims under the definitions section, N.J.S.A. 2C:25-19(d). Its protections extend only to people who qualify as victims of "domestic" violence; the word "domestic" is a key threshold that first must be met before there is a broad construction of the Act's terms. The statute was never intended to protect against all violence in all contexts; it addresses violence only in a domestic setting. The Appellate Division has cautioned trial courts against stretching the jurisdictional limits to the point of absurdity. Smith, 298 N.J. Super. 121 (holding that two former renters of a summer shore house were not household members under the Act). Accordingly, the statute's ambit goes no further than the violence that takes place in a "family-like" domestic context. N.J.S.A. 2C:25-18. Those relationships covered under the Act might take on unusual forms in the case law, but courts will still avoid a construction that might "torture the English language" by extending the statute beyond its rational limits. *M.A. v. E.A.*, 388 N.J. Super. 612, 618 (App. Div. 2006) (holding that it was impossible to construe a stepfather's sexually abusive conduct as creating a "dating relationship" with his stepdaughter because there must be limits to the phrase "dating").

Instead, when discussing dating relationships in particular, the Chancery Division has established a number of factors that a plaintiff must demonstrate before a court can establish jurisdiction based on a "dating relationship" under the statute. *Andrews v. Rutherford*, 363 N.J. Super. 252 (Ch. Div. 2003). In addition, the appellate courts have refused to grant jurisdiction when the circumstances indicated that there was no potential for future abuse between the parties. *Tribuzio*, 356 N.J. Super. 590.

There are two reasons why the Court should once again refuse subject-matter jurisdiction over the present case. First, Ms. Hawthorne and Mr. Beagle were never in a dating relationship under Section 19(d) of the statute. Second, the facts of this case negate any reasonable possibility of future abuse.

B. The parties' online-only interactions never created a relationship beyond a mere friendship.

The courts have noted that the Act is not concerned with the individual words, neither "dating," nor "relationships"; rather, it is concerned with both words, i.e., "dating relationships." *See* N.J.S.A. 2C:25-19(d); *J.S. v. J.F.*, 410 N.J. Super. 611, 613 (App. Div. 2009); *Andrews*, 363 N.J. Super. at 382. To this end, the Chancery Court in *Andrews* settled on a factor test after conducting a survey of how other jurisdictions define a "dating relationship." *Andrews*, 363 N.J. Super. at 260. Subsequently, the Appellate Division reused the *Andrews* test in *J.S. v. J.F.*, 410 N.J. Super. 611. The factors given in *Andrews* and *J.S.* are:

1. Whether the parties had a minimal social interpersonal bonding over and above a mere casual fraternization;

2. How long the parties' alleged dating activities continued prior to the acts of domestic violence alleged;

3. What the nature and frequency of the parties' interactions were;

4. What the parties' ongoing expectations were with respect to the relationship, either individually or jointly;

5. Whether the parties demonstrated an affirmation of their relationship before others by statement or conduct;

6. Whether there are any other reasons unique to the case that support or detract from a finding that a dating relationship existed.

Andrews, 363 N.J. Super. at 260. The *Andrews* court acknowledged that the factors it proposed were not necessarily exclusive, and the Appellate Division has noted that there may be other factors not mentioned in *Andrews* that may be relevant. *J.S.*, 410 N.J. Super. at 614; *Andrews*, 363 N.J. Super. at 260. The courts use these six factors to determine whether the totality of the circumstances justify labeling the relationship as a "dating relationship." *Ibid*.

In previous cases where the courts have held that the parties were in a dating relationship, there were a number of factual bases that, as a totality, justified the courts' holdings. In *Andrews*, the plaintiff and defendant were in a relationship for five months while the woman defendant had another boyfriend. 363 N.J. Super. 252. The parties held themselves out as a couple in front of the plaintiff's family, but because of the defendant's other boyfriend, they hid their relationship from the defendant's family. *Id.* at 261. They were seen kissing, hugging, and being affectionate, and they went out at least fifteen times over the course of a few months. *Ibid*. They would spend nights together, and they attended a number of social gatherings together. *Id.* at 261–62. The defendant argued that because she was in another relationship at the time, she could not be held to be in a dating relationship with the plaintiff. *Id.* Nevertheless, the court found that the sum of the circumstances sufficiently established that a dating relationship existed. *Id.*

Similarly, in *J.S. v. J.F.* the Appellate Division found that the facts were sufficient to affirm the trial court's conclusion that the parties were in a dating relationship. 410 N.J. Super. 611. The plaintiff in *J.S.* was an exotic dancer whom the defendant may or may not have paid as a hired escort to accompany him to a family Thanksgiving dinner. *Id.* at 616–17. The evidence also included testimony that the plaintiff had gone to the defendant's home and she was introduced to his parents. *Id.* at 617. They went out several times and would spend weekends together. *Ibid.* Additionally, they spent Thanksgiving together with the defendant's parents, and he had given her money "to help her out financially"; she believed that she was in a dating relationship with the defendant. *Ibid.* The Appellate Court determined that the defendant's attempts to characterize their relationship as a professional one would not prevent the court from granting jurisdiction. *Id.* at 617–18.

Previous cases have shown that there is usually a significant period of time, and frequent contact between the parties, before a dating relationship can be found. In *Andrews*, the parties dated for four months, went out on at least fifteen dates, were seen hugging and kissing, and on occasion spent nights together. 363 N.J. Super. 252. In *Tribuzio*, the parties dated for a year. 356 N.J. Super. 590. The parties in *Sperling v. Teplitsky* dated for two to three years. 294 N.J. Super. 312 (Ch. Div. 1996). In *D.C. v. F.R.,* the plaintiff and defendant dated for thirteen months. 286 N.J. Super. 589 (App. Div. 1996).

Since the parties in this case, Petitioner, Arthur Beagle, and Respondent, Elaina Hawthorne, only met briefly in person twice (once at a speed-dating event and a second time by chance at a New Years' Eve party a few weeks later) and were never physically intimate, Ms. Hawthorne is unable to establish that the parties were in a dating relationship. As such, this is a matter outside of the family court's jurisdiction.

1. *There is an absence of a bond that goes beyond casual fraternization.*

Jurisdiction is improper because Mr. Beagle and Ms. Hawthorne never formed the type of bond that is indicative of a dating relationship. All these parties ever did was talk online for six weeks while Ms. Hawthorne sat in her family's den, and with her sister often sitting in on the conversations. Unlike the parties in either the *J.S.* or the *Andrews* case, who each saw the other party in person on multiple occasions, Mr. Beagle and Ms. Hawthorne made no arrangements to spend time with one another outside of their online conversations. Nor did they ever physically manifest any emotional bond. There were no special occasions spent together, and they did not meet each other's family except in the case of Sara Hawthorne joining their online conversations. In these respects, the present case is wholly dissimilar to all cases where the courts have granted jurisdiction.

By her unwillingness to spend time with Mr. Beagle in person, Ms. Hawthorne has demonstrated that she was emotionally detached rather than emotionally invested in their relationship. Instead of spending time with Mr. Beagle, she went to a singles party with her sister on New Year's Eve. When people are in a dating relationship, as Ms. Hawthorne claims they were, they take time out of their schedules to go out together. Based on the frequency of their conversations, it is only reasonable to say that she had the time to meet Mr. Beagle in person, especially during her winter break. The only plausible conclusion from Ms. Hawthorne's conduct is that she wasn't willing to reserve the time to engage in a dating relationship with Mr. Beagle.

Additionally, they did not discuss anything that would indicate that a dating relationship existed. They talked about their jobs, common interests, childhood memories, and they had inside jokes. There is nothing about this that would show that they were anything but friends. It is true that they flirted, but this alone cannot amount to a dating relationship. Although the parties may have been interested in beginning a dating relationship, they never progressed to that point.

Their interactions were frequently marred by misunderstandings and unreciprocated attempts to advance the relationship. When Ms.

Hawthorne's jokes about undressing for Mr. Beagle came to an abrupt end, it indicated that the parties were unprepared to engage in that sort of behavior. Additionally, when Mr. Beagle refused to continue giving "goodbye" kisses over the Internet, he demonstrated that he was uncomfortable with showing affection. Finally, the misunderstanding about the book quote that Ms. Hawthorne posted on her Facebook wall shows that the parties did not know how to be clear with one another about their feelings.

These few, awkward, and misunderstood encounters strongly suggest that there was an absence of the emotional bond that the courts of New Jersey have held is necessary to engage in a dating relationship.

2. The parties lacked a reasonable expectation of a committed dating relationship.

Mr. Beagle explicitly stated that he never believed the parties to be in a dating relationship. Although factor four of the *Andrews* test does not require that the parties agree on whether they were in a dating relationship, it is still important to note that one of the parties did not see a reason to believe that their online conversations amounted to a dating relationship.

Ms. Hawthorne here testified that she believed the parties were in a dating relationship. However, quite unlike the plaintiff's account in the *J.S.* case, in which her account of the parties' interactions reasonably demonstrated a dating relationship, Ms. Hawthorne's alleged belief that she and Mr. Beagle were in a dating relationship lacks a rational basis. For the reasons already discussed above, there is nothing on record to show that the parties were anything but friends, and that their intent was to be friends.

The parties had no expectation of an exclusive relationship. On New Year's Eve they separately, and without telling one another, went to a singles event. Mr. Beagle indicated that he was willing to meet new people and Ms. Hawthorne never indicated that she was not open to do the same. In fact, Mr. Beagle did end up meeting two women, and he and his friend, Mr. Al Gero, sat with them for some time after Ms. Hawthorne left the event to see her family. Although there may have been a mutual interest between the parties, their actions do not indicate that they expected to have a dating relationship.

Furthermore, Mr. Beagle's statements at the singles event indicate that he did not expect to foster any sort of dating relationship with Ms. Hawthorne. When Mr. Beagle saw Ms. Hawthorne at the event, he said to himself, "this isn't going to be a night for romance." When Mr. Beagle said that it wasn't a night for romance, he meant, in addition to other implications, that there would not be any romance between himself and Ms. Hawthorne. Furthermore, when Mr. Beagle tried to appease Ms. Hawthorne because she was upset with him, he may have demonstrated a desire to advance the relationship, but her rebuffs prevented him from believing that the nature of their friendship was changing.

Finally, Ms. Hawthorne's reaction to seeing Mr. Beagle at the singles event does nothing to indicate that the parties had an expectation of being in a relationship. Plaintiff herself never said at trial that she was angry that he was trying to cheat on her; she only said that she was "upset because it looked like maybe he was looking to meet other women." At most her statement reflects her desire to be the object of Mr. Beagle's affection.

3.   *Their friends and family never considered the parties in a dating relationship.*

Both the *J.S.* and *Andrews* courts spent some time reviewing the evidence that family and friends knew about the parties' romantic dating relationship. There was testimony about family events, and photographs and videos of the parties together in romantic poses. In contrast, the evidence in this case is very thin or nonexistent about the parties holding themselves out as anything other than online chatters. No one besides Ms. Hawthorne has stated that the parties were in a dating relationship. Mr. Beagle's friend, Mr. Gero, testified that he had no belief that the parties were ever in a dating relationship, although he was aware of their conversations and the general nature of their interactions. He noted that Mr. Beagle "wasn't all that interested" in Ms. Hawthorne.

Even Sara Hawthorne, who witnessed more of the parties' interactions than anyone else, would say only that they were interested in each other. Additionally, she stated that she never saw the parties being affectionate during their conversations. She further noted that she might have seen the parties holding hands at the singles event. However, "holding hands" conjures an image that runs counter to the actual occurrence. Mr. Beagle held Ms. Hawthorne's hand to help calm her down, but he received only a mild response and Ms. Hawthorne remained "standoffish." Sara Hawthorne also said that Mr. Beagle "nuzzled" Ms. Hawthorne's neck when they saw each other at the singles event. The veracity of this testimony is suspect, however, because no other witness mentioned this when describing the same event. It appears most likely that Mr. Beagle was leaning in to speak to Ms. Hawthorne and it appeared from a distance to be a display of affection.

Without affirmation from the people who are close to the parties here, it would be unreasonable to accept Ms. Hawthorne's characterization of her relationship with Mr. Beagle.

4. *To find that a purely online relationship is a dating relationship would be a significant and unjustified break with established law.*

The facts of this case are without precedent with respect to the online nature of the friendship. In all of the past cases that have dealt with the present issue, the parties' interactions were primarily in person.

A brief examination of the present state of online relationships shows that relationships conducted online are not "dating" relationships. A recent study demonstrated that younger members of society are less likely to view online relationships as being serious. Trent Parker,

How Bad is It? Perceptions of the Relationship Impact of Different Types of Internet Sexual Activities, 25 Contemp. Fam. Therapy 415, 419–20 (2003). This is probably attributable to the ubiquity and anonymity of online interactions that younger Internet users are more accustomed to. In contrast, older members of society are more likely to believe online relationships are serious, which helps to explain why marriages are occasionally harmed by sexual interactions online. *Ibid.* Thus Ms. Hawthorne's thorough reliance on the "generational factors" mentioned in *J.S. v. J.F.* is unsupported by the evidence: Ms. Hawthorne's argument would be more appropriate if the parties were twice as old as they are. 410 N.J. Super. 611.

Online "dating" is not an end in and of itself. The purpose of online dating websites is to meet a person online, develop a rapport, and eventually start an in-person relationship. Match.com's and eHarmony's "success stories" webpages feature lists of couples who met through their services. eHarmony Success Stories, http://www.eharmony.com/success/stories (last visited Apr. 18, 2010); Match.com, Success@Match, http://success.match.com (last visited Apr. 18, 2010).[2] Importantly, the pictures of the successful couples show the couples together in person. The "success stories" are not lists of people who continue to happily talk online; they are lists of people who are happily dating, engaged, and married. The online aspect of the relationships was merely a stepping-stone for the real intimacy that comes with in-person interaction. The parties here have remained on the hypothetical "first stone."

It would be an unprecedented and harmful change in law to apply the Prevention of Domestic Violence Act to the present circumstances. It would allow the courts to call a series of online conversations a "dating relationship" despite the absence of anything that could reasonably be called a "date" and where the situation completely lacks the domestic context that the statute necessarily requires. Extending the statute in this manner would wholly disregard the statute's intended purpose: to protect victims of violence in a family-like setting.

---

[2]N.B.: date left in place from date student author last checked.

Consideration for the factors set forth in *Andrews* shows that there is an absence of any interaction that would justify finding that the parties were in a dating relationship. The jurisdictional limitations and considerations set forth by the Appellate Division are important to effectuate the true intent of the Act. As this Court is surely cognizant, there are no gradations of remedies permitted under the Act: the same nonexpiring restraints and indefinite limitations are imposed on a defendant regardless of whether the alleged abuse was a serious assault or, as was the situation between these parties, merely a mutual verbal argument between two people disagreeing about the professional impropriety of Facebook postings. Thus, courts must dismiss when there is no evidence of a relationship between the parties. In light of the extraordinary and permanent implications of a restraining order, as well as the minimal nature of the parties' acquaintanceship, this Court should grant this Motion for Reconsideration and dismiss this case for lack of subject-matter jurisdiction.

Conclusion

For the foregoing reasons, it is respectfully submitted that this Honorable Court committed an error in denying jurisdiction, and the Court should thus grant Mr. Beagle's Motion for Reconsideration and dismiss this case.

Respectfully Submitted,

1L Student Intern
For Petitioner-Defendant, Arthur Beagle

Plaintiff Elaina Hawthorne's brief in opposition to motion for reconsideration

(student brief)

Elaina Hawthorne,	:	Superior Court of New Jersey, Camden County
Plaintiff	:	Chancery Division – Family Part
	:	
	:	
v.	:	Docket No. FV010-171696
	:	
Arthur Beagle,	:	**Plaintiff-Respondent's brief in opposition to motion for reconsideration**
Defendant	:	
	:	Sat: Hon. Wali Dodes, J.S.C.

Preliminary statement

Plaintiff-Respondent, Ms. Elaina Hawthorne, began this domestic violence case in January 2010, seeking a Temporary Restraining Order (TRO) against Defendant-Petitioner, Arthur Beagle. The TRO was granted, and, per standard procedures, the date for a full hearing on the merits of a Final Restraining Order (FRO) was set for two weeks later. Ms. Hawthorne sought this protection based on Defendant-Petitioner Arthur Beagle's threatening and harassing conduct toward her just after the parties' breakup. Prior to the scheduled FRO hearing date, Defendant-Petitioner filed a motion to dismiss, challenging this Court's jurisdiction to hear the matter. This Court held a hearing on the sole issue of whether the parties' relationship falls under the jurisdictional category of "dating." At the end of that proceeding, and after hearing testimony from the parties, plus two other witnesses, this Court issued a written opinion, concluding that the parties did, in fact, have the requisite dating relationship, pursuant to N.J.S.A. 2C:25-19(d), and that Ms. Hawthorne was entitled to a hearing on the merits of an FRO.[1]

Nevertheless, Defendant-Petitioner has filed, also at the family, trial level, this Motion for Reconsideration of this Court's written opinion finding jurisdiction. This response brief, thus, is filed on behalf of Plaintiff-Respondent, Elaina Hawthorne, in opposition to that Motion for Reconsideration. By liberally construing the Prevention of Domestic Violence Act, this Court's opinion properly gave effect to the Legislature's intent and followed the guidance prior appellate case law. Accordingly, Ms. Hawthorne respectfully requests that this Court deny Defendant-Petitioner's Motion for Reconsideration and move forward with the scheduled hearing on the merits of her application for an FRO.

Statement of the case

Plaintiff-Respondent, Elaina Hawthorne, is a third-year law student at Rutgers School of Law in Camden, New Jersey. (R. at 4.) In November, at a local speed-dating event, Ms. Hawthorne met the Defendant, Mr. Arthur Beagle, a student at the New Jersey State Police Academy. (R. at 4.) The two bonded at the event after finding that they had much in common. For example, both are interested in working for the Gloucester County criminal justice system after each graduates from his or her respective program. In addition to being a student carrying a sixteen-credit load, Ms. Hawthorne spends twenty

---

[1]This brief uses New Jersey local rules of citation, which is what a New Jersey court would expect to see.

hours each week (four academic credits) externing with the Gloucester County Prosecutor's Office and hopes to be offered a job in that office after graduating and passing the bar exam. *Id.* Likewise, after graduation, Beagle aspires to work in either "the Sheriff's Office or as a detective in the Prosecutor's Office" of Gloucester County. (R. at 23.)

Recognizing their shared interests, the two developed their relationship using, with increasing frequency, telephone calls, Skype video phone calls, Facebook, and Yahoo chat rooms. Of those several methods, the parties opted more and more for Skype: within a short time after the parties met they were using Skype several times a week in order to have real-time and face-to-face calls. Skype allowed them to chat with each other in a very personal and one-on-one manner. (R. at 4.) These meet-ups took place over the course of months and occurred up to three times a week, often lasting two hours at a time. (R. at 14, 15.) During their conversations, Ms. Hawthorne and Mr. Beagle talked about common interests, flirted, and traded quotes about love. (R. at 5, 31.) They would also "blow kisses to each other," and once or twice Ms. Hawthorne and Mr. Beagle even went so far as to fully kiss their respective video cameras as if they were "making out." (R. at 6, 20, 24.) During other, more casual conversations, Ms. Hawthorne's sister, Sara Hawthorne, was occasionally present and spoke to Mr. Beagle a few times. She understood that the parties had a "romantic interest in each other." (R. at 18.) At one point during the relationship, Ms. Hawthorne told her sister that she "might be able to fall in love with [Mr. Beagle]." *Ibid.*

Although the parties spoke and interacted quite frequently each week, Ms. Hawthorne and Mr. Beagle each were also balancing their busy end-of-semester studying schedules and had little time for a lot of social activity. (R. at 24.) Ms. Hawthorne testified that grades were very important to her because of her goal to become a prosecutor and that she studies and prepares for classes at least two or three hours each day. (R. at 4.) In November and December, students at Rutgers

Law are busy preparing outlines for final exams. Her fall semester course schedule kept her at school from early afternoon until 8 or 9 p.m. two days each week,[2] and her fieldwork externship at the Gloucester County Prosecutor's Office meant that she was working in a law office two or three other weekdays. Ms. Hawthorne also holds a part-time waitressing job with hours on some weekend nights and some weekend mornings. (R. at 5.) Mr. Beagle was likewise in class during the week, commuting over an hour each way to school (R. at 24), and Ms. Hawthorne, in addition to attending her regular classes and externship, was working on law school outlines and final exams. Additionally, numerous serious snowstorms occurred during the same period of time. As the newspaper reports demonstrate, 2009 was the "Snowiest Winter in History" in Philadelphia.[3] Given all that was happening at that point in the academic year, the parties were unable to schedule more traditional dates during November and December. Thus, Skype became a very easy and efficient way for the parties to nurture their relationship.

Ms. Hawthorne and Mr. Beagle also engaged each other through Facebook, even though Ms. Hawthorne was new to it. (R. at 17.) On one occasion, Ms. Hawthorne posted her status as "why is love intensified by absence," which she testified referred to her absence from Mr. Beagle. He responded on Facebook that he "liked" it. (R. at 6.) Nevertheless, Ms. Hawthorne remained listed as "single" on Facebook during her relationship with Mr. Beagle. (R. at 17.) When asked why she was listed as "single" despite the fact that she believed she was in a dating relationship with Mr. Beagle, Ms. Hawthorne noted that she had been advised by others, "it is better to say single no matter what" on Facebook. (*Ibid.*)

---

[2]RUTGERS SCHOOL OF LAW, Camden Academic Calendar 2009–10, http://camlaw.rutgers.edu/cgi-bin/academic-calendar.cgi (last visited Apr. 18, 2010) (N.B.: last-visit date left intact from student's brief).
[3]Vince Lattanzio, It's Officially the Snowiest Winter in History, NBC PHILA., Feb. 11, 2010, available at http://www.nbcphiladelphia.com/news/breaking/Its-Officially-the-Snowiest-Winter-in-History-84065947.html.

It was after seeing this particular status that Mr. Beagle asked Ms. Hawthorne to undress in front of the camera during a Skype session. (R. at 6, 21, 25.) She agreed to wear a tank top for their next video phone call, but would not go further. Ms. Hawthorne was reluctant and uncomfortable, she explained, for two reasons. First, the video camera was located in a common area of her house. (R. at 6.) Second, Ms. Hawthorne's personal belief system involves a pledge of chastity before marriage. Mr. Beagle was aware that Ms. Hawthorne is a member of the Facebook group "Purity." (R. at 25.)

Ms. Hawthorne and Mr. Beagle saw each other in person during a New Year's Eve party at T.G.I. Friday's. (R. at 7, 26.) Ms. Hawthorne attended the party because Sara Hawthorne, her sister, asked for company. (R. at 7.) Mr. Beagle attended with his friend, Al Gero, as a "wingman." (*Ibid.*) Ms. Hawthorne testified that she was "unhappy" to see Mr. Beagle at the event, particularly because this was only a few days after the conversation in which he asked her to take off her clothes. (*Ibid.*) Mr. Beagle, however, seemed happy to see her and immediately asked his friend to please let Mr. Beagle and Ms. Hawthorne have some alone time. (R. at 33.)

Both parties testified that they sat down next to each other—side by side—in a booth. They began talking and holding hands. (R. at 8, 21, 27.) Ms. Hawthorne's sister testified that she saw the parties "being kind of cuddly" and that Mr. Beagle "nuzzled her neck once." (R. at 20, 22.) Later, both of the Hawthorne women needed to leave for a family dinner. (R. at 7.)

Although Mr. Beagle told her that he was at that New Year's Eve event only as a "wingman" for his friend, Ms. Hawthorne was somewhat upset that she saw him at the event. (R. at 9, 7.) Nevertheless, the parties continued their relationship via Skype just as they did before. (R. at 9.) During one such Skype session, Mr. Beagle again asked Ms. Hawthorne to undress. (*Ibid.*) It was then that Ms. Hawthorne began to become skeptical of Mr. Beagle and posted on her Facebook wall "Arthur is really Weasely," which, she testified, was an obvious, joking reference to Harry Potter. (R. at 1.) Both parties are readers and belong to online chat rooms about popular books. (R. at 8.) Mr. Beagle was angry about the post, however, because he had previously told her about being teased for his name earlier in his life. (R. at 23.) He called Ms. Hawthorne, admonishing her for that, and also for not being "more physical" in their relationship. (R. at 27, 10.) In response, Ms. Hawthorne then told Mr. Beagle "we should just be friends," to which Mr. Beagle responded "sure, OK." (R. at 10.) Ms. Hawthorne viewed this conversation as "that's when we broke up." (R. at 10.)

The next day at her externship, Ms. Hawthorne expressed frustration to her co-workers that Mr. Beagle did not understand a simple joke. (R. at 10.) Mr. Beagle became aware of Ms. Hawthorne's comments through mutual friends and, the very next night, appeared, uninvited, at Ms. Hawthorne's house. He had never been to her house prior to that time. (R. at 11.) Mr. Beagle banged on Ms. Hawthorne's door so loudly that it appeared to Ms. Hawthorne and her sister that he was using his nightstick, although Mr. Beagle denies this. (R. at 10, 20, 29.) Ms. Hawthorne answered the door and found Mr. Beagle "so mad that he was shaking." (R. at 11.) He screamed "don't you dare call me stupid to my friends! And don't post things about me on Facebook! That can hurt a person's professional reputation! I am really good at what I do, you know!" (*Ibid.*) Ms. Hawthorne testified that this particular statement worried her because "he is a very good marksman. So I knew what he was suggesting—that he might hurt me. Because he is such a good marksman." (*Ibid.*) In his testimony, Mr. Beagle has agreed that he "takes great pride in his ability to shoot guns accurately." (R. at 19.)

Adding to Ms. Hawthorne's unease at the scene, Mr. Beagle presented her with a bouquet of dead, headless flowers. (*Ibid.*) Trying to defuse the situation, Ms. Hawthorne said she was "sorry that it had not worked out between us." Mr. Beagle was upset and responded, "no, this is not working and it is just too bad." (R. at 12.)

After he left her house, Ms. Hawthorne called the police and sought the restraining order. Although admitting that their relationship was nontraditional, Ms. Hawthorne testified:

> This thing I had with Arthur was not just friends. It was definitely much more than that. We were in a relationship. And now I am scared about what he might do to me—we could very well end up seeing each other all the time because of the line of work we are both in.

[(R. at 12).]

Despite the Defendant's challenge to this Court's jurisdiction, the Honorable Wali Dodes ruled that this matter can be adjudicated under the New Jersey Prevention of Domestic Violence Act. Specifically, Judge Dodes reviewed the applicable case law interpreting the "dating relationship" language in the Act, before he held that "plaintiff and defendant showed affection through words and actions, they outwardly demonstrated their relationship, and they spoke regularly for long periods of time (albeit on the Internet). These actions undoubtedly reflect typical behavior in a dating relationship as outlined by our statute and by prior decisions." (Tr. Op. at 2.) Because Judge Dodes's ruling accurately reflects the state of the law, this Court should likewise deny Defendant-Petitioner, Arthur Beagle's current motion to the same court for reconsideration of that jurisdictional ruling.

Legal argument

A. The Defendant-Petitioner is unable to show any sort of error in this Court's previous ruling that would give rise to an appropriate reconsideration under *R.* 4:49-2.

Defendant-Petitioner's Motion for Reconsideration is premised upon a narrow view of modern dating trends. This Court, on the other hand, has already properly concluded that under the expansive reach of the Prevention of Domestic Violence Act ("the Act"), these parties were dating.

The standard for Motions for Reconsideration are codified by New Jersey Rule 4:49-2, which states:

> [T]he motion shall state with specificity the basis on which it is made, including a statement of the matters or controlling decisions which counsel believes the court has overlooked or as to which it has erred.

[(*R.* 4:49-2).]

There was neither an overlooked fact nor a legal error in this Court's ruling on Defendant's Motion to Dismiss. Rather, the parties' relationship satisfies several of the factors approved by the Appellate Division in *J.S. v. J.F.*, 410 N.J. Super. 611 (App. Div. 2009). Because this Court's prior holding correctly applied the germane case law, this Motion for Reconsideration should be denied and Ms. Hawthorne should receive a hearing to argue the merits of a FRO.

B. This Court has already properly effectuated the broad intent of the Act's scope and the courts' expansive interpretation of "dating relationship" when it took jurisdiction over the case.

This Court can comfortably deny Defendant-Petitioner's Motion for Reconsideration because its initial ruling was well within the purview of what the Legislature intended. The pertinent law indicates that a "victim of domestic violence" includes "any person who is 18 years of age or older or who is an emancipated minor who has been subjected to domestic violence by a spouse, former spouse,

or any other person who is a present or former household member."
N.J.S.A. 2C:25-19(d). The New Jersey Legislature amended this
provision in 1994 to include protection for individuals who have
"been subjected to domestic violence by a person with whom the
victim has had a dating relationship." *Ibid.*

The pertinent section of the statute does not provide a definition of
what constitutes a "dating relationship." Interpreting courts have
rejected the notion of an absolute or plain meaning to the phrase.
Instead, courts will interpret it in light of the policy set out by the
New Jersey Supreme Court to look at the Act through a broad lens.
Cesare v. Cesare, 154 N.J. 394 (1998). The New Jersey Supreme
Court has stressed the importance of a liberal interpretation "to
achieve its salutary purposes" so as to "assure the victims of
domestic violence the maximum protection from abuse the law can
provide." *Id.* at 399.

Because the Legislature has called for a liberal construction, courts
have developed and use an expansive and liberally construed factor
test to determine when parties are in a dating relationship. There
are relatively few opinions that look at the specific issue of what is or
isn't a dating relationship in New Jersey. Each of the cases, however,
has agreed that a broad factor test is the appropriate analysis
vehicle. The most often cited opinion, though trial level, outlined a
series of factors after considering the various tests used in other
states. *Andrews v. Rutherford*, 363 N.J. Super. 252, 260 (Ch. Div.
2003). Those factors, though broken out into six separate parts,
really boil down to some sort of romantic attachment between the
parties beyond that of "mere casual fraternization." *Ibid.*

1. Was there a minimal social interpersonal bonding of the parties over
   and above mere casual fraternization?

2. How long did the alleged dating activities continue prior to the acts
   of domestic violence alleged?

3. What were the nature and frequency of the parties' interactions?

4. What were the parties' ongoing expectations with respect to the relationship, either individually or jointly?

5. Did the parties demonstrate an affirmation of their relationship before others by statement or conduct?

6. Are there any other reasons unique to the case that support or detract from a finding that a "dating relationship" exists? *Ibid.*

A recent Appellate Division opinion, covering some of the same ground, found the *Andrews'* decision factors "useful" though not mandatory. *J.S. v. J.F.,* 410 N.J. Super. 611, 616 (App. Div. 2009). The appellate court, reminded that the Act calls for liberal construction, declined to adopt any exclusive formula, because it worried that doing so would potentially fall short of embracing a broad enough category of people covered by the Act's protections. Rather, the Appellate Division encouraged courts to combine a factor analysis with an examination of "the parties' own understanding of their relationship as colored by socio-economic and generational influences" in order to best achieve the broad relief that the Legislature intends. *Id.* at 616; *see also Andrews,* 363 N.J. Super. at 260 ("in the interest of interpreting the Act broadly as required by Cesare and the statute itself, these factors should also be liberally construed.").

Those relationships covered under the Act might take on unusual forms but, so long as they still demonstrate some romantic connection, can provide a jurisdictional basis for the family court to consider a restraining order. For example, the Appellate Division in *J.S. v. J.F.* easily affirmed the family court's finding of jurisdiction, regardless of the defendant's claim that the nature of the relationship—and the physical affirmations—were based in finances rather than romance. 410 N.J. Super. 611. The defendant in *J.S.* claimed that the plaintiff, an exotic dancer by profession, was his paid escort at his family's Thanksgiving dinner. Even if he had paid for her Thanksgiving company, the Appellate Division reasoned, "the fact that a person receives monetary benefit from engaging in a relationship does not automatically disqualify that person from the Act's benefits." Indeed, the Appellate Division opined, in dicta, that *au pairs* should be considered household members under the Act even when the relationship's foundation was financial. *Id.*

Instead, the Appellate Division focused on the relationship's other qualities that tended to weigh in favor of calling this a dating situation. *Id.* at 615. Enough of the other factors were present to merit the family court taking jurisdiction. The parties admittedly had a romantic and physical relationship. They shared time together and spent a holiday together in the presence of the defendant's family—the Thanksgiving dinner for which he allegedly paid her to attend with him. *Id.* at 617. The court, without much pause, affirmed the family court's finding that these facts amounted to a dating relationship.

Similarly, a couple may still be in a legally defined dating relationship even when one of the partners has multiple other dating partners and no real expectations of permanency or exclusivity with the other party. *Andrews*, 363 N.J. Super. at 265. A court in that situation will still look at the overall romantic nature of the parties' relationship. In *Andrews*, the defendant denied dating the plaintiff because she had another, publicly acknowledged boyfriend. The plaintiff, according to the defendant, was just someone whom she spent time with and had physical relations with. When the *Andrews* court set aside the existence of the defendant's other boyfriend, the relationship between the parties met other factors. The parties sustained a relationship over the course of several months that included "the typical conduct of young people who are exploring the limits of each other's feelings for one another." *Id.* at 265. The family court found that the parties demonstrated an interpersonal bonding over and above a mere fraternization by the fact that they "saw each other regularly" in a noncasual fashion and had physical affirmations of their romantic attraction to each other, evidenced, by way of example, in a video of the parties enjoying themselves in a hotel room during a late night New Year's Eve party. *Id.* at 264. The evidence also demonstrated other examples of romantic and physical attraction to each other. *Ibid.* The plaintiff had introduced the defendant to his friends and family, even though she had not reciprocated with her friends or family. The family court used the commonsense reasoning that these parties were dating because the presence of the other factors counterbalanced the nonexclusivity of the relationship, and ultimately controlled the legal conclusion. *Id.* at 260, 265.

Moreover, in one of the very few unpublished opinions on point, the Appellate Division recently held that a dating relationship was present in a case in which the only factor that was considered was the sixth "catchall" factor outlined by the *Andrews* court. *Jensen v. Baratta*, No. A-3805-07T3, 2009 LEXIS 3185 (N.J. Super. Ct. App. Div.). In Jensen, the parties met at a five-day real estate class and had several lunches together in the company of other attendees. *Id.* at *2. The parties also went out to dinner once, though the relationship fizzled after this meeting. *Ibid.* Six years later, the defendant was seen in his car outside the plaintiff's house with a loaded gun, $10,000 in cash, and a notebook that said "real-estate girl." *Id.* at *3. The Appellate Division agreed with the family judge, who "gave great weight to number six of the *Andrews* factors, that is, other reasons unique to the case that supported the finding that a 'dating relationship' existed." *Id.* at *6. Thus, a court's discretion is broad enough to find a dating relationship solely under just one of the factors, if the circumstances warrant it.

The only limitation that a court has ever mentioned with respect to dating relationships are those situations, far different from the romantic situations our parties are in, where the ruling would be "absurd." *M.A. v. E.A.,* 388 N.J. Super. 612 (App. Div. 2006). The appellate judge in that case was speaking about a very different set of circumstances—a sad situation in which a mother was trying to obtain a restraining order for her teenage child, who was being sexually abused under circumstances not covered by the New Jersey child abuse statute. Although recognizing that the facts fell into a gap between the two statutes, and although reluctant to leave the child with no recourse, the appellate panel was forced to agree that sexual molestation could not, nor could it ever, be considered a "dating relationship" because such a finding would "unacceptably torture the English language and euphemize the hostile nature of defendant's alleged behavior." *Id.* at 618. The M.A. case, therefore, is typically considered outside of the dating relationship panoply of decisions.

Under the courts' holistic and liberal examination of dating relationships, this Court properly concluded that these parties had a dating relationship. From the first meeting of the parties at the speed-dating event—an event whose very purpose was to further the attendees' goal of finding someone with whom to have a dating relationship—these parties moved beyond a mere casual fraternization. The courts have already determined that they will disregard one unusual factor if the overall tone of the relationship is romantic. That is exactly what characterizes this relationship.

First, the parties interacted frequently over the course of their months together. Given the limited amount of free time that either party had during November and December, they chose to spend quite a lot of it with each other. They were in each other's company for numerous hours, juggling their individual time constraints and their obligation–restrictions in order to be with each other. The parties were stymied by school, studies, and unexpectedly bad weather. Throughout their relationship, Ms. Hawthorne was a busy third-year law student, taking evening courses, studying, waitressing, and working twenty hours each week at the very office where she hopes to work after graduation. She was also studying for her finals during many of those weeks. The Defendant-Petitioner spent several hours of his week with Ms. Hawthorne even with his own studies and three hours of commuting time each day. The level of commitment the parties demonstrated to each other was at least as serious, if not more so, than the dating relationships in the *J.S.* and *Andrews* cases.

The nature of the parties' frequent interactions also bears the hallmarks of a dating relationship, even if some of their dates were not the traditional dinner-and-a-movie. There was just as much, if not more, alone time for this fledgling couple. In addition to other means of communication such as traditional phone calls and Facebook, the parties Skyped with each other quite often—typically three times a week for almost two months, with some sessions even lasting as long as two hours. During that time, the parties demonstrated the type of "clear romantic attraction to each other" noted as important in the *Andrews* case. Mr. Beagle and Ms. Hawthorne talked about each other's interests, flirted, and even traded love quotes. Moreover, they kissed each other albeit via a computer screen and camera. The video calls were intimate enough that Mr. Beagle asked Ms. Hawthorne several times to undress in front of the camera. People do not kiss casual acquaintances on the lips; nor do they ask them to undress.

Both Ms. Hawthorne's sister and Mr. Beagle's friend testified that they were aware of the parties' frequent communications. Ms. Hawthorne's sister had personal knowledge of the communications because she had been invited into some of them. Likewise, just as the holidays in the two reported cases played a role in demonstrating the dating relationships, the New Year's Eve event at T.G.I. Friday's similarly demonstrated to friends and family that their romantic interest in each other was beyond "mere casual fraternization." Both Mr. Beagle's friend, Al Gero, and Ms. Hawthorne's sister concur in their testimony that the parties were sitting alone together, holding hands, cuddling, and "nuzzling necks." Defendant-Petitioner himself asked Mr. Gero if he could have some time alone with Ms. Hawthorne, forsaking his promised role as "wingman" for Mr. Gero, helping him meet women.

Courts must continue to broadly define "dating relationships" and recognize that technology will play an increasingly significant role in dating practices. To do otherwise will soon render the Act largely irrelevant to the modern world. This case is a perfect example of why the court must continue to construe "dating relationship" broadly. The presence of technology in this relationship is merely a sign of modern times. In every other way the bond looks like a traditional dating relationship. The Legislature, in leaving "dating relationship" undefined, purposely deferred to future courts to refine the contours of the term to reflect future understanding of dating. As the appellate court in *J.S.* has signaled, modern relationships should be understood and colored by "generational influences." Skype was just a vehicle to let the parties be in the same room with each other in real time.

Even if these parties fall under the category of "online dating," that is still within the new boundaries of this era and this Court has plenty of discretion to include online dating as falling within the jurisdiction of the Act. That is why the sixth "catchall" factor in the *Andrews* case exists. Online dating is a growing trend that shapes the structure of dating relationships. The New York Times has reported,

> Since the current recession began, the popularity of online dating has surged—memberships are up and new matchmaking portals have emerged to take advantage of the demand—industry growth of up to 30 percent is expected in the next year or two, according to the tracking site DatingService.com.

[Scott James, *In Calculations of Online Dating, Love Can Be Cruel*, N.Y. Times, Feb. 12, 2010, at A25A.]

In 2007, the online dating industry was estimated to have generated $900 million in revenue.[4] This number is estimated to grow to over $1.9

---

[4]BUSINESSWIRE.COM, JupiterResearch Sees Steady Growth for Online Personals, *Despite Explosion of Social Networking* (Feb. 11, 2008),

billion by 2012.[5] The practice has become so common that to provide protection for online daters, the New Jersey Legislature passed the Internet Dating Safety Act in May 2007.[6] Just as the Legislature did, the Judiciary should act to provide protection for online daters.

Thus, this Court had sufficient legal justification to conclude that this relationship is covered by the New Jersey Prevention of Domestic Violence Act. There is nothing in either the law or in the facts of this case that would warrant a ruling in favor of Defendant-Petitioner's Motion for Reconsideration. Rather, this case should proceed to the hearing on the merits of granting a Final Restraining Order.

Conclusion

For the foregoing reasons, Respondent, Elaina Hawthorne, respectfully requests that this Honorable Court deny this Motion for Reconsideration and reschedule the remainder of the Final Restraining Order hearing.

Respectfully submitted,

1L Law Student Intern

for Plaintiff-Respondent, Elaina Hawthorne

---

http://www.businesswire.com/portal/site/home/permalink/?ndmViewId=news_view&newsId=20080211005037&newsLang=en.

[5] *Ibid.*

[6] The Internet Dating Safety Act requires that online dating sites tell customers whether they do background checks on their members.

Plaintiff's brief in support of plaintiff's motion for summary judgment and in opposition to defendant's motion for summary judgment

(student brief)

In the Superior Court of
Marion County, Indiana

The Gloucester Hotel of Indianapolis, a Delaware corporation,	
Plaintiff	
v.	No. 1531-GD-2012
Save Our Forest Trees, Inc., a California nonprofit corporation,	
Defendant	

Plaintiff's brief in support of plaintiff's motion for summary judgment and in opposition to defendant's motion for summary judgment

I. *Preliminary statement*

The Gloucester Indianapolis Hotel is a relatively new luxury hotel in downtown Indianapolis, with a growing reputation in hosting meetings for nonprofit and business organizations. In summer 2011, it agreed to be the host hotel for a two-day conference of 75 to 100 members of the organization Save Our Forest Trees, Inc. The Hotel entered a contract to hold 150 room nights open for the organization's members, thereby forgoing the opportunity to book other organizations for that same time period. The contract included a provision that required SOFT to sell 90% of the reserved block to its members. If it failed to do so, SOFT would be responsible for the difference between 90% of the reserved block (or 135 room nights) and the actual number of room nights sold to SOFT guests, at the contracted room rate (a discount from the hotel's normal rate).

SOFT guests in fact reserved only 82 room nights, far less than the contractually required 135 room nights. Accordingly, the Hotel invoiced SOFT for the 53 room nights it had promised to sell but failed to use. When SOFT refused to pay the invoice, this litigation ensued.

Since these essential facts are all undisputed, both parties have moved for summary judgment.

II.   *The facts of the case*

The Gloucester Indianapolis Hotel is part of the Gloucester Worldwide hotel group, a growing chain of luxury hotels and resorts. The Indianapolis hotel, which opened in 2007, achieved an 82.3% occupancy rate in 2012, the second highest in the entire Gloucester Worldwide chain and well above the Indianapolis average rate of 68.2%. Mason Dep. 5:11–6:19, Aug. 20, 2013.

Sometime in August 2011, Julius Mason, the General Manager of the Gloucester Indianapolis, received a call from a representative of a nonprofit organization known as Save Our Forest Trees, Inc., headquartered in California. *Id.* at 10:1–14. The organization wished to host a conference on the campus of Indiana University Purdue University Indianapolis (IUPUI) in July 2012 and wished to reserve a block of rooms for up to 75 out-of-town participants who were expected to attend (a total of 150 room nights for the two-day conference). Since this was well within Gloucester Indianapolis' capacity of 250 rooms, Mr. Mason negotiated a group rate of $159 per night, a discount from the normal summer rate of $189 per night. He prepared the standard hotel contract for a group reservation and mailed it to SOFT's headquarters in Eureka, California. *Id.* at 11:10–14. It was returned by mail about ten days later, and the reserved block was entered into the hotel's reservation system. *Id.* at 12:3–6.

The contract signed by SOFT included this paragraph:

> **Reservation Deadline:**   June 1, 2012
>
> In order to qualify for the guaranteed room rate, individuals must reserve rooms on or before the Reservation Deadline specified above, and must specify the Group Name. After the Reservation Deadline, rooms not reserved in the Group Name will be returned to the Hotel's general inventory and may be sold by the Hotel to any guest at normal Hotel rates. Group acknowledges that it may forgo the opportunity to reserve those rooms for other guests prior to the Reservation Deadline, and that the Hotel will incur costs in reselling rooms, and that these damages are difficult to ascertain. In the event that the Group fails to reserve 90 % of the Room Block Reservation specified above by the Reservation Deadline, Group agrees to pay as liquidated damages, and not as a penalty, the difference between the actual number of rooms reserved by Group guests and 90 % of the Room Block specified above, at the Guaranteed Room Rate, such payment to be due 15 days after the Reservation Deadline.

Contract for Room Reservations, Aug. 15, 2011, attached to Freebird Dep. Ex. 1, Aug. 20, 2013.

Less than a month later, Mr. Mason received a call from the Hoosier Club, an organization of Indiana small- to mid-size business leaders interested in promoting Indiana businesses to global markets. Mason Dep. 15:6–19. The Hoosier Club met annually, usually in Indianapolis, and usually drew as many as 200 participants to its summer meetings. It wanted to schedule its 2012 conference at the hotel, on the same weekend previously booked by SOFT. However, due to the preexisting commitment to SOFT and a few other contractual obligations, Mr. Mason could offer only 125 rooms per night to the Hoosier Club, so the group elected to book rooms at another nearby hotel. *Id.* at 17:2–21.

Shortly after June 1, 2012, Mr. Mason checked the pickup report for the SOFT conference and learned that only 82 rooms had been reserved from the SOFT block, far fewer than the total of 150 reserved by SOFT. *Id.* at 22:17–23:4. Per the contract, Mr. Mason instructed his staff to invoice SOFT for the shortfall, but for reasons that he cannot explain, that invoice was not sent until July 27, 2012. *Id.* The invoice was for $9480.38, representing room charges and tax for a shortfall of 53 rooms (90% of the block of 150, less the 82 rooms actually reserved by SOFT guests). Freebird Dep. Ex. 3.

Luckily for the Gloucester Hotel, the Hoosier Club meeting that weekend was larger than usual. Gloucester was able to accommodate many of the overflow guests attending the Hoosier Club meeting, at the hotel's normal room rate of $189 per night. Mason Dep. 26:5–16.

SOFT has paid no part of the July 27 invoice and has indicated verbally to Gloucester that it does not intend to pay any part of it. Freebird Dep. 42:17–24. Gloucester therefore filed this action to collect the amount due under the contract provision. After the completion of discovery, both parties agreed that the basic facts are undisputed, and both parties have filed Motions for Summary Judgment that are now before the Court for resolution.

III. Issues

A. Is a liquidated damages clause enforceable on its face when it was freely bargained for and when the hotel would be unable, at the time the contract was signed, to predict how much it would be damaged if the booking party breached its promise to generate stated room revenue? *Suggested Answer:* Yes.

B. Is the amount of the liquidated damages stipulated in the contract reasonable since it is proportional to the extent of the breach by the booking party? *Suggested Answer:* Yes.

IV. Argument

Summary judgment should be granted where there is no genuine issue of material fact, and where the moving party is entitled to judgment as a matter of law. Ind. Trial Rule 56(C). Construction of a written contract is generally a question of law for the court, and summary judgment is a particularly appropriate means for resolving such cases. *Ancich v. Mobil Oil Corp.*, 422 N.E.2d 1320, 1322 (Ind. Ct. App. 1981). It is undisputed that SOFT signed the Group Contract for a conference to be held July 13 and 14, 2012, at the Gloucester Hotel, and that it failed to sell 90% of the rooms reserved to its guests, so summary judgment is appropriate in this case.

Liquidated damages provisions are enforceable when, if a breach occurs, the resulting damages are uncertain and difficult to ascertain, and the sum stipulated as liquidated damages may fairly be allowed as compensation for the breach. *Gershin v. Demming*, 685 N.E.2d 1125, 1127–28 (Ind. Ct. App. 1997). The designation in a contract of a sum as "liquidated damages" in the event of a breach indicates the parties' intention to limit their recovery to only the amount of the stated damages. *Beck v. Mason*, 580 N.E.2d 290, 293 (Ind. Ct. App. 1991). Where the sum stipulated in the agreement is not greatly disproportionate to the loss likely to occur, the provision is valid. *Nylen v. Park Doral Apts.*, 535 N.E.2d 178, 184 (Ind. Ct. App. 1989).

In this case, the damages that the Gloucester Hotel might have suffered if SOFT did not sell the required block of rooms was uncertain and difficult to ascertain. The liquidated damages clause in the contract was intended by the parties to be the exclusive remedy in the event of a breach, and the sum specified is directly proportional to what the actual damages likely would have been. The clause is therefore enforceable.

A.   The liquidated damages clause in this contract is valid and enforceable

Whether a contractual provision stipulating damages in the event of a breach is a valid liquidated damages clause or a penalty is a question of law for the court. *Mandle v. Owens*, 164 Ind. App. 607, 330 N.E.2d 362, 364 (1975). In determining whether a stipulated sum payable on breach of a contract constitutes liquidated damages or a penalty, the court will consider the facts, the intention of the parties, and the reasonableness of the stipulation under the circumstances of the case. *Nylen*, 535 N.E.2d at 184.

In this case, the parties freely entered into a contract knowing that it contained a liquidated damages clause, not a penalty. Because the amount of actual damages in the event of a breach were, at the time the contract was negotiated, difficult or impossible to ascertain, and because the contract provides for no other remedy besides payment of liquidated damages, the clause is valid.

1.   *The clause was freely bargained for and is unambiguous*

Indiana courts presume that contracts represent the freely bargained agreement of the parties. *Grott v. Jim Barna Log Sys.–Midwest, Inc.*, 794 N.E.2d 1098, 1102 (Ind. Ct. App. 2003). Nothing in this record suggests that this contract was not freely bargained.

Absent ambiguity, courts need only examine the contract itself to determine the intention of the parties. *Kincaid v. Lazar*, 405 N.E.2d 615, 620 (Ind. Ct. App. 1980). Here, the contract unambiguously includes a liquidated damages clause, specifying the amount of damages that SOFT should pay in the event that SOFT attendees did not reserve 135 rooms (90% of the block of 150).

The Executive Director of SOFT testified that she did not read the entire contract before signing it, Freebird Dep. 9:2–10:14, but that is not a defense to enforcement of the unambiguous provisions of the contract. In *Sanford v. Castleton Health Care Center*, 813 N.E.2d 411 (Ind. Ct. App. 2004), the plaintiff sought to avoid enforcement of an unambiguous provision of a contract with a health care institution for the care of her mother. The plaintiff brought her mother to the Castleton Health Care Center for treatment. During the admission process, her mother, who suffered from Alzheimer's, became agitated and aggressive; in addition, the plaintiff had to care for her own children who were with her as she completed the form. As a result, she signed the health care contract without reading it, although she admitted that nobody at the care facility prevented her from doing so. *Id.* at 415. The court held the contract enforceable on its terms.

Here, SOFT has even less reason to avoid the unambiguous contract language than did the plaintiff in *Sanford*. Ms. Pat Freebird, the SOFT Executive Director, testified that she received the contract in the mail in her office in Eureka, California, and that she had enough time to review its provisions to be sure they conformed to her understanding of the reservation she wanted to make. Freebird Dep. 9:2–10:14. There was no chaos or confusion, or really any sort of time pressure; the contract was returned to the hotel ten days after it was sent. Mason Dep. at 12:3–6. Accordingly, the contract is enforceable on its own terms.

2. At the time the contract was negotiated, actual damages for a possible breach were difficult to ascertain

A liquidated damages clause provides for the payment of a stated sum of money upon breach without proof of damages. *Gen.*

Bargain Ctr. v. Am. Alarm Co., 430 N.E.2d 407, 411 (Ind. Ct. App. 1982). Courts hold such clauses to be appropriate where, in the event of a breach, the resulting damages would be uncertain and difficult to ascertain. *Id.* For example, a provision in a residential lease requiring the tenant to pay a late fee of 1% of the monthly rent per day a rent payment was overdue was held to be an enforceable liquidated damage provision because it fairly compensated the landlord "for the administrative expense and inconvenience associated with untimely rent, including late payment notices and additional bookkeeping, and for the loss of use of rental income," all of which are uncertain and difficult to ascertain. *Gershin v. Demming*, 685 N.E.2d 1125, 1130 (Ind. Ct. App. 1997).

Likewise, the administrative expenses and inconvenience occasioned by SOFT's breach in this case were uncertain and difficult to ascertain. Gloucester had no way of knowing, at the time the contract was signed in August 2011, how many rooms short SOFT might be in June 2012. It could not predict what advertising costs or expenses it might incur to find additional guests to purchase the unsold rooms in an effort to mitigate damages. Nor could it know in advance what room rate the hotel might get for reselling those rooms; in fact, common sense suggests that finding substitute guests at the last minute might require the hotel to deeply discount its rooms in order to sell them. In addition, most guests at Gloucester also purchase meals and other services during their stay, all of which generate revenue for the hotel. It is impossible to determine how much revenue was lost from those ancillary sources as a result of SOFT's breach. Mason Dep. 22:2–23:19.

It is true that another organization, the Hoosier Club, was hosting a very popular event in a nearby hotel at the same time as the SOFT meeting, and that Gloucester was able to sell rooms to overflow guests from the host hotel for that meeting. *Id.* at 31:12–18. But this lucky circumstance does not save SOFT. For one thing, it should be noted that SOFT's preexisting contract for rooms at Gloucester prevented the hotel from contracting with the Hoosier Club to be the host hotel for that meeting. *Id.* For another, the relevant time period for determining the foreseeability of actual damages is the date of signing the contract, not the date of breach. In *Zalewski v. Simpson*, 435 N.E.2d 74 (Ind. Ct. App. 1982), the court upheld a liquidated damages provision where it determined "[t]he purpose of the provision was not to force compliance with the contract, but rather to compensate in the event of breach for damages which were uncertain and difficult to ascertain *at the time the contract was executed.*" *Id.* at 77 (emphasis supplied). In August 2011, when this contract was signed, Gloucester had no knowledge that the Hoosier Club was going to host a meeting on the same weekend, and therefore could not have predicted whether it would be able to resell any rooms in the event SOFT breached its contract. Mason Dep. 31:12–18.

3. *The parties intended the liquidated damages clause to be the exclusive remedy*

In some cases, a dispute has arisen as to whether a liquidated damages provision is the exclusive remedy or whether a nonbreaching party may seek relief in addition to liquidated damages. *See, e.g., Beck v. Mason*, 580 N.E.2d 290, 293 (Ind. Ct. App. 1991) (holding that describing an earnest money deposit in a real estate sales contract as "liquidated damages" was sufficient proof that the parties intended to limit their remedies to that clause); *accord, Rogers v. Lockard*, 767 N.E.2d 982 (Ind. Ct. App. 2002). In our case, however, Gloucester seeks no remedy other than payment of liquidated damages. Pl.'s Compl. ¶21, Apr. 17, 2013, and *ad damnum* clause.

Accordingly, since the parties intended to create a liquidated damages clause, and since damages in the event were uncertain and difficult to ascertain, this Court should enforce the liquidated damages clause.

B. The sum specified as liquidated damages is proportional to the actual damages

SOFT, in its First Affirmative Defense, alleges that Gloucester was fully sold out on the nights of the SOFT conference and that therefore it has suffered no damage. Def.'s Answer, May 10, 2013, First Affirmative Defense. But this is not a sufficient defense.

First, as noted above, the purpose of liquidated damages clauses is to fix the amount of damage in the event of breach. *Gershin*, 685 N.E.2d at 1127 ("[a] typical liquidated damages provision provides for the forfeiture of a stated sum of money upon breach *without proof of damages*.") (emphasis supplied). The amount of actual damages incurred therefore is irrelevant, when the court determines that the liquidated damages clause is enforceable.

The most common argument made by those seeking to avoid application of the agreed-upon liquidated damage clause is that the amount of the specified damages is disproportionate to the amount of the actual damage that may occur. *See, e.g., id.* at 1128; *Czeck v. Van Helsland*, 143 Ind. App. 460, 241 N.E.2d 272 (1968). But it is important to remember that this determination is evaluated as of the time of the signing of the contract, not at the time of breach. *Rogers*, 767 N.E.2d at 991 (liquidated damages clauses are unenforceable where the payment specified "is grossly disproportionate to the loss *which may result* from breach") (emphasis supplied); *Gershin*, 685 N.E.2d at 1128 (liquidated damages clauses are enforceable where the payment specified "is not greatly disproportionate to the loss *likely to occur*") (emphasis supplied). Both of those formulations of the rule use predictive language, proving that the relevant inquiry is from the time the clause is agreed to by the parties.

As noted in section A-2 of this brief, *supra*, in August 2011 the amount of damages that Gloucester might suffer as a result of SOFT's brief was difficult or impossible to predict. When

Gloucester entered into the contract, it gave up the opportunity to sell those rooms to other groups (like the Hoosier Club) that may have been planning meetings in Indianapolis over the same weekend. It had no way of determining in advance how many rooms SOFT members might fail to book, nor whether it would be able to resell those rooms to anybody, or at what rate. But, rather than arbitrarily specify a flat amount as liquidated damages, it agreed to a formula that directly proportioned the amount of damages to the amount of the shortfall in room sales. Thus, rather than being "grossly disproportionate" to the possible future loss of revenue, it was directly proportionate.

The formula specified in the contract is not, however, a measure of actual damages. As noted previously, it was impossible for Gloucester to know in advance how much advertising or other work it would need to do in order to resell the rooms, or how much ancillary revenue (food service and similar revenue) it would lose from having vacant rooms. Setting the amount of liquidated damages at the contract room rate times the number of unsold rooms was a reasonable estimate of the actual loss that would be occasioned if SOFT breached the agreement. Therefore, the contract provision is reasonable and should be enforced as a valid liquidated damages provision.

V.   Conclusion

SOFT freely entered into a contract in which it reserved the exclusive right to book a specific number of rooms at the Gloucester Indianapolis Hotel for its guests. The Gloucester Hotel, relying on that promise, gave up other business opportunities, in exchange for a reasonable liquidated damages provision expressly proportioned to estimate the actual loss that might occur if SOFT failed to sell the number of rooms it promised to sell. The mere fact that SOFT may now regret its agreement is not a sufficient reason to avoid the contract. This Court should enforce the liquidated damages clause and enter judgment in favor of the Gloucester Hotel in the amount of $9480.38.

Respectfully Submitted

_____

Sara Bellum, Esq.
4321 East Broad Street
Indianapolis, IN

Defendant's brief in opposition to plaintiff's motion for summary judgment and in support of defendant's motion for summary judgment

(student brief)

In the Superior Court of
Marion County, Indiana

The Gloucester Hotel of Indianapolis, a
Delaware corporation,

Plaintiff

v.

No. 1531-GD-2012

Save Our Forest Trees, Inc., a
California nonprofit corporation,

Defendant

Defendant's brief in opposition to plaintiff's motion for summary
judgment and in support of defendant's motion for summary
judgment

I. *Preliminary statement*

Save Our Forest Trees, Inc., is a small nonprofit organization
devoted to raising public awareness about the effects of deforestation
on global warming, as well as facilitating scientific exchanges of
research on this topic. It sponsored a conference in Indianapolis in

summer 2012 at the Gloucester Hotel Indianapolis, part of the Gloucester Worldwide chain of hotels. The Hotel is seeking $9,480.38 from SOFT under a Group Contract for guest rooms it claims SOFT reserved but did not use; it claims that amount pursuant to a liquidated damages clause in the contract. However, the Hotel has admitted that it was sold out on the nights of the conference; as a consequence, numerous attendees of the SOFT conference had to find rooms elsewhere. The Hotel in fact suffered no loss of revenue.

Both parties have filed Motions for Summary Judgment, which are now before the Court for decision. The facts giving rise to this dispute are described in more detail below.

II. Statement of the facts

Global climate change has been the subject of a great deal of scientific inquiry and discussion in recent years. Many scientists have explored possible causes of the phenomenon and possible steps that society might take to slow or reverse the trend. One theory is that deforestation contributes to the problem by removing large numbers of trees that could otherwise convert a notorious greenhouse gas, carbon dioxide, into oxygen. One nonprofit organization, Save Our Forest Trees, Inc. ("SOFT") has devoted its existence to promoting an exchange of ideas and information among climate scientists working on this issue.

In summer 2012, SOFT hosted a two-day conference at the Gloucester Hotel Indianapolis. However, because Gloucester had booked other events at the same time and sold out the entire hotel on the nights of the conference, SOFT conference attendees were not able to purchase the number of hotel rooms specified in the contract between SOFT and the Gloucester Hotel. Gloucester's attempt to charge SOFT for the rooms its members could not buy has led to this lawsuit.

A.   Save Our Forest Trees

Ms. Pat Freebird, now thirty-two years old, formed SOFT shortly after being awarded a bachelor's degree in biology and volunteering her time with other nonprofits and environmental advocacy groups. While her title is Executive Director for SOFT, in fact she is the organization's only employee, working long hours to realize its mission of connecting scientists and environmentalists to share their research findings and discuss ways to bring awareness to the problem of deforestation and climate change. Freebird Dep. 2:14–3:9, Aug. 20, 2013.

SOFT's headquarters are in Ms. Freebird's home, although she charges no rent to SOFT. Operating costs are kept to a bare minimum by communicating and advertising primarily over the Internet and through e-mail. Ms. Freebird herself earns only $30,000 in income, although she is a full-time employee. *Id.*

In 2011 SOFT had nearly $160,000 in total revenue. Freebird Dep. Ex. 1. Nearly $100,000 of that revenue came from the registration fees at four national conferences, usually held at universities where space is donated. About $30,000 of the revenue came from membership dues of $25 per member; the remainder of SOFT's income came from charitable donations. *Id.* Over the ten years it has been in existence, SOFT has accumulated a fund balance of only $25,000; in most years, its income and expenses have balanced out. Freebird Dep. 15:6–16:10. The organization currently has about 1200 dues-paying members. Membership benefits include access to one another's contact information and publications, quarterly newsletters by e-mail, and invitations to SOFT's national conferences. Def.'s Answer to Interrog. ¶5, Aug. 8, 2013.

To date, SOFT has held more than twenty successful national conferences. In 2012, conferences took place in four major cities: Miami Beach, Portland, New York City, and Indianapolis. *Id.* ¶7. A typical conference will draw around 200 registered participants. In a given year, usually at least half of SOFT's members, currently around 1500 people, attend one or more of these conferences. Freebird Dep. 12:6–21. Most conferences generate revenue of between $10,000 and $15,000 in excess of conference expenses, although some have generated net income as high as $18,000. Def.'s Answer to Interrog. ¶8. Participants are expected to make their own arrangements for hotel accommodations, but Ms. Freebird always arranges for a nearby hotel that offers a discounted rate to registrants. The main cost to SOFT is the cost of the opening reception where participants network and share ideas. Freebird Dep. 13:2–8.

Ms. Freebird has frequently arranged for hotel rooms through the Gloucester chain for group discounts, partly because it has hotels in most major cities, but also because it has a corporate policy of being "green." For example, it gives its guests the option of not washing linens and towels, serves only Fair Trade coffee, and offers a wide selection of fully organic meals, mostly from local farms, in many of its restaurants. *Id.* at 8:3–9:16.

B.   The Indianapolis conference at the Gloucester Hotel

In summer 2011, SOFT selected Indianapolis as the site for a conference. Ms. Freebird called the Hotel to inquire about conference dates in July 2012. She requested a block of 150 rooms to be held over for July 13 and 14, 2012 (approximately 75 per night). *Id.* at 7:13–8:9. Based upon that number and the dates requested, the reservation agent for Gloucester told Ms. Freebird that the Hotel could offer a rate of $159 per night, which represented a significant discount from the hotel's normal rate of $189 per night. *Id.* at 8:1–6. Shortly after that phone call, a form contract arrived in the mail entitled "Group Contract," dated August 15, 2011 ("the Agreement"). Ms. Freebird checked the form to ensure that the room rate and block were accurate, and then signed it and returned it in the mail. *Id.* at 9:2–10:14.

Ms. Freebird did not read the contract in detail before signing it but testified at her deposition that "most of those contracts are all the same; just a bunch of legalese." *Id.* Based upon past arrangements with other hotels in the Gloucester chain and in the hotel industry generally, Ms. Freebird believed that the Agreement was meant to be simply a confirmation of the earlier conversation with the person she spoke to on the telephone. She believed that a signature was necessary to ensure that her group would get the discounted rate. *Id.*

In late June 2012, several SOFT members contacted Ms. Freebird to tell her that Gloucester was already sold out. *Id.* at 21:13–19. Ms. Freebird assumed from this information that the block of rooms under the Agreement had all been reserved by other members. She then recommended to the callers that they seek accommodations at another nearby hotel. *Id.* at 22:2–18.

When Ms. Freebird and the other participants arrived at the Hotel for the July conference, many SOFT guests were unable to check in on time. *Id.* at 26:1–27:16. Guests Carla Johnson and Milton Jones were both told by a clerk at the registration desk that the Hotel was "completely sold out." Johnson Aff. ¶4, Aug. 7, 2013. Many conference attendees were told that their rooms were not ready for the 4:00 p.m. check-in time they were promised; in fact, many participants did not get into their rooms until after 6:00 p.m. Freebird Dep. 19:2–14. On account of the "chaos," many of the out-of-town guests staying there missed the conference's opening reception and the catered refreshments. *Id.*

C.   Pat Freebird returns to Eureka

Attendance at the conference turned out to be lower than Ms. Freebird had expected. Instead of 200 registrations, there had been only 152; and several of those were from Indiana residents who did not stay overnight at the Hotel. Because of the lower-than-expected attendance, the conference generated only about $5800 of income over expenses. Def.'s Answer to Interrog. ¶11 and Ex. 2 thereto.

A week or so after the Indianapolis event, SOFT received an invoice from the hotel charging $9480.38 for "attrition for unused guest rooms." The invoice claimed that there were 53 "unused" rooms. Freebird Dep. Ex. 3. Ms. Freebird was unsure how there could have been a shortfall if the hotel was turning away guests and claiming that it had been full, so she called the Hotel for an explanation. Nobody provided her with any information. *Id.* at 29:14-30:2.

Ms. Freebird then spoke with some of the people who had registered for the conference and found that several of them had been charged $189 per night rather than the discounted conference rate for their rooms; she assumed this was because the reserved block had sold out and that the guests then bought rooms at the regular Hotel rate. *Id.* at 31:15–23. She also discovered that at least a dozen SOFT members had been unable to book rooms at Gloucester during the conference and had to stay in other nearby hotels. *Id.* at 32:16–20.

Since she had not gotten a satisfactory answer on the phone, Ms. Freebird wrote a letter to the Hotel requesting a list of the participants who had reserved rooms, including how many were counted as part of the group. *Id.* Ex. 4. She hoped she would be able to determine from that list whether everybody who should have been counted toward the room block was in fact counted. *Id.* at 32:3–7. But instead of the guest list, about a month later, an attorney for the Hotel sent a letter insisting upon full payment of the entire amount within one week. *Id.* at 32:17–21 and Ex. 5. The attorney claimed that the amount sought represented liquidated damages for unused rooms ("attrition"), based on this clause in the contract:

Reservation Deadline: June 1, 2012

In order to qualify for the guaranteed room rate, individuals must reserve rooms on or before the Reservation Deadline specified above, and must specify the Group Name. After the Reservation Deadline, rooms not reserved in the Group Name will

> be returned to the Hotel's general inventory and may
> be sold by the Hotel to any guest at normal Hotel
> rates. Group acknowledges that it may forgo the
> opportunity to reserve those rooms for other guests
> prior to the Reservation Deadline, and that the Hotel
> will incur costs in reselling rooms, and that these
> damages are difficult to ascertain. In the event that
> the Group fails to reserve 90% of the Room Block
> Reservation specified above by the Reservation
> Deadline, Group agrees to pay as liquidated damages,
> and not as a penalty, the difference between the
> actual number of rooms reserved by Group guests and
> 90% of the Room Block specified above, at the
> Guaranteed Room Rate, such payment to be due 15
> days after the Reservation Deadline.

Contract for Room Reservations, Aug. 15, 2011, attached to Freebird Dep. Ex. 1. The Hotel then instituted this action when SOFT refused to pay for the allegedly unused guest rooms. Pl.'s Compl., Apr. 17, 2013.

During discovery in this case, the Hotel admitted that it was in fact sold out on both of the nights in question. Pl.'s Answer to Req. for Produc. of Doc. ¶6, July 18, 2013. It claimed, however, that it had turned down another conference for the same dates shortly after SOFT had signed its contract. Pl.'s Answer to Interrog. ¶13, July 18, 2013. It also claims that SOFT guests purchased only 82 room nights, rather than the 135 required by the contract (calculated as 90% of the 150 rooms in the original contract block). *Id.* at ¶15. While SOFT disputes both of those claims, even if the jury resolves both claims in favor of the Hotel, the Hotel cannot recover, and thus those disputes of fact are not material to the resolution of SOFT's Motion for Summary Judgment.

III.   *Issues*

1.   Is Gloucester's claim for additional payment from SOFT a penalty, and therefore not a valid liquidated damages clause? ***Suggested answer:*** Yes.

2. Since Gloucester sold all of its available rooms on the nights of the SOFT conference, has it been damaged at all? **Suggested answer:** No.

3. Did the sale by Gloucester of all available rooms on the nights of the SOFT conference make it impossible for SOFT to perform its obligations under the contract? **Suggested answer:** Yes.

IV. Argument

The attrition clause in the contract is a penalty rather than a liquidated damages clause; it is therefore unenforceable. Payment of the invoice by SOFT would be grossly disproportionate to damages (if any) suffered by the Hotel as a result of the shortfall in bookings by SOFT and result in a windfall to the Hotel. Moreover, the Hotel was not damaged because it was able to resell any rooms not reserved by SOFT guests, presumably at a higher price, and was therefore likely put in a better position than it would have been if SOFT's guests had filled the 53 "unused" guest rooms at the contract rate. In addition, by selling all of the rooms not reserved by SOFT, the Hotel made it impossible for SOFT to perform the contract.

A.   The hotel seeks to enforce a penalty because the amount claimed is disproportionate to the actual damages and is easily calculable

To recover for a breach of contract, a plaintiff must prove that (1) a contract existed, (2) the defendant breached the contract, and (3) the plaintiff suffered damage as a result of the defendant's breach. *Collins v. McKinney*, 871 N.E.2d 363 (Ind. Ct. App. 2007). The plaintiff bears the burden of proof as to the amount loss resulting from a defendant's breach. The parties to a contract, however, may stipulate a sum in advance to be recoverable for a breach of contract where the loss suffered would be uncertain or difficult to ascertain. A liquidated damages provision "provides for the forfeiture of a stated sum of money without proof of damages." *Harbours Condo. Ass'n v. Hudson*, 852 N.E.2d 985, 993 (Ind. Ct. App. 2006).

However, a contract provision that claims to be a liquidated damages clause will not be enforced if it is in reality a penalty for nonperformance. This determination is made on a case-by-case basis, without the benefit of strict guidelines. *Gershin v. Demming*, 685 N.E.2d 1125, 1127–28 (Ind. Ct. App. 1997) ("In determining whether a stipulated sum payable on a breach of contract constitutes liquidated damages or a penalty, the facts, the intention of the parties and the reasonableness of the stipulation under the circumstances of the case are all to be considered.").

Here, the "attrition clause" sought to be enforced by the Hotel bears all the hallmarks of an unenforceable penalty. "[W]here the sum named is declared to be fixed as liquidated damages, is not greatly disproportioned to the loss that may result from a breach, and the damages are not measurable by any exact pecuniary standard, the sum designated will be deemed to be stipulated damages." *Jaqua v. Headington*, 16 N.E. 527, 528 (Ind. 1888). Further, there must be some nexus between the amount claimed and the damages flowing from a breach: a "stipulated sum will not be allowed as liquidated damages unless it may fairly be allowed as compensation for the breach." *Sterne v. Fletcher Am. Co.*, 204 Ind. 35, 49–50, 181 N.E. 37 (1932).

In one case, a hotel was required to refund the plaintiff's deposit because of the otherwise disproportionate loss that the plaintiff would have suffered. *2625 Bldg. Corp. v. Deutsch*, 179 Ind. App. 425, 385 N.E.2d 1189 (1979). In that case, the plaintiff reserved six hotel rooms during the weekend of the Indianapolis 500 race and, upon doing so, paid $1008.00 to the hotel, representing the full cost of the rooms. Two months prior to the reservation dates, the plaintiff cancelled the reservations and requested a refund. The hotel refused to return any of the advance payment. *Id.* at 1190.

Although the contract in that case was oral and thus included no express liquidated damages clause, the court held that allowing the hotel "to retain damages representing payment for use of all the rooms, regardless of the fact that damages could be ascertained, would be to enforce a penalty or forfeiture." *Id.* at 1192. Moreover, "assessing Deutsch for the full amount of his room payments would cause him to suffer a loss which was wholly disproportionate to any injury sustained by [the hotel]." *Id.* at 1193. The court therefore ruled that the defendant hotel was required to refund the plaintiff's deposit.

In the recent case of *Corvee, Inc. v. French*, 943 N.E.2d 844 (Ind. Ct. App. 2010), a collection company obtained a default judgment for an unpaid $8500 hospital bill and further sought to recover $3400 in attorney fees under a liquidated damages provision. The hospital admission form imposed responsibility on the patient for forty percent (40%) of the outstanding balance in connection with any attempt to collect the money due. The trial court awarded only $1000 in attorney fees to the collection agency as the reasonable fee for the default judgment collection action. Determining that the contract unambiguously required payment of the $3500, designated as attorney fees, the court of appeals considered whether the provision was an enforceable liquidated damages clause.

The Court of Appeals considered three factors relevant to the determination as to whether the liquidated damages provision was valid or an unenforceable penalty: (1) the difficulty of ascertaining damages resulting from a breach; (2) whether the stipulated sum can be "fairly allowed as compensation for the breach"; and (3) whether the party seeking enforcement of the liquidated damages clause has shown a correlation between the liquidated damages and actual damages, which is necessary "to assure that a sum charged may fairly be attributed to the breach." Reasoning that the calculation of attorney fees incurred during litigation should not be considered difficult to ascertain, and that the amount must be reasonable (even under a contractual provision), the court of appeals upheld the award of reasonable attorney fees. The court further stated that to allow the attorney pursuing the default judgment to recover the stipulated amount—in the absence of evidence that the fees were actually incurred—"gives rise to the possibility that [the attorney] will enjoy a windfall at [the defendant's] expense." *Id.* at 848.

In this case, the liquidated damages claimed by the Hotel fail to meet the legal requirements of an enforceable liquidated damages provision and should therefore be considered an unenforceable penalty provision. Just as the court in *2625 Building Corp.* found that damages in the event of a breach were easily ascertainable, damages in this case are easily ascertainable: the Hotel sent an invoice to SOFT for exactly 53 unused guest rooms. Freebird Dep. Ex. 3. More important, however, just as the court in *2625 Building Corp.* held that charging the patron who reserved the rooms but did not use them for the full value of those rooms was wholly disproportionate to any injury sustained by the hotel, charging SOFT with the full value of the rooms its members did not use is grossly disproportionate to any loss the Hotel might suffer. This is because the Hotel admittedly resold the rooms not reserved by members of SOFT. Pl.'s Answer to Req. for Produc. of Doc. ¶6. When reselling those rooms, the Hotel was no longer obligated to offer them at the lower rate called for in the SOFT contract; instead, it was free to sell the rooms at its standard rates. The Hotel therefore stood to make more money by reselling the rooms than by seeking liquidated damages. Any damages awarded to the Hotel would therefore likely result in a windfall to the hotel.

But even if the Hotel had been forced to sell the rooms at rates lower than those specified in the SOFT contract, they were not given away for free. Thus, the Hotel's damages, if any, were less (and likely far less) than the total cost of the rooms that the Hotel now seeks to recover from SOFT. Thus, the damages claimed are grossly disproportionate with the actual damages suffered, and therefore this liquidated damages clause is unenforceable.

B. The Hotel has not been damaged because it sold all of the rooms in the SOFT reservation block to other guests

To maintain a cause of action for breach of contract, a plaintiff must prove that it has been damaged. *Collins v. McKinney*, 871 N.E.2d 363 (Ind. Ct. App. 2007).

As noted in the previous section, the Hotel has admitted that it was sold out on the nights of the SOFT conference; in all likelihood, it sold the rooms at a rate higher than the contract rate. (There is in fact some evidence that several SOFT guests paid the higher rate of $189; *see, e.g.*, Johnson Aff. ¶6.) The Hotel has not claimed in any of the discovery materials in this case, nor in any of its pleadings or briefs, that it was forced to sell rooms at a rate lower than the contract rate in order to fill the hotel on the nights in question.

Since there is no evidence that the Hotel suffered any damage at all, its cause of action for breach of contract must fail.

C. The Hotel made it impossible for SOFT to perform by selling all of the rooms in SOFT's block to other guests

Where, after a contract is entered into, something happens that is not the defendant's fault but that renders defendant's performance of the contract "absolutely impossible," the defendant is excused from performing. *Krause v. Bd. of Trustees*, 162 Ind. 278, 283, 70 N.E. 264 (1904); *Kruse, Kruse & Miklosko, Inc. v. Beedy*, 170 Ind. App. 373, 394, 353 N.E.2d 514 (1976).

Most of the cases dealing with impossibility of performance deal with acts of God or other unforeseen events that are the fault of neither party to the contract. *See, e.g.*, *Krause*, 162 Ind. at 265 (fire caused by lightning strike made it impossible for building renovation contract to be completed). However, the rule should apply with even greater force when one contracting party, by its own actions, renders it impossible for the other party to perform the contract. Stated another way, if one party to a contract engages in conduct that makes it impossible for the other party to perform the contract, the party creating the impossibility should not be allowed to recover for the breach it caused. *Cf. Prather v. Latshaw*, 188 Ind. 204, 122 N.E. 721, 722 (1919) (apparently accepting the proposition that a party to a contract is not bound to perform it where performance is rendered impossible by the act of God, by the law, or by the act of the other party to the contract).

Here, Gloucester admits that it sold all of the hotel rooms it had on the nights of the SOFT conference to non-SOFT guests. Pl.'s Answer to Req. for Produc. of Doc. ¶6. Since the contract did not prohibit SOFT members from purchasing rooms after the reservation deadline, Gloucester's sale of those rooms made it impossible for SOFT to sell rooms to its own guests. Accordingly, Gloucester should not be allowed to charge SOFT with a breach of contract consisting of a failure to sell those rooms.

V. *Conclusion*

The Hotel's admission that it was sold out on the nights of the SOFT conference is fatal to its claim in this case, for a number of reasons. First, the contract language in this case does not create a valid liquidated damages clause since any damages would be easily calculable. Instead of liquidated damages, therefore, the Hotel is limited to any actual damages that it can prove. But it cannot prove any damages at all since it was able to resell all of the rooms originally reserved for SOFT guests. Second, the Hotel's act of selling all of the available rooms rendered it impossible for SOFT to perform its obligation under the contract. The Hotel should not be allowed to profit from its actions by demanding that SOFT pay it a second time for rooms that it has already been paid for by other guests.

This Court should grant SOFT's Motion for Summary Judgment, deny the Hotel's Motion for Summary Judgment, and dismiss this action with prejudice.

Respectfully Submitted

Amanda Reckonwith, Esq.
1234 West Main Street
Indianapolis, IN

Index

(Figures, notes, and tables are indicated by f, n, and t following page numbers.)

Ruth Anne Robbins, *Distinguished Clinical Professor of Law, Rutgers LawSchool.* Professor Robbins teaches first year and advanced legal writing courses and clinical courses. She has received the Lindback Foundation Award for Distinguished Teaching at Rutgers University and was one of the *New Jersey Law Journal's* Women Lawyers of the Year in 2016. She is a past president of the Legal Writing Institute and is the co-Editor in Chief of *Legal Communication & Rhetoric: JALWD.* Professor Robbins co-founded and organizes the Applied Legal Storytelling international conference series. She lives in South Jersey, which is neither North Jersey, nor Central Jersey. In an act of whimsy, she and her family taught their puppy to jump up on his hind legs in response to the command, "Wingardium Leviosa!".

Steve Johansen, *Professor and Director of Legal Analysis and Writing, Lewis & Clark Law School.* Professor Johansen teaches 1L legal writing, contract drafting, and professional responsibility. He is a past president of the Legal Writing Institute and a co-founder and organizer of the Applied Legal Storytelling conference series. In 2009, he received the Thomas Blackwell Memorial Award from the Legal Writing Institute and the Association of Legal Writing Directors. He shares his office with his dog Quigley and likes his Sox red and his beer black.

Ken Chestek, *Professor of Law, Assistant Director of the Center for the Study of Written Advocacy, and Director of Externships, University of Wyoming College of Law.* Professor Chestek was a trial lawyer in Pennsylvania for 21 years before teaching at the University of Michigan, Indiana University McKinney School of Law, and the University of Wyoming. He served as President of the Legal Writing Institute from 2010–2012 and has published several articles studying the impact of stories on judicial decision making. In 2018, the nonprofit, nonpartisan organization he co-founded and chairs, Wyoming Promise, received a National Citizen Leadership Award from the national advocacy group American Promise. He has 3 states left to complete his lifetime quest of running a marathon in all 50 states, but isn't sure whether completing the quest will make him a hero or some other type of character.